D0616985

# Arbella

# Arbella

## ENGLAND'S LOST QUEEN

### Sarah Gristwood

HOUGHTON MIFFLIN COMPANY
BOSTON · NEW YORK

Copyright © 2003 by Sarah Gristwood

First published in Great Britain by Bantam Press,
a division of Transworld Publishers, in 2003

For information about permission to reproduce selections from
this book, write to Permissions, Houghton Mifflin Company,
215 Park Avenue South, New York, New York 10003.

Visit our Web site: www.houghtonmifflinbooks.com.

*Library of Congress Cataloging-in-Publication Data*
Gristwood, Sarah.
Arbella : England's lost queen / Sarah Gristwood.
p. cm.
Originally published: Great Britain : Bantam Press, 2003.
Includes bibliographical references and index.
ISBN 0-618-34133-1
1. Stuart, Arabella, Lady, 1575–1615. 2. Great Britian—Kings and
Rulers—Succession—History—17th Century. 3. Women political
prisoners—Great Britain—Biography. 4. Great Britain—History—
Elizabeth, 1558–1603. 5. Great Britain—History—James I, 1603–
1625. 6. Nobility—Great Britain—Biography. I. Title
DA391.1.S9G75 2005
942.06'1'092—dc22 [B] 2005040300

Printed in the United States of America

MP 10 9 8 7 6 5 4 3 2 1

The extract on page 390 from *1066 and All That* by W. C. Sellar
and R. J. Yeatman is reproduced with permission of Methuen
Publishing Ltd; copyright © W. C. Sellar and R. J. Yeatman.
The extract on page 45 from Dorothy L. Sayers's *Gaudy Night*
is reproduced with permission of Hodder & Stoughton.

# Contents

# Preface

On a dank October day, under the eyes of the famous ravens – and of the flocks of tourists – a crowd a hundred strong has gathered to watch a moment from history, coming to life on the spot where it first took place. The Tower of London is staging 'Escape from the Tower' for a school-holiday audience. Four times a day ('Each Escape lasts approximately forty minutes') the performance reconstructs the most dramatic episode from Arbella Stuart's story.

'Imprisoned for love!', the publicity had trumpeted. 'Lord William Seymour is held in the Tower for the crime of marrying the king's cousin. His wife, the Lady Arbella Stuart, has a scheme to set him free. Can you come up with a better plan?' As the years rolled back to 1610, we, the spectator-accomplices, were caught up completely. As we witnessed a stolen meeting between Arbella and William (he in dandified crimson, she with the long rope of pearls she would sell to pay his expenses), the Lieutenant of the Tower appeared, to ask whether we had seen the couple do anything guilty. 'They killed the queen!' yelled one excitable six-year-old. The actors improvised gracefully around this unforeseen conspiracy theory.

It was an impressively accurate show. Up and down the Tower's steps, to the very room where William was held, decorations still hanging on the medieval walls, though that great glass gonad, London's new city hall, peers oddly through the window today. Of course the actors had to telescope events a little, and William was not 'Lord' William, if we are to hold out for total veracity. But at an event like this, really, who cares? The emotions rang true. And it is possible to get too hung up on the factual details of history.

In the last two years, since the first publication of *Arbella,* I have grown used to coming upon her unexpectedly. As a subject on a popular quiz show or recreated on a TV documentary, she is, it seems, once again a figure in currency. Yet each time is a curious and enlightening experience, like meeting someone you thought you knew – suddenly, out of context – and seeing a different side of her personality.

And Arbella Stuart's personality, for me, was always the key to writing her tale. The attraction of her dramatic public life almost paled beside that of her passionate and complex character. I loved the woman who fought for her independence – 'I must shape my own coat according to my cloth', she wrote in a letter once, 'but it will not be after the fashion of this world but fit for me' – and the Tower reconstruction lit up this spirit, this energy. But there was a darker side to Arbella Stuart's nature. 'I dare to die, if I be not guilty of my own death, and oppress others with my ruin too', she wrote in a later letter, when spirit and energy had failed her finally. It is her letters that, four centuries on, still give her a claim to posthumous fame in her own private identity.

It would, of course, be a crime to rifle through a volume of centuries-old letters as though it were an airport paperback. You would certainly never get the chance (so vigilant are the staff of the British Library's Manuscripts Room) with the hefty tome labelled 'BL Harl. MS 7003'. But in just one way, it would be an interesting experiment. Those letters that were written by Arbella Stuart would leap out at you instantly.

Amid the cramped, indecipherable hands of many of her contemporaries, often as inaccessible to the novice reader as if they had been Linear B, Arbella's writing stands out first for its sheer size. Capitals are as tall as the top joint of a finger, and never larger than when she is writing something – like the huge *S* of 'my Selfe' – that proclaims her identity. Not only her neat, schooled 'presentation' script but also her more frequently seen informal hand are as clear as a bell to read (even to someone who habitually tosses out friends' postcards on the grounds of illegibility).

No doubt it would be a mistake to deduce too much from her letters' appearance, especially at a time when the vagaries of a quill might change writing considerably. But it is hard to avoid when, at the end of an appeal to the king, her complimentary closing words are split in two, so that 'your Majesty's' appears right after the text, followed by half a sheet of blank space before 'most humble and faithful subject and servant' comes with her name at the bottom of the page. These were the letters Arbella wrote from her own imprisonment, and the management of space was surely a device to prevent anyone else from adding a treasonable postscript and getting her into worse trouble than she was in already.

One archivist mentioned to me that Arbella obviously cared how her letters were laid out on the page. Another, peering over my shoulder in the library at Longleat, asked, 'Did she actually send that?' – horrified, clearly. But curiously enough, both reactions make sense. Often Arbella Stuart's letters begin in an elegant presentation hand, then degenerate into an angry scrawl as her feelings carry her away. Afterthoughts are squashed sideways in the margin, where a calmer spirit might have broached another sheet. Letters are addressed, on the outside, with the self-conscious formality due a great lady; but they are marred on the inside with the heavy scratchings-out of one who desperately fears being misunderstood – and marred, all too frequently, with the blots of tears. Many of Arbella's letters are something more profound than mere practical communications. There were times in her life when it seems she may have been trying to write her way to sanity. Certainly, she wrote of herself with a freedom manifested by no other royal woman, and rarely seen again in any woman until the twentieth century.

It would be a treat to have such an intimate portrait of any woman born four centuries ago, even were there no political dimension to her life. And it might have been possible – looking back, with hindsight – to have written a different version of 'the Arbella Stuart story'. This would not be the story of dynasty, of the succession struggles of the late sixteenth century. Instead, it would let you skip the brief genealogy lesson of the second chapter and go right to the splendours and savage emotions that were Arbella's childhood; would let you, indeed, skip straight to Part III of this book as it now stands, where Arbella starts to speak in her own voice and visibly to take control of her own destiny.

This other version of Arbella's tale would be the picture of a woman striving to find a place for herself amid crushing pressures: ambition and apprehension, power and poverty, and the difficult proximity of some of the age's most forceful figures. The story of a woman driven to madness, hauling herself up again by sheer determination, only to fall, finally. Battering against the political realities of the late Elizabethan age with the folly, perhaps, of a butterfly beating against a windowpane, but with a courageous obstinacy. Perhaps the courage, as well as the obstinacy, were recognized in her own day. Perhaps, after all, Arbella's inner journey has already been told, by John Webster, her contemporary – was a source (so critics have long believed) for *The Duchess of Malfi*.

When *Arbella* came out, interviewers would often say to me, What a tragic story, a spirit crushed, a life wasted. But for them to see her as just a victim puzzled me, even angered me. If Arbella Stuart gambled for the throne of England, then she did not, could not, win. Perhaps the same is true if she were fighting only for her own autonomy. In that epoch she was constrained twice over: as a woman and as a vessel for the royal blood that held as much menace as promise. She demanded 'those ordinary rights which other subjects cannot be denied of', but she demanded in vain. Yet surely, to have fought as long and hard as she did is in itself a kind of victory.

In one sense, Arbella's is Everywoman's tale. But in another, her problems were those of her precise place in history. In the end it is how, and to whom, she was born that determined her destiny. Shakespeare wrote of Hamlet that he was 'subject to his birth', unable to carve his own path as 'unvalued persons' may. The same was true of Arbella Stuart – is true of all royalty, even today. The subtitle of this book, 'England's Lost Queen', is something of a deliberate provocation. But like every exaggerated statement, it contains a kernel of truth. In her own day, many prominent commentators took Arbella's chances of inheriting the crown very seriously. History has an unamiable habit of losing the losers; and today few recognize that Arbella might have set the Stuart dynasty on a different path from that taken by her cousin James, with huge consequences for England, Scotland, and indeed the colonization of the distant Americas. But I see no chance of understanding Arbella unless we give her political importance the weight it had for herself and her contemporaries; no chance (at a moment when new nations were being forged) of understanding the politics of her country.

It seems ironic now that my interest in Arbella was first sparked by my study of her grandmother Bess of Hardwick and of Bess's relations with two great queens: her friend and mistress Elizabeth I of England, and her prisoner, Mary, Queen of Scots. I saw in my mind a curious pattern, like an irregular diamond, each of its four points bearing a miniature of one of the four women whose destinies were intertwined. Two of the Tudor 'type' and two of the Stuart: Bess and Elizabeth, Arbella and Mary. Bess has the great house of Hardwick as her stone memorial. Elizabeth Tudor and Mary Stuart are the stuff of legend, offering an emotive alternative – the charismatic or the romantic? – to every amateur of history.

My own allegiance was always to the Tudor model. I never heard the Stuart siren song, and to find myself having written the biography of a Stuart still fills me with a kind of incredulity. But the shadowy Arbella – in whose veins ran the blood of all the other three – provoked in me a nagging sense of a story missed, a road not taken. Though her writing had sparked interest in academic circles, the general public showed no recognition of her name, and I was bewildered that she could have disappeared so completely. Now, to me at least, she is a less shadowy figure. If others could say the same, I would be happy. Arbella Stuart deserves better than to be just one of those ghosts who linger on the edge of memory.

In attempting to bring Arbella Stuart's life to a wider audience I have of necessity made certain practical decisions, like modernizing spelling and punctuation to a degree. Selective source notes are given at the end of the book, but precise calendar dates are at a premium, partly because of the endless explanations necessitated by the two different calendars in use at that time, and partly because so many of the relevant papers are in any case undated. The capitalization of titles has been kept to a minimum in the interest of readability, and I describe the protagonists by whichever forename, surname or indeed nickname distinguishes them most clearly. These were difficult times for a biographer, with the same names recurring endlessly through a family tree, so that 'William Cavendish' could describe Arbella's grandfather, her uncle, or two of the cousins with whom she had most to do. (It seems a particularly malign disposition on the part of Providence that the three noblemen unrelated to Arbella who were most instrumental in her career should be the earl of Northampton, the earl of Northumberland, and the earl of Nottingham, two of whom share the surname Howard and two the forename Henry.) Courtiers of the Jacobean years changed titles with promiscuous frequency – but Robert Cecil (who in the space of a mere fifteen years became successively Sir Robert Cecil, Baron Cecil, Viscount Cranborne and the earl of Salisbury) remains Robert Cecil throughout the story, just as Gilbert and Mary Talbot remain Gilbert and Mary Talbot even after they followed their parents as earl and countess of Shrewsbury.

There are many people I want to thank for their help with this book, besides Deanne Urmy at Houghton Mifflin and Selina Walker and

Sheila Lee at Transworld in England, Araminta Whitley and Celia Hayley at LAW agency in London, and my American agent Emma Parry. First Margaret Gaskin, who gave me not only huge amounts of her time and skill, but also her knowledge of the period and her collection of books on the sixteenth century. Alison Weir for her unfailing kindness and support to a novice in the field she herself has explored so very successfully; Carole Myer, Leonie Flynn, and Daniel Hahn for their practical help and constructive comments; and Peter Bradshaw for the title. A handful of experts have given of their time and knowledge: Luc Chaput, Pauline Croft, Alan Cromartie, James Daybell, Kenneth Fincham, Jeffrey Boss, Ralph Houlbrooke, Heather Wolfe at the Folger Shakespeare Library in Washington, Kate Harris at Longleat, Robin Harcourt Williams at Hatfield, and Anna Keay and Jeremy Ashbee at the Tower of London, who steered me towards some important conclusions. Their generosity is their own; any mistakes I may have made in interpreting their suggestions are all mine. When it comes to interpretation, I owe special thanks to Duncan Harrington for his help in transcribing those texts which – unlike Arbella's own – did prove quite beyond me. And I should like to thank Bethan Tomlinson and the other actors of the troupe Past Pleasures, who gave me so much pleasure at the Tower that day.

The support of family and friends tends to be taken for granted. But I have also met with kindness from many strangers, from John Entwistle and Kate Wheelden at Hardwick Hall, who understandingly took me behind the scenes to see Arbella's own room, to the chance-met lady in Great Bedwyn Church who let a total unknown walk away with the records of the local historical society. Thanks for permission to use quotations from Arbella's letters are due to the British Library; to the Marquess of Bath, Longleat House, Wiltshire, for the use of quotations from the Talbot Papers; and to the Marquess of Salisbury, Hatfield House, Hertfordshire, for quotations from the Cecil Papers.

The source notes show what I owe to Arbella's other biographers – but that hardly seems adequate to acknowledge one particular debt. In 1994 Sara Jayne Steen's edition of the letters of Arbella Stuart was published by the Oxford University Press. Her insight, her commentary, her interpretation represent a huge gift bestowed upon anyone else who approaches Arbella's story.

To all these, and more – I only hope the book is worthy.

S. G.

*London, November 2004*

# Tudor and Stuart Line of Succession

HENRY VII

James IV of Scotland  m.  Margaret  m.  Archibald Douglas

HENRY VIII

Charles Brandon  m.  Mary
Duke of Suffolk

MARY I

EDWARD VI

ELIZABETH I

Henry Grey  m.  Frances Brandon

JANE  Catherine  m.  Earl of Hertford  Mary

Sir William Cavendish  m.  Bess of Hardwick

James V of Scotland  Margaret  m.  Matthew Stuart
4th Earl of Lennox

Charles Stuart  m.  Elizabeth Cavendish  Lord Beauchamp
5th Earl of Lennox

Edward Seymour

Mary Queen of Scots  m.  Lord Darnley

Arbella Stuart  m.  William Seymour

JAMES VI and I

Greenwich Palace from the north bank of the Thames, 1544

# Prologue

EVEN IN THE HEIGHT OF SUMMER, THERE IS ALWAYS A BREEZE OFF THE Thames – and this was still early in the season. When the small party put out onto the river from Blackwall at eight o'clock in the evening, the sun had already set. The tension, and the cold salty air off the water, each brought its own chill.

It was more than eight long hours' rowing from Blackwall to the ship that lay waiting by the open sea. Long enough for the clunk and scrape of the oars in the rowlocks, the slap and suck each time the blades sliced through the tiny waves, to become a torment of monotony. Long enough to suspect that every light and every craft threatened pursuit, every curious question from the watermen betokened a government spy.

Behind them to the west lay the swamps of the Isle of Dogs, and beyond that, the City. Somewhere in the dark down to the south lay Greenwich Palace, where king and court would be sleeping. One of the little group upon the water should by rights have been there among them, lapped in the comfort and homage due to royalty. But her goal lay elsewhere.

At least she and her followers had already accomplished the first leg of their illicit journey. On the afternoon of Monday, 3 June 1611, at around three o'clock, a party of three had ridden out of a 'sorry inn' near the village of East Barnet, towards the Great North Road. The ostler who had held their stirrups later recalled that one young rider, as he swung his leg over the saddle, seemed 'very sick and faint'.

'The gentleman would hardly hold out to London,' the ostler remarked, none too perceptively. For, beneath the male attire, the rider was no gentleman, but the Lady Arbella Stuart, kinswoman to King James I. She would have to 'hold out': her aim was to flee the country. A leading contender for the English throne and throughout her life the focus of plot and intrigue, Arbella had recently dared to wed – secretly, and without the permission of her royal cousin. It was an act that, in one so close to the throne, was accounted virtual treason, especially since her choice of husband seemed more than suggestive to the authorities.

At the age of thirty-five, Arbella had fallen in love with a man twelve years her junior: William Seymour, who, like Arbella herself, had a prominent place in the English succession. The news of their marriage had, a twelvemonth before, sent the king into a frenzy. Since then, they had been kept apart – William held under lock and key in the Tower of London, Arbella under a kind of house arrest. Now, a double escape had been arranged, and this disguised ride was Arbella's first stage in her plan to start a new life abroad with a young man whom she loved sincerely.

'We may by God's grace be happier than we look for in being suffered to enjoy ourselves with his Majesty's favour,' Arbella had written to William from her imprisonment, 'but if we be not able to, I for my part shall think myself a pattern of misfortune in enjoying so great a blessing as you so little a while.' No separation but death, she continued, 'deprives me of the comfort of you, for wherever you be, or in what state so ever you are, it sufficeth me you are mine . . . Be well,' she ends her letter, 'and I shall account myself happy in being your faithful loving wife.' Perhaps James need not have been so quick to suspect a coup. Love had come late to Arbella, and from an unlikely source – but this hardly sounds like a match born of mere political expediency.

Arbella had been appalled when word came to her custodian in London that, for even greater security, she was to be taken north to Durham – 'clean out of this world', as she wrote despairingly. She had written to the lord chief justice of England, claiming the right of *habeas corpus*, and demanding 'such benefit of justice as the laws of this realm afford to all others'. Arbella, with brains and education, was never one to give up easily – but it was no use. The great right enshrined in the Magna Carta was denied her by her very royalty. Next, she besieged with letters all those who might intercede for her with James. 'Sir, though you be almost a stranger to me . . .' began one missive, desperately. After hopes failed her one by one, she resorted to simple stubbornness. When the time came to set out for Durham, she refused to leave her bed, and the king's men had to carry her into the street, mattress and all.

But the journey north gave her an opportunity. Barely ten miles outside the city, in Barnet, she fell ill and the party had to halt. King James suspected that she was faking. But her physician Dr Moundford declared that, while she might yet be 'cherished to health', she could not undertake long travel. Unable, so it was said, to walk the length of the room unaided, she was not closely guarded. She had, moreover, lulled the vigilance of her captors with 'a fair show of conformity'. She had then deceived her female attendant – Mrs Adams, a minister's wife – with the tale that she was going to the Tower, to bid her husband goodbye in 'a private visit'. The unsuspecting woman 'did duly attend her return at the time appointed', recounted one contemporary. But there was never to be any return. On that June morning Arbella pulled a pair of 'great French-fashioned hose' over her petticoats, feeling for the first time the stiff unaccustomed padding of fabric between her thighs. She donned 'a man's doublet, a man-like peruque with long locks over her hair, black cloak, russet boots and a rapier' – and, with her gentleman servant William Markham, simply walked away.

Even the mile and a half's trudge to the inn where the horses and her trusted steward Crompton waited must have tried Arbella in her weakened state, unused to exercise for some weeks; and to ride her 'good gelding' astride, in masculine fashion, was an awkward new experience. 'Yet the stirring of the horse brought blood enough into her face,' as the courtier Sir John More, in the long account he wrote to a friend, reported vividly. South and east they rode, through the suffocatingly lush greenery of early June . . . until, at six o'clock in the evening, the trio clattered into Blackwall on the River Thames, fourteen miles away.

In a life that often followed the pattern of a tragedy, this dashing ride seems like a scene from an altogether more rumbustious style of drama. Arbella, normally studious and easily distressed, could behave with courage and vigour on occasion, and all her adult life she fought against the unjust exercise of authority. 'I must shape my own coat according to my cloth,' she once wrote defiantly, 'but it shall not be after the fashion of this world but fit for me.'

At a tavern in Blackwall more of her servants were waiting, with baggage and a change of clothes. But there was no sign of William, whose carefully arranged escape from the Tower should by this time have brought him here in safety. For an hour and a half – as one of the watermen later told it – the group lingered, fearfully. At half-past seven Arbella's companions urged that night was falling, the tide would soon turn, and they must be away. They were to be rowed downriver to where a French captain called Corvé would wait until nightfall, equipped with a password by which to know their party.

Arbella insisted on giving William yet another half-hour's grace before she would leave Blackwall. She had no means of knowing what had happened to him – delay, capture, even a change of heart. The phrase 'time and tide wait for no man' can never have made itself felt more agonizingly.

Eight o'clock on a moonless night, and still no sign of William. They had to go now, or wait until morning. Leaving a pair of servants behind to direct William on after them, two boats put out onto the water, the one rowed by 'a good pair of oars' for Arbella and her companions, and the other for the luggage that had been smuggled out of William's lodgings. They slipped past Woolwich, through deserted marshland and down the flat featureless banks of the Thames estuary. At Gravesend the tired boatmen, wearied with dodging shoals and obstructions, refused to row further in the dark and had to be persuaded on with a double fare. Even then they insisted upon stopping for a drink at Tilbury, while the fugitives waited miserably in the boats.

As the oarsmen steered blindly in the dark, the river widened until the further shore would have been almost out of sight even on the brightest day. They were navigating a path through a maze of creeks and inlets, with the great beds of eelgrass blurring river and land, and sticky mudbanks to trap the unwary. Trying to find one ship among such a watery wilderness must have seemed like seeking a needle in the hay.

Dawn, heralded by the cries of the estuary birds, was breaking as they approached the tiny port of Leigh around four o'clock on Tuesday morning. But the light was a potential danger, too. Soon men would be stirring in the shipyard. (Vessels – the *Mayflower* among them – would soon regularly be plying the New World route.) Corvé's ship should lie a few miles further on; but would he still be waiting there?

Seeing a brig close at hand, they hailed the master, John Bright, and asked him to take them to Calais. Bright refused – but the curious incident stuck in his memory. Later, he described the five passengers in vivid detail. Among the three men, he noticed one for his long flaxen beard, and the steward Crompton for the urgency with which he pressed on Bright a large sum of money. There were two women, he said. One, 'bare faced, in a black riding safeguard with a black hat', he took to be the notorious thief and cross-dresser Moll Cutpurse, already the Roaring Girl of stage fame, 'and thought that if it were she, she had made some fault and was desirous of escape'. It was rather a fantastical guess on the part of Bright, but still not as dramatic as the real story.

The other woman, Bright reported, 'sat close covered with a black veil or hood over her face or head. He could not see her – only that under her mantle she had a white attire and that, on pulling off her glove, a marvellous white hand was revealed.' Forty years before, it was the whiteness of a hand that had betrayed Arbella's aunt, the queen of Scots, in one of her vain attempts to escape across Loch Leven.

But Arbella herself was not caught yet. Eight miles beyond Leigh, she finally reached Corvé's barque, hung with the pre-arranged flag, in safety. Arbella begged for another delay but, with a contrary wind blowing over high seas, the 'importunity of the followers' convinced her they had to get away. In fact, the tides held them for another two hours before, through the advance whisper of a rising storm, they weighed anchor and set sail for Calais.

Behind them in England – though Arbella's party had no means of knowing it – William had indeed escaped the Tower. He was even now on the water, not far away. But the alarm had been raised soon after his departure. The king had been alerted and a proclamation issued against the fleeing couple for their 'divers great and heinous offences'. Letters were dispatched to ambassadors abroad, 'describing their offence in black colours, and pressing their sending back without delay'.

Everyone connected with the pair was brought in for questioning: Dr Moundford; the gullible Mrs Adams; even the man who had made Arbella's wig was urgently sought. The fugitives' route was easily traced – thanks, in part, to the observant John Bright – from Blackwall to Leigh. Every vessel in the port was searched, every house in Leigh. In London, the earl of Nottingham, the lord high admiral, reassured James that, the wind being against them, the party could hardly have reached Margate. But nothing could abate the king's panic and fury. The messengers who were sent scurrying to order the pursuit had 'Haste, haste! Post haste! Haste for life. Life' written on their dispatches, with the figure of a gallows ominously scrawled alongside. The admiral of the fleet, Admiral Monson, hastily flung after Arbella every vessel he could raise in a hurry – one for the Flanders coast, one towards Calais. He even ordered an oyster boat, loaded with six men and shot, to set out while the bigger ships were still getting under way, and himself put to sea in a light fishing craft to watch the action from as close as may be.

Nottingham, the experienced hero of the Armada, had been right about the winds; but pursuers and pursued alike, knowing that each hour mattered, had to battle on over the choppy sea. Most of Arbella's life had been lived far inland. As the brisk, short waves of the estuary waters softened into the deeper swell of the open sea, perhaps the wide expanse around her convinced her that she really had got clean away. The little barque bucked its way across the Channel to within sight of Calais; but there again she insisted on waiting. This time, the pause was fatal.

Griffen Cockett, captain of the English pinnace *Adventure*, sent from the Downs, was not 'half channel over' when he first saw a sail ahead. 'Under the South Sundhead we saw a small sail, which we chased,' he reported afterwards to Monson. It was indeed Arbella's vessel, which lay 'lingering for Mr Seymour'. But the winds would not let the *Adventure* overtake its quarry; so the resourceful Cockett packed his men, armed 'with shot and pikes', into a smaller boat, and it must have been this that Arbella's party saw being rowed towards them over the sea.

It cannot have been, on the face of it, a very dramatic sight. But it was definitive enough, in its way. Corvé threw out all his sail and tried to make a run for it, but again the winds were against Arbella's party, and the French barque hardly moved. The *Adventure*'s boarding party opened fire. Corvé bravely endured several volleys. ('Thirteen shots straight into his vessel' was how Sir John More, safe at home in London, heard the story later. Perhaps the small sea battle had been turned into something more spectacular along the way.) It was against the tinny rattle of musketry that Arbella at last came forward and surrendered herself, still defiant: 'not so sorry for her own restraint as she should be glad if Mr Seymour might escape,' wrote Sir John, not unadmiringly.

Resistance was at an end. Corvé stood to and struck his flag. The party from the *Adventure* had to commandeer the larger French barque to take the whole party, prisoners and captors, back to Sheppey. Monson sent for 'his Majesty's directions how to dispose of my lady, for that I am unwilling she should go ashore until I have further authority'. But in the meantime, he said gallantly, 'she shall not want anything the shore can afford, or any other honourable usage.' It was the last time she was to be treated so courteously.

# I

## 1574–1587
## *'So good a child'*

'Your sweet jewel is so good a child as can be this day.'

Elizabeth Wingfield to her half-sister Bess of Hardwick

# 'The hasty marriage'

TODAY, RUFFORD ABBEY IS AN EVOCATIVE RUIN, INCONGRUOUSLY set in a neat country park run by the local authority. The bulldozers that moved in during the 1950s seem to have sliced cleanly through the huge Nottinghamshire house, exposing the strata of the centuries: clear as the layers of rock in a geologist's sample, and just as illustrative of history.

Half buried in the ground are the remains of the twelfthcentury Cistercian abbey, where birds now fly straight through the glassless windows of the cellarium. Above them gawp the gigantic windows – ruined in their turn – of the Tudor mansion built by the noble Talbot family, after the Cistercians were turned out in the dissolution of the monasteries. The hound dogs of the Talbot crest still prance above the stable doorway. The formal grounds, and yet more brickwork, were laid out in time for the royal house parties of Rufford's second, Edwardian, heyday: the epoch which led D. H. Lawrence to borrow it for 'Wragby Hall', oppressive home to his Lady Chatterley. Finally – after the Second World War, after the county council took over – there were added the railings and notices, the disabled access ramps, of the late twentieth century.

Rufford has everything, including a ghost. Several of them, actually, including a clammy baby, with a penchant for nestling up to lady guests, and a huge Black Monk – blame him for the man buried in a nearby churchyard, who 'died after seeing the

Rufford ghost', as the parish register solemnly records. There is also a White Lady, flitting through the trees and weeping in classic style. This, so the guide books say, is Arbella.

But there seems no particular reason why Arbella Stuart's spirit, however restless, should choose Rufford for her return. Surely Hardwick Hall – or the Tower of London – would be more likely? On the other hand, Rufford Abbey was where it all began. This, almost forty years before that wild June ride to the river, was where Arbella Stuart's parents met and married. Another 'hasty marriage', another source of controversy. But no-one will ever be sure whether the brief drama enacted at Rufford in November 1574 was a romance or a political story.

Rufford lies a mere twenty-odd miles from Sheffield Castle and Chatsworth – the principal homes Arbella's grandmother (Bess 'of Hardwick', as she is usually known) shared with her fourth husband, George Talbot, the sixth earl of Shrewsbury. It lies, too, hard by the Great North Road along which the widowed countess of Lennox, with Charles Stuart, her only surviving son, set out from London to visit their Yorkshire estates that autumn. On the way north they stopped at the house of an acquaintance at Huntingdon, and Bess, who was visiting Rufford, made the comparatively easy trip down to join them. No surprises there, surely. Company fresh from the court was always welcome – and there had, after all, been some talk of marriage between Bess's daughter Elizabeth and 'young Bertie', son of the Huntingdon acquaintance. No surprise at all that Bess should invite the Lennox party to pause again at Rufford, and make another break in the wearisome winter journey.

So far, so likely. But Bess also happened – happened? – to have brought Elizabeth, her only unmarried daughter, with her to Rufford. And Lady Lennox no sooner arrived at the Talbot house than she found herself so fatigued by travel as to keep to her rooms for several days with Bess in close attendance, thus leaving the young people to each other's company. It would have been easy for them to lose themselves in Rufford – especially if no-one were trying to find them. The house was 'a confused labyrinth, underneath all vaults, above entries, closets, oratories . . . I was never so puzzled in my life,' reported a neighbour,

Sir John Holles, the then sheriff of Nottingham, disgustedly.

Did Bess have an ulterior motive in issuing her invitation? Did Lady Lennox have an ulterior motive in accepting? Elizabeth Cavendish (Bess's daughter by her second marriage) was twenty years old to Charles Stuart's nineteen. Perhaps the young people, thrown thus together, did start to fall in love. Whatever the feelings of the two principals, Bess had not got where she had by failing to seize an offered opportunity, and within days the wedding ceremony was performed at Rufford, with a speed that reflected the need for secrecy.

Young love was certainly the version of events their families offered to the authorities in London, when news of the sudden marriage was broken at court. But only a few vulnerable lives stood between Charles Stuart and the English, as well as the Scottish, throne. The unlicensed marriage of a possible royal heir was something like treachery; and each of those two formidable dames, the Ladies Lennox and Shrewsbury, had a past history that made a plot seem likely. When news of the match reached court, the queen and the privy council, her closest advisers, were unconvinced, and furious. A wave of arrests, accompanied by threats of the Tower and of torture, surrounded Arbella Stuart's conception.

Trouble was in her very bloodlines; and it dwelt with one blood relative particularly. The real concern over the events played out at Rufford Abbey was the suspicion that they were just one move in a deep-laid plot involving that perennial bugbear of Elizabeth's reign, the imprisoned Scots Queen Mary. Not only had Charles Stuart's elder brother been that Lord Darnley who had married Mary, but now the deposed queen was being held in English custody, just a few miles away from Rufford, by no other than Bess's husband, the earl of Shrewsbury.

Mary's arrival in England in the spring of 1568 had signalled a fresh series of shocks to the realm's stability – a stability never easily preserved by a small Protestant land in a continent of covetous Catholic superpowers. In 1574 it was only three years since the queen of Scots had plotted Elizabeth's murder; two since the duke of Norfolk had gone to the block for his part in that conspiracy. Just two years ago, in 1572, the St Bartholomew's Day

Mary Stuart, queen of Scotland, and Henry Stuart, Lord Darnley,
Charles Stuart's brother and Arbella's uncle

Massacre in Paris had seen thousands of Protestants slaughtered for their religion; now a new wave of Catholic missionary priests had begun to infiltrate England from the Jesuit seminaries. One year ago Queen Elizabeth had turned forty, and the chances of her marrying and bearing a child were beginning to look scant. The uncertainty about England's future, and in particular the danger of a Catholic challenge, explain why events at Rufford were taken so seriously at court.

From the isolation of the midlands, exculpatory letters were galloped south. Lord Shrewsbury wrote to the queen's chief minister Lord Burghley (William Cecil) that the young people 'hath so tied themselves upon [their] own liking as they can not part. The young man is so far in love as belike he is sick without her.' Shrewsbury – unlikely to have been included in any scheme of Bess's devising – was at a disadvantage here. Relaying his tale of young love to Burghley, he appended, dismally, 'as my wife tells me'. He wrote to Queen Elizabeth herself that the marriage:

> was dealt in suddenly, and without my knowledge . . . my wife, finding herself disappointed of young Bertie . . . and that the other young gentleman was inclined to love with a few days' acquaintance, did her best to further her daughter to this match, without having therein any other intent or respect than with reverent duty towards your Majesty she ought.

Lady Lennox wrote in a similar vein to Burghley: 'Now my Lord, for the hasty marriage of my son after that he had intangled himself so that he could have no other . . .' But as she wrote she was already on the way back to London, delayed only by her 'overlaboured mules'. She had been ordered south, with her son and new daughter-in-law, while the authorities conducted an inquiry into the affair.

She knew as well as anybody what had frightened Queen Elizabeth so severely. It was, as Lord Shrewsbury put it trenchantly, 'not the marriage matter . . . that makes this great ado. It is a greater matter.' But he firmly dismissed the possibility of any 'liking or insinuation' with Queen Mary. He was sticking to his story of young love. He added a significant comment: that surely 'that benefit any subject may by law claim' should also be given to his family. All her life, Arbella's rights as an individual would come up against her royalty.

One can hardly blame the council for their suspicions. Around the proffered picture of a romantic young couple entwines a cat's cradle of strings pulled by older and more powerful people: the two queens, of England and of Scotland; and those two forceful ladies, Arbella's grandmothers. The latter were to be the dominant influences on her early life. It was certainly they – rather than Arbella's short-lived parents – who most concerned Queen Elizabeth and her advisers.

Bess of Hardwick, Arbella's maternal grandmother, was by now almost fifty. This greatest of all the Elizabethan dynasts had been born into small gentry obscurity, but the cumulative gains of four marriages had made her one of the richest women in the land. The second, to Sir William Cavendish, had produced her children. The third had helped make her wealthy. Her fourth, to the earl of Shrewsbury, put her in a position to purchase for her daughter an alliance with royalty.

Bess and her fourth husband had not long been married when Queen Elizabeth found herself in need of a custodian for the deposed queen of Scots, newly landed in England. The choice fell on Shrewsbury – loyal, incorruptible and wealthy – and it was at his country houses (Sheffield Castle, Sheffield Lodge, Chatsworth) that Mary spent the next several years. Mary and Bess struck up a kind of friendship, and though the earl assured Lord Burghley that their talk together was all of 'indifferent trifling matters', they were much in each other's company. If Bess did later scheme to see her grandchild Arbella on the throne, then perhaps her dream was born here, as she sat at her needlework in the exalted company that in her obscure girlhood would have seemed so unlikely.

Arbella's grandmother on her father's side, Margaret, Lady Lennox, came from a very different background. Like Queen Elizabeth, Lady Lennox was a granddaughter of Henry VII of England, and hers was the illustrious bloodline that made Arbella's birth a matter of such moment. The survivor of nearly sixty years of intrigue and catastrophe, Lady Lennox was a bitter and disappointed woman, one with whom life had dealt harshly. In contrast to the ever-rising Bess, Lady Lennox was facing an old age of poverty – poverty, at least, for one who never forgot that she was royalty.

She was born from the second marriage of Henry VIII's elder sister Margaret Tudor (whose first marriage to James IV of Scotland had produced the Scottish royal line). It had been a stormy match that saw the dowager queen finally hounded out of Scotland, and Margaret Lennox's youth had not been happy. As a teenager, 'Little Marget' had been taken by her uncle Henry VIII to be brought up with his daughter Mary, and there was a time (after both Mary and her half-sister Elizabeth had in turn been declared illegitimate) when Margaret, though herself a Catholic, was officially her uncle's heir. At the same time, unfortunately, she was thrown into the Tower for an unsanctioned betrothal to Thomas Howard, a near relation to the disgraced Anne Boleyn. (This, interestingly, was the alliance which prompted parliament to pass an act imposing the death penalty for royal marriages undertaken without the monarch's approval.) Then the birth of Prince Edward released her from her perilous pre-eminence in the succession, Thomas Howard died of 'Tower fever', and Margaret was thrust into a diplomatically useful alliance with Matthew Stuart, earl of Lennox, a powerful Scottish noble with a good claim to be the next heir to the Scots crown after the infant Mary.

Lennox was 'a strong man, of personage well proportioned . . . very pleasant in the sight of gentlewomen'; Margaret was 'sensible and devout'. Their arranged marriage in 1544 turned into some sort of love-match. But their life was far from easy, for Lennox's alliance with the English cause cost him his Scottish lands. The couple lived as pensioners of the English throne in Yorkshire, Margaret's fortunes rising during the reign of her fellow Catholic and old classmate Mary Tudor (who gave her precedence, in court and succession, over the Protestant princess Elizabeth) and sinking when Elizabeth came to the throne. As the likelihood of acquiring power in England diminished, the Lennoxes' eyes turned again north of the border. In 1564 Lord Lennox was allowed to return to Scotland and attempt to repossess his confiscated lands there, but Lady Lennox, remaining in England, was soon in trouble, suspected of disloyalty, and spent a second period in the Tower for her part in planning the match between her eldest son, Lord Darnley, and Mary, queen of Scots.

The Lennox or 'Darnley' Jewel – still in the British royal collection – was made to commemorate the changing fates of Matthew and Margaret's royal claims. 'Who hopes still constantly with patience shall at last obtain victory' reads the Latin motto. A winged crown reposes amid figures of the optimistic virtues, Faith and Hope. The locket case is inlaid and enamelled with a whole anthology of emblems: a crowned salamander (the creature which, like the much-enduring Lennoxes, can survive scorching flames); the phoenix risen from the ashes. But flames and ashes were indeed the end of the marriage between Darnley and the queen of Scots. In 1567 he was murdered in an explosion at Kirk o' Field, possibly with the connivance of his royal wife, and the ensuing scandal forced the Scots queen to flee.

Whatever their personal grief, the Lennox family briefly held on to power, the earl ruling Scotland as regent for his infant grandson James. But the earl himself was assassinated in 1571, his bleeding body carried past the young boy. The darker emblems on the Lennox Jewel had begun to look more appropriate: the pelican in her piety, plucking her own breast that her young might feed from her blood; united hearts wounded by arrows. A demon dragging a distressed woman by her hair is considered to represent Time, and by 1574 Margaret Lennox, long since released from imprisonment on compassionate grounds, must have felt time had run out on her and her own chances of success or happiness.

There remained only the dynasty. When Lady Lennox petitioned to be allowed to visit her northern estates for that fateful trip, broken at Rufford with such dramatic consequences, her request was at first regarded dubiously. 'I greatly suspect that she has no other purpose than to transfer the little prince [James] into England,' Fenelon, the French ambassador, warned his master darkly. Permission for the journey was reluctantly granted, however, on condition that Lady Lennox did not attempt any communication with the queen of Scots along the way. She retorted that she had no wish to speak with the woman who had murdered her son. A feint? When the court learned of the marriage of Lady Lennox's son to the daughter of the Scots queen's companion, it seemed all too likely.

While Shrewsbury couldn't leave his post as custodian to Mary, while Bess was left at large, Lady Lennox obeyed her summons south, lamenting all the way. Back in London, she found herself committed to the Tower for the third time in her life. 'Thrice I have been cast into prison, not for matters of treason but for love matters,' she complained sadly.

The affair did not quickly die away. The queen's spymaster, Sir Francis Walsingham, himself drew up a list of questions to be put to Lady Lennox's steward Thomas Fowler:

'Whether about midsummer last he was not sent to his mistress' house at Templenewsam.'

'If he was, for what cause.'

'Whether during his being at Templenewsam he went to speak to Lady Shrewsbury . . .'

Charles Lennox's secretary was also subjected to 'some kind of persuasion cunningly used'. But the authorities failed to uncover any plot involving the queen of Scots; any 'large treasons'. There is no evidence that Bess (who seems to have maintained an obstinate silence throughout) suffered any punishment beyond a vague house arrest. It was simply too embarrassing to have the wife of the Scots queen's gaoler herself thrown in prison, as Bess herself was probably well aware.

Even the luckless Lady Lennox was soon released to her house in Hackney, where the young couple were living very quietly. The new countess Elizabeth was already pregnant. A family friend of the Shrewsburys visited them there in the spring and found all well. 'I trust very shortly that the dregs of all misconstruction will be wiped away, that their abode there after this sort will be altered,' commented Shrewsbury's son Gilbert piously.

The precise date and place of Arbella's birth are uncertain, but on 10 November 1575 Lady Lennox was writing to the Scots queen from Hackney: 'I yield your Majesty my most humble thanks for your good remembrance and bounty to our little daughter here.' The unexpectedly warm tone of the letter may well have given pause to the authorities when, inevitably, it was intercepted by Burghley. Lady Lennox signed herself affectionately 'Your Majesty's most humble and loving mother and aunt', and the young countess Elizabeth added obsequious prayers for Mary's 'long and happy estate' from one 'who loves and honours your Majesty unfeignedly'.

Arbella's unusual name stands out from the usual Tudor litany of Elizabeths, Margarets and Marys. (Latinizing it to Arabella, as became usual in later centuries, doesn't help to explain it away.) It is true that the sixteenth century did have a colourful range of Christian names to set beside the old favourites: the *Casebooks* of the astrologer and doctor Simon Forman featured an Appellina Proudlove, an Aquila Gould and an Actaeon Dove. But Arbella's name may have been chosen for the Queen Annabella (Drummond) who had featured in the annals of Scottish royalty. She had, after all, a good claim to the Scottish throne, as well as to the English one.

James the heir, Arbella the spare . . . Perhaps, after all, the more hopeful prophecies of the Lennox Jewel were beginning to look a little more likely.

# 'Most renowned stock'

ARBELLA'S SEX WAS PROBABLY A DISAPPOINTMENT TO HER GRAND-mothers – though not, perhaps, to Queen Elizabeth. A boy might have become a candidate for the throne attractive enough to threaten an ageing, childless woman. But, male or female, Arbella had an important place in the convoluted web of debated rights that constituted the English succession in the late sixteenth century.

The Elizabethans loved genealogy. Historians laboured to trace the queen's descent from King Arthur of Round Table fame. Lord Burghley (though himself short of illustrious forebears) had a chamber of his great house Theobalds painted with trees, one for each county in England, and hanging from the branches the coat of arms of every noble who dwelt there. Arbella's family tree was one of particular complexity; but she would have grown up knowing every detail of it.

Since Queen Elizabeth had neither child nor surviving sibling, the chain of succession stepped backwards a generation. Discounting the Spanish royal family, who claimed distant rights through the fourteenth-century John of Gaunt, and distant Plantagenet descendants, there were at the time of Arbella's birth four principal English families who could contend for the position of heir, deriving from the two sisters of Henry VIII.

The most prominent claimant, and chief among the descendants of Henry's elder sister Margaret, was Mary, queen of

Scots herself. In 1575 she was widely held to be Elizabeth's immediate heir. But as a Catholic, a foreigner and a prisoner, her claim was obviously problematic in practical terms. The children of Margaret Tudor's marriage to the king of Scotland, moreover, were as foreigners technically excluded from any rights in the English throne. By contrast, Arbella's grandmother Margaret Lennox (sole surviving child of Margaret Tudor's second marriage), had the advantage of having been born in England. Against that stood the fact that her father was already betrothed elsewhere when he married her mother: a serious matter in the sixteenth century, and enough to lay Lady Lennox open to the slur of illegitimacy. But no claim at this time was squeaky clean. The throne was still a prize to be played for, in a game of politics and pragmatism.

Within a few years from 1575 the claims of the contenders on Margaret Tudor's side had crystallized in a younger generation. The claim of Mary, queen of Scots passed to her son James, so usefully a Protestant. The claim of Margaret Lennox passed either to her grandson, that same James – thus doubly entitled – or to her son Charles and then to his daughter Arbella. James may have had the advantage of seniority, but he could easily have found himself excluded by his foreign nationality. The boy king of Scotland, moreover, was the target of repeated assassination attempts, while Arbella grew up in seclusion and safety.

So much for the descendants of Margaret Tudor. The descendants of Henry VIII's younger sister Mary Tudor might be assumed to take a lower place in the succession. But Henry, in his latter years, specifically decreed that, in the event of his own children dying without heirs, the throne should pass to Mary's line. (Opinion was divided as to whether the crown really could be thus willed, like a piece of private property.)

Mary Tudor had been married off young to the ageing French king, Louis XII. Widowed without child, she married again and gave birth to two daughters, each of whom in turn had a family. The child of her younger daughter married into the Stanley family, the earls of Derby. Her offspring were not only the most junior line of inheritance, but those potential heirs who sought the throne least consistently; nor did they interact much with the other three branches of the family tree. There was, moreover, the taint of Catholicism about them. We can set them aside, for the moment.

The situation was different in the case of Mary Tudor's elder daughter, who married Henry Grey and gave birth to the tragic Grey sisters: Jane, Catherine and Mary. Unequivocally English and ardently Protestant, Lady Jane Grey went to the block in 1554 for her proximity to the throne. In the early years of Elizabeth I's reign Catherine Grey had been widely regarded as Elizabeth's heir apparent, her claim set above even that of Mary, queen of Scots. Elizabeth herself talked of adopting Catherine – but then Catherine made a clandestine marriage with Edward Seymour, earl of Hertford, son to the lord protector who had dominated Edward VI's minority (and himself descended, through his mother, from Edward III). When their secret wedding was discovered, the marriage, for lack of proof, was declared invalid, and Catherine was sent to the Tower, where her baby, Lord Beauchamp, was born. Hertford too was imprisoned, but the couple still managed to meet with their gaolers' connivance, as proved by the birth of a second baby.

Catherine was the only one of the three Grey sisters to produce sons and grandsons – men whose fate was to be closely inter-twined with that of Arbella. Catherine died in disgrace in 1568; her story would be one with which Arbella grew up, and which affected her deeply. In 1575 the Seymour claim seemed to have been buried with Catherine. Her sons seemed disqualified by the taint of illegitimacy. There was no thought of reviving her claim in her hunchbacked sister Mary – who was in any case herself similarly disgraced for an unlicensed marriage, and died in 1578.

But claims which could be set aside in the early days of Elizabeth's reign, when it still seemed likely that the queen would marry and have heirs of her own body, loomed up again a few decades later. The Seymours, the Scots royal line and Arbella remained locked in a decades-long dance of relationship and rivalry. In her own generation, Arbella's claim to the English throne was by no means the worst of the three on the table. But she – the only woman left in the race – was the individual who would suffer most bitterly.

*

The apparent love-match of Arbella's parents was in many ways an ominous start. Her family background reflects a familiar, frightening, leitmotif: an intimate association of love and death, sex and violence, that echoed in the events which followed Charles and Elizabeth's wedding day. Illicit and controversial marriage runs like a fault-line through the chronicles of the Tudor family, erupting in Henry VIII's appalling marital history; Mary, queen of Scots' romantic disasters; and Queen Elizabeth's early encounter with Thomas Seymour, the earl of Hertford's uncle, whose attempted seduction of the young princess brought him to the block. Margaret Lennox saw the marriage of her parents end in divorce and armed conflict; her first love Thomas Howard died in the Tower – a 'gentle beast' who had lost his will to live, as the poet-earl of Surrey described him movingly. Her own subsequent marriage was almost torn apart by political necessity. Catherine and Mary Grey both married for love and died, in direct consequence, under lock and key. Catherine Grey's son, Lord Beauchamp, was himself kept three years under house arrest by his own father for marrying against his wishes.

This was a pattern that would recur in Arbella's life, too. And yet, it was itself only one aspect of a violent heredity. When the baby Arbella was christened at the parish church of Chatsworth, her only recorded godparents were maternal aunts and uncles – in bleak contrast to the royal sponsors who had attended the baptisms of Bess of Hardwick's own children. Few of the near relatives on her father's side who might have been represented at the font were alive and at liberty. It was a bloody heritage.

# 'My jewel Arbell'

THE PORTRAIT OF ARBELLA STUART AS A TODDLER WHICH STILL HANGS in Hardwick Hall is surely too idiosyncratic not to have been painted from life. This is no mere map of the fashionable standard of beauty; not even infant beauty. Her hair neatly coiffed under a jewelled cap, she stands almost as broad as she is high in her embroidered robes. Pearls drip from the heart of each twining flower (the Cavendish eglantine?) on the padded sleeves; but her wide blue eyes, unmoved by all this grown-up glory, stare un-compromisingly from a face so square the pointed chin juts out like an afterthought. Not a toddler to tangle with, you would say. But court fashion has its place in her accoutrements: one podgy hand clutches a doll in the elaborate formal dress that was called the Spanish style, and the red-gold of the doll's hair – and of Arbella's own, whether by nature or artifice – reflects that of the queen.

Family pride, too, looms large. On a massive triple chain around the infant's neck there swings a shield with a gold countess's coronet upon it, and the ominous Lennox motto, *Pour parvenir, j'endure*: 'I endure in order to succeed'. (Perhaps it fits her better than the Cavendish motto: *Cavendo tutus*, 'Safe by taking care'.)

Along with the sitter's exact age – twenty-three months – the picture is labelled, rather defiantly, 'Arbella Comitessa Leviniae' – countess of Lennox. Arbella's gender would win her no favours in the patriarchal world of the sixteenth century; nor yet would her youth be granted much indulgence. Childhood, to the Elizabethans, was merely the tiresome prologue to the play, to be got over speedily. But her rank was another matter. Arbella had been born into the very highest rank of a hierarchical society. The nobility still attracted to themselves not only troops of lesser men (an earl of Shrewsbury earlier in the century had been able to raise four and a half thousand of his own forces), but a satellite horde of client gentry. Many a knight was glad to wear an earl's livery.

That title, the Scottish earldom of Lennox, had belonged to Arbella's father. Charles Stuart, always sickly, died of consumption in early April 1576, at the house in Hackney. It is hard to know how much was lost with his death. A portrait of an ethereally fair child standing next to the elder brother he resembled, Lord Darnley, is one of the few sources of information about Charles Stuart. But while it would be unfair to deduce his character from that of Darnley – 'wilful, haughty, and vicious', in the words of one Scots courtier – he was clearly not the perfect son. When Charles was a difficult fifteen-year-old, his widowed mother described him as the 'greatest dolour' in a life not free from trials. 'His father's absence so long time in his riper years hath made lack to be to him in diverse ways . . . he is somewhat unfurnished of qualities needful and I being now a lone woman am less like to have him well reformed at home than before.' A year later his new tutor, more optimistically, wrote that he 'gives great promise for the future'. If he did, it was never realized.

Charles left his wife Elizabeth widowed after eighteen months, and his daughter a baby. The Lennox title and lands now belonged to Arbella – or so her relatives in England felt. But the Scottish government claimed differently. Citing the minority of young King James, which might be held to make all grant of title and estate provisional, and Arbella's English nationality, they instantly moved to repossess the Scottish Lennox property.

Old Lady Lennox begged Queen Elizabeth's intercession with the Scottish regent in a letter full of bullet points: '1st. How the dower can be avoided by their laws. 2nd. How the regent can disinherit the daughter of Charles Stuart. 3rd. If he will not permit the dower to be answered.' Elizabeth was sympathetic; she could afford to be, since she, at least, was being put to no expense. A message was sent off to the effect that 'The queen finds it very strange that any disposition should be intended of the earldom to the prejudice of the only daughter of the late earl of Lennox.'

The queen of Scots likewise spoke out on her niece's side. In a draft will she wrote: 'I give to my niece Arbella the earldom of Lennox, held by her late father; and enjoin my son, as my heir and successor, to obey my will in this particular.' It was perhaps unhelpful that she had previously tried to will the Scottish crown itself to Charles, Arbella's father, as next heir after James. In any event, in the matter of Arbella's inheritance, as in so much else, James disappointed his mother. On 3 May 1578 the twelve-year-old king bestowed the earldom on the old and childless bishop of Caithness, Charles Stuart's uncle. Shortly afterwards, with the bishop's connivance, a deal was struck by which the earldom of Lennox was handed on to James's cousin and favourite, Esmé Stuart, the fascinating Lord D'Aubigny.

The Lennox title was one thing; the Lennox lands another, and in practical terms even more important. In letters a quarter of a century later Arbella herself, suffering from a lack of the independence money might have brought her, would make repeated reference to 'my long desired land'. Her early background, indeed, was one of comparative poverty. Until the spring of 1578, Arbella and her mother seem to have lived much of the time with Lady Lennox in Hackney. The young Stuarts had never set up their own establishment, probably lacking the money; and Lady Lennox's own means were limited indeed. Her poverty, indeed, may explain her compliance in her son's match with Elizabeth Cavendish: a rich girl, but only gentry-born. Lady Lennox's records showed regular payments to Bess, probably on a considerable loan, and she had also repayments due on debts to the crown.

Elizabeth Lennox should have had her own dowry of three thousand pounds from her stepfather, the earl of Shrewsbury; but, her marriage having been arranged 'suddenly and without my knowledge', the earl – also somewhat strapped for cash, despite his huge land holdings – refused to pay.

Then, in the first days of March 1578, the old countess of Lennox fell ill with sharp pains. Granted a brief respite, she none the less called her household together to say goodbye. On 9 March she died. Wardship of the infant Arbella was given to her mother Elizabeth – though for a noble orphan to be placed in the care of its relatives was by no means a foregone conclusion. Rights in a child's estate and person, with the future right to dispose of them advantageously in marriage, fell to the crown and could be given or sold on by the master of the wards, Lord Burghley. In this case, however, the Shrewsburys had made their request just a few days beforehand, with a prescience that struck some contemporary observers rather oddly.

On the day she fell ill, Lady Lennox had dined with Robert Dudley, earl of Leicester, Queen Elizabeth's perennial favourite. This conjunction of events produced vague rumours of poison; but there were always rumours of poison after the sudden death of any person of note. The story surfaced a few years later in a scurrilous Catholic propaganda publication called *Leicester's Commonwealth*, which suggested that Robert Dudley had put several people away.

It is true that in the next decade Leicester – a man so often disappointed of the crown he sought, and an old friend and ally of Bess – would seek a match between his son and Arbella. If Lady Lennox opposed such an alliance, he would indeed be better off with her out of the way. But there is no evidence for this, nor any real reason to impugn Leicester's reputation – especially since, while Lady Lennox's death is commonly described as 'sudden', one contemporary remark places it rather in the context of a 'languishing decline'.

She certainly wasn't murdered for her money. Lady Lennox's death left Arbella theoretically the richer of some jewels; but jewels apart, she didn't even leave enough to pay for her funeral expenses. Still, she was buried in Westminster Abbey with the full panoply of royalty: the herald to proclaim every one of her titles; nobility in attendance. On her glorious painted tomb kneel the figures of her dead children – the half-dozen who died in infancy, Darnley with the crown above his head, and Charles, who had himself been interred in the same vault two years before.

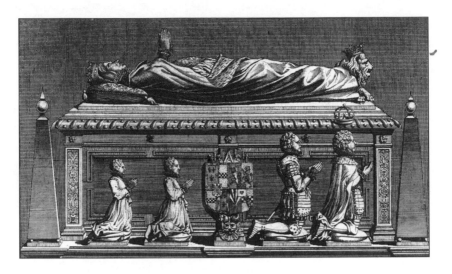

The tomb of Margaret, countess of Lennox,
Arbella's paternal grandmother

*Invicta anima* and *patientia incomparabili*, read the tributes; and indeed, an undefeated spirit and an incomparable patience were exactly what the much-tried Lady Lennox had required.

The notoriously parsimonious Queen Elizabeth, unusually, picked up the bill for the funeral. Relations between the two women had not been easy. But Elizabeth had won. She was the queen; Margaret had died in poverty. And to have her buried other than as befitted her lineage would damage the queen's own dignity.

Dignity was one thing. Practicality was another. In recompense, she said, for the funeral expenses, Elizabeth seized the remaining, English, Lennox lands. In this she was behaving in just the way she had deplored in the king of Scotland, but what was sauce for the gander wasn't always sauce for the goose. As the contemporary historian Camden records it, the queen 'would not give ear to those who affirmed that the Lady Arbella, daughter to Charles the king's uncle and born in England, was next heir to the lands in England'. There was more of the undignified squabbling over rights that seemed to follow any death in the Elizabethan nobility. Arbella retained the estate of Smallwood, and its revenues of perhaps three hundred pounds a year. But even her grandmother's jewels were to be another source of controversy.

Lady Lennox's will ordained the jewels – twenty-odd items 'with other things that be not yet in memory' – should be delivered to Arbella when she was fourteen. They included 'a jewel set with a fair table diamond, a table ruby and an emerald with a fair great pearl . . . a clock set in crystal with a wolf of gold upon it . . . buttons of rock rubies to set on a gown'. The jewels were in the charge of her steward and executor Thomas Fowler – the same Thomas Fowler who had been questioned over the marriage of Arbella's parents. (Later, his son was to care for Arbella. These Fowlers were one of the satellite families whose fate trailed Arbella's own story.) Mary wrote to him in her own hand in the autumn of 1579: 'Be it known that we, Mary, by the grace of God queen of Scotland, do will and require Thomas Fowler, sole executor to our dearest mother in law and aunt . . . to deliver into the hands of our right well-beloved cousin Elizabeth, countess of Shrewsbury, all and every such jewel . . .' This was to be another of those ineffectual pronouncements the queen of Scots was so fond of making. Fowler, instead, made his way to Scotland, where he was – he claimed – waylaid and robbed. The jewels ultimately found their way into King James's possession. They remained the focus of yet another longstanding dispute.

At least in her grandmother Bess Arbella had an able protector, one who would defend her rights all the way. It was Bess who ensured that Queen Elizabeth was eventually persuaded to provide an annual pension for mother and child: four hundred pounds for Elizabeth and two hundred for Arbella. Lady Lennox's death had certainly brought Arbella – and her mother – more directly into Bess's turbulent orbit. In the autumn of 1578 Bess was writing to Walsingham of 'my little Arbell': 'I came hither [Sheffield] of Crestoline's eve and left my little Arbell at Chatsworth. She endured very well with travel and yet I was forced to take long journeys to be here with my lord afore ye day.'

The great Elizabethan households were by their nature peripatetic; in an age with little plumbing, houses had to be periodically vacated for 'sweetening'. One has here a particularly vivid sense of the young Arbella swept along in her grandmother's turbulent wake; uncomplainingly 'enduring' the hard journeys in horse litter or unsprung coach, wooden wheels jouncing along roads often little better than waterlogged tracks. There is no mention of whether Arbella's mother travelled with them; to judge from one letter Elizabeth wrote to her mother when Arbella was rising two, the relationship between Bess and Elizabeth may have foreshadowed that of Bess and Arbella all too neatly.

In the matter of some unknown dispute, Elizabeth Lennox was furiously resentful that Bess had not given her the benefit of the doubt she would have accorded to others: 'I have not so evil deserved as your Ladyship hath made show.' In a postscript to one letter, thanking the earl of Leicester for his efforts in the matter of the Lennox inheritance, the 22-year-old Elizabeth shows a young woman's resentment of parental authority. 'My mother hearing of the infection at Chelsea, whereof, although there was no great danger, yet her fear was such, as having not any fit house that for necessity I must presently come hither [to Newgate Street] by her commandment which I have obeyed.'

All three generations were together for the Christmas of 1581 in Sheffield. But during the Twelfth Night celebrations, Elizabeth Lennox fell sick; and on 21 January 1582, she died. Five days earlier, already 'sick in body', she had made her will. 'In her extreme sickness,' as Bess put it, 'and even at the approaching of her end (which I cannot without great grief remember) [she] did most earnestly sundry times recommend to her Majesty's great goodness and favour that poor infant her only care.'

The young countess left behind her entreaties that Leicester, Sir Christopher Hatton, Burghley and Walsingham – Queen Elizabeth's four closest courtiers – should continue their 'wonted favour' towards her 'small orphan'. To the queen herself she left her 'best jewel set with great diamonds'; to her mother, her white sables; to Shrewsbury, whom she thanked for being a good father both to her and to Arbella, her gold salt cellar.

Touchingly, she arranged gifts to be given to her brothers and sisters against the next New Year. Arbella, by the queen's good grace, she left to Bess's charge. Elizabeth Lennox was buried in the parish church of Sheffield; from now on, Arbella's primary relationship was to be with Bess.

There is no record of the six-year-old Arbella's feelings about her mother's death, just as there had been none of the young Queen Elizabeth's feelings at the violent death of her mother Anne Boleyn. But the countess Elizabeth (unlike Anne the queen) had by Bess's testimony been with Arbella almost constantly. It is easy to believe that the relationships between aristocratic parents and children, distanced as they were by servants, were less close than those among the less privileged classes. But in the 1570s one Peter Erondell (in a volume of dialogue, *The French Garden*, written as a translation exercise) painted a different picture. His noble heroine Lady Ri-Melaine goes to supervise the wet-nurse who is bathing her baby son, her 'little boykin', with a display of tenderness that still moves today: 'O my little heart! God bless thee, rub the crown of his head, wash his ears, and put some fine clout [cloth] behind them to keep them dry and clean . . . What a fair neck he hath! Pull off his shirt, thou art pretty and fat my little darling, wash his arm-pits: What aileth his elbow? O what an arm he hath!' If this tenderness was in any way reflected in the relationship between Arbella and Elizabeth Lennox, the child's loss was great indeed. None the less, it is the feelings of Bess, not those of the orphaned Arbella, about which we hear. Shrewsbury wrote to Walsingham that Bess 'taketh her daughter's death so grievously and so mourneth and lamenteth that she can think of nothing but tears'. He added – piteously but, given Bess's wealth, unconvincingly – that the child Arbella was now destitute.

Seven days later, Bess was sufficiently recovered from her grief to think of the future. 'Your Lordship', she wrote to Burghley, 'hath heard by my lord how it hath pleased God to visit me; but in what soever is to lay his heavy hand on us we must take it thankfully.' She thanked Burghley, too, for his many favours: 'how much your lordship did bind me, the poor woman that is gone, and my sweet jewel, Arbella, at our last being at court, neither the mother during her life nor I can ever forget.' Now she asked another favour: that the four hundred pounds' pension paid to Elizabeth Lennox be added to Arbella's two hundred for 'her better education'. 'Her servants that are to look to her, her masters that are to train her up in all good learning and virtue, will require no small charge.' Bess never got the extra money. But her justification for requesting it – Arbella's relationship to the queen – was a theme upon which Bess harped repeatedly. The child, she wrote to Walsingham, is 'well near seven years old and of very great towardness [precocity] to learn anything and I very careful of her good education as she were my own and only child, and a great deal more for the consanguinity she is of to her Majesty'.

To Burghley, Bess wrote again: 'Although she were everywhere her mother were during her life, I can not now like [Arbella] should be here nor in any place else where I may not sometimes see her and daily hear of her, and therefore [I am] charged with keeping house where she must be with such as is fit for her calling.' The little girl was 'very apt to learn and able to conceive what shall be taught her', added Bess, encouragingly.

Bess could not have been an easy woman to live with, or one with whom a child would necessarily feel at home. In a letter of 1577, her son-in-law Gilbert Talbot described to Bess the effect she had on his toddler George. The child, he said, 'drinketh every day to Lady Grandmother'; but 'if he have any spice, I tell him Lady Grandmother is come and will see him; which he then will either quickly hide or quickly eat; and then asks where Lady Danmode [Grandmother] is.' The effect is of a formidable personality – a family martinet, if not actually a bogey.

Ten days after Gilbert had written that letter, little George died. Shrewsbury wrote to Burghley unsympathetically that 'I doubt not my wife will show more folly than need requires.' To Walsingham he wrote: 'my wife is not so well able to rule her passions, and has driven herself into such a case by her continual weeping as is likely to breed in her further inconvenience.' Bess seems to have been a woman of untrammelled feelings; and in the orbit of such a one, it is difficult for a younger and more fragile personality to develop freely. But there is another warning bell sounding here. The earl's letter also indicates the growing lack of sympathy between the Shrewsburys themselves.

# 'Good lady grandmother'

WE CANNOT, AT THIS POINT IN HER STORY, FEEL THAT WE HAVE REALLY 'met' Arbella. Perhaps it would not even help if we could step back through the distance of the centuries. She was, after all, still only six years old, and anyone who has spent time with children knows how their gaze – the wide, unreceptive gaze of the toddler in the portrait – seems to interact only briefly with the adult world and then move on, fast as sun and showers on an April day. But if we look forward to the Arbella of the adult letters, we can see some of the traits she would display marked out already.

We can see how she came by her powerful head of anger, and her refusal to settle for the hand her life had dealt. We can see her curious blindness to other people's reactions, her intelligence and her emotional timidity. It is harder to see her playfulness and her independence, her capacity for self-mockery. But these were not qualities of which the Elizabethans wrote. Contemporaries praised Arbella for her goodness and her gravity: censured her only for haughtiness, or for her failure to understand and accept the politics of her day – for her failure, in other words, appropriately to assess her position in relation to other people. Perhaps that, too, is something she learned from her family.

Her childhood – nature and nurture alike – gave her many gifts. But neither was calculated to make her life easy. Hers was a fractious family. As early as 1575 the earl of Shrewsbury was reported by his son Gilbert as being 'often in great choler upon slight occasion'. By the time the six-year-old Arbella came wholly into Bess's care in 1582, the situation had deteriorated yet further. A gentleman servant of Bess's wrote seeking new employment on the grounds that 'this house is a hell.' And Arbella was to be another cause of strife between the earl and countess. In the usual way of marital disputes she was used as pawn, to be placed on the board wherever necessary. 'My lord sending the little lady Arbella to me,' grumbled Bess to Lord Leicester, 'being a thing I desired much the contrary . . .' As Robert Beale, clerk to the privy council, wrote: 'The matter of the Lady Arbella's remaining with [the earl] might have been well brought to pass if the countess could have [been] brought to have sought it at his hands in humble sort.' But Bess was not well acquainted with humility.

Portraits of Bess from the time of Arbella's youth show a spare woman dressed in uncompromising black, her sandy hair turning grey. She is not uncomely; but the sharp nose and thin rigid mouth bespeak a formidable severity. The antiquarian Edmund Lodge called her 'a woman of masculine understanding – proud, furious, selfish and unfeeling'. It was a harsh judgement on the woman who was to raise the young Arbella; a man's judgement, maybe, resentful of a woman who had achieved what Bess had achieved in terms of power and property. In the eighteenth century, Horace Walpole had a malicious rhyme for her:

*Four times the nuptial bed she warmed*
*And each time so well performed*
*When Death had spoiled each husband's billing*
*He left the widow every shilling.*

Bess was indeed a triumphal survivor – but her life, while successful, had not been easy. Her father, John Hardwick of Hardwick Hall in Derbyshire (then a simple manor house), died in 1527 in Bess's infancy, and the family was left in penury. His widow married again, but her new husband was himself imprisoned in the Fleet for insolvency just a few years later. Perhaps her early experience of struggle to overcome disruption and hardship hardly encouraged Bess, later, to regard the troubles of a more privileged granddaughter with particular sympathy.

Bess was not yet fifteen when she married her first husband, Robert Barlow, a young man whom she nursed devotedly when he fell sick in the house where she was staying. But Barlow died in 1544, still a minor. Her second husband was Sir William Cavendish: a widower and father already, a rising man knighted by Henry VIII and profiting from the dissolution of the monasteries. He was twenty-two years older than her, but by all accounts they were very happy. Children came quickly – six surviving to adulthood – and in 1549, through family connections, they bought the manor of Chatsworth in Derbyshire and began to purchase lands around it, close to Bess's family. They rebuilt Chatsworth as a grey castellated block (itself long since replaced) with meagre windows, framing a central court; the old style from which fashion was only just moving away.

The advent of Catholic Mary, 'Bloody Mary', to the English throne was a blow to the Cavendish family. But Sir William's death in 1557 put an end to an official inquiry into his professional dealings. Bess recorded her own feelings, on this occasion, with a mixture of emotion and efficiency. 'Memorandum. That Sir William Cavendish Knight my most dear and well beloved husband departed this present life the 25th day of October . . . I most humbly beseech the Lord to have mercy and rid me and his poor children out of our great misery.' Bess, some thirty years old, was left with six young children, two stepdaughters and five thousand pounds owing to the treasury. Yet perversely, it may have been now that the preoccupation of her life was born – to continue what her husband had begun and found a great dynasty.

After two years of widowhood, Bess married again. Sir William St Loe was one of the most ardent supporters of the new Queen Elizabeth. He was well-to-do, a successful courtier, and besotted with Bess to the point of folly. He appears gladly to have taken on not only her family commitments but the further beautification of the Cavendish home in Derbyshire; he dowered Bess's stepdaughter, arranged her boys' entry into Eton, and jokingly addressed letters to 'my own dear wife Chatsworth'. Bess's huge influence over St Loe, and his expressed intention of leaving all his lands to her, led to accusations of sorcery being bandied around his family. His death – after some five or six years of marriage – left her very rich indeed.

Bess's fourth and last marriage, concluded three years later, was to be her grandest. But her alliance with George Talbot, sixth earl of Shrewsbury, a wealthy widower whose massive property in the north and the midlands ran close by Bess's own, was to end so badly that it shook the country.

At first Shrewsbury, like his predecessors, seemed to fall happily under the spell of Bess's forceful personality. 'Of all earthly joys, that hath happened to me, I thank God chiefest for you,' he wrote to her soon after their marriage. But the earl's onerous new duties as custodian to the Scots queen placed an enormous strain on the family. There were, from the start, essentially three people in the Shrewsburys' marriage, since the earl was never allowed to be far away from Mary. From Shrewsbury's main home at Sheffield, the party moved between Tutbury, Wingfield, the springs at Buxton and Chatsworth, as dictated by orders from London and the pressing need to clean the overcrowded houses – some forty-eight moves in sixteen years, made in mounting disharmony.

Queen Elizabeth's insistence on having as few people as possible near the Scots queen multiplied alarmingly the number of establishments that the earl had to maintain in order to house his children ('heavy burdens, although comfortable', he called his off-spring). There were an 'infinite number of hidden charges' brought on by his position, and by the early 1580s the supposed richest man in England was in such difficulties that he wrote of having his old plate melted down to pacify his creditors. But his pride was wounded even more sharply. To the demands of Mary's custody was added, he increasingly came to feel, Bess's determination to enrich her own children at his expense. 'My riches they talk of are in other men's purses,' he said grimly.

When the two great landowners had married, the financial settlements had been complicated beyond belief. All Bess's property (other than the entailed Chatsworth) naturally became Shrewsbury's. In return, however, he made her promises of in-heritance and upkeep, including the settlement of a large sum on each of her two younger sons, William and Charles, when they

George Talbot, sixth earl of Shrewsbury, Bess's fourth husband

came of age. A few years down the line, this agreement had been amended by mutual consent, so that Shrewsbury instead then and there returned to his wife's ownership a certain percentage of the lands that had been her own. He thus gave back to Bess her financial independence; and, shrewd businesswoman that she was, she used her holding wisely. But as his countess became richer, the earl's wealth decreased, and he resented it furiously. Only 'brawling' finally brought Bess her daughter Elizabeth's disputed dowry. And 'brawling', increasingly, was the way she communicated with her husband.

Their feuding even became physical. Bess's son Charles Cavendish had to take refuge in a church steeple for twenty-four hours after being attacked outside Chatsworth by a party of the earl's servants. In July 1584 (when Arbella was eight, and able to understand the servants' gossip) Shrewsbury and a party of armed men tried to take forcible possession of Chatsworth, and were repulsed by Bess's favourite son William, 'with halberd in hand and pistol under his girdle'. Shrewsbury, outraged, complained to the queen's advisers. 'It were no reason that my wife and her servants should rule me and make me the wife and her the husband,' was how he tellingly described the insult.

The authorities, to placate Shrewsbury, clapped William Cavendish into Fleet prison, since 'it was not meet that a man of his mean quality should use himself in a contemptuous sort against one of his lordship's station and quality.' In view of his position as Queen Mary's gaoler, the great earl was always dealt with as tenderly as could be. But the class dimension to the indictment is interesting: Shrewsbury himself would sneer at his wife's 'base stock'. The Cavendishes (whose blood it was that mingled in Arbella's veins with that of the royal Stuarts) really were Johnnies-come-lately – like Burghley, Leicester, Ralegh and so many of the Elizabethan mighty.

The younger generation, Arbella's aunts and uncles, were drawn into the quarrel between the Shrewsburys. When Bess and George had married in 1567, two more alliances had been built into the deal, to make an indissoluble partnership of persons and property: Shrewsbury's son Gilbert Talbot married Bess's daughter Mary, while Bess's eldest son Henry Cavendish married

Shrewsbury's daughter Grace. When the split came, Gilbert sided with his stepmother (and mother-in-law) against his own father. Shrewsbury blamed the influence of Gilbert's dominating wife Mary. With far more enthusiasm, Henry Cavendish flung himself onto the other side, beside his stepfather (and father-in-law) Shrewsbury, against his mother. 'My bad son Henry', Bess later described him angrily. Arbella's uncle, and ally in her first rebellion, Henry was an interesting character: a volunteer soldier in the Low Countries; a rake who would be described as the 'common bull' of the district; a sometime traveller whose servant's journal of his voyage to Constantinople in 1589 still survives today. (They travelled through Germany, Venice – 'a most foul stinking sink' – and Dalmatia; and Poland on the return journey.) He was the heir to Chatsworth and his hostility may have played a part in driving Bess, who had already quit the Shrewsbury stronghold of Sheffield Castle, out of that territory also.

Once sharing a home with Shrewsbury ceased to be a possibility, Bess (with her son William, his family, and often Arbella too) went back to her childhood home of Hardwick. In 1583 she bought the house outright, for nine and a half thousand pounds, from the estate of her brother James who had died bankrupt. This was the core of Hardwick Old Hall, as it is known today, to distinguish it from Hardwick Hall, which gave Bess her famous sobriquet. The quarters must have been cramped. One way and another, even the redoubtable Bess was feeling the strain. 'For herself she hopes to find some friend for meat and drink and so to end her life,' she wrote to Walsingham in April 1584, melodramatically.

But it was Shrewsbury who was really isolated. Bess, over the years, had carefully kept in touch with all the powers at court: Walsingham, Burghley, Hatton and the earl of Leicester, her old ally. Visiting the springs at Buxton for his health, bravely trying to mediate between the Shrewsburys, Leicester advised the earl to make up with the countess. 'She is your wife and a very wise gentlewoman.' The bishop of Coventry put it more bluntly: 'If shrewdness and sharpness be a just cause of separation between man and wife, I think few men in England would keep their wives long.' The prolonged dispute drew in the privy council and even the queen herself, always coming down on the side of Bess who, with no desire for a formal separation, painted herself as a patient Penelope.

What brought matters into the public domain was, of course, the issue of the Scots queen. In the autumn of 1583, rumours had begun to spread of an affair between the earl and his royal charge. Mary believed Bess had spread the rumours and, through the French ambassador, begged that Queen Elizabeth would 'see justice done to me'. The famous scandal letter saw the Scots queen's anger burst its banks. Her declaration that she was writing 'without passion and from motives of true sincerity' must draw one of the hollowest laughs in history. Bess (said Mary) had accused Queen Elizabeth herself of licentiousness, sexual malformation and a vanity so extreme that Bess and her daughter Elizabeth had trouble concealing their laughter at the courtiers' extravagant compliments. Gossip from over the embroidery frames was dredged up and set in the harshest possible light, for the most dangerous possible audience. Bess (wrote Mary) had said:

> Firstly that one to whom she said you had made a promise of marriage before a lady of your chamber, had made love to you an infinite number of times with all the licence and intimacy which can be used between man and wife. But that undoubtedly you were not like other women . . . and you would never lose your liberty to make love and always have your pleasure with new lovers.

This was dynamite – but there was no explosion. It seems likely Burghley prudently kept the letter from Queen Elizabeth, or that Mary herself thought better of sending it. But in December 1584 Bess and her sons William and Charles were called to court to deny, in public, that they had initiated the rumour that Mary had had a child by Shrewsbury.

The days when the countess and the Scots queen had sat together at their embroidery were very far away. Now Arbella, once perhaps their common project, had her share in Mary's vituperation. 'Nothing has ever alienated the countess more from me', Mary wrote in one of her letters to the French ambassador in March 1584, 'than the vain hope she has conceived of setting

Sir Robert Dudley, earl of Leicester

the crown on her granddaughter Arbella's head, even by marrying the earl of Leicester's son.'

The charge, up to a point at least, was true. In 1584, Bess and her old friend the earl of Leicester did speak of arranging a marriage between Arbella and Leicester's son Robert, Lord Denbigh; Leicester's visits to Buxton and Bess had not been only in his self-imposed role of mediator. In March 1584 Lord Paget wrote to the earl of Northumberland: 'A friend in office is very desirous that the queen should have light given her of the practice between Leicester and the countess for Arbella, for it comes on very lustily, insomuch as the said earl hath sent down the picture of his baby.'

That match died with young Robert himself only weeks after it was spoken of, but Leicester's presumed ambitions in promoting it were already common knowledge. A doggerel verse entitled 'Leicester's Ghost' circulated during the earl's lifetime:

> First I assayed Queen Elizabeth to wed,
> Whom divers princes courted, but in vain;
> When in the course unluckily I sped
> I sought the Scots' queen's marriage to obtain;
> But when I rept no profit for my paine,
> I sought to match Denbigh, my tender childe,
> To Dame Arbella, but I was beguiled.

The next verse suggests that Bess and Leicester between them were preparing 'a new triumvirate':

> If Death awhile young Denbigh's life had spar'd
> The grandame, uncle and the father-in-law,
> Might thus have brought all England under awe.

Mary also believed that the countess had schemed more grandly still: 'even that my son should marry my niece Arbell'. Bess, she said, had commissioned an astrologer, who foretold Mary herself replacing Elizabeth, to be followed by King James and Queen Arbella on the English throne. In 1585 the marriage of Arbella and James was indeed mooted by Walsingham himself,

and in many ways it does seem the perfect solution to the problem of the succession. The idea of uniting in wedlock the English
and Scottish kingdoms was by no means a novel one; the marriage
of Arbella's Lennox grandparents had been made with half an eye
to that possibility. The marriage of Edward VI of England and the
infant Mary, queen of Scots had been suggested; and Queen
Elizabeth had lamented aloud that neither she nor Mary were a
man, so that they might marry each other. But nothing came of
any James–Arbella project. Had Elizabeth herself stepped in –
never as keen as her ministers to see the direction of the succession signalled too clearly? Or was James simply not ready for
matrimony? Whatever the government's deeper plans, after these
early ventures Bess seems to have been warned off further match-
making. In all her dynastic games, Arbella's marriage was one
gambit closed off to her.

A few years on – just weeks before his death in 1590 –
Shrewsbury would speak bitterly of Arbella as 'this lady who will
bring trouble to his house'. Prophetically, he coupled Bess with
her daughter Mary Talbot as being responsible for the storms
ahead. Arbella had often stayed with her aunt and uncle, Gilbert
and Mary Talbot, since her mother's death; the couple had three
daughters of their own, though the eldest was still some years
younger than Arbella, and she was sometimes in their company.
It is true that even with the Talbots, Arbella seemed affectionate,
teasing . . . but never quite easy. But then, that sort of unease was
very characteristic of the Cavendish family. And Gilbert and
Mary – especially Mary – were to play a vital part in Arbella's
later life as correspondents and allies.

Gilbert Talbot (heir to the earldom after his elder brother died
in 1582) repeatedly tried to act as mediator between the battling
elders. Despite his incessant quarrels with friends and relations,
he emerges as not unlikeable from Arbella's many later letters to
him. 'I will not be restrained from chiding you (so great a lord as
you are),' she could tease him gently. In his own letters through
the years of Arbella's childhood, his passion for hunting and
hawking sits oddly alongside a chronicle of his many minor
ailments. The medical man Simon Forman treated a Gilbert
Talbot and found him 'full of cold humours', melancholy in his

stomach and plagued with cold phlegm; a well-intentioned man, but a weak one, maybe.

By contrast, Mary Talbot resembled her mother Bess in temperament: a formidable woman, famous in her day for her ambition, her learning and her grim defiance of authority. It was Mary Talbot, rather than Bess, who, in *Gaudy Night*, was the foundress of Dorothy Sayers' fictional Shrewsbury College in Oxford. Sayers, in the persona of Harriet Vane, recalled that

> Bess of Hardwick's daughter had been a great intellectual, indeed, but something of a holy terror; uncontrollable by her menfolk, undaunted by the Tower, contemptuously silent before the Privy Council, an obstinate recusant [Catholic, and non-attender at the Anglican church], a staunch friend and implacable enemy and a lady with a turn for invective remarkable even in an age when few mouths suffered from mealiness. She seemed, in fact, to be the epitome of every alarming quality which a learned woman is popularly credited with developing. Her husband, the 'great and glorious Earl of Shrewsbury,' had purchased domestic peace at a price; for, said [Francis] Bacon, there was 'a greater than he, which is my Lady of Shrewsbury'.

And that, 'of course', was a dreadful thing to have said about one, remarked Sayers/Vane sardonically.

Her family mattered to Arbella, and not just in the clannish sense of her day, in which the extended family unit was a source of financial support and political security. Her later letters show that she felt a close and personal interest. She would attempt to mediate among her quarrelsome relatives, as well as to promote their interests with the powers in the land.

But the matriarchal world in which Arbella was raised was to serve her badly in later life, when it came to dealing with the masculine atmosphere of James's court. She was surrounded by strong, not to say inimical, female authority figures: Bess of Hardwick, Margaret Lennox, Mary Talbot . . . to say nothing of the watching queens, Elizabeth and Mary. The old earl felt the pressure: 'I am removed to the castle, and most quiet when I have fewest women here,' he once wrote misogynistically. Towards the end of his life he was to thank Elizabeth for setting him free of 'two devils' – his wife and Queen Mary. The young Arbella, as she grew up, must often have felt like a mouse in a cattery.

She was surrounded, too, by unsuccessful marriages (remarkably unsuccessful even in a society where one in three among the country's older peers were estranged from their wives, officially or unofficially): the Shrewsburys themselves; the relationship of Grace and Henry ('There is no good agreement between Mr Henry Cavendish and the lady his wife; he hath lately charged her to be a harlot with some of his men and named the men to her', a family retainer would later report); Mary Stuart's disastrous alliances; Mary Talbot's domination over her husband. In later life, Arbella would write of an acquaintance who was 'as near a free woman as may be and have a bad husband'. Really, old Lady Lennox, in her lifetime, had presented the nearest thing to a successful role model. 'Sweet Mage', her husband had addressed her in his letters. But he was writing from distant Scotland, while she was held in another country, hostage for her husband's good behaviour. Even theirs was not exactly a happy ever after story.

# 'Little Lady Favour'

WE DO HAVE A SUNNIER PICTURE OF ARBELLA FROM THE EARLY 1580S. Sir Walter Mildmay, the chancellor of the exchequer, writing to his brother-in-law Walsingham from Hardwick on 17 June 1583, gives evidence of the little girl's progress in a postscript:

> Sir – After the closing up of my other letter to you, I received this little enclosed paper written with the hand of Lady Arbella, daughter of the late earl of Lennox. She is about seven years old and learned this Christmas last, a very proper child, and to my thinking will be like her grandmother, my old Lady Lennox. She wrote this at my request, and I meant to have showed the same to her Majesty, and withal to have presented her humble duty to her Majesty, with her daily prayer for her Majesty, for so the little lady desired me.

'My little Lady Favour' was how Robert Beale, clerk to the privy council, described her charmingly. Arbella seems habitually to have been presented to important visitors. Bess must have been eager to show her off to anyone who had access to Queen Elizabeth's ear and could report favourably. This was a woman whose very considerable energies were focused on the future of her family, and in that dynastic firmament Bess's 'jewel', as she so often called the little girl, was potentially the brightest star. In these years the Fugger newsletters (reports circulated privately around the great German banking house) repeatedly mention the young girl cousin 'who, after the queen's death, will be next heiress to the throne'.

In the letters of the Cavendish family one can trace an oddly mixed attitude to the orphaned relative who could grow up either an overwhelming asset or a liability; a celebrity, or a glamorous cuckoo pitched into their nest. For the child, this cannot have been easy. But on a day-to-day basis, there is no reason to assume Arbella was not tolerably happy. A report from Bess's steward describes her as 'merry'. A great-aunt, Elizabeth Wingfield, on two separate occasions described her Arbella as being 'as good a child as ever there was'. She adds in a minatory tone that no efforts of hers will be spared to increase the little girl in virtue, but she also takes care to reassure Bess that her grandmother's 'jewel' is in good health. The suggestion is that there was no overt difficulty. If Arbella suffered the pressure of high expectations, she also enjoyed the privileges of luxury: nurses; tutors; toys. She was taught to ride out with hawk and hounds (Mary and Alethea Talbot were famous huntresses), as well as to embroider, to sing, and to play the lute and the viol. Music was an important part of any social education, but Arbella's was a particularly musical family.

In many ways, Arbella was lucky in the people who arranged her upbringing. The stories and successes of her cousins suggest that in the Cavendish households there was no painful division between learning and love of life. For example, her cousin William (Charles Cavendish's eldest son, the future duke of Newcastle) would exchange verse letters with his own children; a pleasurable game for all the family. The philosopher Thomas Hobbes became a friend as well as tutor to his whole household – a household famous as much for skill in horsemanship and swordplay as for the mathematical genius of Charles Cavendish's younger son, the little cousin Charles whom Arbella would mention fondly. So the young Arbella's tastes were far from entirely cerebral. She wasn't another Jane Grey, famously found indoors while her family were out at sport, and glorying in her distaste for finery. Arbella heartily enjoyed the pleasures of the world: clothes, food, flattery.

But there are similarities between the two girls. In the end, it was her books which Arbella would call 'my dead counsellors and comforters'; a consolation in a life of many difficulties. Lady Jane had told Roger Ascham, tutor to the princess Elizabeth, that 'One of the greatest benefits God gave me is that He sent me so sharp and severe parents and so gentle a schoolmaster, for when I am in the presence of either father or mother, I think myself in hell till the time comes when I must go to Mr Aylmer.' Arbella would later take refuge in literature in much the same way. 'I go rather for a good clerk than a worldly wise woman,' she was to say, a little ruefully.

Sir John Harington would later write of Arbella's 'virtuous disposition, her choice education, her rare skill in languages, her good judgement and sight in music, and a mind to all these free from pride, vanity and affectation, and the greatest sobriety in her fashion of apparel and behaviour as may be, of all of which I have been myself an eyewitness'. Arbella's cousin, the composer Michael Cavendish, dedicating a book of songs and madrigals to her, wrote of her 'rare perfections in so many knowledges'. Poets were later to dedicate volumes to Arbella. 'Great learned lady' was how Amelia Lanyer would hail her in the dedication to *Salve Deus Rex Judaeorum*: 'Rare Phoenix, whose fair feathers are your own, / With which you fly, and are so much admired.' Though the extravagant nature of the compliments may be put down to contemporary court politeness, it is still noteworthy that all the compliments tend the same way.

The sixteenth century boasted a small but highly significant minority of very learned ladies. Queen Elizabeth had been educated in this tradition, and made scholarship fashionable in the aristocratic world where she set the time of day. 'The stranger that entereth into the court of England shall rather imagine himself to come into some public school of the universities than into a prince's palace,' said one observer wonderingly. Bess of Hardwick's own cultural tastes were simple, and a few religious texts are the only books listed in her possession in the household inventory: Calvin on Job, Solomon's Proverbs, a book of Meditations. But she knew what was due to her upwardly mobile family, and when it came to Arbella's schooling, the queen would have been Bess's role model in every way.

For Arbella, this was fortunate in the manner of her education as well as its content. In 1570, Elizabeth's great tutor Roger Ascham had published his book *The Schoolmaster*: a how-to manual for anyone desirous of educating a Renaissance princess. Besides his method and curriculum, Ascham laid down principles of education that seemed like sparing the rod and spoiling the child to many of his contemporaries. Learning, he wrote, 'is robbed of her best wits by the great beating'. He suggested praise and encouragement rather than chastisement: 'I assure you there is no such whetstone to sharpen a good wit and encourage a will to learning.'

The glory of a well-educated Renaissance princess lay in arts and languages, and knowledge of classical antiquity. The beginning of Elizabeth's day, wrote Ascham, 'was always devoted by her to the New Testament in Greek, after which she read select orations of Isocrates, and the tragedies of Sophocles, which I judged best adapted to supply her tongue with the purest diction, her mind with the most excellent precepts, and her exalted station with a defence against the utmost power of fortune.' In Latin, the princess read 'almost the whole of Cicero and a great part of Livy'.

Like Elizabeth, Arbella was taught to speak, as well as to read, French and Italian as well as the classical languages. Ascham favoured a double translation method: turning one language into another and then back again. His methods obviously worked, since the queen, and later Arbella, could both dictate Latin *extempore*. By the time she was thirteen, Harington noted that Arbella 'did read French out of Italian, and English out of both, much better than I could'. Harington, who had translated Ariosto's *Orlando Furioso* into English, added that Arbella had caused him to read her part of the work 'and censured it with a gravity beyond her years'. She, like the young Elizabeth, was praised for her 'towardness', her precocity.

There was, after all, a tradition of female learning in Arbella's family. She was related to many of the 'learned ladies' of the day. Her grandmother Lady Lennox had been a poet, whose verses to her imprisoned lover Thomas Howard surpassed the fashionable norm. One poem of Margaret's displays the sentiments upon which her granddaughter Arbella was to call when, in 1603, she struggled to invent an idealized fantasy lover of her own.

> *I may well say with joyful heart,*
> *As never woman might say before,*
> *That I have taken to my part*
> *The faithfullest lover that was ever born.*
>
> *Great pains he suffers for my sake*
> *Continually night and day*
> *For all the pains that he does take*
> *From me his love will not decay.*
>
> *With threatening great has he been paid*
> *Of pain and eke of punishment,*
> *Yet all fear aside he has laid:*
> *To love me best was his content.*

Decades later, the educator Bathsua Makin, in her treatise on learned ladies (following the lead of Lanyer, who wrote of Arbella as accompanied by the Muses), specifically listed Arbella (like Jane Grey) among the poets – tantalizingly, since no poems of hers, if any there were, survive today.

On the Cavendish side, Cousin William would write plays, as would his daughters. William's second wife was the famous duchess of Newcastle, the author of philosophical publications like *Nature's Pictures* and *The Description of a New World*. She was mocked as 'Mad Madge', a notable eccentric, but her husband warmly supported her efforts. Two of the three girl cousins with whom Arbella would have had most to do, the daughters of Gilbert and Mary Talbot, became published authors. All three – Elizabeth, Mary and Alethea – married men from intellectual families: in Mary's case that earl of Pembroke who was Shakespeare's patron, the nephew of Sir Philip Sidney and son of the countess of Pembroke who has been credited with more or less of her brother's *Arcadia*.

Elizabeth Talbot, whose marriage later made her countess of Kent, was famous for her medical cures and recipes: distillation of watercress and of spearmint made up with beeswax, wines or oils. 'To take away hoarseness: take a turnip, cut a hole in the top of it and fill it up with brown sugar-candy, and so roast it in the embers and eat it with butter.' After her death in 1651 they were published under the title of *A Choice Manual, or Rare Secrets in Physick and Chirugery Collected and practised by the Right Honourable the Countess of Kent, late deceased*. It was still in print fifty years later, despite the daunting nature of some of the recipes: 'Take three round balls of horse dung, boil them in a pint of white wine.' 'Take a hound's turd . . .'

The youngest Talbot sister, Alethea, married the earl of Arundel, famous for his collection of antiquities, and patron to Inigo Jones, who brought the fruits of the classical revival to England. But she also published her own volume of medical recipes, *Natura Exenterata*, which had a more scientific found-

Alethea Talbot and the title page of her book

ation than those of her sister, setting chemical experiments alongside the more traditional recipes and advice on planting and horse-breeding. She was painted proudly holding the instruments of navigation as well as the pearls of medicine.

Elizabeth and Alethea took their interests from their mother; the traditional female skill of brewing remedies was one Mary Talbot pursued most enthusiastically. 'My invective against pancakes causeth my wife to send you a little glass of her cinnamon water,' Gilbert Talbot later wrote to his friend Robert Cecil. 'Inflame it will not, for there is no wine in it, but cinnamon in borage water only.' Arbella would likewise have had an earthier element to her education among the herb gardens Bess caused to be laid out at Hardwick. She would later draw on metaphors from the domestic life she knew, writing of conceits which time and experience 'have grafted in my heart and I have watered in tears'. She would send to Gilbert the 'stoppingest [most constipating]' dish she ever did see. On another occasion, she drew an extended metaphor from needlework, describing how a case against her has been made by

patching up every idle word to every foolish imagination . . . lining it with secret whisperings and shaping it as best pleaseth their fantasy who have made you present her Majesty with a misshapen discoloured piece of stuff fitting none . . . slubbered up in such haste that many wrong stitches of unkindness must be picked out and many wrong placed conceits ripped out.

Arbella, like every girl of rank, was taught the art of embroidery. She wrought pieces which, sent to the queen as a New Year present, displayed the child's skill and played their part in the important gift culture of the sixteenth century. She was, after all, surrounded by notable needlewomen; not just Bess, in whose draughty homes there were many walls to fill, but the Scots Queen Mary, who stitched away the hours and years of her captivity.

The influence of the queen of Scots on the young Arbella is hard to assess. It is unclear just how much time the fugitive queen and her young niece ever spent together. Mary Stuart flitted like a ghost through the story of Arbella's early life; perhaps more present in her legend than in actuality. There is a widespread belief that the queen of Scots enjoyed (as Antonia Fraser once put it) 'a pleasant quasi-maternal relationship' with Arbella. But in sober truth it is hard to find documentary evidence to support the idea that they saw each other from day to day.

Certainly – until she fell out so spectacularly with Bess – Mary thought and wrote kindly of 'Arbelle, ma nièce'. There was much in her own situation which might incline her to do so: hurt at the way her own son James had rejected her; the boredom of imprisonment, which led her to lavish affection on lapdogs and ornamental birds; even, at first, pride and ambition, if she really had been party to making a match between Arbella's parents. But how much of a relationship was there beyond notes or gifts, an auntly request for news, or to see the latest piece of embroidery?

Over those long years of confinement the Scots queen did develop a rapport with the Shrewsbury family. But access to her, or even to any household where she was in residence, was at times restricted with the utmost severity. In February 1575 the wretched Shrewsbury had had to excuse himself to Queen Elizabeth for having allowed even the midwife to come to the house to attend on his daughter-in-law, and pleading pathetically that he and two of his children had christened the baby themselves, rather than bring in a priest. Burghley's initial instructions to Shrewsbury had run to several pages of prohibitions. 'The queen of Scots may see the countess, if she is sick, or for any other necessary cause, but rarely. No other gentlewoman must be allowed access to her.' Shrewsbury's eldest son Francis once told Queen Elizabeth that the queen of Scots was kept so close that none of his family had seen her 'for years'.

The level of security surrounding Mary obviously ebbed and flowed according to the political situation, and to her own level of clandestine activity. The rules Burghley made for her custodians may not have been kept consistently. But given Arbella's political importance, her access to the Scots queen would surely have been monitored with especial care, while the presence of the little girl's tutors and servants in any house where Mary was also staying would be a strain on security. We have seen how Bess left Arbella at Chatsworth while she went to Sheffield, where Mary was chiefly held; and we have seen how, on another occasion, the earl sent the little girl away. 'It seems her Majesty has no liking our children should be with us where this queen is,' as Shrewsbury wrote bitterly. Nevertheless, whenever they were in the same household, Arbella must have been perpetually aware of the existence of the captive queen whose presence explained so much that seemed odd about the Shrewsbury establishment – all the more so, perhaps, if Mary were kept shut away like the mad-woman in the attic; the aunt Arbella was never allowed to see.

Even if the relationship between Arbella and her aunt is set at its lowest, dismissing any idea of companionship or affection, the events of the late 1580s cannot but have made a powerful im-pression on a child. In September 1584 the queen of Scots had been removed from Shrewsbury's gentle care and placed in the more stringent conditions that presaged her road to trial and execution at Fotheringay. For sixteen years she had been a dominant factor in the household Bess and the earl still occasion-ally shared; its enforced *raison d'être*. Now she was gone. Two years later Mary was brought to her death through her complicity in Anthony Babington's plot to place her on the English throne; young Babington, that inept air-dreamer of a conspirator, had once, during Arbella's babyhood, been a page in Shrewsbury's household. When he was hung, drawn and quartered the news must have touched those around Arbella – as, in the spring of 1587, must Mary's own end at Fotheringay.

As earl marshal, it was Shrewsbury's painful duty to give the signal for the axe to fall on his former charge. No wonder he turned his face away. It was one of his sons who galloped to carry the news to court. Mary Talbot, and Shrewsbury's daughter Lady Mary Savill, were among the chief mourners at the funeral, and among the English ladies who were seen to kiss the queen's griev-ing Scotswomen kindly.

A terrier had nestled in the folds of Mary's skirts when she knelt to the block at Fotheringay. Its fur had been soaked and matted with the blood that gushed from her severed neck. The ladies had taken it away and washed it, but they said it had pined and died from shock and misery. It was the kind of whispered story that would run up and down the servants' stairs, repeated with ghoulish relish.

Arbella must have known – think of Babington! – that beheading was not the worst form of execution. (Not even when your head stayed on through the first stroke; or when you had to fumble blindfold for the block, like Lady Jane Grey.) She must surely have wondered, hearing of her own aunt's fate, just how much it hurt, and whether it was true, as they told Anne Boleyn – another dead queen – that the pain was 'very subtle'; wondered what you would feel when you saw that lump of polished wood in front of you, when you had to step firmly up to it and quietly kneel, when every instinct swore at you to scream, to fight, to run away.

In the time of her own danger, years later, Arbella was to make an oblique reference to Mary's fate. Queen Elizabeth always claimed that her officials exceeded her wishes in rushing through an execution she had never really intended. Wrote Arbella:

Let me lose my head . . . which her Majesty hath threatened to take . . . Her Majesty I know would be highly offended to have such a matter effected without her Highness liking but what will not or cannot one of [the councillors] do and gild over with some colourable rule of policy, or officious pretence of superabundant love?

Whatever their relationship while she lived, Mary left to Arbella her *Book of Hours*, a devotional-volume-cum-diary which she had brought with her from France. On the blank sheets she had written notes and poems, and had inscribed it in her own hand: *Ce livre est a moy, Marie Reyne.* (Arbella, towards the end of her life, would send it to her husband in Paris, inscribed from 'Your most unfortunate, Arbella Seymour'.) We do not know when she was given it, or with what words or ceremony. But the removal of the Scots queen had taken her another step closer to the crown. The political events following Mary's execution were to precipitate Arbella's first steps onto the public stage – and her formal introduction to the woman whose throne she might inherit.

# II

## 1587–1602

## *'Lawful inheritress'*

'She would be the lawful inheritress.'

M. de Châteauneuf, French ambassador, 1587

# 'She will one day be even as I am'

EVERY PROMINENT ELIZABETHAN NEEDED A FRIEND AT COURT. THE man without eyes and ears there – without a voice to plead his cause – was 'like a hop without a pole', as Lord Burghley said pityingly. The provident Bess was never likely to neglect such an obvious provision for her family. Amid the web of important contacts she nurtured so carefully, she did not disdain the regular letters from her half-sister, Elizabeth Wingfield, in London.

In one December of the mid-1580s Elizabeth Wingfield sent Bess a significant bulletin, a sprawling sheet of paper crammed with news aplenty. Concerning the important seasonal present Bess would make to Queen Elizabeth, 'Lady Cobham does not advise a gift in money,' while the queen had given 'many good words' what she would do for Bess in the matter of 'my lord's hard dealing' – referring to Bess's quarrels with Shrewsbury.

Having thus dealt with Bess's grand affairs, Mistress Wingfield moved on to a more domestic matter. Seven yards of green velvet were needed to make a dress for Arbella – on the brink of her teens – but the tailor had only five yards and a quarter. This too, in its way, was an important business. Clothes mattered in the display culture of the sixteenth century. Dress was tied to status so directly that sumptuary laws decreed what rank was required before you could wear silk or velvet, and then how much of it: a velvet trimming? A cap? Or – like the royal Arbella – a whole gown? If clothes always mattered, Arbella's had begun to matter acutely. The time was approaching when she could be expected to make her curtsey at court. Now, if ever, was the time for finery.

You went to court with a fortune on your back – literally. An outfit could be worth more than an estate. ''Twere good you turned four or five hundred acres of your best land into two or three trunks of apparel,' wrote Ben Jonson sardonically. Contemporary portraits show Sir Walter Ralegh, for example, in short capes almost solid with pearls. If he had indeed laid his cloak down in the mud for the queen to walk over, he would have been making a gesture grandiloquent enough to be worth remembering in story.

The gowns Elizabeth herself wore for formal show – and she had three hundred of them – are sewn with eyes and ears, flowers, whole menageries of mythical animals. Even lesser ladies, on public occasions, wore their dresses tricked out with ornamented buttons, knots of ribbon, elaborate embroidery, the fabric itself 'pinked' or 'paned' (cut in a decorative arrangement of holes, or slashed to show a different material underneath). Roger Ascham once praised the young Elizabeth's 'simple elegance', her contempt for 'show and splendour'. Perhaps it is lucky Ascham never saw the style later chosen by his pupil. When we read Sir John Harington's praises of the young Arbella's sobriety in dress as well as behaviour, we have to remember that everything is comparative; in later life Arbella, too, would order four hundred pounds' worth of pearls to be embroidered on a single gown. She would fantasize about courtiers bowing before her and marvelling at the 'sudden and gorgeous change of my suite', as she revealed herself in metaphorical garments, 'strange and new and richly worth more than any lady in this land'.

The princess Elizabeth had worn simple gowns in black and white, suitable to a Protestant's modesty; her hair plain, no cosmetics except a faint marjoram scent, in ostentatious contrast to her Catholic sister Mary's gaudy finery. A portrait of Arbella painted in her early teens shows her too clad in a white satin gown decorated with trimmings of black. But the magnificent double rope of pearls around her neck, the outsize pendants in hair and ears, belie any suggestion of economy. Bess would have seen to it that Arbella had everything of the finest. The old lady knew how to spend money where it counted.

Fashions reached new heights of extravagance in the later years of the century, and it was no sinecure to dress an Elizabethan lady. The gown itself came like a self-assembly kit; the lavish unwashable fabric was to be used and reused, and preserved very carefully. From the skin up Arbella would have worn first a chemise or 'smock' of cambric or silk finely embroidered, and maybe perfumed. (Drawers were commonly worn only by fast Italian ladies.) Over that came a corset, made in two parts and thus described as a pair of 'bodies', stiffened with wood or whalebone, and with a rigid centre piece projecting the long line of the 'stomacher' downwards. Then came the petticoats, tied by 'points' or laces to the bodies. The petticoats were held out by the bell-shaped farthingale, which was itself supported by a strip of padding or rope tied around the hips below the waist, and commonly known as a bum roll. Over this went the gown itself, a sleeveless coat-like garment hooked onto the stiff front panel. The huge padded sleeves were attached separately, and that is even before ruffs and cuffs had been pinned into place . . . Getting a court lady into her clothes was something like kitting a knight out in his armour. Contemporaries noted the martial quality of a lady's 'privy coats by art made strong'. 'Were they for use against the foe/Our dames for amazons might go!' wrote one Philip Gosson.

As Arbella's attendants latched the cumbersome fabric around their young mistress, the girl standing doll-still in the midst of the activity would have known that when she went to court she would indeed be entering a battleground. Court was the arena in which power, position and lucrative employment were won. It stood alone as the only source of advancement; the 'only mart', said the poet Gabriel Harvey, 'of preferment and honour'. Failure could be terminal, and mistakes were public: the earl of Oxford, breaking wind as he bowed, retired to his estates for seven years (only to be greeted, on his return, by a mischievous queen: 'My lord, I had forgot the fart,' she said). The very fury with which the rejected railed against this place of 'glittering misery' told its own story. 'Go tell the court it glows and stinks like rotten wood,' wrote Sir Walter Ralegh.

The ritual of the court was to figure largely in Arbella's life, and though later she would be a fish out of water in King James's riotous establishment, she had a certain taste for splendour. She could be unusually free and unassuming with subordinates, but her letters reiterate a great pride in her 'renowned stock', the 'most royal lineage' she shared with the queen. She was 'not ignorant of either my birth or my desert', she would write proudly. In the summer of 1587, when she faced the exciting challenge of her presentation, she knew she was facing an encounter even more significant for her than for most girls. Was ambition – even an aspiration to the throne itself – nurtured when, at the impressionable age of eleven, she saw the queen in glory?

In 1587 Elizabeth I was approaching her thirtieth year on the English throne. She had lost none of that famous wit, but she was fifty-three and, defy age as she may, the image of the potent, ever-youthful Virgin Queen was beginning to petrify into the mask-like persona she would maintain till her death: the beruffed and bejewelled Gloriana. Though ten years later a bedazzled German visitor still found that in looks and vigour the queen need yield little to a girl of nineteen, Nicholas Hilliard, with his unsparing painter's eye, told a different story. His 'Ermine Portrait' of 1585 shows a face already sagging into the idiosyncratic contours of age, in bitter contrast to the delicate, lush framework of lace and embroidery around it. Her fifties had brought a check to her driving energy and the queen was becoming 'daily more unapt to bear any matter of weight', as Walsingham had noted recently. Her motto was *Semper eadem*, always the same; but she could no longer easily impose the fiction on her court. Men, she noted grimly, turn always towards the rising sun.

To write, even to speak, of the future of the realm was treason. The queen was notoriously sensitive about 'the curious and dangerous question of the succession'. To ask her to name her heir, she once told the Scottish envoy, was 'to require me in my life to set my winding sheet before my eye'. But, in a world where the succession had been for decades the most important topic of secret speculation, no-one could fail to know that Arbella Stuart had a claim to the throne second only to that of her cousin, the Scottish king, James VI. If James were to be excluded from the succession by his foreign birth, Arbella would be the 'lawful inheritress', reported the French ambassador urgently. When Arbella appeared at court, every officer and suitor knew that this unknown child could well be their next sovereign.

It was an extraordinary moment in history. Elizabeth Tudor had never met her rival Mary, queen of Scots; would never meet Mary's son James. But now she confronted a representative of the dynasty that would succeed her; a living reminder of her own mortality.

Arbella, for her part, was facing the nation's 'dread and sovereign mistress'. It was an ordeal for anyone. Age had not made Elizabeth less formidable: 'When I see her enraged against any person whatever, I wish myself in Calcutta,' wrote an ambassador apprehensively, 'fearing her anger like death itself.' But Arbella had more reason than most to be afraid. This was the woman she had been raised to emulate, the one who held her fortune in her hands. What is more, she curtseyed before the terrifying figure who, just five months before, had ordered the beheading of her royal aunt Mary, whose unburied body still lay stinking at Fotheringay.

Mary's ghost haunted Arbella's visit in more ways than one. It was the tense political situation that followed the execution that lay behind the young girl's summons to court, like a skull just discernible beneath the painted skin. But she could not be expected to think of politics, when faced by such a dazzling scene; and in some ways, perhaps, Arbella got off lightly. Instead of the vast, forbidding – and almost entirely male – crowd that might have greeted her in London, she met a court in holiday mood. The queen was on her summer progress, engaged on one of those extraordinary annual jaunts by which as many as two hundred courtiers and the entire apparatus of state trailed laboriously and expensively around the southern counties. Arbella, sponsored probably by her uncle and aunt Gilbert and Mary Talbot, joined the royal train at Theobalds, the quasi-palace created near Enfield by Lord Burghley.

Even by the standards of the great Elizabethan 'prodigy' houses – infinitely theatrical, imaginative and expensive – Theobalds was the wonder of its age. Large as a village, fantastical as a dream, it

63

The façade of Theobalds, drawn by John Thorpe.

was a place where stone and wood were bent to imagery. To entertain his queen, Burghley 'thought no trouble, care, nor cost too much'. The green leaves of high summer in the magnificent grounds were echoed inside for Elizabeth's pleasure. An entranced visitor described the presence chamber decorated with oak trees, their foliage so convincingly painted that when the windows were open (and Elizabeth could not endure closed windows) birds 'flew into the hall, perched themselves upon the trees and began to sing'. The ceiling was laid out with the sun, stars and signs of the zodiac, the whole working its course 'by some concealed ingenious mechanism' and functioning as a planetary clock. This great chamber, wrote Arbella's uncle Charles Cavendish, had 'at the nether end a fair rock with duck and pheasants and divers other birds which serves for a cupboard'. Luxury abounded: a container in the gatehouse was made to look like a bunch of grapes and, during the queen's visits, ran constantly with wine, white and red.

But every gaudy 'device' contained hidden layers of meaning. There was a grim subtext to the royal visit itself. This sojourn of an unprecedented month, longer than ever before, was designed to mark Elizabeth's eventual forgiveness of her host for his part in pushing through the execution of the Scots queen. Truly, as Arbella trod between the carved snarling lions which decorated Burghley's wide stone stairs, the complexity – as well as the fascination – of a wider world than she had hitherto known could hardly have been presented to her more vividly.

Her reception was encouraging beyond dreams. The child was given an honour after which ambitious men had sighed for years. Arbella was invited to dine in the presence – seated beside the queen herself. 'Majesty', said Elizabeth, 'makes the people bow.' So the food and table furnishings were borne in to the sound of trumpets and kettledrums. A lady in waiting prostrated herself three times before the queen's seat – whether or not Elizabeth was actually present – before rubbing the plate with bread and salt and giving each guard a taste of the dish in case of poison. At home, Arbella was served on bended knee, and addressed as 'Highness' at her grandmother's insistence. She was used to ritual. But nothing like this, surely. It was a test, and she performed well. Charles Cavendish reported to his mother Bess – detained at home in the midlands on one of those enforced, unsuccessful reconciliations with her husband on which the queen still insisted – that her family's young hope 'can behave herself with great proportion to everyone in their degree'.

'I believe she will dance with exceedingly good grace,' he added. This was an accomplishment particularly important in Elizabethan society. The queen herself had been an expert performer, and remained a critical spectator. A number of manuals promoted the art on both philosophical and practical grounds. ('Dancing is practised to reveal whether lovers are in good health and sound of limb,' wrote one author; 'a pleasant and profitable art which confers and preserves health', said another.) But Elizabethan dances required a good deal of training as well as considerable athleticism. The stately processional pavane might be designed primarily to display, peacock-like, your clothes, but a livelier form left you inventing solo steps according to your own skill and your dancing master's fantasy. One version of the galliard required a man to leap in the air and kick a tassel held above shoulder height; in la volta, he twirled the woman off the ground with a single arm around her waist, and broken legs were not unknown among the clumsy. A woman's costume spared her the more terrifyingly active of these public feats, but a lady had elegantly and discreetly to manage her farthingale or her train. She had, moreover, to know whether the Italian custom, whereby a lady could invite a man to dance, was really common practice in England; and how to comport herself when neither inviting nor, worse, invited. Arbella acquitted herself admirably.

The newcomer did not lack notice from the grandees of the court. Her host Burghley, the lord treasurer himself, received her very kindly. The political 'fox', as his enemies called him, was in private life a paternal and domestic man, and an ally of Bess's to boot. 'My lord treasurer bade [Arbella] to supper,' Charles wrote to Bess:

> He spoke openly and directed his speech to Sir Walter Ralegh greatly in her commendation as that she had the French, the Italian, played of instruments, danced, wrought [embroidered] and wrote very fair, wished she were fifteen years old. And with that rouned [whispered] Mr Ralegh in the ear, who answered 'it would be a happy thing.' At supper he made exceeding much of her, so did he in the afternoon in his Great Chamber publicly.

This was a time, Charles wrote, when the court was 'in that height' – on the very brink of change, the balance of power shifting between the figures of Elizabeth's prime and those who surrounded her in her twilight years. The older generation – men like Leicester and Hatton, Walsingham and eventually even Burghley himself – were to give way to a younger set. Leicester's stepson the earl of Essex, newly arrived at court at this time, was already so intimate with the queen that 'he cometh not to his own lodging till birds sing in the morning,' as his servant reported triumphantly. Leicester had been Bess's friend; Essex was to be Arbella's ally. They may already have met: the young earl had accompanied his stepfather when Leicester visited the spa at Buxton. He was, of course, half-brother to the youthful Lord Denbigh for whom Arbella had briefly been intended.

Essex's great rival for the queen's favour was Sir Walter Ralegh, but Ralegh – as Charles Cavendish noted – was 'in wonderful declination yet labours to underprop himself by my lord treasurer'. Hence, no doubt, his attentive presence at Burghley's supper party.

The bold and bearded captain of the queen's guard, dressed in jewels worth a king's ransom, Ralegh was a dashing figure, fit to dazzle older and wiser eyes than those of the youthful Arbella. But, on trial for his life in later years, accused of plotting to place Arbella on James's throne, he declared that she was 'a woman with whom he had no acquaintance'. This was one aspect of court life to which Arbella (like Ralegh himself) never grew accustomed – the falsity, the political necessity that would make yesterday's friend into today's enemy. 'What fair words have I had of courtiers and counsellors,' she later recalled in her misfortunes – adding bitterly: 'and lo they are vanished into smoke.'

But without the dubious benefits of hindsight, 1587 seemed a time of unalloyed personal triumph for Arbella; a time when the queen 'by trial pronounced me an eaglet of her own kind', as she put it dramatically. In fact, her own qualities were hardly the point. With one potential claimant, Mary, out of the way, it was important to demonstrate that James did not stand alone in the succession. So even that expensive education was hardly touched upon. 'Her Majesty examined her nothing touching her book [lessons],' Charles wrote. It was Arbella's royal blood, not her brains, which was in demand here – except, of course, in so far as her accomplishments made her a more marriageable commodity.

Over the next fifteen years, Arbella's name would be coupled in international gossip with those of every single prince in Christendom. Promise of her hand (and implicitly of the succession) would become an invaluable tool in Queen Elizabeth's lifelong game of diplomacy; Arbella was to be Elizabeth's deputy in the long courtship ritual that had proved the queen's best political weapon. Elizabeth had kept one foreign power after another in line with the promise of her hand, and her kingdom along with it. Now the 'best match in her parish' could no longer plausibly play that game. 'I am an old woman to whom paternosters will suffice in place of nuptials,' she told her courtiers pathetically. But she could offer an alternative match – Arbella. The young relative whom she always preferred to keep out of sight in Derbyshire could be transformed, when diplomatic necessity required, into 'a near cousin of her own, whom she loves much, and whom she intends to make her heir and successor', as the French ambassador would later describe her. The second-best match in the parish, in effect. It meant that Elizabeth, as she looked at Arbella now, was reminded not only of mortality, but of the loss of her own sexuality. But politically, it was a good card – and this was a moment when Elizabeth had to play her hand especially skilfully.

By 1587, with his great Armada already in preparation, the Spanish King Philip's envoy to Elizabeth, Mendoza, had already broached the possibility of a marriage between Arbella and the duke of Parma's son, Rainutio Farnese. Now, with England facing a war it could not afford, such a diplomatic solution was very appealing. But in Scotland, the idea had alarmed King James. Professing indignation at his mother's death, he incensed Elizabeth by demanding to be named as her heir. Having got wind of the proposed Farnese match, he demanded, furthermore, 'that the Lady Arbella be not given in marriage without the king's special advice and consent'.

More Scottish unrest must have struck Elizabeth as an un-necessary complication at this difficult time. She had dubbed Mary Stuart the 'Daughter of Debate'; Mary's niece showed every irritating sign of proving just such another figure of controversy. But Elizabeth, though she could harbour an unjust grudge, never let it stand in the way of policy. It was certainly time to give the girl a brief moment in the limelight. A visit to the court at Theobalds, an acknowledgement of Arbella's rank, would increase her value for the king of Spain – and teach the king of Scotland not to count his chickens before they were hatched.

Arbella could hardly have been fully aware of such consider-ations, but her relatives were better placed to assess the situation, and had no intention of letting the hopes of their thrusting house rest on a single curtsey. Over the next year Arbella spent much of her time in the south, in the care of Gilbert and Mary in their London homes. Just a month after her appearance at Theobalds,

Arbella's few household goods were on the road back to Derbyshire: 'two beer jugs, gilt with covers; one great bowl, gilt with a cover; two livery pots, parcel gilt; eleven spoons . . .' But if she went with them, it was only briefly, for on 10 October Sir Henry Goodere wrote to Mary Talbot (who was away with the court) concerning Arbella, left with her ladies in London and in his care. Arbella's 'diet' was putting him to considerable cost, he wrote: 'my housekeeping doth stand me in five marks every week now more than I spent before the ladies came to Newgate Street.' Just so did courtiers complain about the far greater charge of playing host to Queen Elizabeth – though most of them felt it more than worth the expense.

And Arbella, after all, was the young lady of the hour. She had come away from her first court visit carrying with her the heady whiff of flattery. The queen herself, in the end, had awarded the palm, though it was typical of her not to praise the girl directly. Instead, she placed her words where they mattered politically. To Madame de Châteauneuf, wife of the French ambassador, Elizabeth made a calculatedly tantalizing remark. She asked the Frenchwoman whether she had remarked the little girl who had dined at her own table. Madame de Châteauneuf agreed she had, speaking politely of Arbella's grace and charm. Indicating Arbella, the queen said: 'Look to her well: she will one day be even as I am and a lady mistress [*une maitresse dame*]. But I will have gone before.'

These were words of the kind that spread rapidly through a court and beyond. To Arbella and her family, if they heard them, they would have sounded like a promise. To James of Scotland, and to Elizabeth's ministers, they would represent a threat. In either case, they came to prove a most uncomfortable prophecy.

# 'Court-dazzled eyes'

THESE WERE HALCYON PUBLIC DAYS FOR ARBELLA. COURT VISITS, A plethora of marriage proposals – it seemed likely her fortune would map out in accordance with the wildest dreams of her hopeful family.

There seemed none to challenge her among the other English candidates for the succession. The Seymour line had been brought low when Lord Beauchamp – elder son to the earl of Hertford and the ill-fated Catherine Grey – had made an illicit love-match with a 'lady of much lower quality', as the Spanish ambassador reported disapprovingly. His bride was the daughter of Sir Richard Rogers – a notorious smuggler, no less, whose title of knight concealed the fact that he owned several pirate ships. Queen Elizabeth, moreover, had never acknowledged the legitimacy of Hertford's sons: Lord Beauchamp bore his title by courtesy and common usage only. As for the Stanleys, they were always the line least likely to succeed. Not only were they the most junior, but their candidate was another ageing woman: the 47-year-old Lady Derby, granddaughter of Mary Tudor. Lady Derby, moreover, had recently spent several years in custody for having treasonably caused an astrologer to predict the date of the queen's death, and the name of her heir.

If Elizabeth wanted a check on James's vaulting ambition, Arbella was the only realistic choice. But to Arbella herself, the widening of her horizons probably presented itself less as a political opportunity than as a chance to escape from her grand-mother's charge – what she would later call her grandmother's custody.

One letter Arbella wrote to Bess in the early months of 1588 offers an insight into the relationship between them. She was stay-ing with Gilbert and Mary much of that Armada year, and a stilted bread-and-butter note she wrote, in French, to Burghley from the Talbots' house in Coleman Street still survives. Her letter to Bess is very different. In many ways it is a domestic epistle. 'My cousin Mary hath had three little fits of an ague, but now she is well and merry.' Enclosed are the ends of Arbella's hair, 'which were cut the sixth day of the moon, and with them a pot of jelly which my servant made.' (Bess, who kept an astrologer in her household, presumably wanted Arbella's hair – thus dated on the lunar calendar – for astrological or magical purposes; or else, perhaps, to prevent their being obtained by any ill-wisher hoping to cast his own spell.) The letter ends: 'thus with my humble duty unto your Ladyship and humble thanks for the token you sent me last, and craving your daily blessing, I humbly cease . . . Your ladyship's humble and obedient child'. So many 'humbles' in one sentence suggest a formidable recipient, even making allowance for the rhetoric of the sixteenth century. Above all it is still a child's letter, with a child's uncomfortable approach to an elder.

But Arbella was starting to grow up – not always easily. In the early summer of 1588 she made a second visit to the court, now at Greenwich, again with the Talbots. A marriage between Arbella and Parma's son was again spoken of as a possibility, and though it might have been little more than diplomatic obfuscation, the gambit had at least to seem to be taken seriously. Spain's mighty Armada was already on the seas. The mood of the court was darker than when Arbella had made her first visit to it at Theobolds. Astrologers had always predicted (said the chronicler Holinshed) 'most wonderful and very extraordinary accidents' for 1588, and events looked like proving them right. Throughout the early months of the year the country had begun to move onto a war footing. Ships were built, stores requisitioned, a network of warning beacons set up on hilltops across the land.

For Arbella, too, a personal crisis was approaching. Her trip to Greenwich with the Talbots ended badly. Arbella's own later comment that she had been 'disgraced in the presence at Greenwich and discouraged in the lobby at Whitehall' showed that the incident still rankled fifteen years later. Further inform-ation is frustratingly vague, but perhaps the inexperienced Arbella had taken the queen's flattering words upon her last visit a shade too seriously. In 1603, when she was again in trouble, the Venetian ambassador relayed an old story that at Greenwich, the twelve-year-old Arbella had

> displayed such haughtiness that she soon began to claim first place; and one day on going into chapel she herself took such precedence of all the princesses who were in her Majesty's suite; nor would she retire, though repeatedly told to do so by the master of ceremonies, for she said that by God's will that was the very lowest place that could possibly be given her. At this time the queen in indignation ordered her back to her private existence without so much as seeing her before she took her leave.

The ambassador, when he wrote this, had only just arrived in England; he was recounting hoary hearsay. But beneath a layer of exaggeration – the ambassador adds, inaccurately, that the queen never saw Arbella again – the story has the ring of plausibility. By the rules of court protocol, the insistent Arbella had a point – and she had been raised to value her rights highly. (This, moreover, is the kind of mistake to which royal heirs were prone; just so had a younger Elizabeth furiously censured Catherine Grey for her 'arrogant and unseemly words'. And Catherine Grey was con-siderably older, and used to the ways of the court.) If the story is true, then Elizabeth – frantically trying to conduct peace negotiations until 17 July, just two days before the Armada was sighted off The Lizard – must have been exasperated by such an ill-timed storm in her domestic teacup. Since the Farnese marriage was clearly off, the girl's presence may have seemed redundant, even embarrassing.

But the earl of Essex seems to have spoken up in support of Arbella. Essex was Elizabeth's new favourite, her 'wild horse'; but

A contemporary view of the Spanish Armada
and the thanksgiving celebrations afterwards

even he, as Arbella herself later recalled, though 'then in highest favour durst scarce steal a salutation [with Arbella] in the Privy Chamber'. It seems possible that Arbella showed signs of becoming too close to one of the queen's favourites – an offence Elizabeth always punished swiftly.

Not yet twenty, Essex was tall and pale, ardent, athletic, religious and egotistical, given to attacks of prostration and melancholy. Stepson to Leicester, kinsman to the queen and royally descended from Edward III, he was proud of his birth, bitter at the rise of the 'bare gentleman' Ralegh, and resentful of Elizabeth's power over him at the same time as he exploited his power over her. It is hard to envisage a man more sure to be chivalrously sympathetic towards Arbella's attempt to claim preeminence as a princess of the blood; and, slight though the incident may have been, Arbella many years later remembered it keenly, recalling with gratitude 'My noble friend who graced me . . . in his greatest and happy fortunes, with the adventure [at the risk] of eclipsing part of her Majesty's favours from him'. Whatever the risk to Essex's own standing with Elizabeth, his championship – indeed, the whole episode – would hardly have endeared the young girl to the ageing ruler.

As the Armada bore down upon England, Arbella was sent north to Derbyshire: away from the danger, but also away from the centre of activity. She was old enough to know that if the Spanish army did land in Kent, or sail up the Thames to take London – and all England was aghast at the very real possibility – then she, pawn or prisoner, would be one immediate target for the invading army. But now the preparations to repel invaders, the great victory on the sea – all these could reach her only as rumour. Because of her relatives' importance, perhaps she heard the news with just enough tantalizing freshness to bring home what she was missing; a Shrewsbury-owned ship, the *Talbot*, had been sent to join the fighting. The earl of Leicester wrote directly to the earl of Shrewsbury about the queen's famous speech at Tilbury. 'Our gracious Majesty hath been here with me to see her camp and her people, which so inflamed the hearts of her good subjects as I think the weakest person amongst them is able to match the proudest Spaniard that dare land in England.' Arbella had been an important figure, a featured player, in this stirring episode – but now the most insignificant courtier, soldier or inhabitant of a southern coastal town must have experienced the great events more directly.

In November, the month of the official victory celebrations, Arbella was at Wingfield in Derbyshire, attended only by servants. It was a great block of an old house, perched on a craggy eminence – but the mood of the place obviously did not affect her unduly. On 5 November the steward Nicholas Kinnersley wrote to Bess: 'My Lady Arbella at 8 o'clock this night was merry; and eats her meat well; but she went not to ye school these six days: therefore I would be glad of your Lady coming.'

But Bess, like the queen herself, was suffering from a personal loss in the death of the earl of Leicester, cruelly timed at the very moment of the victory rejoicing. Arbella knew the earl – but she is more likely to have been ruffled by a sense of events passing her by. Did she have another cause for wildness at this time? It is tempting to speculate that Arbella's wilful mood might have been connected to the recent kindness of the most romantic young man in England, Leicester's stepson, Essex; tempting to anyone who has ever lived through the years of adolescent fantasy.

In all events, Bess came to Wingfield, gladdening the heart of her steward, and swept her recalcitrant granddaughter back to Hardwick. There are suggestions that she may from this point have treated her 'jewel' less deferentially. Arbella, the old earl of Shrewsbury told his confidential servant in 1590, 'was wont to have the upper hand of my wife [Bess] and her daughter Mary, but now it is otherwise (as it is told to me), for that they have been advised by some of their friends at the court that it was misliked.' Perhaps, as Arbella began to grow up, her grandmother began to find her less easy to handle.

Bess had, moreover, other fish to fry. The quarrels of Arbella's family had once again become a public scandal. When the old earl of Shrewsbury died in November 1590, Arbella cannot have felt it too much. He had long ceased to be a part of her life. But his departure was the cue for fresh disputes among the Cavendish/Talbot clan. Bess's attempt to claim what she felt was due to her from her husband's estate thrust her into fresh conflict with the new earl and countess of Shrewsbury, Gilbert and Mary Talbot, and the rest of the family flung itself into the debate. Gilbert could not – or would not – give Bess the portion to which she felt she was entitled by her marriage settlement. For Arbella, this can only have led to some fracturing of old rapports, pitting her almost filial relationship with Mary and Gilbert against the loyalty she owed to Bess. But perhaps, in that family, fractured relationships felt like normality.

Bess had commissioned another portrait of Arbella, to hang in her new picture gallery at Hardwick, alongside other illustrious relatives and ancestors. This is the picture in which Arbella wears that long and lavish rope of pearls, tied with a black ribbon bow at the throat to show up the whiteness of her skin. These jewels may have belonged to Bess: the fabulous pearls feature in enough Cavendish portraits of the era to suggest they were loaned around the family. Heavy restoration in the early part of the twentieth century damaged the painting of the face, and the only character-istics of Arbella that remain are the long nose and beautiful hands, so like the sovereign's own.

Arbella stands with books to her hand and a tiny dog (symbol of loyalty) at her feet. Her light brown hair hangs loose down her back: a symbol of virginity and marriageability. But the key feature, for Bess the indefatigable campaigner, may well have been the inscription painted in one corner. Above the date and Arbella's age (thirteen and a half) are the same old words that had been used on the toddler's portrait: 'Arbella Stuart, Comitessa Leviniae'. Countess of Lennox . . . Bess could cling on to family rights with the determination of a bull terrier, and her grand-daughter inherited the trait.

She was now the subject of more marriage negotiations than ever. At fourteen or fifteen, Arbella had reached the age where she (like Shakespeare's Juliet) might be considered marriageable. (Betrothals were often contracted between high-born children but these, being unconsummated, could be broken.) Almost every week, accordingly, she was mentioned in dispatches, in the conversations of ambassadors and the reports of spies. In 1588 and again the following year King James, frantic for alternatives to the ever-threatened Farnese alliance, suggested that Arbella should marry Ludovic Stuart, son of his first favourite Esme and one who, he promised, 'longeth after Arbella'. This idea Elizabeth squashed quickly, 'with harsh words and much contempt': to have Arbella a Scottish pawn would quite obviate her value as counterweight to James's pretensions.

There was a kind of grim appropriateness to James's proposal, for it was Esme Stuart who had been given, and who had passed on to his son, that Lennox earldom which Bess always felt should have been Arbella's anyway. Perhaps in consequence of this issue being broached, Burghley and Walsingham were moved in the summer of 1590 to attempt again to retrieve from James the Lennox jewels, which her grandmother had willed to Arbella. 'Sundry times have I moved the king that the jewels appertaining to the Lady Arbella might be restored to her,' wrote the English ambassador wearily. 'Nevertheless I am still deferred.' That same year, reports circulated abroad that Arbella had secretly married the earl of Northumberland, Henry Percy, nicknamed the 'wizard earl' for his interest in strange science. This was a dangerous rumour, being coupled with claims that the Catholic Percy, in line with his family history of raising rebellion in the papist north, was to proclaim Arbella queen and restore England to the old faith.

Although Arbella was away in Derbyshire at this time, temporarily out of sight, she can hardly have been out of Elizabeth's mind, much though the queen may have wished she could be. And as the 1590s dawned, the scene of Arbella's life shifted southwards again. She returned to London and to the court – and this time it would be for a longer stay.

# 'Exile with expectation'

BY 1591, PARMA'S SON WAS ONCE AGAIN BEING SPOKEN OF AS A MATCH for Arbella. The Spanish war still sapped England's resources, and a double agent employed abroad in the matter begged for a picture of Arbella by 'Hildyard' (Nicholas Hilliard) with which to promote the match. Arbella would be needed for sittings. Bess herself accompanied her granddaughter south. She had to recruit friends and consult legal counsel over the highly public lawsuit that had ripened out of the dispute over Shrewsbury's legacy, while the furnishing of Hardwick, now that her additions to the original manor house were nearing completion, demanded an extensive spending spree on plate and tapestry.

Bess probably also hoped to discuss Arbella's future with her old friend and mistress Elizabeth. If the queen would not pair Arbella off, surely she could at least increase her income? The two hundred pounds a year allowed to a baby princess had now, for a sixteen-year-old, begun to look distinctly scanty. Arbella's gaffe at Greenwich seemed to have been long forgotten: only a year later, the queen had asked after her most kindly. So Arbella and her waiting gentlewoman Mrs Abrahall were among the ladies who went south that autumn in Bess's cumbersome coach. Charles and William Cavendish, with their wives, went too; the forty sheep and two fat oxen sent from Bess's estates in Leicestershire travelled separately. This was to be an extended, eight-month visit, and a retinue of some forty persons, including

Bess's cook and brewer, made up a quasi-royal procession.

Bess's account books tell the story of the journey, from 'my lady's setting forth', across the Trent by the Sawley ferry, through Loughborough, Leicester and Northhampton ('pears 1d'), down Watling Street and into London via Barnet, jolting over roads still 'very deep and troublesome', as a contemporary put it. They took almost a week on the journey. Towns rang out their bells in welcome at the first sight of the distinctive Cavendish livery.

The party was ultimately making not for London itself, where the family had two residences, but for Shrewsbury House in rural Chelsea: a great three-sided structure facing onto the river, surrounded by pasture. 'The manner of the most gentlemen and noblemen is to house themselves in the suburb of the city, because the air there being somewhat at large, the place is healthy; and through the distance from the body of the town, the noise not so much and so consequently quiet,' wrote one observer, praising the 'gardens and orchards very delectable'. Hasty building work had been necessary to accommodate so very large a party – stables were converted into dormitories – but the place had one great advantage: upriver to Richmond, or downriver to Whitehall or to Greenwich, access to the court was easy.

Before the ladies could make their appearance, a little preparation was necessary. Londoners, wrote the duke of Württemburg, 'are magnificently apparelled . . . The women have much more liberty than perhaps in any other place; they also know well how to make use of it for they go out dressed in exceedingly fine stuff, and give all their attention to their ruffs and stuffs.' Fifty yards each of velvet and damask, forty yards of satin and more were purchased, and Tasker, the household's London tailor, was summoned for a hasty refurbishment of country wardrobes. Johns, the queen's own tailor, made the yet grander dress designed as a New Year gift for Elizabeth. It cost a sizeable £59 14s, plus another fifty pounds for embroidery.

'The women-folk of England lay great store by ruffs and starch them blue, so that their complexion shall appear the whiter,' wrote Thomas Platter in his *Travels in England* of 1599; and starch both blue and white appears in the household's account book in their first London days. Armed with their face-flattering finery, the Shrewsbury party joined the court at Whitehall: a palace built astride a highway, with the main road from Westminster to the City passing through its very gates. Curiously public though it was, Elizabeth's principal residence showed no lack of luxury. Two thousand rooms straggled over its twenty-three acres; out of doors there were the huge tiltyard, the cockpit, King Henry's tennis court and the privy gardens, adorned with heraldic beasts atop painted pillars.

Arbella and her grandmother were at Whitehall for the twelve-day Christmas festivities: dancing, music, gaming and jesting (Bess gave twenty shillings to the queen's jester Ramsey), and every night a play. Lady Ri-Melaine in *The French Garden* describes one such social evening: 'We have been long at supper, then afterwards we have had dancing . . . then came a mask [masque] which made a fair show. They played at cards, at cent, at primeroe . . . at tables, at draughts, at chess.' But despite the cheer of the Christmas season, the court had changed since Arbella's last visit. There was already an imperceptible decline from the energy of the Armada days, when first the tension of crisis, then the flush of victory, had for a time masked the reality of an ageing queen, a weary country.

Leicester's death had been only the first of a series of bereavements as much political as personal. Elizabeth lost her spymaster Walsingham, her 'Moor', in 1590, and Chancellor Christopher Hatton, her 'Lids', in the November of 1591. A counsellor a year . . . Both men died bankrupted in the service of their sovereign. They were the old guard, the team with whose help Elizabeth had first governed – now were represented primarily by Burghley, and even he was slowly ceding place to his son Robert Cecil.

In January 1592 the earl of Essex returned to court from the French wars. There is no record of whether he and Arbella met, but it seems a probability. Back in Shrewsbury House, her family was not short of company. Bess's visitors were people of fame and influence: Lady Sheffield (she who once claimed she had been secretly married to Lord Leicester, and was mother of his 'base son'); Sir Fulke Greville; Lady Walsingham; Lady Warwick, the queen's old friend; Charles Howard the lord admiral; the new lord chancellor. The circles in which Arbella was moving were certainly exciting compared to those in the country.

The talk in town in these months was of the Spanish army's advance in France, and of whether the papists or the puritans really represented more of a danger; of the Catholic priest, tortured by the queen's rackmaster Topcliffe, who at his execution claimed Topcliffe had boasted to him of 'very secret dealings' with the queen, 'having not only seen her legs and knees but felt her belly'. (The dreaded, fanatically Protestant Topcliffe was a friend and correspondent of Bess, and the Shrewsbury household would have been scandalized by that story.) There was talk, too, of Robert Greene's new book of 'conny catching', in which he set out to warn his fellow Londoners against the practices of criminals ('the nip and the foist [cutpurses], the priggar [horsethief], the Vincent's law [cheating at bowls], the courber [lifter of goods from open windows], and the black art [picking of locks]'); of the petition against playhouses in the City; and of the king of Scotland's investigation into the witch Agnes Sampson, who confessed to having gone to sea in a sieve the Hallowe'en before, with two hundred of her fellow witches, and sailing to the kirk of North Berwick where they landed and danced a reel

When it came to Scotland, Arbella was in the gratifying position of herself providing fresh food for gossip. In December 1591 – perhaps in lieu of returning her jewels, perhaps disturbed by news of her fresh presence around the court – James thought it politic finally to initiate a correspondence with his cousin. He wrote to her an effulgent Christmas letter from Holyrood House:

As the strict band of nature and blood, whereby we are linked [one] to other, craveth a most entire good will and mutual intelligence to be entertained betwixt us, so we have of long time carried a most earnest desire to contract that acquaintance by letters, as witness of the conjunction of hearts which our so far distant bodies will not permit . . .

The earnest desire might, one thinks, have been achieved rather earlier; but, interestingly, James offers as an excuse the uncertainty of knowledge 'as to the sure place of your abode'. Was Arbella kept in such secrecy?

News of 'the rare parts [abilities] it has pleased God to endow you withall . . . to the great honour of that house whereof we are both issued' came as a great pleasure to Arbella's 'kindly affected kinsman', he wrote, perhaps rather disingenuously. In the secretary's copy which may have replaced his own rough draft, James promised to 'the more frequently visit you by my letters . . . expecting also to know from time to time of your estate by your own hand'. Sadly, there is no record of such a correspondence being continued on either side.

In the spring the court moved away, but it seems Arbella, with her grandmother, stayed in London. It was then, most likely, that she sat for her portrait, though Bess's accounts show it was summer before the painters were paid: 'Given 27th of July to one Mr Hilliard for the drawing of one picture, forty shillings. Given unto the same Mr Hilliard, twenty shillings. Given unto one Rowland for the drawing of one other picture, twenty shillings.' 'Rowland' was Hilliard's sometime apprentice Rowland Lockey, who may well have been employed to make a copy of the master's work. The twenty shillings given to Hilliard after the original fee represents the amount of Bess's habitual tip. Clearly, this was a picture with which to be pleased.

But the cost seems small when you consider that over those eight months Bess had spent an astonishing £6,360. Two hundred pounds had gone on jewellery to make a show at court ('five little jewels at 14s a piece, for an other little one of a bee 6s 8d'); £321 6s to the heirs of the bankrupted Sir Christopher Hatton for the seventeen Gideon tapestries which would eventually line the long gallery of Hardwick Hall. (Thrifty Bess managed to get a five-pound reduction on the strength that Hatton's arms would have to be replaced with her own.) The household's smallest expenses are diligently chronicled: on one Friday fast day, oysters 5d, lampreys 6d, half a saltfish 6d, a chicken 6d, a capon 2s 8d, butter 9d, grapes 4d, 1 quart French wine 4d. There were more weighty transactions, too – 'about my Lady's law matters, £40' – and other incidental expenses: a hundred pounds to found a clergy scholarship and thank the bishop of Bristol for loan of his barge to move the party to court down the river. In February Mrs Digby, Bess's lady in waiting, had a baby. 'At christening of the child,

£4; the midwife and nurse, 10s each; given by Lady Arbella 40s.'

Just after Easter more velvet and lace were purchased, along with some pairs of the perfumed gloves the queen had made fashionable, and Spanish leather shoes. Authors like Philip Stubbes in his *Anatomie of Abuses* railed against the elaborate dress that made women 'puppets' ('sleeves hanging down to their skirts, trailing on the ground, and cast over their shoulders like cow tails . . . three or four degrees of minor ruff, all under the master devilruff'). But Arbella would have been a strange sixteen-year-old had she objected to finery.

The Shrewsbury party spent three Whitsun weeks at court, which had now moved downriver to Greenwich; a smaller, luxurious palace and one of Elizabeth's favourites. From the privy apartments, with their direct access to the water, Elizabeth would wave to her ships as they passed by. The hive was abuzz with rumours about the latest scandal – the queen's maid of honour, bold Bess Throckmorton, who had left court fat on a plea of sickness and had returned two months later without her swollen belly. Ordered to reveal the father of her child, she fearfully named Sir Walter Ralegh. The queen sent a furious summons to recall Ralegh from the high seas. It was another object lesson in the perils of unlicensed love – if Arbella hadn't seen enough already.

It must have been with some regret that Arbella returned from court to Chelsea. But Bess took her train to pay a last official visit to court on 11 June; a visit heralded by the usual flutter of tailors, and the purchase of a 'powdered ermine gown' – for Arbella, probably. Her grandmother stayed at Greenwich until the middle of the next month (well after Sir Walter and his wife had been sent to their separate cells in the Tower), finally setting out northwards on 31 July. Arbella stayed on in the south after her grandmother left – but only briefly.

As she travelled north, she had no reason to think she would not soon be back. She was, after all, reaching the age of matrimony. No-one could have predicted then how long she would dwindle in Derbyshire, in 'exile with expectation', as she later called it bitterly. No-one could have predicted that, with the final demise of the Farnese proposal, Arbella had already missed her best chance of making an approved marriage; of accepting an uncontroversial and appropriate destiny. But time would prove that Arbella was entering a new and less hopeful phase of her life. It cannot have been long before the walls of cramped Old Hardwick began to close in around her after her long sojourn away.

The 1590s were to prove a difficult decade for everybody; so much so that the historian John Guy identifies the years from 1585 to 1603 as the 'second reign' of Elizabeth I, distinct from her earlier success story. Those years, he writes, were characterized by 'ambition, apprehension, expectation, insecurity, authoritarianism, self-interest'; discord, aggression, resentment, venality, paranoia and claustrophobia. 'The nasty nineties', Patrick Collinson, an essayist in the book Guy edited, calls them even more bluntly. To the political and social problems was added a pervasive uncertainty. In 1592, of course, no-one knew that the queen would still be alive as far ahead as 1603; in 1589 Essex had claimed, in a secret letter to James of Scotland, that she could not live 'above a year or two'.

Arbella was an important figure in the tide of intrigue that ebbed and flowed. The political machinations of the decade are vital to understanding her fate – why the girl who was bred for queenship wound up with so different a destiny. But as regards her own life, we have less information about her own thoughts, feelings, actions over these long years than we have for a single month – a week! – later in her story. Where Arbella herself is concerned, ten years go by in a few stray facts, and we can appreciate the significance for her of these static years only when, later, her suppressed emotion burst its banks and we have the evidence from which to understand the full force of her personality.

To contrast reports of the life Arbella had so recently been living in London with a report of her time at Hardwick in the 1590s is to feel an abrupt sense of dislocation. While her portrait was being touted round the courts of Europe, while reports of spy after spy mention her name familiarly, her own existence contrasts most bitterly with the wide debate about her. The division between the figurehead – that marriageable, malleable puppet 'the Lady Arbella' – and the girl's private reality would become ever more sharply apparent. The one was known in every court of

Europe; the other was restricted even beyond the normal rules of her age and sex. While the turn of the decade had been for Arbella a time of possibility and excitement, the 1590s ticked by in inactivity. Surely it was here, in this time at Hardwick, that the seeds of her later rebellion were sown. Over these years her life would come to look increasingly freakish, her royal blood cutting her off from the usual female pattern of matrimony, even as her sex damaged her royal expectations.

For the next decade, there are few records of Arbella leaving Derbyshire. In a region still considered so remote from London that Burghley had once written to Bess at Chatsworth urging her not to live so solitary 'there amongst hills and rocks of stone', Bess was building not one but two houses. By 1592 her modest family home was well on the way to becoming a grandiose pile with tall new wings and vast glittering windows grafted haphazardly onto the old core. Work on Hardwick Old Hall continued on and off into the mid-1590s, long after the foundations of the yet grander Hardwick Hall had been laid just a few hundred yards away. Here Arbella studied Hebrew and Spanish, reading Virgil and Plutarch as well as the Bible, cramming her mind with the stories and the figures who would live again from her own pen: Pope Joan; the Greek Camilla, who abjured marriage to lead a troop of warrior women; Esther, who became a queen to set her people free.

It was not a harsh life. The Cavendish households were never short of lighter pleasures. Arbella's cousin William, brought up at his father Charles Cavendish's seat at nearby Bolsover, later wrote to King Charles II advising him, on his restoration, to bring back 'all the old holidays, with their mirth and rites set up again' that he obviously remembered from his youth: 'May games, morris dances, the Lord of the May, the Lady of the May, the Fool and the Hobby Horse, also the Whitsun Lord and Lady, carols and wassails at Christmas, with good plum porridge and pies'. There were cards and board games, laid into the design of a table that still stands at Hardwick; there were the gardens, with their orchard and nuttery, their pavilions where a dessert course of white sugar candy or caraway comfits, prunes and strawberries, could be taken on a warm day.

A seventeenth-century drawing of Hardwick Old Hall;
the New Hall is just visible over the wall on the left.

Household accounts show Arbella buying a set of viols; visits from the musicians in service with the earls of Rutland and of Essex; visits from the local waits. (Her uncle Henry kept a private orchestra notable even at a time when the standard of English performance was famously high.) Bess's accounts a few years later show payment to a quartet of men and boys come to sing four-part songs: 'Given to them that plays of music with Will, 20s.' Bess's payments also mention 'those that built the bower' – maybe the set for a masque, with all its attendant ceremony. The Queen's Players visited Hardwick in 1596 and 1600, as did Lord Thomas Howard's and Lord Ogle's troops and those of the earls of Huntingdon and of Pembroke; not the best companies at the height of their reputation, but enough to fire a girl's imagination. Arbella had the habit of describing her life in theatrical terms. She and those around her would be 'actors'; she herself one who had not yet learned her part in the play. But increasingly, over the

years ahead, she would discover in herself the desire to write her own lines; not simply to rehearse those laid down by her family.

The mating game in which Queen Elizabeth used Arbella as a pawn carried a huge human cost, and it was Arbella and her grandmother who had to pay. It was in the queen's interest to keep Arbella out of the way at Hardwick, where faction was less likely to form around her. She had suffered under the open intrigues of Catherine Grey. But from Arbella's standpoint, the life that seemed agreeable enough at first must have palled eventually. Everything we know about the beliefs Arbella's upbringing had fostered in her suggests that she had not been raised to expect a quiet private destiny. And now – just at a time when her horizons should have been broadening – she found herself instead suffering a lack of freedom and privacy that even her contemporaries came to find extraordinary. Bess (to whom Arbella was clearly still a child) wrote to Lord Burghley a description of their life that is all the more chilling for being quite unconscious of its cruelty:

I have little resort to me, my house is furnished with sufficient company: Arbell walks not late; at such time as she shall take the air it shall be near the house, and well attended on: she goeth not to anybody's house at all: I see her almost every hour in the day: she lieth in my bed-chamber. If I can be more precise than I have been I will be.

It is almost a surprise when Bess adds: 'I find her loving and dutiful to me.'

# 'Slanderous and unlikely surmise'

IT WAS THE RUMOUR OF A CATHOLIC PLOT TO KIDNAP HER THAT HAD seen Arbella packed off back to the fastness of Derbyshire for her own – and the nation's – security. One Sir William Stanley, an English Catholic renegade living at the Spanish court, had warned a companion (so a captured Jesuit revealed under torture that August) that 'he must do service with a lady'. The companion asked who that might be. With Arbella, Stanley answered, 'who kept with the earl of Shrewsbury'.

'It is Arbella . . . who they most certain would proclaim queen if her mistress [Elizabeth] should happen to die, the rather as they might still rule after their own designments under a woman's government, and if they had her most of their fears would be passed, for any that would hinder them in England.' Semple and Rowlston, two Scots Catholics, had promised 'to convey her by stealth out of England into Flanders: which, if it be done, she shall shortly visit Spain'.

Stanley's plan, for an armed invasion of England by Spanish forces, was probably designed not to place Arbella on the throne but – having cleared her prior claim out of the way – rather to install a Catholic claimant; perhaps his cousin, Lord Strange. As Stanley passed on to Rome, so he talked again, telling another table of Catholic diners that 'one young lady, as yet unmarried, was the greatest fear they had, lest she should be proclaimed queen, if it should so happen that her Majesty should die.'

This, to most of Arbella's contemporaries, seemed a perfectly realistic prediction. In the event James of Scotland acceded peacefully, and history (never interested in also-rans) has glossed over any other possibility. But at the time, as one of the modern authorities, Howard Nenner, puts it, there was 'simply no contemporary agreement as to whether the crown ought to pass automatically at the death of Elizabeth to the next in hereditary line; whether the next in hereditary line might be passed over because of a "legal" incapacity to rule; whether the next monarch ought to be determined in parliament; or whether the queen should be exhorted in the waning days of her life to nominate her own successor'. (The same confusion, presumably, is reflected in the declaration of the hereditary heir Hamlet that in the imminent 'election' for the throne of Denmark, Fortinbras had his dying voice.) There was no consensus as to whether the throne went by strict order of birth; by greatest suitability (out of the shortlist of the blood royal); or by divine selection – and the third was the most uncertain of interpretation. 'Set him king over thee, whom the Lord thy God shall choose,' said Deuteronomy – but simple success (in battle or otherwise) was the most obvious evidence of favour, surely? Henry VIII's daughters had both laid stress on parliament's ratification of their title: James, by contrast, would come to the throne in defiance of that legislation which Henry's parliament (and Elizabeth's) had laid down. No wonder that, in the last years of Elizabeth's reign, a positive snowstorm of pamphlets attacked the problem, most urging the queen to declare her successor. But if the constitutional issue offered an interesting philosophical problem, it was the religious struggle – a Protestant heir or a Catholic one? – that gave the question its point, its impetus and its vitality.

In the last quarter of the sixteenth century, as the tides of the Counter-Reformation lapped against England's shores, the midlands had become a centre of covert Catholic activity. Disguised missionary priests found hiding places in the homes of sympathetic gentry. There were several such helpful households close to Hardwick: Lady Foljambe at Chesterfield; the notorious Vaux sisters; the Fitzherberts; the Markham family near Rufford, whose names figure later in Arbella's story. The Jesuit priest John

Gerard described thrusting himself hastily into one such 'priest's hole' below the floorboards, where he hid for four days, sustained only by 'a biscuit or two and a little quince jelly', while officers unavailingly searched the house. The arrival of these Jesuits, well educated and highly motivated, heralded a fresh wave of missionary activity in the 1590s. 'There is', wrote the Jesuit Henry Walpole in 1591, 'a great hope and inclination to the Catholic faith of late in England, in court, camp and country.' Many of the gentry and nobility (many ladies, especially) found their old faith renewed or reactivated by these persuasive men, and among them was Arbella's aunt Mary Talbot, who from this time was repeatedly cited for her open papistry.

Nor was she alone within her family; through the centuries ahead, indeed, Catholicism continued to run deep through the Talbot line. But it must have been yet another source of controversy within a divided clan. Bess was a stalwart of the Protestant party, and the old earl of Shrewsbury's reputation was such that in 1590, shortly before his death, the notorious persecutor of Catholics Topcliffe could write to him, excusing his late arrival at Shrewsbury's home on the grounds that he was on the trail of a Catholic suspect – sure that this excuse would be sufficient. (Though what, in this context, is one to make of the queen of Scots' sometime claim that Shrewsbury, like the other northern earls, was secretly of her party?)

Soon after the old earl's death, when Gilbert and Mary Talbot had become the new earl and countess of Shrewsbury, the family letters reflect accusations of recusancy. Bess's daughter Frances was one target, along with her husband Henry Pierrepont. Next comes an allegation that Gilbert himself had seen a book of the sacrament 'and did not mislike it'. Gilbert was never openly taxed with Catholicism. This was true of most of the senior nobility whose support, after all, was essential in maintaining order in distant parts of the country. But another letter suggests that his wife's open papistry might put an end to his political career; and indeed, for one of his rank, he did long languish in comparative obscurity. Suspicion touched Charles Cavendish, favourite brother to Gilbert and Mary. The tactless Lady Cook urged Mary not to be 'deaf like an adder' in matters of religion; clearly,

Mary had taken up this cause with her accustomed obstinacy.

The religious beliefs of the sixteenth century are hard to grasp from a twenty-first-century perspective. We have to come to terms with the simultaneous existence of passionately held and mutually incompatible modes of belief as well as with the fact that men and women were prepared to die in agony over subtle differences in religious practice. Even among the most committed, it must have been hard to keep up with the changing doctrines of the century. The earl of Essex was emerging as the figurehead of the Protestant party; yet his mother's new husband was a Catholic, and he himself increasingly found it politic to extend some protection to imprisoned Catholics, thus endearing himself to the continental royalty.

Many, of course, took the pragmatic line. 'In 1580 there were 66 English peers,' wrote the historian Lawrence Stone; '20 of these were Catholic recusants, about 10 were of strongly Puritan sympathies, about a dozen were supporters of the Anglican settlement, and the remaining 24 were relatively indifferent to religious issues and anxious only to back the winner.' Queen Elizabeth preferred, as she put it, not to open windows into men's souls. 'There is only one faith and one Jesus Christ; the rest is a dispute about trifles,' the queen declared once, shockingly. In 1593 Henri IV, the Protestant king of France, converted to Catholicism in order to bring peace to his country and power to himself. 'Paris is worth a Mass,' he said cynically. One Catholic commentator on the succession would sum up Arbella's own position pragmatically: 'I know it not, but probably it can be no great motive, either against her or for her' – in other words, it was likely to be negotiable. There was, moreover, a secret but influential group of thinkers in London whose beliefs tended towards what the sixteenth century called atheism and we might call free-thinking. Prominent among them was Sir Walter Ralegh, who was to be important in Arbella's story.

Arbella, in later life, was to say frankly that she would go with 'papists, Turks, Jews or infidels' if they would help her have her liberty. Could the diverse influences of her background have bred in her a broad tolerance – a genuine indifference to precise religious forms? William Seymour, the man she eventually chose for her husband, was described by a Jesuit who met him abroad as ignorant of religion to the point that marked him rather an atheist than a heretic; atheist (or agnostic) even in modern terms, since he apparently expressed doubts about the immortality of the soul.

Bess obviously raised her granddaughter in the established faith. (If proof were needed, Bess's accounts, while in London, once mention 'given for my Lady Arbella and Mr Cavendish unto the parson of Chelsea for their communions, 10s'.) The French ambassador, usually to be relied upon for a common-sense summary, stated clearly, later in her life, that he saw no reason to doubt Arbella was of the religion usually practised in her country. But time and time again, among more excitable spirits, there was to be speculation as to whether Arbella was or was not 'inclinable to papistry'. This, of course, was the politically interesting possi-bility; for the Protestants already had a candidate – James – handy. As far back as 1589 an all-purpose informer named Barnes was reporting on the feelings of the English Catholics, for whom 'all platforms fell to the ground on the death of the queen of Scots. Their next design will be built on other ground than religion, and they harp much on Lady Arbella, despairing of the king of Scots.' Had she married Parma's son, wrote a member of the Catholic Arundel family, 'all would be holiday.'

For her own part, Arbella once described herself, perhaps not too seriously, as being half a puritan, and her wide reading of the Bible would fit with that Protestant tradition. Though her later alliances tended the other way, this may have been mere ex-pediency. Then again, the Catholic influence in her childhood had been strong. Lady Lennox had been a Catholic who raised her son Charles in that faith until the authorities intervened, and there were usually disguised Catholic priests in the household of the ardently Catholic Queen Mary.

So Burghley, after the unmasking of the Catholic Stanley plot, wrote to Bess in late September, warning her to look to the secu-rity of the neighbourhood. Bess, scouring the district for 'traitor-ous and naughty persons', wrote triumphantly of her victory over 'one Morley', who, having attended on Arbell, and read to her for the space of three years and a half, showed to be much discontented since my return into the country . . . saying he had lived in hope of having some annuity granted him by Arbella out of her land, or some lease of ground to the value of £40 a year, alleging that he was so much damnified by leaving of the university.

Seeing that Arbella herself had not the power to give it, he had the temerity to request of Bess some payment for this long service. Bess promptly 'took occasion to part with him'. But the day after leaving Hardwick with his things 'Morley' was back, begging for work again and 'very importunate to serve' even 'without standing upon any recompense', as Bess recounted incredulously, and suspiciously. This merely heightened Bess's doubts as to his 'forwardness in religion' – 'though I cannot accuse him of papistry', she added scrupulously.

'Morley' may well have been simply a man who, in those years of reading and making music with Arbella, had become fond of her; fond enough to serve without salary . . . Returning tail between legs to Hardwick, at least he would get his bread that way. If this were the case, then his dismissal would have been just one more brick in the wall of what would become Arbella's increasing isolation. However, Morley-the-tutor has been speculatively identified with a Catholic spy, 'Morley, the singing man . . . who has brought divers into danger', and/or with Thomas Morley of St Paul's, the organist and composer. (A Catholic letter now in the State Papers, intercepted in the autumn of 1591, complains that the St Paul's organist seemed to be a good son of that church; and yet word was that in his new post he had turned coat, and was responsible for Catholics being arrested.) But that particular road leads nowhere. The organist Morley *may* be a spy of Catholic background; Arbella's Morley *may* be a spy with Catholic leanings as well as a musician; and yet the dates make it most unlikely that Arbella's Morley is the St Paul's man, whose work must have kept him in London almost constantly. (There remains the possibility that, as an acquaintance of Michael Cavendish, he may have introduced a relative into the Hardwick family.) But the conception of Arbella's Morley as a spy opens the

way to another, even more interesting, possibility. For Morley-
the-tutor has also been identified with another spy: the playwright
Christopher Marlowe, to whom he bears a number of circumstantial and biographical similarities. (*See Appendix A for discussion.*) It remains a possibility, though not a probability. But it is
true that in these years there would be many watching Arbella,
and her religion, carefully. Ironically, her political profile was
never higher than for much of this twilight of Queen Elizabeth's
reign, just as her own personal horizons dwindled. Never was the
name 'Arbella Stuart' bandied around the continent more vigorously.

The early 1590s saw the rise of a new generation of men at
court who would decide Arbella's future, but with whom her
grandmother's established contacts would not help. In her youth
and middle age Bess had carefully cultivated powerful friends –
Burghley, Walsingham, Leicester – but they had all faded too
early. Bess and Queen Elizabeth had alike outlived most of those
old allies. Down in London, new men would take their place. But
while the pieces of English politics were recombined like the
picture in a kaleidoscope, Arbella was mewed up in Derbyshire, a
long way from the seat of power.

Change had already been in the air when Arbella left London.
Lord Burghley, old and wracked with gout, begged his mistress
for leave to retire. The queen would not allow it – but increasingly, over the years to come his son Robert Cecil would take over
his functions as secretary. From the start of 1593 (when the latter
was sworn in as a privy counsellor) Burghley's son faced
Leicester's stepson Essex across the council table. At first, perhaps, it was hoped that the two younger men would help their
elders to recreate the working alliance that, in Elizabeth's younger
days, had bound together men of very different methods. At first,
with his own son still in the background, Burghley helped and
supported the young earl whose guardian he had once been. At
first, it was still possible for courtiers like Gilbert Shrewsbury to
steer a prudent middle way, juggling the friendships of both
younger men. But increasingly, as Robert Cecil rose in importance,
and as it became ever clearer that Essex sought pre-eminence, not
cooperation, it became obvious that the two were oil and water.

They would not mix easily. The court politics of the 1590s saw important divisions in terms of politics and ideology; but personalities, too, were part of the story.

Robert Cecil was a bureaucrat, an administrator of vision and 'a courtier from his cradle'; a man of smooth and gentle manners whose physical appearance, however, was damaged by a slight hunchback and tiny build. The queen (who could be cruel) called him her Elf, or Pygmy. By contrast, Essex's tall and flamboyant person was his chief attraction. If he really were the model for Nicholas Hilliard's 'Young Man amongst Roses', with its long limbs and delicate face, then he had the kind of ravishingly romantic looks that glow right down through the changing fashions of the centuries. He never mastered the skills of the court; indeed, he despised them ostentatiously. And yet Essex was no longer just another pretty favourite but prospectively 'a great man in the state', as his new assistant Francis Bacon put it clearly. That very ardour, that youthful crudeness, may have been part of his attraction for an ageing queen whose palate was jaded of smoother flattery.

In 1590 Essex had married the widow of Sir Philip Sidney when England's parfit gentil knight died on the battlefield of Zutphen. But, having made the grand gesture of giving his protection to his comrade's widow, he did not allow the wedded state to curb his sexual freedom, and Elizabeth, who always fought for a high moral standard at her court, had to wink at many infidelities. Born into an ancient but impoverished Welsh family, entirely dependent on the queen's favour, Essex had been dubbed 'the poorest earl in England'. But that did not mean his ambitions could be bought off cheaply. Indeed, he sucked in honours and power 'too fast like a child sucking on an over-uberous nurse', as one courtier later put it unforgettably.

Cecil sought above all else the safety of the English crown. This he saw as lying in a cessation of the endless war with Spain, and, when the time came, in a smooth passage on to the next dynasty. Essex hungered for personal glory, and gathered around him the puritan hawks, who believed that the conflict with Spain should be pursued aggressively.

It was among these new men that Arbella's future had

constantly to be renegotiated. We know from Sir John Harington that rumour linked Essex's name politically with Arbella's. Arbella herself, in one of her later letters, suggested that if her cousinly affection for James were mistaken for something warmer, such misunderstanding would be no more than fit return for his 'unprincely and unchristian giving ear to the slanderous and unlikely surmise of the earl of Essex and me'. We also know, from Arbella's own later writing, that *in her mind* at least, she and Essex were linked personally. 'Shall not I say I never had nor shall have the like friend?' She remembered him, on the anniversary of his death, as 'My noble friend . . . who graced me in his greatest and happy fortunes [at the risk of] eclipsing part of her Majesty's favours from him'. This edifice of emotion was built, perhaps, on very slight foundation. But Arbella, in the 1590s, was living the empty kind of life in which a tiny happening could be blown up into the most vivid fantasy.

There were rumours that the earl of Essex sought royal power for himself; 'wore the crown in his heart these many years', as the earl of Northumberland later put it jealously. If so, Arbella was a pawn Essex could hardly fail to consider in his game, if not actually to play. Were he not already married, it might have been suspected that he had his sights, as Arbella's husband, on the crown matrimonial – of the same sort Darnley had demanded from Mary; the same sort Leicester had dreamed of winning from Elizabeth. But history would not repeat itself so easily.

Arbella and Essex were very alike, in too many dangerous ways – both setting great store by their noble birth; both erudite; both with a streak of hysteria never far below the surface; both potentially self-destructive (Essex was forever risking the queen's favour on wild, quixotic missions to win attention for friends and family); both all too apt, when things went wrong, to hurl wild accusations at a third party. Both unapt for policy, they were both, in their different ways, potentially dangerous to the realm's stability.

There are no surviving letters between them, nor any real evidence that such existed. If there were any correspondence, of course, it would have been conducted in deepest secrecy. Few of Arbella's letters survive, before she sprang so prolifically into print in 1603; and Essex spent the last hours of his liberty in burning his secret papers, determined they 'should tell no tales to hurt his friends'. The impact of their relationship on Arbella's life must be explored in emotional, rather than objective terms. If the friendship born of a few kind words at court never meant as much to him as it did to her – if the flame of his easy interest flickered briefly and early went out – she did not know it. From the distance of the midlands, how would she? If the manoeuvrings for the succession were like a battle fought out on a chessboard, then the last ten years of Queen Elizabeth's reign represent the endgame. And this was a game Arbella, in Derbyshire, was literally in no position to play.

# 'The disabling of Arbella'

LATER IN HER LIFE, THE FINALE OF ARBELLA STUART'S STORY WOULD find dramatic reflection in one of the most famous plays of the day. Indeed, Sara Jayne Steen, who edited her letters, has convincingly argued that she was an inspiration for Webster's *The Duchess of Malfi* – first performed in her old home of Blackfriars at a time when rumours were rife that Arbella had been driven mad by her incarceration just a mile away. That came further down the line, in the time of marriage and flight, captivity and insanity – a time when Arbella, like the Duchess, had begun to ask:

> *Why should only I,*
> *Of all the other princes of the world*
> *Be cas'd up, like a holy relic?*

But the play strikes one note that echoes even as early as the 1590s. The Duchess's jealous brother Ferdinand placed Bosola as a spy in her establishment to 'note all the particulars of her 'haviour: what suitors do solicit her for marriage / And whom she best affects.' By the same token, the records show many paid watchers circling Arbella. At a time when information was currency, the tutor Morley is only one candidate for an informer within her very household. It is hard to believe the whole endless business passed her by. In later years Arbella herself would jocularly write of an employee as 'my old spy'.

In the days before England had newspapers, anyone who wanted to know what was going on anywhere had to pay someone to tell him. This was the service the professional news reporter Peter Proby offered to Gilbert Talbot in 1592, boasting that he already sent news to the earls of Hertford, Pembroke and Derby. The Cecils, it is true, had access to the printed Italian news-sheets – but only erratically. 'Intelligence can never be too dear,' said Elizabeth's great spymaster Walsingham, who often had to foot the bill himself and died so impoverished he had to be buried at night, lest creditors hold his corpse to ransom. After Walsingham's death, different camps competed to be first with the story. The Cecils had their own intelligencers; the earl of Essex, helped by the Bacon brothers, Anthony and Francis, also found that an intelligence operation of his own, such as his stepfather Leicester had maintained, was a useful route to 'domestical greatness'. He paid highly for information, and by 1592 he was able to bring news to the queen on a regular basis – of the Spanish king's health; of the progress of the religious wars in France; and, indeed, details of the kidnap plot which had sent Arbella north so dramatically.

This was a time when Queen Elizabeth would have herself painted in a cloak ominously decorated with human eyes and ears, reminding all who looked on it that she saw and heard everything happening within her realm; an age when the suspected Catholic Ben Jonson, epigrammatically inviting a friend to supper, felt it worth offering assurance that they would be safe from spies:

> *No simple word,*
> *That shall be uttered at our mirthful board*
> *Shall make us sad next morning: or affright*
> *The liberty, that we'll enjoy tonight.*

For the intelligence gatherers, it was a risky business. Payment was only by results. Protection of the law was not guaranteed. Many of those who reported for the government on Catholic activity were themselves Catholic. Letter after letter reflects this uncertainty. An Elizabethan agent was not a highly trained and paid professional, answering only to one controller. Many followed other professions – as merchants, diplomats, servants, painters; or, of course, tutors (like, perhaps, Morley). Each frantically clamoured for commissions as he tried to get his news heard – and make a little income on the side.

During this period, any number of powerful men would have wanted to know the details of Arbella's associates, and of any approaches made to her. In 1589, during two months alone, the State Papers reflect a flurry of queries directed to the informer Barnes. Barnes is instructed to discover 'what party Arbella and her favourers adhere to, and how they mean to bestow her in marriage'. Barnes relates how James 'needs not Arbella's marriage to advance his title, though he has been scared with her to keep him in order'. Barnes is checking that Lady Arbella's friends are 'unlikely to take part with any new opinion not countenanced by the state'. Now, in 1592, the two or three years were approaching in which the claim of Arbella Stuart to the English throne was debated most vigorously. But the evidence, though plentiful, is deeply confusing; apt enough for this decade, maybe. Reports contradict each other; letters are written to obfuscate (and one has always to remember that in a small and densely intermarried world, the political and religious alliances that live in print often came into conflict with family loyalties). Any attempt to interpret the sheaves of correspondence which fluttered around the desks of powerful men is further complicated by the frequency with which their assistants and agents used a manner of speech so elliptical as to amount almost to a code. Thus Francis Derrick, an exile in Antwerp, would write incomprehensibly to the earl of Essex's secretary Henry Wickham in the autumn of 1594 of his plans to sell his commodities 'at the rate of Arbella'. Among the merchants involved, 'the principal offered first the Car. Allen; another offered Fitz; another Throk; and another, Jacques; but in the end all are agreed to give Arbella.'

No-one could see clearly, even at the time. No-one knew what Francis Bacon aptly called 'that deep and inscrutable centre of the court, which is her Majesty's mind'. Essex was demanding information and sending messages with a speed that left his own stance uncertain, while Cecil in particular – pacing the corridors with 'his hands full of papers and his head full of matter' – was always careful to avoid 'unsecrecy'. None the less, in the correspondence of the time, the name of Arbella Stuart was mentioned, at first, most forcefully.

In the summer of 1593 Robert Cecil's agent in Rome reported a conversation with a priest in the staff of Cardinal Allen, leader of the Catholic exiles. 'England is gone,' the priest mourned; 'we know of their secret proceedings; they expect a new queen and another Cecil' – that is, a Robert Cecil who would be to Queen Arbella what his father Burghley had been to Queen Elizabeth. In those months Allen had been offering himself as a mediator between England and Spain, and when, the next year, Francis Derrick wrote to Henry Wickham that 'the traffic of Arbella is accepted. Allen is the principal merchant,' it seems possible she was to be built into that deal. Married to a Spanish satellite, she could have secured a Catholic England. Yet here too the evidence is contradictory. A letter from a Captain Duffield to the Cecils, in November 1593, described how there was 'small account made' of Arbella; how he had enquired of a third party 'whether there were any liking or good will between the king of Spain and the Lady Arbella or not, and he said he knew not of any.' The Catholic Church did not speak with one voice in the closing years of the sixteenth century. The Jesuits supported Spain, while the Catholics of France and Italy did not always love the Jesuits. The English Catholics, especially after the death late in 1594 of Cardinal Allen, were in disarray; 'in the briars, not knowing the way out,' as one would put it dismally. Into the chasm dropped an important source of potential support for Arbella's claim. And in other ways, too, things were not going hopefully.

In years to come one anonymous but – from his analysis – clearly experienced observer was to suggest that the main opposition to Arbella would come from those who 'have been offended by, or have offended' her family. Arbella's relatives the Shrewsburys do seem to have been scheming on her behalf, but this in itself was almost unhelpful, especially since the main agitator seems to have been the aggressive Mary Talbot. A letter from London in 1593 reported that 'The queen here daily bears more and more a bad conceit of the earl of Shrewsbury and his countess for the sake of the Lady Arbella, which has been evinced in a late quarrel between his lordship and the Stanhopes.'

The feud with the rising official Sir John Stanhope grew to embroil not only the Talbots but Mary's brother Charles Cavendish. Charles challenged Sir John to a duel, only to cancel the affair in disgust when Stanhope turned up in an excessively padded doublet for protection; a whole six years later, Stanhope took a party of twenty horsemen to attack Charles near his midlands home. Mary Talbot, never one to take an injury lying down, sent Sir John a message wishing that 'all the plagues and miseries that may befall any' should light upon one who had 'for your wickedness become more ugly in shape than the vilest toad'. Such flamboyant quarrels were not unusual; Essex himself had been in several violent brawls and affairs of honour. But the Cavendishes and the Talbots made up a particularly turbulent family. When, in 1594, Gilbert Talbot challenged his own brother Edward to a duel with rapier and dagger, alleging that Edward had slandered him, even Essex wrote advising calm.

Such counsel might seem rather a case of the pot and the kettle, given Essex's own impetuosity; but Essex, these days, was 'a new man, clean forsaking all his youthful tricks'; a privy counsellor and, at Essex House on the Strand, centre of a glittering circle gathering around him. No-one at court, least of all Essex, could fail in these years to be weighing up the various claims; each problematic, but each a possibility. As Sir John Harington later recalled: 'My Lady Arbella also now began to be spoken of and much commended, as she is well worthy for many noble parts, and the earl of Essex in some glancing speeches gave occasion to have both himself and her honourable friends to be suspected of that which I suppose was no part of their meaning.'

What the gossips did not know, as they linked Essex with Arbella – what she did not know herself – is that the earl had long been in secret communication with James of Scotland. As far back as 1589 his sister Penelope had started sending James letters on her brother's behalf – along, rather blatantly, with a portrait of her famously beautiful self. By 1593 Essex himself had caused Francis Bacon to open a correspondence with a confidential servant of James VI, and the relationship progressed so warmly that Essex, it was said, carried James's letters in a black silk bag around his neck.

It is still possible, given the convoluted nature of the political scene, to speculate about his motives. One Catholic exile, aware of Essex's advances, none the less believed he was deceiving the Scots, and, seeking the crown himself, 'takes [James] for his competitor'. It is true that one of Essex's agents claimed his master was in favour of the Stanley claim, probably only to discover the plans of Sir William Stanley. But in the case of James, perhaps the approach should be taken at its face value. It is true that Essex, always a weathercock, may have been trying to cover all eventualities. He would certainly, with his lifelong anti-Spanish stance, have been appalled by the much discussed possible accession of the Spanish infanta – a child of Philip of Spain to whom, rejecting her own Protestant son, the queen of Scots had tried to will her rights in the succession. He was just as certainly hostile to the Seymour claim; indeed, it is arguable that to have seen *any* fellow subject elevated thus far above him would have tried him unbearably.

But if from this point Essex ignored Arbella's claim, he may have been reflecting a shift of mood already in existence. In June 1594, in the course of one long report to 'Mr Robyn', one John Brystone reported to the Cecils that 'Arbella is out of request.' The events of the year ahead conspired to put that point more forcibly.

In 1594 there was printed, in Antwerp, a highly controversial book entitled *A Conference about the Next Succession to the Crown of England*; its ostensible author 'Doleman' was usually taken to be a pseudonym for the leading Jesuit commentator and agitator Father Parsons. Banned in Elizabeth's realm, the book filtered only slowly into English circles. It was the following November before Elizabeth showed a copy to the earl of Essex, who had almost certainly seen one (and prudently remained quiet about it) some months before.

The book provocatively called upon the earl to play the kingmaker (or queenmaker) after Elizabeth's death; no other figure, it claimed, 'could have a greater part or sway in deciding of this great affair'. This was a backhanded compliment indeed, and the shock was such that Essex immediately took to his sickbed. In

A CONFERENCE

# ABOVT THE

NEXT SVCCESSION

TO THE CROWNE OF ING-
LAND, DIVIDED INTO
TVVO PARTES.

VV H·ER E-O F

THE FIRST CONTEYNETH THE
difcourfe of a ciuill Lavvyer, hovv and in vvhat manner
propinquity of blood is to be preferred. And the fecond
the fpeech of a Temporall Lavvyer, about the particuler
titles of all fuch as do or may pretende vvithin Ingland
or vvithout, to the next fucceffion.

*VVhere vnto is alfo added a nevv & perfect arbor or genea-*
*logie of the difcents of all the kinges and princes of*
*Ingland, from the conqueft vnto this day, vvhereby each*
*mans pretence is made more plaine.*

DIRECTED TO THE RIGHT HO-
norable the earle of ESSEX of her Maiefties
priuy councell, & of the noble order of the Garter.

Publifhed by R. DOLEMAN.

Imprinted at N. with Licence.

M. D. XCIIII.

Title page of Doleman's *A Conference about the Next Succession
to the Crown of England*

fact, he suffered no real harm. But one way and another, the book turned a spotlight on all the possible candidates for Elizabeth's throne, and few were shown up flatteringly. When, in the autumn of 1595, the old earl of Hertford tried once again to win legal recognition for the validity of his marriage to Lady Catherine Grey, and thus for his sons' legitimacy, the queen had them all clapped in the Tower. Was the harshness of her reaction inspired by the fact that Doleman had described the Seymours as the popular candidates for the throne? It cannot have helped, certainly. Nor can the fact that the lieutenant of the Tower, Sir Michael Blount, was arrested after he was found stockpiling supplies to hold the fortress for the Seymours after Elizabeth's death.

It seems unlikely Arbella read Doleman's book. But the ideas it contained may still have filtered through to her, slowly. As a supporter of the Spanish infanta's claim, Doleman found or invented proof against all the Protestant claimants. (He also suggested that the crown should go less by strict right of lineage than by suitability.) Thus, against Arbella he alleged the double illegitimacy of her grandmother Lady Lennox, whose parents, he claimed, had both been secretly married to other people at the time of their own wedding. Cecil's chief legal adviser, Sir Edward Coke, wrote in the margin 'note the disabling of Arbella' beside Doleman's assertion that 'it was intended to prove bastardy against Arbella.' But both Elizabeth and Mary Tudor had survived far more damning declarations of bastardy; and James was attacked in a similar way. No-one ever took this seriously enough to cast it up against Arbella later in life. She was handi-capped more fatally.

Doleman was if anything rather polite – in a patronizing sort of way – about Arbella herself: 'in that she is a young lady, she is thereby fit . . . to procure good wills and affections, and in that she is unmarried she may perhaps by her marriage join some other title with her, and thereby also friends.' It was he who, prag-matically, had suggested that her religion was 'no great motive, either against her or for her,' being presumably 'tender green and flexible yet, as is her age and sex'. But Doleman also unerringly put his finger on the real weakness of her position. No-one ever accused the Jesuits of being fools. Arbella, he wrote, 'is nothing at all allied with the nobility of England, and except it be the earl of Shrewsbury, in respect of friendship to his old mother-in-law . . . I see not what noble man in England hath any band of kindred or alliance to follow her.' Her kindred on her father's side being 'mere Scottish', she 'hath only the Cavendishes by her mother's side, who being but a mean family for a princess, might cause much grudging . . . to see them so greatly elevated above the rest'. The real question, as the exiled Derrick had phrased it, was 'what support Arbella hath in England or is like to have'. It was a question that could only be answered discouragingly.

Arbella herself, meanwhile, could neither act nor speak in her own cause. She was growing up in seclusion, as Bess settled into old age far from the seat of power. Through all those years of Arbella's childhood, Bess had tried to give her granddaughter the training and trappings of a princess; to fit her for an offer which never came. But now something more active was needed, and Bess had no means (or perhaps, at her age, no volition) to move thus aggressively.

Queen Elizabeth had lived too long. One can never say for certain that Arbella's chances of the throne would have been better had the moment of decision come early in the 1590s. James was always the stronger candidate. But yet there is a sense of a chance slipping away; of the throne being decided (as one historian put it) by 'time, survival and delay'. While Arbella sat at her stitchery, all but incommunicado at Hardwick, the king of Scots, from a greater geographical distance, was manipulating, offering, corresponding; doing deals and demonstrating royal authority. He began hinting that he might tolerate Catholics in return for their support, and in 1594 his position had been strengthened by the birth of his first son, Henry. Now, besides Tudor blood, the male chromosome and experience of government, he could also offer a dynasty.

At this dangerous point, in the summer of 1595, came evidence of more unhelpful scheming on the part of Mary Talbot. A man called Nicholas Williamson, an imprisoned Catholic, was under investigation for suspicious activities. Amid the mass of documents in the Cecil papers bearing his name is a declaration he made in June of that year, attempting to buy favour by giving, as was demanded, 'the smallest particular' of any 'plot or practice for the succession'. Paragraphs of his lengthy statement chronicle various of Mary Talbot's dealings, like her quarrel with the Stanhopes – for fear of poisoning by whom, she said, Gilbert would not dine much abroad when he visited London shortly. (The Stanhope family, that year, were offering Williamson a place in Essex's service if he provided damaging information against Gilbert and Mary.) He ran over all the old plots, and the points raised in Doleman's *Conference*. But he also retailed Scottish gossip to the effect that the queen 'would never set Lady Arbella up in regard to [because of] her Majesty's love of the now lords of her council, who, or most of them, were then sure to be displaced.'

> For her Honour's friends by her father's side would then be her chiefest enemies, and her chiefest friends those by her mother's side, the chiefest of whom (naming my lady) was of so imperious a nature and so conceited against the most of the council . . . that when she should have a ruling hand she would overrule those whom now she least affecteth.

Asked what, if anything, he had ever heard spoken 'touching any expectation to the succession', he could only relay some tittle-tattle Mary Talbot had given him concerning the poverty of the earl of Huntingdon (descended from the Plantagenets) and the recent suspicious death of the earl of Derby (Ferdinando, Lord Strange, claimant of the fourth main, the Stanley, line). But at a time when telling the queen's horoscope was treason, even that could seem dubious.

One Edward Thurland wrote to Gilbert in August warning him that he was in trouble for rumours concerning Arbella; adding, in the same letter, that Mary too was at some risk, being known to have heard mass in her husband's house. In this year Gilbert Talbot, Arbella's only highly placed English relative, seems to have been warned off any activity on his niece's behalf. Essex was pro-Scottish, the Talbots' hands were tied . . . Doleman believed Burghley favoured Arbella, but it seems more likely that the Cecil interest would be dedicated to ensuring an uncontested succession by whoever the front-runner should prove to be. Moreover, thanks to Elizabeth's longevity, Burghley's would not in the end be the relevant voice. Warmly though Arbella's claim might be discussed abroad, there seemed suddenly to be no person or party of power in England with real reason to support her candidacy at home.

# 'This my prison'

AT THE END OF 1595 ARBELLA STUART HAD JUST TURNED TWENTY. The years of her autonomy – of action, attempt, adventure – were still far ahead. And yet something seems already to have died – the phantasm, perhaps, of the life for which she had been raised. It seems almost apt that at the end of 1595 James in Scotland heard that she was 'not like to live', though we do not know what her illness, if any, may have been. It is dangerous (if all too easy) to view Arbella's life only from the political perspective; to see her stamped by failure here, so early in her adulthood. But if we do ask 'what went wrong' with her hopes of ruling the country, the answer lies in these years, surely.

If it is true that Arbella Stuart had at one time been an important candidate for the throne, it is probably also true that by the start of 1596 the most influential of Elizabeth's court had ceased to take her seriously. Among later historians, Joel Hurstfield in 1961 saw James, Arbella and the Spanish infanta as the three among the many contenders who went on counting through the 1590s. Today, Pauline Croft makes a significant distinction between the inner circle – for whom Arbella was never a likely prospect – and the outer circle, the majority. And, as she points out, death or disaster could bring an outside hope into the lead all too easily. But most of Arbella's contemporaries could never have known that she had been ruled out of the game. Nor, crucially, could she.

For the remainder of Queen Elizabeth's reign, Arbella Stuart was the victim of a campaign of obfuscation, baffled by the smokescreen the queen and her ministers successfully threw up over the question of the succession. She was still spoken of for this or that foreign prince – more princes than ever – and the crown would go with her, surely? But somehow, all the promises came to nothing. The deception was probably not aimed at Arbella herself, or even at those who might support her; Elizabeth's desire to keep everyone guessing was ingrained, the result as much of temperament as of international policy. But then again, if enduring hope kept any potential supporters from building an aggressive party, then that was a good thing – from the viewpoint of those in power.

Ironically, it was the very length of time Arbella Stuart spent in hopes of the crown of England that would finally drive her to rebellion. We need not imagine her waiting at Hardwick in tranquil passivity. If we borrow for a moment the Elizabethan belief in human nature as dominated by four humours, hers – like her uncle Gilbert's, like her cousin James's – fits the pattern of the 'melancholic' temperament all too neatly. Melancholy man or woman was studious and solitary; steadfast in choice though 'long a-choosing', subject to 'perpetual sadness' or irrational joy. It was proper to all melancholy men, wrote Robert Burton, the author of the *Anatomy of Melancholy*, 'what conceit they have once entertained to be most intent, violent and continually about it'. The fixed conceit in which Arbella had been reared – this troublesome, this obsessive conceit – was that of her royalty.

The pieces on the board were taking on a new shape, and James was pulling far ahead. Much, though, still depended on the way the powerful men in London played their game; and between them, the factions (wrote one courtier, Sir Thomas Lake) were 'never more malicious'. For both Essex and Robert Cecil, 1596 saw significant advances. But they were holding very different territory.

While Cecil had become 'the greatest councillor in England', Essex was ever more 'wearied' of the 'dissembling courses' of the court. Essex was the man of war, seeking the bubble reputation in the cannon's mouth. Cecil was the man of peace. In the summer of 1596 Essex (together with Sir Walter Ralegh; two natural enemies thrust into a brief alliance) set off on a raiding expedition towards the Spanish coast. Their flamboyant achievement was to capture and sack the port of Cadiz and destroy the fleet the king of Spain was building towards another Armada. It was a feat tailor-made to give English morale a useful boost in these gloomy years. But they missed, to Elizabeth's fury, their chance to capture the laden Spanish treasure fleet. Essex always had the capacity to snatch defeat from the jaws of victory.

The balance of power was shifting in the Cecils' favour. The day Essex set sail from Cadiz was the day Cecil was sworn in as secretary of state. Robert Cecil's intelligence network was coming to rival that of Essex, and at the beginning of 1597 Francis Bacon, Essex's chief agent and adviser, transferred his allegiance to Burghley. It was becoming increasingly likely that the next head to wear the English crown would be the one that enjoyed Cecil support; but still no-one knew whose it might be. The smoke-screen still kept the future from view. Arbella still seemed to be of importance to almost everybody.

Essex's own spy network threw up evidence of another abortive plot to kidnap Arbella – a feeble one, but it may further have focused his mind upon her: 'how beautiful', as the agent noted, 'how virtuous and how inclined'. Essex's voyage had been one move in the anti-Spanish alliance Elizabeth cemented that year with Henri IV of France – and Henri (seeking a divorce from his barren wife Marguerite de Valois) was looking for a new bride. That summer, the rumour mill was busy – especially when Arbella's uncle Gilbert was chosen to lead the celebratory embassy. James in Scotland was said to suspect 'that the queen of England would persuade the French king . . . either to divorce or kill his wife and to marry himself with the Lady Arbella to bring him into the succession of England'.

But Henri the shrewd saw it more realistically. As he told his minister Sully:

> I should have no objection to the infanta of Spain, however old and ugly she might be, provided that with her I could marry the

Low Countries; neither would I refuse the princess Arbella of England, if, since as it is publicly said the crown of England really belongs to her, she were only declared presumptive heiress of it. But there is no reason to expect either of these things will happen, for the Spanish king and the English queen are far from making such plans.

Just how far was proved when – perhaps flushed with the honour done her husband – Mary Talbot dared to ask if two of her daughters could be appointed maids in waiting to their cousin. The right to have maids of honour was granted only to the heir presumptive, and Elizabeth ordered the Talbot party home immediately.

It was characteristic of Mary to push too far, too fast. The same was all too true of Essex, and 1597 saw his position shift for the worse. A year which began with a flaming quarrel between queen and favourite (he took to his bed sick; she visited him; he recovered) continued with the disastrous 'islands voyage', which failed in its object of sinking the Spanish treasure fleet, through a cocktail of ill luck and ill judgement. The earl's behaviour, indeed, was by now so erratic that historians have speculated on the insanity which comes from advanced syphilis.

But still the common people cheered him to the rafters whenever he showed his handsome head. These middle years of the 1590s were trying times. Endemic corruption in the palaces combined with economic hardship in the land as the high taxation consequent on campaigns abroad combined with a string of harvests so bad that children died of famine and inns could not afford to brew beer. These are the conditions that focus hate on bureaucrats: 'pen gents', as the Cecils were contemptuously described. These are also the conditions that breed popular heroes – demagogues – and Essex fitted the bill perfectly. His victory in Cadiz had given him 'a charter of the people's hearts'. He knew it, and fostered it, all too visibly.

The deals, the diplomacy were all spectacles Arbella could watch only from a distance. We can never know how much information she was able to obtain; but it was not enough, as events ahead were to prove, to enable her to judge her chances appropriately. Indeed, the high ridge on which Bess built her Hardwick homes seemed to lend its own bedazzlement to the eye. Looking out from Hardwick over the empty landscape, one might easily imagine that other figures would be as easily placed as pieces in a board game; might lose touch with any sense of reality.

While agents and ambassadors spoke of Arbella's moving across the seas to France or Spain, at the end of 1597 she and her grandmother were preparing for a journey of a few hundred yards. But even that was to be marked by triumphal music, played by members of the Hardwick household (two of whom, the chaplain James Starkey, and Bess's confidential servant John Good, or Dodderidge, were to be intimately involved in Arbella's story). And perhaps, after all, the event was significant enough in its way. Their new home, Hardwick Hall, was at last ready.

More space must have been needed urgently. Not only Arbella and her own attendants but William and his family were living at Hardwick, and the records of 1597 show Bess dressing seventy-four servants in her livery of blue or 'mallard colour'. But space, one feels, was only a part of the story. This was an age when men ruined themselves in mortar, as the late Sir Christopher Hatton had done at Holdenby. Building, wrote Francis Bacon in 1594, was the only way 'to cure mortality by fame', and Bess had always been interested in her properties, even beyond the norm of her day. The very stone of Hardwick proclaims her identity. A repeated device around the roof of the Hall, standing high on a Derbyshire escarpment ('exposed to all the malice of the heavens', as the queen of Scots had said of Tutbury), exalts a countess's coronet and the initials E.S. – Elizabeth Shrewsbury – to the sky.

'Hardwick Hall/More glass than wall', as the mocking jingle had it, must have astonished the countryside. Bess even, for the sake of symmetry, squandered the costly glass on fake windows to mask the chimneys. Thus lavishly endowed, Hardwick had to excess the 'largeness and lightsomeness' Burghley had praised in Hatton's Holdenby, but it cannot have had warmth. A later owner wrote that it was icy. The windows grow ever larger as you rise through three stories. On the ground floor was to be found the service area – kitchens, pantry – and also the nursery, where William's children were taught by the chaplain Starkey, along with the base level of the tall hall and chapel. The first floor was the dwelling space of the family, and of some of the upper servants and visitors. The second floor held the great Gallery, the High Great Chamber – the most lavishly decorated room in the house – and the bedroom which would be given to any visiting royalty.

There is a theory that Bess was building a fitting backdrop for a Queen Arbella, but it is hard to walk around the house and still subscribe to that story. The only sign of Arbella's presence is her own coat of arms – tucked in above the larger Hardwick shield – in the back room she was to call her study. It is a pleasant room, with large windows overlooking lawns, but accessible only through Bess's private suite. In that, it was a 'disadvantageous chamber', Arbella would grumble bitterly.

The inventory Bess had drawn up in 1601 lists the contents of the room precisely. There was little solid furniture – a cupboard, a square table, a joined stool – but a lavish array of textiles: 'Six pieces of hangings of yellow, blue and other coloured damask and sating wrought with gold flowers and lined with canvas'; a carpet 'of needlework wrought with antiks'; another 'of russet velvet paned with gold and silver lace and layed with gold and silver lace and fringe about, lined with yellow and green satin bridges'. Some of the household's attendant ladies obviously crammed in to sleep here and in the tiny room that abuts the chamber, for the inventory lists several beds. But Arbella herself, under 'a canopy of darnix blue and white with gilt knobs and blue and white fringe', was still sleeping just across the passageway, in her grandmother's room; a crowded space packed with the huge number of coverlets needed to warm so old a lady. (A closet off it held their private closed stools.) In an age of shared chambers and even beds – an age before corridors, when only the curtains of a four-poster protected its inhabitants from traffic through the room – a lack of privacy must have been something Elizabethans took for granted; until, perhaps, some particular stress of circumstance impressed it on them forcibly.

Hardwick Hall, compared to the great houses of the day, is tiny; less than half the size of Bess's Chatsworth. In practical terms that didn't matter. The Old Hall still stood only yards away to act as overflow accommodation and servants' quarters, and to perform some of the functions that made a great house resemble a small city. Bess's account books show that the two houses were run as one household, and in the courtyard of the Old Hall were to be found the dairy and slaughterhouse, stables and smithy. But the occupants of the new Hall must have found it hard to get away from each other – in particular, to get away from Bess.

In Bess's home, her granddaughter would always be a subordinate. The inventory of contents shows each of the rooms Bess habitually used furnished with one – just one – high chair and footstool. The high back was not just for comfort; it was a symbol of authority. Arbella's chair, though upholstered in cloth of gold, was described as small. This was another queendom in which she could never wield power.

Hardwick in all its appointments, in every departure from usual arrangements, proclaims that it was built for the convenience of one ageing and autocratic woman. No wonder Arbella came eventually to hate 'this my prison', as she would later describe it bitterly. Sequestered inside its glowing golden stone, amid the painted tales and embroidered images chosen by Bess to reflect her own past, Arbella must have wondered what was to be *her* story.

Arbella was later to claim that she was shut up in Hardwick with only 'ancient gentlewomen' to attend her. She begged for some young company. She had her own immediate attendants among the community and later, when the great row came, she was to make a sharp distinction between those servants who owed allegiance to her – 'my regiment' – and her grandmother's great majority. But loyal though these attendants may have been (even prepared, Arbella suggests, to give and take blows for her sake), she clearly came to feel that there was something lacking in their society.

For the first part of the 1590s, for many months of the year, Hardwick bustled with William's family: the three young sons and three daughters born to his first wife Anne Keighley. We know little of Anne – 'the most excellent of women', in the words of the tombstone erected by her second son. But while perforce considerably older than Arbella (she married William in 1582, when Arbella was only seven), she must also have been younger than her husband, who was nearing fifty with the turn of the century. Perhaps Anne was a companion for Arbella, and a conduit of London news and gossip after the couple's visits to their Holborn house.

But in February 1598, soon after the birth of her youngest child, Anne died. Two of her daughters did not long outlive her. And in 1599, Bess's accounts record the charges for the 'full furnishing' of Oldcotes (or Owlcotes), the house she had built for William just a couple of miles away. William, as his mother's lieutenant, may have spent much of his widowerhood still at Hardwick; in 1602 he promised his eleven-year-old son Will a rapier, dagger, embroidered girdle and spurs if he would speak Latin with his cousin Arbella until Lent Assizes. But the house was not getting any livelier, as the long years of the 1590s passed away.

# 'They are dead whom I loved'

AS THE QUEEN CONTINUED TO AGE, MARRIAGE PROPOSALS FOR Arbella as her possible heir were never likely to diminish in frequency. In 1599 the chief candidate was Matthias, brother to the Archduke Albert (heir to the Holy Roman Empire). Albert had married the former Spanish infanta, and since the death of her father King Philip II in September 1598 the pair jointly ruled the Spanish Netherlands, so this was a potential alliance powerful enough to cause the watchful James some panic in prospect. In 1600 the Venetian ambassador in Germany wrote home of a new theory about fresh plans for an alliance with France. In Rome they said that 'the marriage treaty between the French king and the great duke [of Tuscany] cools, for the queen of England has promised a near cousin of her own, whom she loves much, and whom she intends to make her heir and successor.'

In the event, Henry went ahead with the lucrative Tuscan marriage, but he put forward instead for Arbella one of his bastard sons. Sir John Harington was gallantly horrified at the idea that Arbella, 'a goodly young lady, aged about twenty four years, should be so disparaged as to be matched with a bastard of France under fourteen'. Such a match, he suggested, might 'make a new Helena to burn our Troy dormant, and run away by the light'. But in fact Arbella – besides being flattered by the comparison with Helen of Troy! – may well have been grateful for the fruition of this or any other of all these tantalizing possibilities.

The most interesting proposal passed without remark, to be revealed only in an inquiry held later, in 1603. At that time, a gentleman called David Owen Tudor – a satellite of Arbella's family, who subsequently sent his young son to be her page – admitted that he had, 'three or four years past', been approached by the earl of Hertford's solicitor 'to move a marriage between the Lord Beauchamp's eldest son and the lady Arbella, which this examinate utterly refused to do'. The solicitor then asked Owen Tudor at least 'to help him to the speech of the said lady Arbella', but again Owen Tudor refused. He was prudent to do so. A marriage between Arbella and Beauchamp's son – the grandson of Hertford and Lady Catherine Grey – would unite two important claims to the throne, and could only be viewed suspiciously. At the time, the matter seems to have faded away – except that Arbella herself, as later events would prove, did not let it slip from her memory.

These were the years when deals and dangers came thick and fast. As the sixteenth century drew to a close, everyone knew the queen's life must soon end; but no-one knew when – or what would happen afterwards. Still came the stream of admonitory literature: 1598 had seen the posthumous publication of Peter Wentworth's *Pithy Exhortation to Her Majesty for Establishing her Successor to the Crown*, urging that neglect of this duty could only condemn her Majesty's people to the 'merciless bloody sword'. Still, James in Scotland told his parliament that he expected to need force of arms to push through his claim. Still, no-one knew for sure even who the Cecils favoured. Doleman had believed that old Lord Burghley favoured Arbella – but then, at almost the same time, had he not married his granddaughter to a claimant of the Stanley line? In the summer of 1598 Burghley had finally died, urging his son Robert on his deathbed that 'three things thou have before thy eyes,' last and hardest of which was to invest a 'true and lawful successor'. Robert Cecil was thus bearing 'the whole weight of the state' as another crisis burst upon queen and country.

Ireland had always been the running sore of Tudor foreign policy. Essex's father had died there, worn out by his efforts to claim Ulster for Protestant colonists and for the English crown.

Since the middle of the 1590s the powerful Irish Catholic lords had been in open rebellion under the earl of Tyrone. In 1598 came the appalling news that, at the Battle (or Massacre) of Yellow Ford, almost a thousand English soldiers lay dead at Tyrone's hand – and, even more dangerous, that Tyrone had appealed for help from Spain.

Essex had by now a strange love/hate relationship with Elizabeth; indeed, his greatness was said to arise as much from her fear as from her love. 'The Queen's conditions are as crooked as her carcass,' he said of her once in anger. At one notorious council meeting he turned his back on her, she boxed his ears and he, momentarily, reached for his sword. Both, by any normal etiquette, had behaved unforgivably. And as Essex retired, furious, to the country, he sent to a friend a letter that voiced dangerous ideas. 'What, cannot princes err? Cannot subjects receive wrong? Is an earthly power or authority infinite? Pardon me, pardon me, my good lord, I can never subscribe to these principles.'

Nevertheless, in this new Irish crisis, Essex was recalled. He was still England's premier soldier. Early in 1599 he accepted the post of lord lieutenant of Ireland, and left London at the head of the largest army sent abroad in Elizabeth's reign. But he took the command with uncharacteristic pessimism. This, he knew, was a poisoned chalice of an appointment. He was, in his own words, 'tied by my own reputation to use no tergiversation', but: 'You might rather pity me than expect extraordinary successes from me,' he told the council grimly.

All Essex's exploits, and most of his titles, were military: earl marshal, master of the horse and of the ordnance. But those who live by the sword see their reputations die by the sword. Essex, sent over the sea without adequate supplies, led a campaign so disastrous he lost three-quarters of his men without ever engaging the main body of the enemy. Worse still, against express orders, he agreed a disastrous truce with Tyrone. There had always been speculation that his real business in Ireland was just that: to make an alliance with the rebel leader and, with his help, to seize the English throne. Now, it seemed all too likely.

Horrified by news of how his treaty had been received in England, Essex abandoned his post to return to London and

The most noble ROBERT Earle of Eſſex and Ewe, Earle Marſhall of England, Vicount Hereford and Bourgcher, Lord Ferres of Chartley, L. Bourgcher and Louayn, and her Maieſties lieutenant, and Gouernour generall of the Kingdome of Irland. 1601.

HIC TVVS ILLE COMES GENEROSA ESSEXIA NOSTRIS QVEM QVAM GAVDEMVS REBVS ADESSE DVCEM.

A triumphant Essex with past campaigns in the background

explain himself to the queen in person. After four days of frantic gallop he reached the court at ten in the morning, brushed his way through the layers of courtiers who should have protected the queen's privacy and forced his way into Elizabeth's very bed-chamber, catching her in an old woman's state of undress. An 'unmannerly (but I think in any lovers opinion) pardonable' offence, Arbella later described it naïvely, disregarding the fact that in the bedroom, as much as he had done in the bogs of Ireland, Essex was displaying a subversive contempt for authority. But one of the things he had in common with Arbella was a conviction that, if they could only win through to the queen's side, all their misdeeds would instantly be forgiven them. Instead, he was dismissed from all his offices of state and placed in custody at York House.

Crowds of well-wishers flocked to see him, until forbidden by the authorities. Tyrone in Ireland confirmed that Essex had been working against his own government, and Essex vainly appealed to James in Scotland for armed support. By now he had severed all ties of loyalty to Elizabeth. But what finally pushed him over the brink was that hoary old Elizabethan chestnut – lack of money. Way back in the heyday of his favour, in the summer of 1590, the queen had granted him the decade-long right to license the selling of sweet wines, and the core of his income (his only income, now he was stripped of all offices) derived from this monopoly. At the worst moment possible, the licence now ran out. The queen refused to renew it – and Essex knew despair. The new post he had hoped for, the mastership of the court of wards, had been given to Cecil while he was away.

It was said of Essex that he had only one enemy – himself – and one friend: the queen. Now the friend had turned her back and he was left with the enemy. 'Ambition thwarted in its career doth speedily lead on to madness,' Sir John Harington wrote of him, in words which could shortly have been applied to Arbella also. But Essex (like Arbella, again) saw his life as barren of viable options. In the autumn of 1600 he appealed again to the unwilling James, weighting his plea with the unwelcome news that Cecil, as he now believed, was promoting the succession of the Spanish infanta, now archduchess in the Netherlands. Probably Cecil was merely pursuing his lifelong policy of bringing to an end the war with Spain, and going about it, as ever, discreetly. (Or was he indeed trying to counterbalance the menacing prospect of a James–Essex alliance by implicitly holding over James's head a threat mightier than poor Arbella could present: an infanta riding into London at the head of an unanswerable foreign army?) In the first week of February 1601 Essex's patience, never extensive, ran out. For years his home had been the headquarters for a motley band of the disaffected: deserters, malcontents, puritans and papists. Now Essex and his followers planned a coup. Their pretext was to rid the queen of her evil advisers, like Secretary Cecil. But they ended by seeking her overthrow, even if it could only be had bloodily.

It is impossible to read of the Essex rebellion without disbelief, so nearly does its conduct verge on the farcical. When their plans were suspected Essex panicked, locked into his house the officials sent to reason with him, and took to the London streets with some 150 supporters, crying that his life was in danger. But the popular uprising he had anticipated failed to materialize. It was one thing to cheer the romantic Essex. But risk your life for him? That was another story.

In the City, the rebels faced more disappointment. One Sheriff Smyth, so Essex believed, had promised a band of citizenry – but no leader of Essex's crew had actually checked this with the sheriff, who now denied all thought of complicity. As the earl's daunted band fought their way back to the Strand, the government troops were assembling. Essex barricaded himself inside his house and set about burning his papers; gunpowder was brought from the Tower, to bring the house down around his ears if necessary. At around ten in the evening Essex surrendered. The rebellion had died as abruptly as it was born – thanks, as one contemporary put it, to 'the providence and celerity of the secretary', Cecil.

Essex was brought to trial on 19 February 1601. Sir Edward Coke accused him of having hoped to be 'Robert, king of England'. 'He has been devising five or six years to be king of England,' Cecil had said a few days earlier. Essex denied it hotly. 'God, which knoweth the secrets of all hearts, knoweth that

I never sought the crown of England . . . only seeking to secure access to the presence of the queen, that I might speedily have unfolded my griefs unto her Majesty against my private enemies.' He had done, he said, only what 'the law of nature and the necessity of my cause' forced him to do. But he was sure to be found guilty. The French ambassador, indeed, gave an uncomfortable description of the jury of peers. 'While the earl and the counsel were pleading my lords guzzled as if they had not eaten for a fortnight . . . they went into a room to give their verdict, stupid with eating.'

Essex had hangings, bedding, pewter and a Bible brought into the Tower, where he was held. But his was to be a brief stay. His execution was set for Ash Wednesday, 25 February. It was – most unusually – to be a private beheading, within the Tower walls. London had not risen for the earl but now it seethed with sympathy. So the headsmen (two of them, so that 'if one faint, the other may perform it') were smuggled in secretly, and separately from 'their bloody tool'. The queen had turned her face away. 'Those who touch the sceptre of princes', she said, 'deserve no pity.'

But a later letter suggests that Arbella felt the event deeply. On the second anniversary of his death, writing out of what was by then her own dire trouble with the crown, Arbella described herself as the earl of Essex's friend. 'They are dead whom I loved, they have forsaken me in whom I trusted, I am dangerous to my guiltless friends . . . How dare others visit me in distress when the earl of Essex then in highest favour durst scarce steal a salutation in the privy chamber' – a reference to that occasion, long ago, on which Essex had stood up for her at court. She wrote of her own 'virtue . . . whither it be a native property of that blood I come of, or an infective virtue of the earl of Essex', before describing how greedy he was of the queen's favour, 'as I protest he ever said to me'. Now 'The newdropping tears of some', she said, might 'make others remember his goodness . . .'

Cecil suffered a fresh wave of unpopularity and a neighbour of Arbella's, Sir John Byron, reported that in nearby Mansfield the 'Robin with the bloody breast' as he was dubbed, was openly blamed for Essex's fall, and armed vengeance threatened.

Mansfield was the town nearest to Hardwick Hall, and the rumours must have reached the household – unless, indeed, the news was dispersed from there, which is perhaps more likely.

Had Essex's mourners seen more of him in his last days, perhaps they would have had less sympathy. On the scaffold he denounced his former life, ambition and womanizing especially. Histrionically, he blamed himself, upon the scaffold, for his rebellion – 'this great, this bloody, this crying, this infectious sin'. In the days before his execution, he went so far as to denounce his own sister for having urged him to conflict – that same Penelope who out of her 'exceeding love' had served his interests 'more like a slave than a sister', as she answered bitterly. Yet the life and death of the ungrateful Essex were attended by the adulation of noblewomen: his wife, his mistresses, mother, sisters, cousin. The queen herself had never been immune to his charm. Why should Arbella be?

# 'Helping myself in this distress'

WITH ESSEX'S DEATH, ONE DOOR CLOSED FOR ARBELLA. PERHAPS IT had never been open that widely. But, as the earl of Northumberland assured James, 'the world assumeth a greater freedom since Essex death to speak freely of your title.' In April James sent ambassadors south, to congratulate Elizabeth on her escape from the late rebellion – and to petition once again for the English Lennox lands. Had Elizabeth granted that request, it would have been a clear signal that she set his claims above Arbella's. Instead, of course, the queen kept the lands – hoping, she wrote crisply, 'to hear no more of these matters' – and ignored James's request that she would do nothing to prejudice his claim to her throne.

But for all of that, the ambassadors took back to Scotland with them one promise, of the greatest value. They had visited Robert Cecil's house in the Strand and with him, in deepest secrecy, hammered out an agreement. By his own lights, Cecil kept his loyalty. Elizabeth was not to be deposed during the period of her natural life. In return for this, Cecil would ensure that James succeeded her smoothly. This he was in a position to do. Cecil, as the popular jingle had it, by now 'rule[d] both court and crown'. He himself was now king of England in effect, James noted shrewdly.

Cecil had chosen. Not, yet again, that Arbella – or, indeed, anyone else – would have known it. At the start of the year, sending thanks for Arbella's seasonal gift, Queen Elizabeth had promised Bess to be 'careful' of Arbella's future, and then insisted that Bess should not speak to anyone of her (vague) promise; a piece of discretion completely excessive in any context other than that of the succession story. Father Parsons – who, as a leading figure in Catholic politics, gathered views from many sources, including correspondents in England – had been told Cecil was now committed to the Stanleys. The secret of the correspondence between Cecil and James was known to no more than half a dozen individuals, and James was warned to opt (unlike Essex) for 'the choice election of the few' rather than 'any general acclamation'. Thomas Wilson, a member of Cecil's staff, wrote sourly in *The State of England, Anno Dom. 1600* that the crown 'is not like to fall to the ground for want of heads that claim to wear it, but upon whose head it will fall is by many doubted' – and a bill was drafted to forbid the publication of any more succession theories.

In the summer of 1601, Wilson prepared for Cecil a list of candidates for the throne. In the first place he put James, in the second Arbella. They were followed – significantly, as it would turn out – by Lord Beauchamp, and then Beauchamp's brother Thomas. The duke of Parma (Farnese) came tenth, and the infanta only twelfth. The ranks of the realistic contenders, from Cecil's viewpoint, were thinning out nicely.

Gilbert Talbot (and who knows what distress this caused to Arbella?) had long since fallen into line behind the secretary. One Rowland Whyte, in 1599, gave a vivid picture of how, the very day Essex was to be called before the Lords to explain the Irish debacle, the two groups – the Essex faction, and Cecil with Shrewsbury – rose and went in to dinner separately. Was it only coincidence that in 1601 Gilbert Talbot, under Cecil's aegis, was finally appointed to the privy council, thereby giving him an alternative means of 'advancement' for his family? Or, as Harington put it:

> If some great counsellors do make some shows, and cast out some words afore fools in favour of Arbella's title for [policy] . . . yet they labour, like oars on the Thames, to row one way and look

another. It is least likely that when it comes to trial they ['my Lord of Shrewsbury, or the countess and her brothers'] will hazard so great estates, so contented lives, so gentlemanly pleasures, so sweet duties, to advance their niece against law, reason, probability, yea, possibility.

An anonymous letter from 1600, intercepted and now found in the State Papers, in discussing the contenders for the throne dismissed Arbella's English birth (she being, as the writer put it, 'otherwise in descent Scottish') as 'too nice a point to stand on', since James, the senior by the same line of inheritance, was 'in every degree jure et dignitate potior' – governed by right and authority. 'Touching Arbella,' it stated firmly, 'no marriage that the Cecilians could build on presented itself.'

There were, however, even rumours of Arbella's marrying Robert Cecil himself: 'Sir R. Cecil intends to be king, by marrying Arbella, and now lacks only the name . . . Lord Shrewsbury, who can remove the blocks from the way of the marriage, is for him, thinking he cannot better establish his house.' But these were surely without foundation, significant only in that they caused Arbella herself to retort that no man in England was her match in rank – untactfully, and, given Cecil's mounting power, unwisely.

One Captain North bragged in the taverns that he 'had commission from her to deal with foreign princes . . . and that her common speech was that she thought no match in England good enough for her'. Was it of this kind of haughtiness, this potentially treasonable course of action, that Henry Howard was thinking when he wrote to James about Shrewsbury's 'idol', who might be made 'higher by as many steps as ascend to a scaffold, if she follow some men's counsels'? Or was it of the dangerous friendship he noted, the 'strong league' among Mary Talbot, Sir Walter Ralegh and Ralegh's wife, 'a most dangerous woman'? This was a connection that a year or two later would resonate ominously.

But Arbella was still held in considerable regard abroad. In 1600 the Fugger newsletters had still been calling her 'successor to the throne' and 'heir to this kingdom'. In the middle of February 1601 they had described (obviously in error) how the queen had issued a decree excluding James, and set about negotiating a peace with Philip III of Spain 'so that she may leave her kingdom at peace and transmit her crown to one of her blood relations and assure her [*sic*] of undisputed possession'. Cecil himself, in his first letter to James, had fostered doubt, warning that Queen Elizabeth (without James's good behaviour and his, Cecil's, watchful care) might yet 'cut off the natural branch [James] and graft upon some wild stock'.

As late as 1601, again, a letter home from the French ambassador in Rome details the Pope's plans for England. Rainutio Farnese, now a married man and duke of Parma, was his first choice – *if*

> his Highness perceives the kingdom of England can be obtained without Arbella. But if, after the queen's decease, Arbella should raise a strong party in England, and that for the easier conquest of the kingdom, it were necessary to join his forces with Arbella's . . . the Pope intends instead of the duke of Parma to bring in the cardinal his brother, who might marry the said Arbella, and by these means they, joining both their forces, would sooner and easier compass their designs.

Another observer (anonymous, but writing in Italian) put together a lengthy analysis of the situation, running to some three thousand words. He was suggesting measures the new young king of Spain might take to protect himself from a rumoured marriage (with England's crown for dowry) between Arbella and the French king's nephew, the prince de Condé.

But, as the first years of the seventeenth century wore away, one by one the powers in England came to recognize the inevitability of James's accession. Northumberland, the 'wizard earl', had once raged to his wife (Essex's other sister Dorothy) that he preferred the king of Scots to be buried than crowned, and that he and his friends would rather take their lives than see her brother's 'great God' rule in England. He was one who might well have supported Arbella's candidacy. But by the spring of 1602 he had changed his mind. A Catholic, he proffered support to James on the tacit condition the new king should tolerate 'a mass in a corner'. Most of the English Catholics 'do declare their affections absolutely to

your title', Cecil told James reassuringly. They had little alternative. For Spain to promote the infanta to the throne of England
now looked increasingly unlikely, though Spain might still have
backed an English candidate – an English *king*, to give the precise
word used in one Catholic letter – who would be supportive of its
policy.

The trouble was that England had had enough of queens. Even
Doleman, despite advocating the infanta, had protested that
Arbella, 'a woman, ought not to be preferred, before so many
men . . . and that it were much to have three women to reign in
England one after the other, whereas in the space of above a
thousand years before them, there had not reigned so many of
that sex.' In 1598, Henri of France's special envoy reported to his
master that the young men of the court, growing restless under
the petticoat government of an ageing woman, declared that they
would not submit to another female ruler. A labourer was seized
for praying for a king – saying poor men could get nothing under
a queen, 'but a woman and ruled by noblemen'. And Catholic
support for Arbella's claim had died away. The bishop of London
was able to send Cecil a reassuring report he had garnered of
attitudes at the Catholic seminary at Douai. 'Lady Arbella is a
notable puritan,' was the word there, 'and they hold the Turk
more worthy of place than she.'

Yet still the bandwagon rumbled on. In the spring of 1602,
London waited for the arrival of the French duke of Nevers. 'I
hear he desire secretly a sight of the Lady Arbella,' the Jesuits concluded significantly, and a house in London was said to be prepared for Arbella's own reception. But once again, the gossips
waited in vain. The duke came late, and Arbella never came at all.
This was just another busted flush; another chimera, another
popular fantasy. Still, in the summer of 1602, a law student called
John Manningham would jot an anagram in his commonplace
book – *Arbella Stuarta: tu rara es et bella*. To a young man around
the city, her name was obviously in currency. But to Arbella herself
at Hardwick the glamorous preparations for Nevers' visit – the
splendid wall hanging taken from the Tower, the entertainments in
rehearsal – might by now have seemed like an absurdity, a message
from another world. This was not her reality.

It seems rather pathetic, and all too telling, that the only certain evidence of her activity in this stirring time was yet more embroidery. (As the imprisoned queen of Scots had put it, the pictures in the work and the diversity of colours made time seem to pass more quickly.) So Arbella became an adept. That gift to the queen in New Year 1601, received by Elizabeth with 'especial liking', was 'a scarf or head-veil of lawn cut-work flourished with silver and silks of sundry colours'. This painstaking cut-work was a technique only for the most proficient – or for those with most time on their hands. Two years later, in the midst of an official inquiry into her potentially treasonable conduct, the government agent took time out to pass on to Arbella a message that the queen wondered how she had made her latest New Year's gift. Obviously, she was still stitching desperately away. We cannot doubt that as she did so, the black dog depression lay all too frequently at her feet. Three years before, her kinsman, the composer Michael Cavendish, had dedicated to her a collection of songs and madrigals.

*Why should my muse thus restless in her woes*
*Summon records of never dying fears?*
*And still revive fresh springing in my thoughts,*
*The true memorial of my sad despairs?*

Even the songs were gloomy.

Perhaps our best picture of Arbella's daily round comes from two contemporary women who kept diaries. Lady Margaret Hoby seems to have been occupied enough; an active puritan and a notable housekeeper, her diary is largely filled with religious exercises. 'In the morning I prayed privately and writ notes in my testament till 7 o'clock then I took order for dinner and things touching the house . . .' Her hours, with prayer listed as much as five times a day, seem if anything to have been over-full: 'I bestowed too much time in the garden and thereby was worse able to perform spiritual duties.'

But for Anne Clifford, a connection of Arbella's writing from Knole in Kent two decades later, the days often lagged. In amid her disputes with her husband, and her litigation to keep her own property, she wrote of saying her prayers in the garden, of playing cards with her steward, of a dog that pupped. But: 'I sat still thinking the time to be very tedious,' she wrote on one occasion, and: 'The time grew tedious so as I used to go to bed about 8 o'clock & did lie abed till 8 the next morning.' Yet again: 'I spent the time as I did many wearisome days besides, in working and walking.'

Clearly, Arbella was not the only lady of the day to find herself often in what she later called a 'dump'. Like Arbella, Anne Clifford felt herself exiled from the court, writing bitterly: 'All this time my lord was in London, where he had all and infinite great resort coming to him. He went much abroad to cocking, to bowling alleys, to plays and horse races & [was] commended by all the world. I stayed in the country having many times a sorrowful and heavy heart.' But Anne, like Lady Margaret, had at least a household and child to keep her busy. By contrast, Arbella's was a life without business, a life on hold; no life for an eager and untried young woman – no matter how fond of her books she might be.

The Venetians left a word picture of Arbella from just after this time. (Elizabeth's court had long been without a resident Venetian envoy. But the ambassador Scaramelli arrived in the last months of her reign, and from that point on the reports of successive Venetian envoys to doge and senate are a vital source of information about Arbella's story.) She was, they said, a woman 'of great beauty and remarkable qualities, being gifted with many accomplishments, among them the knowledge of Latin, French, Spanish and Italian, besides her native English. She has very exalted ideas having been brought up in a belief that she would succeed to the crown.' She had always lived, they said, far from London and in poverty.

Bess tried, at least, to do something about the poverty. It is unlikely she appreciated Arbella's loneliness, but she seems, in the closing years of the sixteenth century, to have tried to make some financial provision of her own for her granddaughter's future. She gave several gifts of capital, and negotiated property in her name. (A typical piece of shrewd dealing, and a gift well worth having, came when in 1594 she lent to the impoverished Sir Francis Willoughby three thousand and fifty pounds, at an annual interest of three hundred. As he had little chance of redeeming the mortgage, Arbella thus gained land worth perhaps fifteen thousand.) In the same year Bess paid to Arbella her mother's long-awaited dowry, plus appropriate interest, and in 1599 gave her more than a thousand pounds to buy land in Lincolnshire. By such means the two hundred pounds allowed by the queen was augmented to some six or seven hundred a year. There were also many smaller gifts of money and of very valuable jewellery: in January 1594 it was a head-dress incorporating thirty highly prized pearls; in 1599, 'Given to my daughter [*sic*] Arbella to buy her a pearl to enlarge her chain, £100.'

In 1601 Bess the provident made her will. She had passed the biblical three score and ten, and her death could not be many years away. Though the serious legacy of Hardwick and its contents went to William and his family, she left to her 'very loving grandchild' a thousand pounds; all her pearls and jewels 'except those as shall be otherwise bequeathed'; an ermine sable 'the head being of gold enamelled'; and a crystal glass set with agate and lapis lazuli. Moreover, with the 'poor widow's mite' Bess willed to the queen (two hundred pounds in a gold cup) she attached a request that the queen should take her 'said poor desolate orphan' back to court. She had already begged Elizabeth to find a husband for Arbella – but perhaps she and Arbella had begun to despair of such an eventuality.

In the year following Essex's death, reports began to spread that the Lady Arbella was mad, that she was heartbroken . . . The latter was true, in one way or another. In that same season, Arbella told the chaplain James Starkey, with whom she read, that she had 'thought of all means she could to get from home, by reason she was hardly used in dispiteful and disgraceful words'. At twenty-seven, she was still being 'bobbed [smacked] and her nose played withall'. Her distress, Starkey said unnecessarily, 'seemed not feigned, for oftentimes, being at her books, she would break forth into tears', as they sat together in the small room she called her 'quondam study'.

In the months ahead Arbella, her grandmother complained, would tell anyone who would listen that she had become a prisoner. But the Venetians show that this was not mere self-dramatization. At Hardwick (they wrote in 1603), 'the unfortunate lady has now lived for many years, not exactly as a prisoner, but, so to speak, buried alive.' Even to contemporaries, her treatment seemed extraordinary.

Arbella had endured years of frustration. In the coming months, she was at last to make her move; to act on no authority other than her own. The earl of Essex, she wrote passionately, had 'the favour to die unbound because he was a prince, and shall my hands be bound from helping my self in this distress?' It proved easy, after the event, for contemporaries and historians alike to decry her plan as folly. But it is surely to her credit that she did attempt to take her destiny into her own hands. Her actions may better be seen as a desperate gamble, made by one who had little to lose, and no great range of options.

Few indeed were the paths open to an unmarried woman in the seventeenth century, when even the law recognized only wives, widows and children. Though England was called 'the paradise of married women', wrote the Dutch historian Emanuel Van Meteren, 'the girls who are not yet married are kept far more strictly than in the Low Countries.' And time was getting on, at least by the norms of the nobility. Anne Newdigate – a gentlewoman her own age with whom Arbella contracted a friendship, writing thanks for 'fine cuffs and kind remembrance' – had been married at twelve, though probably in name only. The summer or autumn of 1602 saw the marriage of the Talbots' daughter Elizabeth, some years Arbella's junior, which must have rubbed salt in the wound. At twenty-seven, Bess had been twice married and a mother; as had Mary Stuart, besides taking and losing power in Scotland. At twenty-seven, Elizabeth had been queen of England for two years.

A century earlier, in a Catholic England, Arbella might at least have had the option of entering a nunnery. Now Robert Burton, in the *Anatomy of Melancholy*, could only suggest half seriously that a benefactor should be found 'to build a monastical college for old, decayed, deformed or discontented maids to live together in, that have lost their first loves, or otherwise miscarried'. Arbella's was a culture that saw marriage as the only successful destiny for a woman, a rule broken by Queen Elizabeth only with great difficulty. The only other career open to a female member of the gentry or nobility was to take service as gentlewoman to a lady of higher rank. But the only woman of higher rank than Arbella was the queen herself; and hers was just the household from which Arbella had been purposely excluded.

What is more, Arbella had been bred in the belief that she might one day rule her country. The Venetians said so very specifically. In the months when the question of the succession became acute – now or never! – it is unreasonable to expect that she should complacently have sat to watch the tide of events pass by.

The question of whether Arbella herself sought the crown – and, if so, with whose aid – can never finally be answered. Earlier biographers chose to believe she did not, preferring her retiring and womanly, but contemporaries judged differently. If they were right, then the phrase 'hope often deferred makes the heart sick' might have been written expressly for Arbella. If the worm was about to turn, the only surprising thing was that it had not done so already.

In the latter half of 1602 Arbella – neither, she said, 'a credulous nor, worse, a fainthearted' fool – contacted unnamed friends in Yorkshire. Is it significant that this was Lennox territory, or even that William Cavendish's wife, Anne Keighley, had come from Yorkshire? And that it was still Catholic to a great degree? Fearing her grandmother would take them, and with them the last chance of seizing independence, Arbella sent her jewels and money away.

# III

January–April 1603

## 'My travelling mind'

'I think the time best spent in tiring you with the idle
conceits of my travelling mind till it make you ashamed
to see into what a scribbling melancholy (which is
a kind of madness) you have brought me.'

Arbella Stuart to Sir Henry Brounker,
9 March 1603

# 'This unadvised young woman'

THE WALLS OF HARDWICK'S COURT ARE HIGH. ON A COLD JANUARY afternoon of 1603, as the weary horseman wound his way up from the road, with the great gold house flaunting itself on the ridge above him and the country rolling away below, the inhabitants can have had little warning of what lay in store. It was outside the gatehouse that Sir Henry Brounker dismounted and flung his reins to the lackey. But as he strode across the flagged courtyard, the arrival of a government officer stained with hard winter travel must have caused an immediate flurry.

He passed into the house, and through the great hall where the servants ate. For once, there can have been no need for the steward to hush the noise with his traditional cry of 'Softly, my masters.' Everyone present must have guessed that Brounker's arrival meant matters of urgency. Walls or no walls – festive season or not – this was one visitor who could not be denied entry.

Brounker sent his name up to Bess. As he waited in the hall, where the stags of Cavendish and Hardwick are carved over the gigantic fireplace, the motto – *Cavendo tutus*, 'safe by taking care' – must have struck him ironically. At once, instructions came back that he should be admitted. Up the shallow stone treads of that wide, dramatic staircase, his route took him past the carved soldier's head at the door to the family chambers, an image meant to signify that Bess and hers were protected from just such intrusions as this.

With a kind of grim appropriateness, the family were on the highest, the state floor. They were in the gallery, lined with portraits of Bess's ancestors and descendants. Designed for dancing, and for exercise in inclement weather, the Gallery at Hardwick Hall is a prodigy of its kind. To stand amid its unheatable expanses is to have the sensation less of a room than of a street, lined with buildings two or even three stories high, and roofed over merely by some whimsy. The massed windows look towards the back of the house, away from the clamour and the trouble that had come so abruptly. But the events of January 1603 made Bess's celebration of her dynasty seem like a mockery.

In the Gallery, under the pictures of the queens of England and Scotland, under the giant alabaster statues of Justice and Mercy, Brounker found Bess and Arbella walking, with their waiting gentlewomen and William Cavendish. The scene bore a brief, transitory resemblance to that which had been enacted at Hatfield some forty years before, when the messenger came to tell the then princess Elizabeth that she was queen. Perhaps Bess even thought for a moment that it would have a similar outcome. Or perhaps not – the brief interval between the announcement of Brounker and the man's appearance was yet long enough for a brief and bitter family conference, a first alarum of controversy.

Arbella, with her secret knowledge, can have had little doubt what Brounker's arrival signified. Just ten days before, she had embarked on a perilous course which was to send waves of consternation through the government, focus a glaring spotlight upon Hardwick Hall and its inhabitants, and bring the threat even of the headsman to her very door.

As she set these events in motion, Arbella, frantic, may have sought no more than, in her own passionate and oft-stressed phrase, 'a small and ordinary liberty'. But it is possible that, in those confused months when even those living remote from court must have guessed Queen Elizabeth's reign was ending, she also sought the English throne. The question which would tax ministers at the time – and historians ever after – was whether this should be dismissed as a private plan, with political implications she was too inexperienced or too desperate to see; or whether it was, rather, a bid to take her place upon the public stage to which she must have believed her birthright entitled her.

By the winter of 1602, Arbella was at the end of her tether. She had lived long enough in obscurity. She had to act – even at the risk of acting foolishly. She had to take control of her own life, even though to do so was to live very dangerously. The project upon which she now embarked was to arrange for herself a marriage with the earl of Hertford's eldest grandson, Edward Seymour – elder brother of the very William Seymour whom she actually did marry in 1610. This was the match that had been mooted three or four years before, a proposal of which Arbella evidently knew.

In the enduring debate over the nature of her intentions, private or political, her choice of bridegroom is suggestive, to put it mildly. This proposed marriage with Edward, unlike her final alliance with William Seymour, could be no match made from personal liking. Not only was Edward Seymour still only in his teens, but the pair had never even met. The inevitable conclusion is that Arbella was drawn not to the boy but to his bloodline; his descent, through his grandmother Lady Catherine Grey, from Henry VIII's younger sister Mary.

It seems possible that the match proposed at the end of the last century had been reborn under the aegis not of the earl of Hertford but of his son, young Edward's father, Lord Beauchamp. Just as Arbella may have sought to bolster her own claim with that of the Seymours, so Beauchamp, more ambitious than his father, may have sought at once to strengthen the position of his own house and to absorb a rival. But Arbella, without in-formation on the internal dynamics of the Seymour family, applied herself to the old earl; and the earl of Hertford, unlike his impetuous son, was a man whom experience had made wary. Few houses, even in Tudor times, had a more troubled history than did the Seymours. Queen Elizabeth never forgot that it was a Seymour queen who had supplanted her mother; and she had had no reason to love Hertford's father, Somerset. In the days of the boy king Edward VI, the earl had seen both his father and his uncle Thomas Seymour die on the block. The earl was only a boy when he first spent time in the Tower for his father's fault; a young man when he fell in love with the Lady Catherine Grey, to be forgiven only when in 1568 Catherine died, still in captivity. Some thirty years later, a legendary entertainment of the queen at his house of Elvetham in Hampshire had bought him a brief return to favour – but not favour enough to save him from the Tower after that attempt, in 1595, to have his marriage to Catherine and his heirs legitimized. Since then, Hertford had trodden very carefully. The last thing he wanted, with little realistic hope of gain, was another dangerous controversy. And what Arbella proposed was not just fantastical – a fantasy of disguised suitors and captive ladies that might have come from one of the popular romances of the day – it was also bordering on treasonable.

Doleman's *Conference about the Next Succession to the Crown of England*, in which he described the Seymours as the popular candidates for the throne, had suggested that Arbella's claim could be strengthened with an alliance to some other title. Tales had already linked Arbella with Edward; with Edward's father Lord Beauchamp; and with Beauchamp's younger brother Thomas, for whom, the Venetian envoy wrote, she had 'a great preference', he and Arbella making a pair 'of like age and of most favourable conditions of mind and body'. In the public mind, it seems, any Seymour would do to make a significant match for Arbella, and the implication does seem to be clear: this is a political, rather than a personal, story. A marriage between a Seymour – any Seymour – and Arbella Stuart would combine two claims, neither of which, alone, was quite strong enough to overbalance that of James. If they were united, it might be a different story. Arbella could hardly have made a more dangerous – or a more ambitious – choice of bridegroom.

In that early spring of 1603, Queen Elizabeth I at last was dying. Since the execution of the earl of Essex she had suffered bouts of depression and a terrible loss of energy. In the country as in the queen, the turmoils of the past few years had given way to a paralysing ennui. In the summer of 1602 Elizabeth had seemed to rally: 'I have not seen her better disposed these many years,' a friend at court wrote to Arbella's aunt Mary Talbot. No doubt it was another turn of the screw to those with reason to await her tardy end. But by the autumn her memory and spirits alike were failing. At Christmas, Sir John Harington wrote to his wife: 'Our dear queen . . . doth now bear show of human infirmity; too fast for that evil we shall get by her death, and too slow for that good which she will get by her releasement from pains and misery.' Elizabeth's will to live had been sapped by the death of favourites and friends; but still she refused to name a successor. 'They were great fools that did not know that the line of Scotland must needs be next heirs,' she told Harington privately – but in public it was still a different story.

In December 1602 Arbella had begged the help, as he later confessed, of James Starkey, the sympathetic chaplain-cum-tutor who had become her ally in the Hardwick household. Swayed first by promises of future reward – that if she were 'translated into another place' he should be her personal chaplain – supported by Arbella's vague boast of 'good friends, and more than all the world knew of', Starkey does seem also to have regarded Arbella with a genuine pity. They were probably much of an age, in a house where most of the gentry were much older, or much younger. One has the sense of shared grievances chewed over as they read together in Arbella's study, both growing more dissatisfied with their respective positions in the household as the years went by. Another malcontent – another Morley. And, of course, another studious man; the type with whom Arbella did seem to be most in sympathy.

As 1602 turned to 1603 Starkey was wintering in London. He had long ago promised to bear messages for Arbella when need be, and in December she sent word to him, asking him to make good his promise. But Starkey's nerve may have failed him at the last for, instead of the helpful envoy she needed, there arrived at Hardwick word that Starkey would not, after all, be coming north until the following Easter. Her ladyship, he wrote, 'knoweth well that I supported her rather to endure her grief and discontent patiently than by an inconvenient course to prejudice herself'. He was backtracking hastily.

When Starkey failed her, Arbella was forced to try another member of the household. John Dodderidge, ironically, was an old and trusted retainer of Bess's; one who, two years before, had even witnessed the old lady's will. Perhaps that duty had reminded him of Bess's mortality, and the need to think of his future; or perhaps he was fond of Arbella. In any event, he agreed to take a message to a lawyer, an agent of the great earl of Hertford. But he was aghast when Arbella asked him, instead, to go directly to the earl himself, as distant in degree as in miles. 'She told me I must go a hundred miles for her. I made answer that I durst not, for fear of my lady's [Bess's] displeasure and endangering of my service,' he wrote in his confession. His instructions were to go to Hertford's house in Tottenham, some eight miles north of London, 'and desire someone of trust about my lord to give you leave to speak to him', then to deliver a verbal message.

When he heard the content of this message, Dodderidge, like Starkey, protested his 'unworthiness and insufficiency' for so complicated a piece of manoeuvring in high society. To matchmake among the nobility was a task far outside his sphere, and this was a match of more than usual sensitivity. But his scruples were overruled. Dodderidge set out on Christmas Day, on a horse borrowed from Arbella's uncle Henry, another rebel in the divided Cavendish family. On that day, as Dodderidge told it, 'presently after dinner [Henry] went out at the gates and, calling me to him, told me his man should deliver me a horse.' Dodderidge, Arbella instructed him, was not to let Hertford think that Arbella was moving in this matter herself, but to imply the idea came from her uncles Henry and William. 'I had no conference with the Cavendishes,' Dodderidge wrote, 'though my Lady Arb. willed me to name her uncles; yet I asked her whether they were acquainted in the matter or not, and she answered me they were.'

It is his confession that provides the first inklings that Arbella was not acting entirely alone. And it is possible Arbella would have been able to call on more help in the neighbourhood. Starkey's note, backtracking on his offer to act as courier to Arbella, was delivered to Hardwick by Frances Pierrepont, Bess's Catholic eldest daughter, whose home was only a few miles away. Old Sir John Byron, residing nearby, might himself be no friend to Arbella, but his son – Brounker later wrote – was 'at her devotion', and his young daughter Margaret soon her most devoted lady. It became apparent, over the weeks ahead, that

Arbella had her networks and her means of communication, enabling her to act with a degree of autonomy.

Dodderidge, Arbella wrote, was to urge that Edward Seymour should at once come to Hardwick secretly. 'The shortness of time will help to keep counsel.' He was to see that Hertford sent with his grandson some 'grave, ancient man' who could distract Bess with talk of business while the two younger people looked to see if they could like. They were to bring with them, as identification, some family heirloom as token; 'some picture or handwriting of the Lady Jane Grey, whose hand I know' – or perhaps even, she suggested, the Greek Testament Jane had sent to her sister Catherine on the day before her execution, with a message inscribed on the blank pages that it would 'teach her to live and learn her to die'. It seems an ominous token for Arbella to invoke thus early in her adventure. But she seems, all too presciently, to have felt a certain identification with the Grey sisters.

The party was to come disguised, pretending that they had come to sell a piece of land. 'If they come like themselves they shall be shut out at the gates, I locked up, my grandmother will be the first shall advertise and complain to the queen.' But it was Hertford himself who did that, and instantly. Arbella had mistaken his attitude completely.

The old earl was bound to panic when Dodderidge arrived in Tottenham at three o'clock on 30 December, still dinnertime at this holiday season, and had him hailed from the midst of his Christmas festivities. Hertford refused even to hear Dodderidge's proposal without two of his own gentlemen servants as witness. So much for secrecy. Kneeling, Dodderidge delivered his memorized message, while Hertford, 'mightily distasting and disliking, grew impatient'. Dodderidge – no doubt bitterly remembering Arbella's assurance that there was no danger in the affair – was shut up in a room to write a full account of the matter. 'Thou art prepared for punishment,' he was told, terrifyingly. With 'weeping tears' he begged to be sent back to 'his lady'.

The next day, Hertford sent his own messenger to the court to alert the privy council. Dodderidge, already repeatedly interrogated by Hertford himself, was sent under guard through the London streets to court, where he faced Robert Cecil's questioning before being locked into the Westminster Gatehouse gaol. Arbella never received the letter he wrote to her, lamenting – with a rather touching absence of reproach – that 'my entertainment here is contrary to all expectation, so that except your honour fully satisfy this bearer, my Lord will not think otherwise of me that I am some counterfeit . . . I beseech your honour therefore to consider the estate I am in.' Instead, without warning, she learnt of the disaster from another source.

The involvement of the privy council could have only one outcome – an official inquiry. Travelling fast despite hard weather, their representative Sir Henry Brounker, personally briefed by the queen, set off for Hardwick to gather evidence. His first impressions were not favourable. There were several men of ill-repute – not locals, but men 'seldom here of many years before' – already clustered around the place, Brounker noted suspiciously. The officer who was ushered into the Gallery on that day of early January was a government hard man of some experience; one of those who had held the City of London against the Essex rebellion and interrogated the populace on the earl's 'seditious and provoking speeches'. He had been employed as Cecil's agent to the Scottish court, and if part of his business in 1600 was to quiet persistent Scottish fears about Arbella's rumoured marriage to Duke Matthias, he probably arrived at Hardwick already weary of her and her marital possibilities. None the less, from the start, he seems to have handled Arbella expertly, juggling harshness with the pretence of sympathy.

Brounker's report sounds a self-congratulatory note as he describes how he dealt with the task of separating Bess from his quarry. 'Then drawing [Bess] on with other compliments to the further end of the gallery, to free her from the young lady, I delivered your Majesty's letter. In the reading thereof I observed some change of countenance, which gave me occasion again to comfort her with the assurance of your Majesty's good opinion and favour.' Bess tried to fall on her knees before him. This was a situation fraught with real danger, as the two women who had seen the Scots queen go to her death would know.

Brounker spoke with Arbella at the other end of the vast room, while Bess could only watch the scene impotently from almost

The portrait of Arbella as a toddler, by an anonymous
artist, still hangs at Hardwick today.

Margaret Douglas, countess of Lennox,
Arbella's paternal grandmother

The young Charles Stuart, Arbella's father,
with his elder brother Lord Darnley.

ABOVE: The Chatsworth Bess built was replaced in later centuries by the present graceful house.

Bess's first building at Hardwick is now a roofless shell. But fragments remain, such as the stairway and the giant statues – Gog and Magog – in the Hill Great Chamber.

MARIA
D G
SCOTIÆ
PIISSIMA REGINA
FRANCIÆ DOWERIA
ANNO
ÆTATIS REGNI
36
ANGLICÆ CAPTIVÆ
10
8 H,
1578

Bess of Hardwick (*above left*) in her sixties in a portrait of the 1590s, and Mary, Queen of Scots (*above right*), the prisoner who changed from friend to enemy.

Many of the embroideries worked by Mary, Queen of Scots (often with Bess of Hardwick) carry a hidden message. The menacing cat here has Queen Elizabeth's sandy colouring.

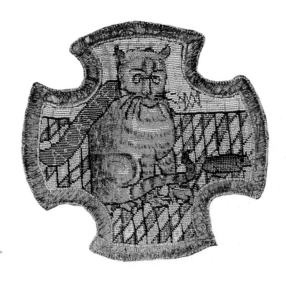

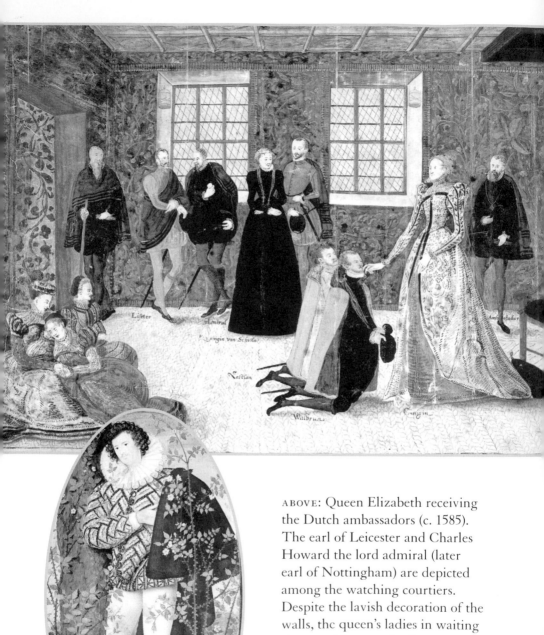

ABOVE: Queen Elizabeth receiving the Dutch ambassadors (c. 1585). The earl of Leicester and Charles Howard the lord admiral (later earl of Nottingham) are depicted among the watching courtiers. Despite the lavish decoration of the walls, the queen's ladies in waiting sit on cushions on the floor.

LEFT: Nicholas Hilliard's *A Young Man Leaning Against a Tree Among Roses* is believed to have been modelled on the earl of Essex.

RIGHT: Hilliard's miniature of Sir Walter Ralegh.

ABOVE: Elizabeth in 1595, and her chief
minister, William Cecil, Lord Burghley.

BELOW RIGHT: Sir Francis Walsingham,
Elizabeth's controller of
intelligence.

In the Hardwick Hall portrait painted when she was
thirteen, Arbella stands with books at her hand
and a tiny dog, symbol of loyalty,
at her feet.

sixty yards away. (Ironically, Brounker may not have realized how sound carries along that great echoing room – but Bess had the ears of an old lady.) First he told Arbella how pleased the queen had been with her New Year's gift. A reassuring message, this, since to accept a gift was to accept the giver; when the queen had rejected the earl of Essex's last Christmas gift, her refusal had struck observers ominously. And yet, Brounker continued, there was a matter the queen 'took unkindly' – one that only 'the naked laying open' of Arbella's heart could clear up satisfactorily.

'During the delivery of this message, it seemed by the coming and going of her colour that she was somewhat troubled yet (after a little pause) she said that the matter was very strange to her.' Brounker asked Arbella if her conscience did not accuse her 'of any late undutifulness', but 'she would by no means acknowledge so much as a thought to offend your Highness.' He asked whether she had had no late intelligence with the earl of Hertford; she denied it, 'but with great show of humility both in words and gesture'.

So it went on. And on, and on. Brounker told Arbella that 'It was not strange for a young lady to err.' That 'that which was past could not be recalled.' That it were better her offence should be discovered to proceed from 'vanity and love of herself rather than want of duty and contempt of your Majesty'. Finding her 'still obstinate', in the end he changed his tone from the paternal to the aggressive and, producing from his pouch Dodderidge's confession, said that rather than having to 'trouble her with many questions' they could both take a shorter way; told her she was foolish to deny everything, 'for it is so openly confessed as there is no denial.' The techniques of interrogation do not change much. Still, Arbella insisted to Brounker that her uncles were innocent in the matter; but by now, she could claim it only 'faintly'. He promised to keep anything she told him from her grandmother – a promise he would break immediately. He told her, too, that 'no extremity was meant to any.' This at last did move her, and as Arbella became more distressed, he decided to let her stew. He told her to go to bed and calm herself, and to write an account of all her dealings, if she was unable to make herself clear any other way.

The statement she handed him the next day was 'confused, obscure and in truth ridiculous . . . not a letter fit for me to carry or for her Majesty to read'. He ordered her to write another draft; together, they went through several and, in the few days he spent at Hardwick on 'this endless business', Brounker became convinced that 'her wits were throughout disordered, either with fear of her grandmother or conceit of herself.' He recruited the help of Bess, to whom 'in duty and discretion' he had disclosed all, and who took the whole story so ill 'as with much ado she refrained her hands' (i.e. from striking Arbella).

The letter Brounker finally carried back to London did not smack of disorder. It was terse, and bold in its brevity. Arbella's aunt, Mary, queen of Scots, had consistently failed to recognize the strength of the forces ranged against her. It seemed to be a Stuart characteristic.

'May it please your most excellent Majesty. Sir Henry Brounker has charged me with many things in your Majesty's name the most whereof I acknowledge to be true and am heartily sorry that I have given your Majesty the least cause of offence.' But she did not sound sorry, despite the rhetorically obsequious sequel – 'I humbly prostrate myself at your Majesty's feet.' And on 15 January, two days after Brounker, delayed on the way by a bad fall from his horse, had arrived back in London 'very secretly', she smuggled out of the house a message for her aunt, Mary Talbot, the countess of Shrewsbury. 'I beseech her to come down with the like speed she would do if my lady my grandmother were in extremity.' Her gentlewoman Bridget Sherland – who found it easier to get outside Hardwick, since Arbella herself was 'restrained from her liberty' – added a yet more urgent plea. If Mary Talbot does not come, 'she will make my lady think that all her friends will forsake her when she hath most need.' Mary Talbot did not come – perhaps because the appeals were intercepted by the authorities. But in fact, she and Gilbert play a puzzlingly vague part during this whole vital episode of their niece's story.

Mary's servant Hacker, the man via whom Arbella sent her letter, was one of the strangers whose presence in the district around Hardwick Brounker had remarked suspiciously. In view of the Catholic Mary's later involvement in Arbella's affairs, it would not be surprising if it transpired that she was party to Arbella's plan. Instead, a few weeks ahead, there would come a report that the Talbots and Cecil had grown 'very great and inward friends' – so great, it would be rumoured that Cecil was conspiring with them to put Arbella on the throne: an absurdity, to anyone who has the access to Cecil's secret correspondence with James that we do today. And it was also even rumoured, again, that Arbella – with the Talbots' connivance – was to marry Cecil himself; or Lord Mountjoy, the confirmed lover of Penelope Rich, Sidney's Stella; or Fulke Greville, a confirmed bachelor nearing fifty.

The vaunted friendship between Talbot and Cecil was in fact of no new date; access to their letters makes it clear that Gilbert had long been Cecil's ally personally as well as politically. Probably his influence went with Cecil's in these months to ensure events at Hardwick ended peacefully. We cannot feel quite as sure of Mary's role, though. Was she at first Arbella's ally in rebellion – a part she would play again later in her story? Even Arbella's own letter to Mary is redolent of a painful uncertainty. It sounds suspicious – even paranoid. But if Arbella were paranoid, she had reason to be.

Like other appeals Arbella wrote at this time, the letter to Mary Talbot was intercepted by Bess's servants, forwarded to Cecil, and a feigned reply dictated. The calendar which lists the Cecil papers for this period makes no bones about it. 'A feigned answer: Am sorry my occasions are so great that I cannot now come to you.' Or when Bridget Sherland wrote to a Mr Bradshaw, to the same effect as she had to Hacker: 'The messenger that was to have carried the abovesaid letter returned a feigned answer by word that Mr Bradshaw was not at home.' The letters were in the same handwriting often seen on Bess's communiqués: that of her trusted steward, Timothy Pusey.

Such surveillance was a commonplace of the times – the Venetians, a few weeks later, casually noted that the queen had intercepted letters from Arbella in her hands – but the swiftness with which the mechanism swung into place corroborates the idea that she was under surveillance already. With such a cloud of deliberate disinformation around her it is hardly surprising if, later in these desperate months, Arbella did lose her grip on reality; hardly surprising, too, that her old childhood affection for her grandmother soured into a resentment that looked very like hate.

She was not the only one weary of the situation. Bess herself wrote to the queen, grumbling at Brounker for his 'preciseness' and Arbella for her 'vanity'. She was seventy-six, and she had grown very tired of keeping her granddaughter, on the queen's behalf, in what had come to look increasingly like custody:

> . . . seeing she hath been content to hear matters of any moment and not impart them to me, I am desirous and most humbly beseech your Majesty that she may be placed elsewhere, to learn to be more considerate, and after that it may please your Majesty either to accept of her service about your royal person or to bestow her in marriage, which in all humility and duty I do crave . . . for I cannot now assure myself of her as I have done.

Bess was another who, like Hertford, had taken risks in her younger life but now wished only to live securely. Nor, herself tough and eminently practical, was she a woman to regard Arbella's impracticable plan and subsequent histrionics with sympathy.

As they waited together at Hardwick, what finally overthrew both ladies' nerves was the intelligence that the queen, represented as annoyed but lenient, none the less wished Arbella to remain where she was. It cannot have helped that the queen was represented, in this case, not only by Cecil but by the vice-chamberlain, Sir John Stanhope – that same Stanhope who had quarrelled so violently with Gilbert and Mary Talbot; or, perhaps, that Brounker, at this stage, was inclined to play down the matter; concluding that 'the poor lady was abused, my Lord [Hertford] guiltless.'

Arbella's follies were officially attributed to convenient (and anonymous) 'base companions' who, 'thinking it pleasing to her youth and sex to be sought in marriage', had led her astray. She herself was warned in future to 'content herself to live in good sort with so dear a parent and so worthy a matron' as her grandmother. Any further involvement in 'such like plots and practices' might not be treated so gently, 'for being of such like blood she is, her Majesty will look for an extraordinary account of her proceedings.'

Cecil and Stanhope expressed their conviction of Hertford's innocence in terms Arbella can only have found patronizing. If the earl's own 'precise carriage' in the matter had not belied any suggestion of his complicity, then 'the incongruity of his grand-child's years ... besides the absurd election of ministers [Dodderidge and Starkey] and course of proceeding' were sufficient to do so. As it had 'a corrupt beginning', so the business had 'a fond [foolish] end', they concluded complacently. To Arbella, surely, insult was added to injury.

Bess, for her part, was warned not to take any overt pre-cautions to secure Arbella for fear of fanning the 'fond bruits' (foolish rumours) already around. Robert Cecil suggested she might instead 'impose some care upon some discreet gentle-women ... and some honest gentlemen, to attend her among the rest, who, without using any extraordinary restraint, may have eyes sufficiently unto her if she do anything unfit'. Bess, the queen advised, should 'remain contented and look to your health'. Ironically, dissatisfaction at these answers may have brought Arbella and Bess nearer into sympathy than they had been for years.

In the middle of January Arbella wrote again to the queen, thanking her for her 'most gracious interpretation of this acci-dent', and giving her assurance that she would never again will-ingly 'yield to grief as I have done heretofore and that very lately, to almost my utter overthrow of body and mind'. None the less, she begged again for 'even that small and ordinary liberty I despaired to obtain of her [Bess] my otherwise most kind and nat-ural parent'. Those things she had done without Bess's knowl-edge, she protested, were things 'she should have had more reason to wink at than to punish so severely', had Bess not been stricter 'than any child how good, discreet and dutiful soever would will-ingly have obeyed'.

In Arbella's 'most distressed state' she had 'with silent and stolen tears implored and expected relief' from the queen. Her only goal, she wrote, had been to end her exile from the royal presence. 'This hath been the principal end of all my desires without which I can think no state happy.' She boasted that, unwise as her proceedings might seem, she had none the less 'preserved your Majesty's most royal lineage from any blot as any whatsoever'. Elizabeth used to boast of being her father's daughter. Arbella, who never knew her father, or many of his kin, had to fall back on the more generalized 'lineage', but that she invoked as frequently. 'I should have adjudged myself unworthy of life if I had degenerated from the most renowned stock whereof it is my greatest honour to be a branch . . .'

It was an attempt at the tone of ritual compliment habitual in elevated Elizabethan society. Elizabeth herself had written of her 'exile' from the presence of her hardly-yet-known stepmother, Catherine Parr. But on this occasion the strained note of tribute failed of its effect, as did any appeal to common emotional ground. The queen was not to be won over. There was no relief, no summons south. It was hardly likely there would be, at this of all unlikely junctures, when the government's interest was to ensure that Arbella – and anyone else in the line of succession – should be kept isolated, well away from the centre of power.

But the conflict between Arbella and Bess had gone too far to settle down as Cecil and Stanhope no doubt confidently expected. By 29 January the situation at Hardwick had reached such a pitch that Bess again wrote again to the queen about 'this unadvised young woman'. Vindictively, or just desperately, she admitted that she 'would not care how meanly soever she were bestowed, so as it were not offensive to your Highness'; for

the bad persuasions of some have so estranged her mind and natural affection from me that she holds me the greatest enemy she hath, and hath given herself over to be ruled and advised by others, so that, the bond of nature being broken, I cannot have any assurance of her good carriage. I cannot but doubt there is another match in working, but who the party should be, I cannot conjecture . . . Sometimes she will say that she can be taken away off my hands if she will.

That there were 'others', that there was 'another match ... working', was an idea Arbella tried hard to promulgate. The friends, like the match, are usually taken to have been imaginary, but Arbella herself was eager to blur the line between fantasy and reality. To keep the authorities' attention on herself, by appearing on the brink of another marriage, may have been her only chance of breaking what had become an intolerable stasis.

# 'A mind distracted'

THE LETTERS ARBELLA STUART WROTE FROM HARDWICK, IN THE LAST
months of what she had come to see as her captivity, are bizarre
and wonderful documents. The longest single letter runs to some
seven thousand words, and the content is often so confused as to
lead contemporaries to question Arbella's sanity. For the
biographer hitherto starved of the subject's voice, this sudden
explosion of words is an *embarras de richesse* hard to handle
gracefully. To pull out only the plums – the vivid, comprehensible
phrases – from what is at times an almost impenetrable mass of
text would fail to reflect the real confusion that so horrified the
recipients. To drag the reader on an enforced route march, line by
line, on the other hand, could be productive of nothing so much
as a bewildered hostility.

Some compromise has to be achieved. The letters Arbella wrote
in the spring of 1603 colour everything else we know about her
story. And out of the morass there emerges in the end the picture
of a personality almost unparalleled among women's writings of
the sixteenth and seventeenth centuries.

The first of her self-explanatory letters amounts to two and a
half thousand words of rhetoric and special pleading, written
a day or two after Bess sent her plaint, and nominally addressed
to the old lady herself. With 'a mind yet distracted between fear
and hope', Arbella 'set down the reason of this my proceeding',
the words often scratched through as the pen raced along in

Arbella's informal, as opposed to her neat 'presentation' hand-writing. Far from being, as she claimed, without 'ceremonies', it is on the contrary so convoluted, so elaborately (and often confusedly) styled as to give the modern reader, on first perusal, little sense of her meaning. On perhaps the fourth reading, it is revealed as the sustained fantasy of a scheme hatched between Arbella herself and a fictional lover; extraordinarily sustained, considering that it was clearly dashed off in a passion.

She described a scheme so complicated one thinks of Shakespeare's plots. Arbella's 'dearest and best-beloved . . . told me he would have me enter into some great action to win myself repute, to try her Majesty's love for me'. This great action was to be the unmasking of traitorous intentions – in persons other than Arbella herself, naturally.

Arbella's approach to Hertford was, she now claimed, her opening gambit in the role of *agent provocateur*. She had wanted to expose – to dramatize, if you will – the consequences of just such a potentially treasonable marriage proposal as that which, she asserts, had indeed been made from the Hertford camp. Her intent was 'to have it known to her Majesty that such a matter was propounded seriously, and by some desired . . . but utterly neglected or rejected by myself from the first hour I heard of it.' Perhaps it *was* the nearest anyone could have got to a viable excuse – whatever doubts one might harbour as to its plausibility.

Ingeniously, she worked in already-known details, like her 'ridiculous' choice of messenger. The council's word there had obviously stung. Now, she claimed that her apparent blunder was a deliberate decision. 'I sent such as I thought likeliest to displease his Lordship [Hertford].' Self-righteously, she protested that she never wished to provoke or produce too much evidence against Hertford. 'I cannot find in my heart to disclose the counsel of any stranger or enemy . . . for all my Lord of Hertford's discourteous dealings with me.'

Arbella professed herself delighted with the result of her plan. 'I thank God it fell out better than I and my dearest and best trusted could have devised or imagined though we have beat our brains about it these three years.' The eyes of the authorities had been opened. 'It was convenient her Majesty should see and believe what busy bodies, untrue rumours, unjust practices, colourable and cunning devices are in remote parts among those whom the world understand to be exiled her Majesty's presence undeservedly.'

There was a little dig here: see what you get for shutting me away in the midlands? Arbella went on to sound the note of warning more openly: 'I cannot rule love and ambition in others as I thank God I can do both very well in my self.' But she did not labour that point. Time and again, her 'device' was presented as merely a piece of 'honest cunning', the queen's anger at which was ultimately to have been converted into laughter. It reads not like a realistic fantasy, but rather like the type of plot contrivance often seen on the stage of the day. Indeed, in this letter Arbella referred to herself and her supposed companion in the language of the theatre – as 'actors' who made themselves merry 'making ourselves perfect in our parts'.

Bess at once forwarded the document to court with a tart covering note. Arbella, Bess wrote, 'hath set down in her own hand this declaration so fraught with vanity. Such as it is I have set it hereinclosed but I could not by any possible means prevail with her to set down the matter plainly, as I desired she would in few lines. These strange courses are wonderful [extraordinary] to me.'

Arbella probably realized her grandmother would submit her apologia to the authorities. In fact, she may well have counted on her words reaching the queen. Such indirection was a not unusual technique; to approach the ruler uninvited, when one was out of favour, was to strain etiquette precariously. So although Arbella later kept up an appearance of anger at the liberty Bess had taken, the manuscript of the letter itself tells a different story. In front of the words 'your ladyship' is a different, abortive, phrase crossed out: 'your Ma . . .'. This is one of several such significant revisions.

Arbella vented her contempt for those who had tried 'what promises, oaths, vows, threatenings, unkindness, kindness, fair means and foul, neglect of others, withdrawing of counsel, hope of redress or anything in the world' could do to persuade one of 'my sex, years and (hitherto) unhappy fortune'. Arbella seems to have loved words for their own sake; an Elizabethan tendency that makes her letters all the harder to assess across a distance of four centuries. They could well be taken as more baffling, more eccentric than they should be – unless you compare them with one of the queen's own elaborate letters, or an allusion-packed speech in a Shakespeare play.

Closer to tragedy than to comedy, surely, was Arbella's detailed pretence of an anonymous lover. In the second half of the letter, she dwelt on him incessantly. The invention of a 'dearest and best beloved' may have been politic, but to flesh out the bones so fully seems unhealthy for a teenager, let alone for a grown woman of twenty-seven. And there is something worrying about the very nature of her fantasy.

This was a man, Arbella boasted, who 'can take nothing ill at my hand . . . [though] I have dealt unkindly, shrewdly, proudly with him'. Shades of the quarrelsome Shrewsbury marriages, in the shadow of which she had been raised? 'I may compare the love of this worthy gentleman (which I have already unrevocably accepted and confirmed) to gold which hath been so often purified that I cannot find one fault, jealousy only excepted.' This was a man

> whom I have loved too well (ever since I could love) to hide any
> thought word or deed of mine from him unless it were to awe him
> a little when I thought his love converted into hate, . . . or to make
> him weary of his jealousy by letting him see it was the only way to
> make him fall out with me.

And yet this paragon is revealed as a Machiavelli, a Polonius figure, who has spoken against Arbella at court in order to disguise their relationship. 'All the injuries he could he hath done me . . .' Carefully, she added that 'he tells me plainly he will not offend her Majesty for my sake, and will rather forsake me forever than incur her Majesty's displeasure, though the time [of it] be never so short.' If he had been a little less scrupulous, we would surely imagine him more enthusiastically.

Arbella refused to name the man; for his safety, she says. 'Secrecy is one of his virtues and he hath as many I believe as any subject or foreign prince in all Europe.' The assumption now must be that he was a fantasy; Arbella herself soon admitted as much, albeit in circumstances that rob her words of their weight. Close-watched as she was, she could have had scant opportunity to form such a relationship (though she would prove able to hold a clandestine correspondence, such as the one with her uncle Henry). Even more persuasive is the fact that had she already fallen in love elsewhere, she would surely never have begun negotiations for Edward Seymour. Certainly no ideal lover 'great with her Majesty' manifested himself in the months ahead. And the initial attention paid to these claims by contemporaries like Bess died away over the days and weeks ahead, as the increasing wildness of Arbella's writing lost her all credibility.

It is elsewhere in this letter one should look for emotional actuality. As Arbella set these words down, 'while I writ, I wept and I marvel it was not perceived, for I could neither forbear weeping at meal times nor in truth day nor night.' No, her romantic lover wasn't real; just a useful figure of fancy who had taken on more life in her imagination than was altogether suitable for a grown woman. But then, a grown woman is just what Arbella was not allowed to be, as she herself complained bitterly.

Consciousness of her years and the indignity of her position were in her mind a few days later, when Arbella wrote to Cecil and Stanhope about her treatment at Hardwick. This is another letter that began in a 'presentation hand' to match the controlled and formal phrasing, but quickly descended into a furious scrawl.

Arbella demanded some ruling be given to Bess,

> whether it be her Majesty's pleasure I shall have free choice of my servants to take, keep and put away ... whether I may send for whom I think good or talk with any that shall voluntarily or upon business come to me ... And whether it be not her Majesty's pleasure I should as well have the company of some young lady or gentlewoman for my recreation, and scholars, music, hunting, hawking, variety of any lawful disport I can procure or my friends will afford me.

These would be in addition – she added, with what in an age of less careful letters would be taken as irony – to 'the attendance of grave overseers, for which I think myself most bound to her Majesty as it is the best way to avoid any jealousy'.

But Arbella wanted more than a companion in her custody. She wanted to know 'Whether, if the running on of the years be not discerned in me only, it be not her Highness pleasure to allow me that liberty (being the 6th of this February 27 years old) to choose my place of abode.' Bound, as she said, in 'an extraordinary yoke of bondage', she now asked the authorities at least to declare how long she should have to wear it, 'and without ambiguity to prescribe me the rules wherby it pleaseth her Majesty to try my obedience'. But that was exactly the kind of definite pronouncement from which Elizabeth's government would always shy.

Dismissing her previous letter as 'the first fruits of my scribbled follies', never meant, she disingenuously claimed, for official eyes, Arbella in this long communication none the less returned to the theme of the lover who had proved so useful, so compelling, a fantasy. Still seeking to address and be addressed in her own right, she said she would reveal her lover's name but only in person, to the queen's own messenger. Time and again, her letters reflect her distaste at being addressed only as Bess's protégée; her rage at finding her own addresses broken against a wall of officialdom.

Even in that first disastrous approach to Hertford, she reproached the earl with having applied to Bess in the matter of her marriage rather than to her own self. Her friends, as she wrote in the message Dodderidge was to deliver, 'think your lordship did not take an orderly course in your proceedings, for it was thought fitter that my Lady Arbella should have been first moved in the matter, and that the parties might have had sight the one of the other, to see how they would like.' The idea that liking should play at least some part in the choice of a marriage partner was slowly coming into currency at this time; but there is another theme here that reverberates through the letters of the sixteenth century. It was the pot of gold at the end of the rainbow to achieve direct communication with the powers that be. Arbella begged for 'two lines' in her majesty's own hand; just so had the queen of Scots sought a meeting with Elizabeth; just so had the young Elizabeth, on her way to the Tower, once begged some direct communication from her sister Mary.

But Arbella had timed her request badly. In London, the death of the countess of Nottingham, Elizabeth's kinswoman and friend, had thrown the queen into a last depression. Her formal robes had long since become too heavy; soon, all too symbolically, the coronation ring had to be cut from her swollen finger. 'All the fabric of my reign, little by little, is beginning to fail,' she wrote to Henri of France. The state of the queen's health naturally increased speculation as to Arbella's position, since Robert Cecil's plans for James's succession were still a close secret. As so often, ripples of gossip spread far beyond Arbella's own circle, to auditors for whom the drama at Hardwick was only a play within a play. Hungry as she was to speak to the outside world, it was as eager to hear her. But it was just such a dialogue the authorities wished to prevent.

King James in Scotland had already expressed concern about Arbella, having been 'credibly informed, that she is lately moved by the persuasion of the Jesuits to change her religion'. He shed what sound remarkably like crocodile tears over 'the frailty of her youth and sex', thus exposed to 'evil company'. In February Cecil secretly sent him a modified reassurance.

> I know not how any minister of state could have made that point [her religion] secure . . . But, Sir, though consciences are secretly wrought in youth . . . yet I assure you (for my own part) I have heard so little proof of her being Catholic, as if I were to speak for a wager I should think it an extravagant information.

Those around Arbella, he added, were notable Protestants – Bess; the chaplain and confidant Starkey. But Starkey himself now added fuel to rumour's flames.

Life had left James Starkey a disappointed man. He had been taken into William Cavendish's household almost ten years before – ten years of 'servitude and bondage' – on the promise of a clergyman's living which, however, had never materialized. The stingy William was notoriously 'sparing in his gratuities'. Starkey's involvement in Arbella's affairs seems to have preyed on a mind already inclined towards melancholy. He had been questioned, perhaps treated harshly. But he had also been 'hardly used by his friends', Cecil himself noted compassionately. In the early days of February, in London, he hanged himself – a decision almost unthinkable in a seventeenth-century cleric, taught that such an act meant eternal damnation. He left a lengthy 'confession' detailing all his dealings with Arbella. He asked her forgiveness, 'being sorry that such a one should be made an instrument of the bad practices of others, whose device was to turn me out of my living and deprive me of my life, the Lord forgive them all', and took pains to exonerate himself and his connections: 'For my own part I was busied about the recovery of my parsonage ... My friends and kinsfolk I protest are blameless and without fault, being unacquainted with this matter.' He added: 'If I had a thousand lives I would willingly spend them all to redeem the least part of her [Arbella's] reputation.'

Perhaps it was this warmth of feeling which led the authorities to tax Starkey with having aspired to Arbella's hand himself. There was the matter of a Bible, the cover of which he had caused to be inscribed with the letters J.A.S. These were his own initials, to be sure (since the A was added only that it 'might distinguish James from John' and the printer erroneously 'set the three letters apart': so trivial had the debate become). But they could also stand for James and Arbella Starkey. This was another ridiculous surmise, given Arbella's respect for her own rank, and her use of Starkey as intermediary in promoting another match. But it shows the climate of suspicion that made the wretched chaplain another victim of Arbella's story.

The French ambassador instantly reported Starkey's death to his king. The Venetians, ever sensational, chimed in a month later. 'In the house of Arbella Stuart they have found the body of her chaplain and tutor with his throat cut. He was the most intimate of all those about her. Rumour says that he killed himself because he was conscious of his own intrigues.' The Venetians were not always accurate as to fact – witness their misinformation as to the means and place of Starkey's death – but they had a greedy ear for gossip. They also reported home that James and Arbella were the real claimants . . . descendants in equal degree. At present the queen has conceived some fear lest Arbella should escape . . . the queen has, therefore, very quietly increased the guards round the castle, fifty miles from London, where the unhappy lady has lived so many years, buried, as one may say. The ministers are anxious on the subject.

Indeed, they had reason to be.

# 'So wilfully bent'

FEW DOCUMENTS SPEAK SO ELOQUENTLY OF DISTRESS AS THE PAGES that lie among the Cecil papers, written by Sir Henry Brounker and labelled 'The Exposition of Lady Arbella Stuart'. In the first days of March 1603, Brounker had returned to confront her again at Hardwick, bringing the council's response to her provocative allegations, and answering an urgent plea from Bess. From Hardwick, he sent back to London a record of his interrogation, setting out Arbella's answers to some thirty questions, quizzing her on everything she had already said. First the reader sees the version over which Arbella and Brounker laboured together – so blotted as to be almost illegible, Arbella's signature and her occasional comments crowded out by Brounker's crabbed hand. Following it comes the neat copy made by Cecil's secretary, evoking a world away from the Hardwick fray. 'Being demanded . . . Being demanded . . . Being demanded' – both documents give a vivid impression of the pounding queries.

It was a far more hostile approach than she can ever have encountered in all her sheltered life. She didn't answer as cannily as the fifteen-year-old princess Elizabeth had done, when Sir Robert Tyrwhitt interrogated her about her relationship with her stepmother's husband, Thomas Seymour. But Arbella was younger than Elizabeth in experience, if not in years. She didn't even answer as doughtily as the princess Mary Tudor had always done, when ordered to abandon her royal prerogative and her faith. But at first she kept her head, and answered quite cogently.

'Being demanded why she was distracted between fear and hope she answered that she feared her Majesty's displeasure by reason of the letters she received from her, and by her innocency she hoped to recover her Highness' favour,' Brounker reported. 'Being demanded who persuaded her to play the fool in earnest she said that that was but a poetical fiction.'

But half a dozen demands in, the questions began to focus more sharply upon personalities. Brounker was trying to discover the identity of her supposed lover. Whenever he asked her for a name, Arbella answered 'the king of Scots'. At first that, too, made a kind of sense. 'Love', after all, could mean the cousinly affection James had professed. (Arbella later complains that courtiers, blind to 'the power of divine and Christian love ... cannot believe one can come so near God's precept ... as to love an unkind but otherwise worthy kinsman so well as nobody else (it seems to your knowledge) doth any but their paramours.') But far beyond this comprehensible point, she was sticking to her story.

> Being demanded what the gentleman was that was so worthily favoured by her Majesty and had done her so much wrong and wherein, she answered it was the king of Scots whom her Highness favoured so much as for fear of offending him she might not be allowed the liberty of the land to sue, nor to send into Scotland to claim an earldom or the [Lennox] lands or recompense for them.

Plausible enough, surely. But by the end of what must have been an exhausting interrogation, her reiterated answer was not so plausible. It was as if the only effect of all Brounker's insistence was to drive Arbella back on her single piteous ploy.

'Being demanded who that gentleman is by whose love she is so much honoured, she sayeth it is the king of Scots.' Was Arbella just panicking, or was this policy? She may just have been casting around for a name with which to silence Brounker. A name which could not immediately be dismissed out of hand, a safe scapegoat who was placed above fear of being hauled over the coals for her accusation. But she may instead have been trying to incriminate a rival – albeit, as so often, clumsily.

Bess could only write apologetically to Cecil and Stanhope:

> It is not unknown to you what earnest and importunate suite my
> unfortunate Arbella hath made for Sir H. Brounker's coming
> down. I was in hope she would have discovered somewhat worth
> his travel, but now she will neither name the party to whom she
> hath showed to be so affectionate, nor declare to Sir H. Brounker
> any matter of moment, spending the time in idle and impertinent
> discourses.

Bess was inclined to take it all as a personal insult: 'them that
have laboured to withdraw her natural affection from me . . .
little respected her undoing so they might overthrow me with
grief.' She begged for Arbella's 'speedy remove': 'it may be that a
change of place will work some alteration in her.' Angry though
Bess was – and, in her attempts at coercion, going just the wrong
way to work with Arbella – she yet displayed some understanding of the girl she had raised for all those years. But Bess's goal by
this stage was just 'to keep her quiet till I may understand further
her Majesty's pleasure', a task not made easier by the fact that
Arbella, as Bess wrote in outrage, had 'most vainly prefixed a day
for her remove'. Set a deadline, essentially.

> Soon after Sir H. Brounker's departure hence, I look she will fall
> into some such extremity of making wilful vows as she did lately.
> She said before Sir H. Brounker that if she had not been suffered
> then to remove hence she would have performed her vow and the
> like I daily doubt she will do at any toy she will take discontent-
> ment at . . . She is so wilfully bent, and there is so little reason in
> most of her doings, that I cannot tell what to make of it. A few
> more weeks as I have suffered of late will make an end of me.

The 'vow' to which Bess so despairingly refers was one which
has echoes in our century. Arbella, Bess had reported to Cecil
towards the end of February, 'is so wilfully bent that she hath
made a vow not to eat or drink in this house at Hardwick, or
where I am, till she may hear from her Majesty'. (The
phenomenon of self-starvation was far from unknown, even

stripped of the saintly religious dimension it might have known in an earlier century. In the 1650s Nicholas Fontanus described women who 'have no stomach to their meat, and being taken with a strong loathing of aliment, their bodies waste and consume'.) For very 'preservation of her life', Bess had to let Arbella be carried in a litter to Oldcotes, two miles away. Bess added that her granddaughter was ill, with 'a sharp pain in her side'. 'Arbella hath a doctor of physic with her for a fortnight together, and is enforced to take much physic this unseasonable time, but finds little ease . . . I see her mind is the cause of all.' It is the first significant mention of Arbella's health – and of her use of self-starvation as a weapon – but these are issues which were to loom large in years to come, and to affect the widely debated question of her sanity.

Throughout her life, and ever since, Arbella has often been spoken of as 'distracted' or, more seriously, rumoured actually to be mad. It is tempting to dismiss the allegation out of hand – like Hamlet, Arbella surely 'knew a hawk from a handsaw'. But her letters do at this stressful juncture in her life exhibit signs of exaggeration or fantasy amounting almost to delusion. She herself called the 'scribbling melancholy' into which she had fallen 'a kind of madness', adding that there 'are many such'.

It has been suggested that as a writer Arbella was deliberately building a fantasy world. 'Writing was a mechanism to maintain self-respect,' wrote Sara Jayne Steen, editor of Arbella's letters. 'In the world she created on paper, a strong and beloved woman rightfully rages against her oppressors.' As a way of counterbalancing the automatic diagnosis of hysteria, imposed by men like Cecil and Brounker, this is a useful theory, which surely contains a good deal of truth. But Bess's letter encapsulates the grounds for several other possibilities.

It has also been suggested that Arbella, in common with her royal Scottish relatives James and Mary, suffered from the then unrecognized disease porphyria, which may also have been responsible for the madness of George III. (*For more on porphyria and the Stuart dynasty, and also on the 'hysteric affection', see Appendix B.*) Genetic and biochemical in nature – emerging usually only after puberty, often in the twenties, more often in women – it can skip generations down the family tree. Mary, during her two most serious attacks, suffered an excruciating pain in her side. A 'very acute pain in the pit of the stomach shooting to the back and sides' was noted by the doctors of George III. Just so Arbella (on 4 March) described herself as 'scarce able to stand what for my side and what for my head'. Later in her life she would exhibit other of his symptoms: the convulsions, the trouble with her eyes, the insomnia. An inability to eat and an excess of speech were also noted in George III. Crucially, of course, she also shared to some degree his pattern of mental disturbance.

Porphyria has been described as an intoxication of the nervous system – and drunk is exactly what Arbella's reeling train of thought often seems to be. (King George's conversation was described rather aptly as being 'like the details of a dream in its extravagant confusion'.) The disease often appears intermittently, with an abrupt onset and an equally rapid recovery, and can be exacerbated by stress, malnutrition or various medications regularly prescribed in the seventeenth century, all three of which conditions applied to Arbella at this time. If she was indeed a sufferer from porphyria, then the situation at Hardwick would have represented a downward spiral which would render attacks ever more acute. But to fix upon the idea of a convenient disease as the sole explanation of Arbella's state may be to narrow the focus unduly.

That the mind could regularly affect the body was a wholly acceptable idea in Arbella's day. Mental distress was given considerable weight in the writings of the sixteenth and early seventeenth centuries. Robert Burton in his *Anatomy of Melancholy* suggested that his age was particularly prone to the 'malady'. One main cause, he said, was study: 'many times if discontent and idleness occur with it [scholars] are precipitated into this gulf on a sudden.' Many of the causes of melancholy Burton offered – solitariness, faction, loss of liberty, ambition – fit Arbella neatly. And 'the mind', Burton wrote, 'most effectually works upon the body, producing by his passions and perturbations miraculous alterations, [such] as melancholy, despair, cruel diseases, and sometimes death itself.'

It is easy, moreover, to find contemporary expressions of distress even more extravagant than those in which Arbella indulged. The queen herself was subject to hysterical episodes and depressive attacks. The earl of Essex experienced attacks of nervous prostration even more acute; on one such occasion he was described by his adviser Henry Killigrew as being in such 'an extreme agony and passion' that his buttons (curious symptom!) burst from his doublet. And Harington wrote that, in the months before his last rebellion, Essex 'shifteth from sorrow and repentance to rage and rebellion so suddenly as well proveth him devoid of good reason or right mind'.

In earlier days Essex, when wishing to bring the queen under his thumb again after some temporary coolness, never hesitated to put his bouts of illness to good employ. By the same token, Arbella's bout of self-starvation came at a time when her other bids for attention seemed to have failed her. The shrewd French ambassador De Beaumont suggested to his employer that the whole affair was being taken too seriously, and he seems not to have been alone in this view, reporting on 26 February: 'What I have written to his Majesty concerning the marriage [sic] of Madame Arbella is confirmed by the judgement of the wisest and most penetrating.' He had earlier noted: 'People are only astonished that the queen has lost her repose for some days about it.'

If Arbella wanted to keep the royal eyes focused upon Hardwick, something more was clearly needed. And if appetite had become for Arbella an instrument of power, then this time, at least, her technique was effective. In her immediate desire, she got her own way. 'I am wearied of my life,' Bess wrote to Cecil, 'and I earnestly pray you to send Sir Henry Brounker hither.' Cecil perforce complied, and Arbella was brought back to Hardwick to face his questioning.

But the open hostility of the interrogation made a bad situation worse. Two days later, on 4 March, Arbella wrote Brounker a long and rambling letter – another document of which Cecil's secretary had to make a tidy copy. But even from this a picture of what life at Hardwick had become emerges all too vividly. Arbella described how she and her cousin Mary (Gilbert and Mary's daughter) had been walking in the great chamber 'for fear of wearing the mats in the Gallery (reserved for you courtiers) as sullenly as if our hearts had been too great to give one another a good word, and so to dinner'. They had talked over the latest rumours – 'spent a little breath evaporating some court smoke'. After dinner she went 'in reverent sort to crave my lady grandmother's blessing' and got instead 'a volley of most bitter and injurious words'.

> At last wounded to the heart . . . I made a retreat to my chamber, which I hoped by your character [authority] should have been a sanctuary . . . I went away . . . a good sober pace . . . though my ears were battered on one side with a contemned and in truth contemptible storm of threatenings with which my lady my grandmother thought to have won my resolved heart . . . and in the other summoned to a parley by my uncle William . . .

The privy council was suggesting to Bess that William – 'a gentleman that can please [Arbella] and advise her in due proportion' – should be asked, or ordered, to take a hand in affairs at Hardwick. They expected 'that he should interpose himself more decently towards the discourtesy of her meaning by these vain letters than he doth'. He should 'ease your ladyship of that continual care which we see you take, the same being a great trouble to yourself and more proper for him, whose company is more agreeable unto her'. But Brounker dismissed William as 'a weak man . . . of little love and respect here'; nor does Arbella seem to have regarded him with particular sympathy.

The row continued all over the house. No room was safe – a particular pressure that Arbella clearly felt keenly. 'I took my way down . . . and there we had another skirmish, where you and I sat scribbling till 12 of the clock at night.' Still besieged by her uncle and grandmother, defended by her gentlewomen, her warrior women, 'a troup of such viragoes as Virgil's Camilla . . . I sat me down in patience and fell a scribbling' – scribbling this very letter while her relatives, baffled, looked on.

Leaving that 'disadvantageous chamber' where no-one could hear her or dared come to help her, she went downstairs to seek 'some of my regiment'. She needed a messenger to carry her letter, but her own servants, she said, were now receiving 'rude entertainment' from those of Bess. None the less, her spirits were raised with the fair words 'of certain hopeful young men who do just as I bid them without either other reason or warrant than my pleasure or service'.

> I went up to the great chamber and there found a troupe of (for my sake) malcontents taking advantage of the fire to warm them . . . My sudden apparition coming alone, through the hall . . . made a sudden alteration and wonderment among them for they that stood shrank back as if they had been afraid of me . . . With a general putting off of hats I should not doubt they should stop their ears against me.

But one young man stepped forward, 'with his hat in his hand and my glove in his hat', and offered to do her bidding. His name was George Chaworth, a family connection, and he continued to be an actor in Arbella's life, and in her letters. An actor, indeed, is how she describes him: 'if you will admit him [to the play] his part is penning.' She said that he speaks 'loverlike and gentlemanlike'; he romantically signed his letters 'Your honour's true servant to death'. If Arbella in her letters liked to fantasize herself surrounded by true and loving friends then she did, in her servants, find just such loyalty. To the end of her life, Arbella inspired great personal affection in her attendants – just like her aunt, the Scots Queen Mary.

Arbella, shut up inside Hardwick all these weeks, must often have felt herself forsaken by all the world. 'How many inquisitive questions are asked of me and how little inquisitive are my friends and acquaintances to what becomes of me?' she asked. It is true her stepuncle Edward Talbot repudiated the appeal she sent to him. 'I protest to Almighty God that I have ever lived a stranger to that lady [Arbella],' he wrote to Cecil angrily, 'without ever having had a thought of anything concerning her, or ever so much as a letter or message from her in all my life.' But many eyes were watching the events at Hardwick. If she were trying to make a noise in the world, to make her voice heard in some way, she clearly succeeded. 'Arbella is diversely reported of . . . Lady Arbella is under guard . . . especially are the minds of the kings of France and Spain well disposed towards her, for neither the one nor the other would willingly see a single sovereign in England, Scotland and Ireland,' the Venetians reported.

By March, after all, Elizabeth was indeed ill with fever, and Cecil had messengers waiting to ride for Scotland instantly. The queen had made her last public appearance on 26 February. Now, though, she refused all that the physicians prescribed; she could not sleep, or swallow food easily. 'The queen for many days has not left her chamber,' noted the Venetian envoy Scaramelli:

> And although they say that the reason for this is her sorrow for the death of the countess [of Nottingham] nevertheless the truer cause is that the business of Lady Arbella has reached such a pitch . . . it is well known that this unexpected event has greatly disturbed the queen, for she has suddenly withdrawn into herself, she who was wont to live so gaily . . . so anxious is she that rumours of this beginning of troubles should not spread beyond the kingdom, that she forbade either persons or letters to leave any of the ports . . .

Other letters seemed to agree. 'The queen's sickness continues, and every man's head is full of proclamations and of what shall come of us after. She raves of Tyrone and of Arbella, and is infinitely discontented,' wrote one observer. The Jesuit Father Rivers wrote to a friend in Venice that 'the rumours of Arbella much affect the queen.' Arbella had achieved one of her minor goals – to be taken seriously.

Only the French ambassador sounded a characteristic note of calm. But even he was reporting that Arbella 'has been brought from Hardwick to be declared Elizabeth's successor'. Two days later:

> Whether Madame Arbella will be brought to this town and there made to live in prison or at liberty, I cannot yet tell you, such is the diversity of opinion and judgement; but I think rather the last than the first. Some call the affair a comedy, others a tragi-comedy. For

myself I confess to you that I cannot yet see clearly enough to give it any name. Still I always keep to my first and strongest opinion that I have sent you – that I see no great cause for alarm.

It sounds as if everyone else were reacting far less coolly.

# 'A scribbling melancholy'

IN THE FIRST DAYS OF MARCH ARBELLA BESIEGED BROUNKER WITH
letters; so many that Brounker suggested 'much writing' contributed to 'the distempering of her brain'. The daunting paragraphs, received as something between a threat and an
irrelevance, must have baffled busy and practical men unbearably.
'I think she hath some strange vapours to the brain,' wrote Cecil
(to whom Brounker, as a good government servant, showed all
the correspondence) on one of her epistles. Even Arbella herself
suggested that her 'scribbling melancholy' was 'a kind of
madness', though today we might interpret it more kindly. 'In the
context of Renaissance composition [such writing] is "madness"
of a kind,' wrote Sara Jayne Steen, 'but it sounds remarkably akin
to what the twentieth century calls freewriting, which can be
therapeutic and cathartic.' She suggested that it allowed Arbella
'to formulate on paper an identity she can accept'.

But Arbella was addressing herself to the wrong audience. The
very length of her epistles was self-defeating, while the frag-
mented syntax and the form, amounting in places almost to
stream of consciousness, are daunting. She herself was well
aware of the particular irony that matter so intimate, so idiosyncratic (one is tempted to say, so essentially feminine), should
be carefully harboured and examined by men who found
such exposure unimportant, irrelevant. They may even have
found it almost indecent, at a time when verbal incontinence

in women was specifically linked to a failure in sexual chastity.

As Brounker set down his brutally businesslike Exposition, she wrote to him a 'declaration' notable first for its tone of profound abasement, the paper blotted with tears. She had learnt some hard lessons in little more than a month.

'I take Almighty God to witness, I am free from promise, contract, marriage, or intention to marry, and so mean to be while I live . . . so far from my liking is it to marry at all that I take God to witness I should think myself a great deal happier in sentence of death.' It sounds rather like one of Elizabeth's own early protestations of virginity.

But Arbella continued with a veiled threat. The only thing that could make her alter her 'long settled determination' is if she were to continue in her grandmother's hands, and 'if her Majesty continue her hard opinion of me'. Abashed or not, Arbella, even when beaten almost to the ground, never gave up trying to argue and to bargain; down but never quite out. Her letters are a contradictory – but very human – cocktail of resentment and placation. Arbella several times referred to herself as a puritan in these weeks, perhaps to disarm suspicions (shortly to be given a strong foundation of probability) that she was in league with a Catholic party. Her repeated hints that the government should look beyond English shores – that she was getting some foreign aid – seem, on the other hand, designed rather to tweak the noses of the government, or at least to make them take her seriously.

Suppose her beloved ('my little, little love') should arrive at a nearby port 'and come attended with 500, as I think that is the lowest number he is answerable for,' she suggested provocatively. She couldn't resist flicking the whip, furious that her 'word and oath' carried so little weight. 'Alas what a dwarf I am thought at court.' It touched her pride nearly. 'You courtiers are wonderfully hardhearted and slow of belief.' From the lines of these letters comes a sense of how very far Arbella has fallen – how strong had been her presumption that she would one day rule England, and how scourging was her present ignominy.

On this occasion she presumed, she wrote, 'to draw Sir Henry Brounker here with an allegory which I have moralised to him'. (One can only imagine his feelings with sympathy.) Being 'in my opinion forsaken of all the world', she felt justified in behaving desperately. Experience, she wrote, 'had taught me there was no other way to draw down a messenger of such worth from her Majesty but by incurring some suspicion and having no ground whereon to work upon but that, and this being love, I adventured.' Having lost, she offered 'expiation', an exaggerated promise of future good behaviour. The stick and the carrot, often in the same letter, seem to have been Arbella's way.

> First I will never trouble her Majesty with any suit hereafter but forget my long desired land [the confiscated Lennox estates], and confine myself to close prison for as little liberty as it shall please her Majesty in the severest rules of wisdom and policy to allot me, and think it the highest favour I can possibly obtain, for I perceive daily more and more to my increasing grief I am and ever hereafter shall be more unfortunate than I lately thought I could possibly have been. Secondly I will make a vow I will never whilst I live, nor entertain thought nor conceal such or any other matter whatsoever from her Majesty . . .

All this on condition she should be granted her 'dear and due liberty'. 'In her Majesty's hand it is to mend it,' she wrote, 'and in God's to end my sorrows with death which only can make me absolutely and eternally happy.'

Earlier in the letter Arbella had written of herself as being 'bound in duty and conscience to make all the means I could to defend myself from perishing'. But she had also written that 'despair may drive me from mere fear to misliked courses,' and that if her actions so far seem bad, she may yet 'do worse'. The words are ambiguous, but a hint at suicide does seem to be a possibility.

References to the possibility of Arbella's own death bedevil her subsequent letters. On 4 March she signed herself off with a quotation in Latin: *Damnata iam luce ferox* – 'furious by daylight, having been condemned'. The tag comes from Lucan's *Pharsalia*; a passage in which, at daybreak, trapped warriors heroically kill themselves to avoid defeat. On 9 March, contrasting her present melancholy in 'this my prison' with the time when

Elizabeth pronounced her 'an eaglet of her own kind', she spoke of desperation, hinting again at suicide: 'now I have lost all I can lose or almost care to lose.'

She harped again on the fate of Mr Starkey: the 'innocent, discreet, learned and godly Mr Starkey', as she later recalled him sadly. But she was still only flirting with the idea of suicide, attracted and repelled simultaneously. On 7 March, complaining that the page she sent to fetch her books had been shut out of her 'quondam study chamber', and that she herself was not allowed to enter to receive the help 'of my dead counsellors and comforters', she declared that such tactics would not prevail. 'If you think to make me weary of my life and so conclude it according to Mr Starkey's tragical example, you are deceived.' Unlike James Starkey, Arbella Stuart did not give up easily.

As Brounker set off back to court again, Arbella began pounding him with letters, each following hard on the heel of its predecessor. Over the next few weeks, the eager young Chaworth was kept busy, as letters pursued Brounker down the Great North Road – letters written on 4, 6, 7 and 9 March. She had, after all, few other friends – and it has often been noted that a strange affinity can arise between interrogator and victim.

His initial tactic of pretended complicity had obviously worked to a degree. 'Sir, as you were a private person I found all humanity and courtesy from you,' she wrote, before warning him in her final epistle: 'If you come as a commissioner, consider what power one mortal creature how great soever hath over another how miserable soever. If as a friend, deserve that holy name before you take it upon you.' She had come to repent 'the trust I have reposed in your sincerity and fair promises', and in a bitter postscript to one note, she added: 'I deal better with you than you with me for I do not torture you with expectation nor promise better than I will perform.' But she had become aware that her letters were received with scant sympathy.

The longest letter of all was the one she wrote to the wretched Brounker on 9 March, Ash Wednesday; a holy day that had grim significance for Arbella. The earl of Essex had been executed on Ash Wednesday. The first gloomy months of the year were over-full of melancholy anniversaries: the deaths of her mother and Lennox grandmother; the execution of the queen of Scots.

Throwing back at him Brounker's opinion which 'I took so very unkindly at your hands, that the more I writ, to the less purpose it was', she conceded (or perhaps one should say boasted) that she 'might utter more welcome matter in 2 words'. But gratifying her correspondent with a simple communication was not her goal, she declared frankly. It would, she assured Brounker, be a great mistake to think

> that my troubled wits cannot discern how unlookt for, how subject to interpretation, how offensive every word [of this letter] will be even to you . . . [But] I determined to spend this day in sending you the ill favoured picture of my grief . . . being allowed no company to my liking and finding this the best excuse to avoid the tedious conversation I am bound to, I think the time best spent in tiring you with the idle conceits of my travelling mind till it make you ashamed to see into what a scribbling melancholy . . . you have brought me . . . If you leave me till I be my own woman . . . then your trouble and mine too will cease.

Sure enough, the letters Arbella wrote after her release from Hardwick were of no more than usual length or fantasy; indeed, the single theme most often reiterated is guilt at having written briefly and tardily. But this was a final verbal fling before the stream of her self-revelation dries up forever; a seven-thousand-word *jeu d'esprit*. 'I will not excuse my prolixity,' she ended her epistle. 'God forgive me my excess – and [you] your defects in love and charity.'

It is important to admit – to stress, indeed – that by this stage the letters have indeed passed the bounds of rationality. The allusions culled from Arbella's extensive reading in the classics are tossed into the screeds she wrote in these few days with a randomness that suggests a mind at once capable of processing a vast range of material with incredible speed, and incapable of so harnessing that material as to interact successfully with another mentality. She was rummaging through the bottom drawer of her own particularly cultured history. One passage in the letter of 4 March, about her supposed lover being 'transported by some

Archimedes to Newstead as miraculously especially to himself as certain Romans (those Romans were full of unsuspicious magnanimity) were hoisted over the walls of the besieged Syracuse', ran on for some dozen more lines before the sentence ends, without ever pausing to explain the allusion in any way. En route it took in: a sideswipe at the court ('you courtiers are wonderfully hardhearted and slow of belief'); a boast as to her own discretion; a threat as to her lover's power; and a promise that she 'will not, no I assure you I will not, no I will be sworn (if you administer the oath) I will not if I can choose see him.'

Perhaps the staggering length of the Ash Wednesday missive is best seen in the context of the events in London, and that strange sense of a time out of kilter – that things could end at any minute, or could go on indefinitely – which attends any prolonged deathbed ceremony. What is more, Arbella was writing in the secret knowledge that she had planned to escape from Hardwick the very next day. She hoped and believed that by the time her extraordinary letter reached Brounker, she would be free and miles away. This means that in the practical sense, it was unnecessary. But Arbella's aim in writing had long passed beyond mere practicality. Communication with the court, with an objective hearer, was no longer her primary aim. The letters had by now a double life: as communiqué, and as diary.

Arbella was writing for her own relief. 'My weak body and travelling mind must be disburdened soon or I shall offend my God' – presumably by suicide. She was wallowing in gloom:

> I have conquered my affection. I have cast away my hopes, I have forsaken all comfort, I have submitted my body and fortune to more subjection than could be commanded, I have disposed of my liberty . . . What harm can all the world do me now? . . . My servants shall be taken from me, then shall I be no more troubled with their troublesome importunity and inquisitiveness. I shall hear of my friends' trouble and by comparison of my own think it nothing.

But she had good reason. In this Ash Wednesday letter Arbella used the metaphors of violence with a frequency that suggests she had been threatened with brutality. 'I shall spit my tongue in my torturer's face . . . lay the axe to the root of the tree in time and let me lose my head . . . this concealed truth which torture whom you list you shall never find.' Indeed, she mentioned threats openly: 'my head . . . which her Majesty hath threatened to take'. She remained defiant: 'I am deaf to commandment and dumb to authority.' But her nerves were wearing thin. 'For the passion of God let me come to my trial in this my prison instantly.'

Thus she came to the real point. Demanding the right to a trial, Arbella Stuart went on to make what amounts to a plea for personal liberty and the right to love. 'When it shall please her Majesty to afford me those ordinary rights which other subjects cannot be debarred of justly, I shall endeavour to receive them as thankfully now as if they had been in due time offered,' the letter launched out hardily. She spoke of those who 'may thank themselves if they have lost all the interest of voluntary obedience they had in me'. 'But [if] I am grown a woman and therefore by her Majesty's own saying am not allowed the liberty of granting lawful favours to princely suitors, how then dare subjects justify their most justifiable affections?'

It is in this letter that Arbella uttered her memorable commitment to her own identity: 'When all is done I must shape my own coat according to my cloth, but it will not be after the fashion of this world, God willing, but fit for me.' With the war of words about to take a different turn – with a physical escape from Hardwick planned – she hoped soon to be able to arrange her own destiny.

# 'Disorderly attempts'

PERHAPS AFTER ALL, IN ALL THOSE YEARS AT HARDWICK, ARBELLA HAD been cobbling together more than her stitchery; had indeed done, as she so casually mentioned, 'very many things' without the knowledge of her watchful guardians. In January 1603, Brounker had noted Henry Cavendish as present in the district around Hardwick and in company, ominously, with a notorious Catholic, Henry Stapleton. From Bess's viewpoint, the Catholic bias of the neighbourhood was a threat. She had written long ago to Lord Burghley of 'one Harrison, a seminary that lay at his brother's house a mile from Hardwick . . . if any such traitorous and naughty persons (through her Majesty's clemency) be suffered to go abroad . . . they are the most likely instruments to put a bad matter in execution.' Arbella, in the years of her confinement, may have come to see their presence rather as an opportunity.

Now, both Henry Cavendish and Stapleton were back near Hardwick, lodging at an inn in Mansfield nearby. With them were some thirty or forty mounted men, hidden in small groups around the country – 'some of them with "dags" [daggers]', Bess observed coolly later. One man had a case of pistols. Another rider was observed by two local men as having 'a little pillion behind his saddle, which he hid with his cloak'. Clearly, the party hoped to carry some lady away.

But before Arbella could be mounted upon the pillion, the con-spirators' first task was to spirit her outside Hardwick. The house may have been built in the newest and most luxurious style, but, notwithstanding the elegant golden façade, its high walls and enclosed courtyard (accessible only through the porter's lodge) fulfilled the function of a fortress.

On 9 March, the day of Arbella's Ash Wednesday letter, Cavendish and Stapleton received an evening visit from Arbella's page, Richard Owen. On the next day, the two men were to ride to the gates of Hardwick where Arbella, on some pretext, would join them. Early in the morning of 10 March the two leaders rode into the hamlet of Ault Hucknall, half a mile from the edge of the Hardwick estate. They had with them just eight men, the rest being concealed in the wooded land thereabouts. John and Matthew Slack, two marksmen employed by a local resident, Mrs Ireton, claimed they saw several hundred men on horseback, but they were probably exaggerating – very pardonably.

Cavendish and Stapleton asked the Slacks to walk the horses while they went across to the vicarage and asked for the church key, hoping from the height of the steeple to see when Arbella had come safely through the gates. But the vicar denied them access and the two men turned discomforted away, remarking with sarcasm that Arbella would thank him for their good entertainment.

The appointed hour had passed by now, and Arbella had not come to their rendezvous. Bess, later that night, reported what had happened with a flatness that purposely mulcts the event of much of its nervous tension. 'At about twelve of the clock Arbell came out of her chamber, went towards the gates (as she said) intending to walk, but being persuaded it was dinner time, did stay.' Arbella had that morning received and burned a letter from London, presumably containing instructions, as Bess discovered subsequently.

Shortly afterwards, Owen and 'old Freake', Arbella's embroiderer, brought a letter to Henry Cavendish at Ault Hucknall. 'She cannot come out this day,' Henry Cavendish was heard to say, before the cavalcade mounted up and rode away. The Slacks heard one of the serving men explain: 'We cannot now come to our purpose, but about a fortnight hence we must come again when these blunders are past, but we must not come with so many near the house.' But Arbella's uncle seems to have decided to make one last attempt there and then.

Bess described the scene in the report she wrote to the privy council: 'At about two of the clock in the afternoon, there came to my gates my son Henry Cavendish and one Mr Stapleton.' The rest of the party waited, 'well weaponed', a quarter of a mile away.

> For that Arbell was desirous to speak with my bad son Henry I was content to suffer him to come into my house and speak with her, rather than she to go to him, but sent him word not to remain here above two hours. I would not suffer Stapleton to come within my gates, for I have disliked him of long for many respects . . .
>
> Arbell and Henry Cavendish had not talked as I think a dozen words together but they both came down and offered to go out of my gates. One of my servants entreated them not to offer to go out until they had my consent. Arbell seemed unwilling to stay, yet at length by persuasion did stay until word was brought to me. When I understood of it, I sent to her that I did not think it good she should speak with Stapleton, and wished her to forbear it . . . She asked if she were a prisoner and said she would see, and so went to the gates and would have gone out, but was not suffered . . .

It is ninety long paces from the doors of the house to the porter's lodge, and Arbella must have felt eyes upon her every inch of the way. And in the lodge, looking through the gates, Arbella could only give to Stapleton 'some vain, idle words of salutation', as Bess put it dismissively. The dowager sent down messages to Stapleton that he should go. Then, when he ignored them, she sent others, for all the world as if he were an importunate dog she were trying to shoo away. Bess also forbade Henry Cavendish from returning the next day, as Arbella had asked; but her granddaughter did not give up so easily. 'He was no sooner gone out of my gates but she made herself ready to walk abroad, which I thought not convenient she should do and so she stayed.' Bess was beginning to repeat her words: for an old lady, it had been a tiring day.

The reader of this acount has the sense of Arbella, and indeed even Henry the experienced soldier, fatally wavering in the face of Bess's habitual authority – authority at once powerful and moral. Forty armed men would probably have been enough to storm the house by force, but its chatelaine was a mother and grandmother, surrounded by well-known and beloved servants who would inevitably have been injured in the fray. The reader cannot but be aware, too, of Bess's repeated use of the possessive – 'my house', 'my gates' – and the affront offered to Arbella's once almost royal dignity. Bess had shown herself mistress of the day. She doubted, though, whether she could win another such: Arbella 'being here one day, I fear I shall not have her here the morrow if I should suffer her but to go without my gates. In my opinion it were better she were removed farther from the north which way I fear she would go.' The north had always been rebellious, Catholic territory. If Arbella were sent south, she would not 'be acquainted with so many to help her as she is hereabouts', Bess suggested practically.

Bess's messenger rode post haste to the court. But Arbella had her own mouthpiece in the south – George Chaworth, the Hardwick servant who had so chivalrously offered to do her service. Receiving word from Arbella on 15 or 16 March, he rushed to take her message round to Brounker. But he found his quarry reluctant to speak with him; the official version of latest events at Hardwick had probably got to him first.

Returning to see Brounker the next day, Chaworth was told the government officer had left town, presumably heading for the midlands. He set off in pursuit. 'I better bethought me of Sir Henry going from court against his promise made to me,' Chaworth wrote to Arbella. 'I presently departed, posted with all speed to the house at Lambeth – he was gone from thence post as they told me into the country – I followed him to know the cause of his sudden going – I overtook him, and as I perceived against his will.' Chaworth pursued the unhappy Brounker on all points, since 'if it be my folly, my love to your honour made me foolish.' As so often, it is hard not to feel sorry for the government envoy.

In the face of Chaworth's protective questions, Brounker denied that there was any hurt meant to Arbella. 'I feigned to him that I had matters reported of his going down . . . as that he went to fetch your honour to the Tower – or to London, or to procure your honour's straight keeping in the country and hard usage from my old lady, all which he with solemn protestations denied.' Brounker told Chaworth, indeed, that he wanted nothing more to do with Arbella, 'because he hath you not at any certainty but in a hundred minds and that you say and unsay and diverse several things'. But the real reason for Brounker's mission was not hard to see: 'to give charge that you be not suffered to pass through the country, or to give charge to the gentlemen in the country or else northwards that none help your honour away'. These, Chaworth adds self-deprecatingly, 'be only my foolish conjectures'. But he was probably in part right, 'for as I hear the post northward be stopped already.' Indeed, his own communication was intercepted, and forwarded by Brounker himself to Cecil.

While still in London, Chaworth had seen his cousin Bridget Carr, a gentlewoman of the queen's privy chamber, entreating her to speak to the queen – 'she is sick, though courtiers say contrary.' In this he was certainly right: on 11 March Elizabeth had lapsed into 'a heavy dullness' and 'unremovable melancholy'. She had, as the French ambassador reported, lost the will to live. Her counsellors begged her on their knees to go to bed, but 'if you were in the habit of seeing such things in your bed as I do when in mine, you would not persuade me to go there,' she told one well-wisher, chillingly.

Every communication now carried an added burden of urgency. Chaworth sent his letter to Arbella by a messenger to whom he gave 'straight charge to post night and day without rest', he added excitably. But the messenger would have had a hard job to beat Brounker, who arrived back at Hardwick on 17 March, having spent a mere two and a half days on the way.

Brounker was indeed armed with a warrant invoking all the Derbyshire authorities to suppress 'unlawful assemblies and disorderly attempts'. He at once sent for Henry Cavendish – but, as Cecil had ordered, tactfully, 'by friendly letter'. Henry was given a generous seven days to prepare his bags to travel to London for further questioning. The whole scenario was to be played *pianissimo*; but 'I have an eye upon Mr Cavendish, that if he may exceed his appointed time, he may know the force of your lordships' commands,' Brounker assured the council grimly. Everyone was interviewed, down to the villagers – except for Stapleton, who had fled. Brounker naturally refused Arbella's request that she should be present at these examinations.

He carried a letter from the council to Bess, cautiously regretting that Arbella's thoughts were 'still no better quieted' and instructing – since the queen (in whose name they still acted) would not hear of her removal from Hardwick – that 'you will deal as mildly with her in words as you can'. Her Majesty would have Arbella 'barred of no thing fit for her . . . as long as those discreet friends of hers, whom you assign to accompany and attend her, can keep her within bounds of temper and quietness . . . Fashion all things as the young lady might not mislike her habitation.' In other words: just keep her quiet. That no more drastic action was taken against the conspirators can be put down to the extreme sensitivity of the situation, with Elizabeth's death expected any day. If the queen did die, then Brounker's warrant, like almost every other piece of authority in the land, might fall into abeyance during an interregnum, calling his right to detain Arbella into question.

In his official report to the council on 19 March, Brounker was reassuring. 'There is no fear of any new practice . . . unless the opinion of her Majesty's sickness, which is here too common, draw on some sudden resolution.' A thorough search found 'neither shot, pikes nor anything else here and the country slow enough and unready'. But the new note sounded here suddenly, of open preparation for armed warfare, is harsh and unexpected. And, along with the emollient report sent to the whole council, Brounker also wrote to Cecil privately.

'I must remember your honour that this Stapleton is a very wilful papist, and had long since practised to convey my Lady Arbella into Norfolk, and there to keep her among seminaries and priests, and to defend her by a strong party if need required, as Arbella herself told me.' Afterwards, Brounker added, she would have denied the last part if she could 'and entreated me to conceal his name'. She really wasn't cut out for conspiracy. Of Arbella herself, Brounker wrote to Cecil, 'she is certain in nothing but her uncertainty. She justifieth herself and desireth liberty.'

Every man's mouth is full of the queen's danger, and Arbella receives daily advertisements to that purpose . . . I suppose her wilfulness (which is greater and more peremptory than before) ariseth out of a hope of the queen's death. I find her so vain and idle as I seldom trouble her, neither doth she much desire my company, though I pretended I came to see her wrongs righted and to compound all matters between her grandmother and her.

He believed that had she managed to leave Hardwick on the tenth, her purpose ('if there were any') had been to head 'for Scotland', since Hull, the nearest shipping place, was forty long miles away. This suggests a flight rather than a coup; but news of the queen's sickness 'may alter her opinion'.

I am verily persuaded that her remove only will stay her practice, which I perceive is resolved by herself and others. If her Majesty should miscarry . . . I do not see how she can be kept in this place two days, and therefore it were good that her remove were thought on in time, if her escape may breed danger.

Even at this late date Arbella's adventure – the whole adventure of the succession – could still have ended very badly. The Venetian envoy pointed out that, Arbella having 'no taint of rebellion or aught but schemes for the future' against her, it would 'in the ordinary course' be impossible to prosecute her. 'All the same', he continued pertinently,

as the situation is growing more serious, and the queen's anger is mounting, many people fear that just as Mary Stuart's first crime was her secret betrothal to the duke of Norfolk, so the joy of Arbella's ill-matched and unconsummated marriage may be changed into a bloody tragedy.

# 'That strange outlandish word "change"'

BROUNKER ARRIVED BACK AT HARDWICK TO FIND THAT ARBELLA HAD shut herself into her room. But she slipped out to him a final blunt letter. 'Pardon me if without ceremony I shut you out of doors, if you will not at my most earnest entreaty forbear to come to me, self-confined within this chamber, till I be absolutely cleared and free every way, and have my just desires granted and allowed.'

Things at Hardwick had evidently gone from bad to worse. Bess, Brounker reported, was 'sickly by breaking of her sleep and cannot long continue this vexation'. On 22 March the council sent orders to Sir Francis Leeke and John Manners of Haddon, neighbours and family connections, to aid in the task of guarding Arbella. But all such decisions were taken in an atmosphere of mounting uncertainty.

It is hard, looking back, to grasp how deeply everyone was dreading the outcome of spring 1603. The world as the Elizabethans knew it was ending, and who knew what the future would be? The contemporary chronicler Thomas Dekker wrote after the event of how easily 'the general terror that [Elizabeth's] death bred' might have been followed by 'the feared wounds of a civil sword'.

> The report . . . like a thunderclap, was able to kill thousands. It took away hearts from millions. For having brought up even under her wing a nation that was almost begotten and born under her,

that never shouted any *ave* but for her name, never saw the face of any prince but herself, never understood what that strange out-landish word 'change' signified – how was it possible but that her sickness should throw abroad an universal fear, and her death an astonishment?

It was in this climate they all stood immobilized, waiting for the lightning. But when it came, they survived – and the Gordian knot of England's future was cut almost immediately.

Even as Brounker rode north again, the queen's condition was deteriorating. As he arrived in Derbyshire, the French ambassador had reported Elizabeth to be 'already in a manner insensible' – seated upon cushions on the floor, one finger in her mouth, her eyes fixed on the ground, silent for hour after hour. 'All agree that she is worse,' he wrote again, showing 'an extraordinary melancholy in her countenance and actions'.

Some attribute the cause of her illness to the extreme displeasure that she has conceived in her mind about what has passed con-cerning Madame Arbella; others about the affairs of Ireland . . . Many also declare that she is seized in her heart for remorse for the death of the earl of Essex, who was beheaded just two years ago.

The old *canard* survived: that Elizabeth was brought low by some special cause (and that cause probably Arbella), rather than by the inevitable intimations of mortality. She spent her nights brooding upon the affair, wrote the Venetians dramatically. But it was becoming clear that, for whatever reason, the end could not be far away. On 20 March – just as Bess in Hardwick was send-ing for witnesses to cut Arbella and Henry out of her will – Cecil sent James a draft of the proclamation proposed to declare him king of England. Perhaps James needed such reassurance, for an official in Berwick on the border was sending his own message south: 'The Scots are very discontented and murmur desperately at a rumour of the Lady Arbella's marriage.' As for the capital, 'London is all in arms for fear of the Catholics,' reported the Venetian envoy.

On 21 March, in Richmond, Elizabeth finally took to her bed.

As she lay there, an abscess in her throat burst and she declared she felt better; but it was obvious that her state was critical. The clerics, whose duty it would be to usher her from one world to the next, were summoned to remain in constant attendance.

On the twenty-third, her ministers again begged the queen to name her successor. She was beyond speech – but it was later said that with her fingers she made a sign (a crown?) above her head; this convenient signal was taken as indicating King James of Scotland. At six in the evening, she signalled for the archbishop of Canterbury to kneel by her bed and pray. At ten she fell into a deep sleep; in the small hours of the next morning she died, departing 'easily, like a ripe apple from a tree'.

One of Queen Elizabeth's ladies removed from her finger a sapphire ring and dropped it out of the window to her brother, Sir Robert Carey, who was desperate to be the first to bring James glad tidings. He handed the token to the king in Edinburgh just three days later, possibly before word had spread to Hardwick, or to the Seymour strongholds in the south-west. This tardy passage of news was to the advantage of the government. The privy counsellors, who had spent the night of Elizabeth's death scattered restless through the corridors, had issued word that no-one was to leave the palace without permission. At dawn, they left Richmond to ride to Whitehall and there, on the green opposite the tiltyard, at ten o'clock on Thursday morning, Robert Cecil proclaimed King James's authority.

The grandees of the land – heralds, privy counsellors, lords, courtiers – then formed up in procession to move down the Strand and through Ludgate to read the proclamation twice more in the City, and formally, in the king's name, to claim possession of the Tower. It was a long walk. For much of the way they were treading the ground Essex's rebels had trod but recently. They must have known that – if Cecil's precautions had failed, if news of the queen's death had leaked out just a few hours early – armed interception was again a possibility. None came. James succeeded smoothly; without so many ripples as might shake a cockle boat, as Cecil put it complacently.

There was an air of pleased astonishment throughout the land. Robert Cecil's elder brother, aware of how very differently things could have gone, wrote to congratulate his sibling. From York, where the news had only just arrived on 27 March, he described 'the fullness of the joy that these parts receive of the expectation of a happy and quiet government'. People had expected, instead, that 'their houses should have been sacked and spoiled'.

Even the thirteen-year-old Lady Anne Clifford was aware that trouble was expected. 'About the 21st or 22nd of March my aunt of Warwick sent my mother word about 9 o'clock at night that she should remove to Austin Friars her house for fear of some commotions,' she wrote in her diary. Instead, the next morning 'King James was proclaimed in Cheapside by all the council with great joy and triumph. This peacable coming in of the king was unexpected of all parts of the people. Within 2 or 3 days we returned to Clerkenwell again,' she reported, anti-climactically.

But there was one last strangled gasp from the revolution that never happened, though the authorities could afford, in the end, to dismiss it fairly lightly. It is at this point that there steps forward from the shadows a figure who (while working always for his own interests) may well have helped to set in motion the events at Hardwick in 1603. Lord Beauchamp, son of the earl of Hertford, father of that Edward Seymour Arbella had sought as husband, had recently been reported by the Venetians as himself betrothed to Arbella. On the eve of Elizabeth's death they also noted that Beauchamp seemed to have left London secretly.

He was another whose hopes may have been raised by Elizabeth's protracted refusal to name James as her successor. The writer of that anonymous letter from 1600 discussing the contenders for the throne while praising James clearly thought that Beauchamp instead would win the prize, though the correspondent regarded the prospect unenthusiastically. Around 28 March there was a rumour that 'the Lord Beauchamp stood out and gathered forces' against James. The same writer, John Chamberlain, continued to the effect that on the thirtieth it was known to be 'a false alarm, for word is come since that [Beauchamp's] father was one of the foremost in the country to proclaim the king.' But in other quarters the story of Beauchamp's resistance was also rife, and not dismissed as quickly. Bess's daughter Frances Pierrepont wrote to her mother that a visitor sayeth that all things in the southern parts proceed peacably; only my Lord Beauchamp is said to make some assemblies, which he [the visitor] hopeth will suddenly dissolve into smoke, [Beauchamp's] forces being feeble to make head against so great a union.

But not that feeble, according to some of the rumours: John Manningham in London heard that Beauchamp's force was ten thousand strong.

The Venetians, too, reported that Beauchamp was 'in the west and raising foot and horse, with the intention of proclaiming himself king in his own right, and more so in that of Arbella'. (They had already said, confusingly, that 'the adherents of Lady Arabella, of the earl of Hertford and the earl of Huntingdon, not knowing what thread to hold on by, are all keeping quiet.' But then, as they put it, the whole affair of the succession, though likely to prove peaceful, was something of 'a hurlyburly'. Confusingly again, they describe both the earl of Hertford and his son as Hertford, in the European fashion.) They alleged that Beauchamp 'was acting at the instigation of France, and the ambassador of his Most Christian Majesty has been put to great travail therein.' A few days later they conceded that Beauchamp's opposition was over – but by the old earl's intervention, rather than his son's own conviction, they said.

> The younger is beginning to yield to the elder and the rumour is dying away, for the elder, crippled as he is, swears that he will have himself carried to London and there sign the proclamation [of James' accession] himself and pledge his son's hand to the same.

It was, so enduring legend says, the name of Beauchamp that had prompted the dying Queen Elizabeth to utter the famous words: 'I will have no rascal's son in my seat.' With hindsight it seems likely that he was at the very least watching Arbella's efforts with sympathy. He does not, however, seem to have suffered any penalties under the new regime – extraordinary, if all the Venetians said was true. Perhaps, after all, he was merely arming his household against civil unrest – a precaution taken by many nobles. In any event, after James's accession he merely fades from view until his death in 1612.

Arbella's precise location in the confusion of these changeful days is uncertain. The Venetians wrote in the old queen's last days that she had already been sent to 'that same castle where Queen Mary of England did at one time keep her sister Elizabeth a prisoner' – Hatfield, or Woodstock, possibly. To confirm this there is no evidence at all. All we know is that word did come that she was at last to move south; it is unclear just when, or to where, initially. Was she moved on Brounker's advice, or by permission of the new king? Suddenly, Arbella's doings were not so well reported, she herself was no longer the subject of such ardent official scrutiny. Suddenly she was irrelevant, to all those who had hitherto watched her so closely.

Events had overtaken any move she might make; but, in fact, she made none. With James proclaimed ruler and her own supporters dispersed, Arbella seemed content to wait on the new regime, or at least to have lost the will to run away. As the Venetian envoy put it: 'Arbella too, no longer mad, writes in all humility from her prison, that she desires no other husband, no other state, no other life, than that which King James, her cousin and lord, in his goodness may assign her.' Had she lost? Or, as she made preparations to leave Hardwick at last, had she won all she really wanted – her liberty? Was Arbella Stuart trying for the throne in 1603? Or was hers a compromise position, seeking only personal goals herself, but desperate enough to compound with a political ally?

Biographers until very recently denied Arbella had any desire other than personal, domestic happiness; have reiterated that there is no evidence she was guilty [*sic*] of so much as a germ of ambition. This is a question to which there can never be a definitive answer (and, *pace* those so-certain earlier writers, it *is* a question). But surely there is only one ground for denying that Arbella was affected by ambition, and that is her own claim to that effect – a claim made in a situation in which she would have been mad indeed to have declared differently.

Follow the first lesson of any detective story, and look at what

Arbella did, rather than what she said, and it seems that she must have had at least half an eye on the throne. Perhaps this perception is a reflection of our age, just as it was expressive of the Victorian biographers' time to feel threatened by the idea of her as a contender. But the opinion of Brounker (an experienced contemporary who would no doubt have preferred to be able to dismiss Arbella as nothing more than a froward girl, so that he himself could get back to the scene of the main action) seems to have tended the other way. His last dispatches show him believing Arbella to be motivated by the queen's imminent death, and suspecting she had powerful allies.

But in truth, even before Arbella began negotiating her marriage, James's accession was essentially a *fait accompli*. England hoped no longer to be governed by 'a lady shut up in her chamber from all her subjects and most of her servants', and the words Sir John Harrington used of the ageing queen also described Arbella all too accurately. Arbella's sex told against her; a barrier that might not have seemed insuperable in Elizabeth's heyday, but which reared its head once England had begun to chafe under petticoat government in the queen's decline.

Nothing, of course, could more effectively have ruined any remaining chance of the throne Arbella Stuart had in January 1603 than the events of the weeks which followed, as rumours spread that she was, as the Venetians reported, 'half mad' – or, as they put it more precisely, is 'or feigns herself to be' half mad. The idea of Arbella's feigning herself to be mad sounds the *Hamlet* note loud and clear. Presumably the Venetians thought she was attempting to avoid blame for the attempted marriage – effectively, to plead insanity. If she were, of course, then her plea worked, in that she kept herself out of the Tower. (And, as a bonus, got to speak her mind under the cloak of lunacy, like one of Shakespeare's Fools.)

There have been three basic explanations for Arbella's distraction: the physiological, the psychological and the sociological; porphyria, pressure and patriarchal oppression . . . Here, a fourth is being added: the legal. The lines of thought are not mutually exclusive; if Arbella were truly terrified by the consequences of her actions, she may have seen an advantage to giving her frantic feelings rein. But surely no-one who has read the letters can believe they were entirely a pretence?

By contrast – and by way of a fifth explanation – Father Rivers wrote to Father Parsons in March that 'they give out' that Arbella is mad, and that is an even more interesting theory. The Venetians added that the faction of the king of Scotland, in order to destroy public sympathy for Arbella, 'are spreading reports defamatory to her good name'. Cecil at one stage instructed Bess to see that Arbella did not write so freely, 'because the dispersing of her letters abroad of such strange subjects is inconvenient in many respects'. But who was so dispersing them, since those that have survived were addressed almost exclusively to men of his own party? Were there other letters, now lost, in which Arbella tried to rally help? Or did Cecil himself strategically leak certain details?

The evidence for Arbella's useful 'madness' is the letters, and no-one can plausibly suggest that they (at that length!) were forgeries. But certainly in the end, Arbella's inept plotting played into Cecil's hands. It *is* going too far to suggest that all the events of that spring at Hardwick were the result of an elaborate conspiracy by Robert Cecil. But is it going too far to suggest that, Arbella's false step having once been taken, he seized his opportunity? Gave Arbella plenty of rope with which to hang herself and her chances? It was a technique the government had used before and would use again: with the earl of Essex's rebellion and the Guy Fawkes plot and, most notably of all, when Walsingham suborned the messengers used by the captive Mary, queen of Scots, and himself used them to build up the collection of letters which would lead to her execution.

We get a hint of some such machinations from the Venetian ambassador, who in the middle of March reported that James's agent at the English court, rather oddly, was 'endeavouring to procure that the council ... should give [Arbella] leave to carry out the marriage'. The Scottish aim, the Venetian implied, was further to weaken Arbella's chances by (a) exposing her as a woman who made a hasty marriage in an ill-advised manner; (b) tying her to one who still suffered the slur of illegitimacy; and (c) bringing her within the treasonable compass of the 'ancient

law' forbidding those of the blood royal to marry without permission, on pain of the capital penalty.

The ambassador may have been over-dramatic, especially in
regard to the 'ancient law'. He himself admitted that as a newcomer to England he found it hard accurately to assess the question of the succession, especially since it could not be discussed
freely. But his suggestion that this Machiavellian Scottish plan
was made 'in concert with those of his friends on the council' is
suggestive to a degree.

One does not, to consider such a theory, necessarily have to
condemn Cecil as a villain. He was a man with a mission –
to secure a smooth succession – and one who would do whatever
was necessary to achieve it. But personally he wished Arbella no
harm. In the months ahead, he was often to stand her ally. It was
thanks in part to him that Arbella, in the short term, gained real
benefit from James's accession – benefit, at least, if you don't look
back, and compare what she got with what she might have hoped
to gain. She rode south with relief in her heart. She would never
again return to her grandmother's custody.

# IV

## 1603–1610

## *'My own woman'?*

'If you leave me till I be my own woman . . . then
your trouble, and mine too, will cease.'

Arbella Stuart to Sir Henry Brounker, 1603

# 'An unknown climate'

LONG AFTER THE EVENT, SETTING DOWN HER MEMOIRS, A COURT lady gave a romantic picture of Arbella's first meeting with the new royal family. She described how at Welbeck – the Derbyshire home of Arbella's uncle Charles Cavendish – Queen Anna, with her young daughter Elizabeth, was surprised by the kind of masquerade in which she delighted.

A band of Arcadian shepherds and shepherdesses, leading a flock of sheep 'whose wool was white as snow', were followed by a troop of huntsmen, leading tame deer whose horns were tipped with gold. These swains told the queen that Diana the virgin huntress, hearing of her approach, invited her to repose herself in the goddess's own bower. The welcoming deity, wrote the anonymous lady, proved to be none other than Arbella herself . . .

It cannot be true, unfortunately. On the dates given, in early May, not only was Arbella known to be much further south, but the new Queen Anna was still in Scotland. The story is as false as the rumours passed on by the Venetian Scaramelli, who on 1 May reported that 'Lady Arbella has been released and gone to meet the king with three hundred horse, after that she will attend the queen's obsequies.' In fact Arbella's introduction was nothing like so immediate, or so unquestionably joyful. But it was dramatic enough in its way. Everything changed for Arbella in 1603.

She was, of course, not alone in the worrying sense of sands

shifting beneath her feet. Everything changed for the country, the
court, the ministers too; and, perhaps most of all, for James VI of
Scotland – now also James I of England – and his immediate
family. In fact, it is tempting to wonder how much of James's
kindness to his new-met cousin was down to sheer fellow-feeling.
In truth, at the English court they were both strangers in a strange
land, though Arbella came south from her extended pupillage,
and he from the barbarous country across the border. They had
both been waiting on the outcome of the same game, and if James
had won, then perhaps that too made him feel magnanimous
towards the loser. Quitting the Scottish capital with unflattering
haste, he surged south into the richer pastures of England on a
wave of universal good feeling – brief though the honeymoon
might prove to be.

Everyone went rushing up to meet him on the way; some seeking titles, some to promote their ideas. James, in waiting, had followed the time-honoured policy of promising all things to all
men; or at least tacitly suggesting he might be amenable to seeing
things their way – whatever that way might be. 'There is a foolish rhyme runs up and down in the court,' John Manningham
wrote,

of Sir Henry Bromley, Lord Thomas Howard, Lord Cobham and
Dr Neville, the Dean of Canterbury, that each had gone to move
the king for what they like –

*Neville for the Protestant*
*Lord Thomas for the papist*
*Bromley for the puritan*
*Lord Cobham for the atheist.*

Even little Anne Clifford wrote of galloping north with her
mother so fast they killed three horses under them with heat on
the road.

Setting out from Edinburgh on 5 April, James worked his way
slowly south through the north country and the English midlands,
receiving hospitality, and granting new honours, all the way. He
took time to think kindly of Arbella – spurred thereto, perhaps,

by a word from Gilbert and Mary Talbot, whose guest he was at Worksop near Sheffield on 20 April. However cautious a part the Talbots had played in Arbella's adventures while at Hardwick, they played a key role in her rehabilitation. She relied upon them in the months ahead – though her letters to them betray flashes of doubt and resentment underneath the surface humility. There was, after all, no-one else to whom she could turn. And they did their best for her, in their own way.

At Worksop the new king was entertained by 'excellent soul-ravishing music', and so much flesh, fish and fowl that Gilbert had to call in supplies from all the surrounding country. Surely the Talbots took the chance to plead for their niece. James loved, wherever possible, to see himself as merciful. Now he could afford to be magnanimous – desirous, as he put it, 'to free our cousin the Lady Arbella Stuart from that unpleasant life which she has led in the house of her grandmother with whose severity and age she, being a young lady, could hardly agree'.

Arbella had by this time been taken to Wrest Park in Bedfordshire, seat of the earl of Kent, whose nephew was married to Arbella's cousin Elizabeth, daughter of Gilbert and Mary Talbot. Kent was a neutral connection – neutral, at least, in the sense of having no direct hand in the Cavendish family controversies. But he was an ageing man and a hardline Protestant who had, as a commissioner at the trial and execution of Mary, queen of Scots, 'showed more zeal for her destruction than befitted a person of honour'. His home is hardly likely to have represented quite the freedom Arbella sought – Kent could so easily have transformed himself from host into severe gaoler. But with the affairs of the country in such flux, with the old regime overlapping the new, Arbella could hardly expect her own life to be anything other than awkward and uncertain still. Presumably she had recovered much of her health: a rapid change, perhaps, but if she had indeed been suffering from an attack of porphyria, just such a dramatic recovery would have been characteristic.

The queen's embalmed body still lay in Whitehall, where the privy council, the Venetians reported without visible surprise, still 'wait on her continuously with all the accustomed ceremonies down to the very table service as if she were still alive, and so will it continue according to ancient custom until the king gives order for her funeral.' Strange stories spread about the queen's last days: that one of her maids of honour had met the dying woman's spirit walking in the corridor; that two of her ladies found a card, the Queen of Hearts, fastened with a nail through the forehead to the seat of her chair. Three days after the death, most gruesomely of all, Lady Southwell described how the queen's body burst inside its coffin 'with such a crack that it splitted the wood, lead and cerecloth, so that today she was fain to be new trimmed up'.

Small wonder that James chose to linger outside the capital until after Elizabeth was finally buried in Westminster Abbey on 28 April. A thousand people followed the procession – the hearse topped by a life-sized wax effigy and followed by her riderless palfrey – through packed streets whose crowds gave up, said the chronicler John Stow, 'such a general crying, groaning and weeping as the like hath not been seen or known'. Little Anne Clifford wanted to be a pallbearer but was not sufficiently 'high'. By contrast Arbella, who as the queen's highest-ranking female relative was invited to be chief mourner and lead the black-hooded peeresses, refused:

> The Lady Arbella Stuart, being of the royal blood, was specially required to have honoured the funeral with her presence; which she refused, saying that since her access to the queen in her lifetime might not be permitted, she would not after her death be brought upon the stage for a public spectacle.

As last words go, it had a devastating finality.

The new king entered London on 7 May; and changes were felt immediately. The very next day, Sir Walter Ralegh was summoned before the council. James's secret allies in England (Cecil and Henry Howard, soon to be made earl of Northampton) had long been poisoning his mind against their potential rivals, the 'diabolical triplicity' of Ralegh, Lord Cobham and the earl of Northumberland, Henry Percy. Now Ralegh was told that his prized office of captain of the guard would be given instead to the Scotsman Sir Thomas Erskine (soon created Viscount Fenton) –

'whereunto Sir Walter in very humble manner submitted himself', ran the official privy council report, with what would prove to be mistaken confidence.

One of the new king's first acts was to release the earl of Southampton and Sir Henry Neville, who had been imprisoned since the Essex rebellion. There had been considerable concern lest James should wreak revenge on those who had promoted the execution of his mother; instead, it was noted with some curiosity, he seemed to take more to heart the death of the earl of Essex. The presses rolled out a belated publication of Essex's *Apologia*, his refutation of the *Conference*, that inflammatory document published eight years before, which had suggested succession did not have to follow proximity of blood. (James's own *Basilikon Doron*, in which he laid out his theories of kingship, had already become a bestseller, needless to say.)

Everyone who had rebelled against Elizabeth was suddenly in favour. Everything that could subtly denigrate the old regime was in vogue. The French ambassador (busy, wrote Scaramelli maliciously, trying to justify his alleged support for Arbella's and Beauchamp's claim on the grounds that he did only 'the duty of every good Catholic – namely, to protect and succour a lady') had attended Elizabeth's obsequies in a mourning cloak six yards long. Granted audience to meet the new king, he was disbelieving when told that his plan to deck all his followers in mourning would be greeted by James with the deepest disapprobation. 'No-one, be he ambassador, Englishman or stranger, is admitted into the king's presence in black; for indeed neither the memory or the name of Queen Elizabeth is nowadays mentioned in court.' Out with the old, in with the new . . . Perhaps it was an unattractive policy. But at least it meant that James could be brought to regard his fellow newcomer – his fellow victim of Elizabeth's procrastination – with a certain sympathy.

On 11 May a letter was sent from the new king to the earl of Kent at Wrest Park:

We have been informed by our cousin the countess of Shrewsbury [Mary] of the great desire which our cousin the Lady Arbella hath to [come] to our presence . . . We do well approve those desires of hers, and for that purpose are well pleased she do repair to our court at Greenwich in the company of her aunt, where we shall be willing to confer [with] her and make her know how well we wish her in regard to her nearness of blood.

When the two Stuart cousins met at Greenwich, Arbella would have seen a middle-aged man with a sparse beard cut square and shrewd, slightly mismatched eyes, his manner an odd mixture of the pontifical and the pawky, reflecting a personality in which arrogance jostled with insecurity. It is the grotesque descriptions of James which live in posterity – the slobbering tongue too large for his mouth; the ungainly weak-legged walk; the hands which he would never wash fiddling constantly around his codpiece. But it is only fair to say that those who saw him thus early in his English career – even those who wrote in secret and had no need to flatter – seem to have noticed no such peculiarities.

As for what James would have seen, when he clapped eyes on his cousin for the first time, the answer is probably a girl; attractive enough but unremarkable, a girl conspicuously nervous in her manner. A *girl*. And James, devoted to his male favourites, never rated the female sex very high. Treat your wife, he wrote in a manual of advice for his son, 'as your own flesh, command her as a lord, cherish her as your helper, rule her as your pupil . . . Ye are the head, she is your body; it is your office to command, and hers to obey.'

The Venetians, who faithfully documented Arbella's coming, made an odd report which accords ill with anything else we ever hear of her. 'Lady Arbella, who is a regular termagent [a virago, in another version] came to visit the king on Sunday last with a suite of ladies and gentlemen.' Perhaps their words can be discredited, since they added implausibly: 'and they say that should the Queen [Anna] die she would be wedded and crowned at once.' But Arbella may have been unusually edgy – have been, even, suffering from the last lingering remnants of her Hardwick illness. Another man, Lord Cobham, was shortly to say that 'when he saw' Arbella, he put aside the ideas he had had in a 'humour of discontentment' and resolved never to hazard his estate for her. And a Talbot retainer hinted at a tumultuous

King James I

pattern of speech, a lack of composure, which did not characterize her behaviour under normal circumstances.

Her future was still very unclear. That same May, while she was at court, Gilbert overheard James saying she should go back 'from wherein she came'. Ironically, it was Cecil (to whom James had every reason to be grateful) who asked the new king 'to deal tenderly' with his cousin. He suggested perceptively that 'she would not go thither nor to any other place as commanded thereunto, for so she might think that she were still under a kind of restraint . . . so it would redouble her grief and affliction of mind wherewith she had been too long already tormented.' Now that Arbella had spoken with the king, Cecil explained, 'if she had not given him satisfaction, she might conceive that she should never be able to give him satisfaction.' But if she were given liberty to choose her place of abode, as she herself had once begged, she could be convinced to choose one convenient to his new Majesty.

James was persuaded to leave Arbella 'to the charge of her own good discretion, assuring himself that she would do nothing of moment whatsoever without his privity and good allowance'. And so from Wrest Park, Arbella moved to Sheen, to the home of Queen Elizabeth's old friend the Swedish-born marchioness of Northampton, the peeress who had taken Arbella's own place as chief mourner at the royal funeral.

Did Arbella resent being passed around like an awkward parcel? Or were events moving almost too quickly? Hers was a nature in which shocks went deep, and she must have been still in recovery from her Hardwick troubles. (If she were actually in recovery from an attack of porphyria, it would certainly account for the 'termagent' of the Venetians' description.) But in any case there were practical reasons for a delay. With Anna still in Scotland, the distaff side of the new royal court had not yet been assembled. Nor had it been arranged how the newly independent Arbella was to support herself in this expensive environment. After the drama and introspection of her letters from Hardwick, the first letters she wrote in her new life are all to do with money.

Arbella's pension had ceased with Queen Elizabeth's death; and presumably she could no longer count on Bess's support. So, on

14 June, from Sheen, she is begging Cecil 'to remember the king's Majesty of my maintenance', as he had promised her uncle Gilbert he would do. By the twenty-second she had obviously had only an unsatisfactory answer and was reduced (since the king seemed to have shifted his mind over a yearly pension) to begging at least for 'some sum of money which needeth not be annual' with which to settle her present debts. The very day after, the twenty-third, she wrote again to her 'honourable good friend Cecil', imploring his help both 'in procuring it as soon, and making the sum as great as may be'.

Cecil, clearly, was no longer the enemy in her mind. But perhaps it was the fear of another flood of letters, the like of which he had suffered earlier in the year, which ensured that Cecil immediately after this did at last extract an interim gift from James. Arbella had written: 'If I should name two thousand pounds for my present occasions it would not exceed my necessity.' She got six hundred and sixty six – but for the moment it would do. Hearing the happy news, she sat down on the twenty-sixth and penned a short note of thanks to Cecil, 'whose important affairs I am constrained to interrupt with this necessary importunity'. On the thirtieth she wrote yet again, to say that she had at last received the funds, 'for which I acknowledge myself greatly bounded to your lordship'. (Cecil had been ennobled by a grateful James.) She had signed the last four letters as 'Your lordship's poor friend' – probably a reminder of her literal poverty. Now, at last, with greater confidence, she signed as his lordship's 'assured' friend.

In July, with Queen Anna arrived in England and the coronation imminent, Arbella at last joined the court. But this was not the settled and stately establishment of Elizabeth's day. Not only were English courtiers jockeying for position with the Scots who had come south in James's train, but it would be winter before the new royal family moved into the London palaces. Perhaps in a perverse way the enforced disruption helped the heterogeneous new court to settle down together. But the reason was terrible. In the capital, the people were dying like flies. The plague, an endemic hazard in London in the summer, had struck with unusual ferocity.

The coronation of King James and Queen Anna

James's very coronation was cut short – 'all parts of that solemnity which are not essential to it are forborne' – and precise limits were set on the numbers of servants officers and noblemen might bring in their train. On 25 July, a rainy St James's Day, king and queen were crowned without the customary feast. The Venetian envoy reported that land access to Westminster Abbey was barred by armed guards and boats forbidden on pain of death to bring visitors from the City. The royal couple came by barge from the Tower, where the monarch traditionally spent the night before the coronation, and the ceremony was performed 'after the ancient manner'. The Garter King of Arms proclaimed James in each of the four quarters of the church, demanding whether the people would have King James their king; the people assented 'with applause, shouting and throwing up their hats'. After a sermon upon the theme that the powers that are, are ordained of God, the king was anointed through specially made gaps in his undergarments; decked in the crown and robes of Edward the Confessor; and installed on the Throne Royal to receive the homage of the peers. When the queen in turn had been anointed and crowned, the party had left for Hampton Court that very night, before setting out on a progress of the southern counties.

Arbella can safely be presumed to have been at the coronation, dressed like the rest in crimson velvet. There is no specific record of her presence, but her absence would certainly have occasioned remark. And she was with the court when they moved on to the medieval bishop's palace at Farnham in Surrey. She was placed, as Scaramelli put it from there on 20 August, near the king and queen as a princess of the blood royal: 'in her appointments, table and rank she takes precedence of all the other ladies at court. She has already begun to bear her Majesty's train when she goes to chapel.' It was a place of honour, albeit one that must have reminded Arbella of what she had missed: the chance to be the one whose train was borne so carefully. Scaramelli himself pointed out that there was a certain mystery in the situation, and that many rumours were occasioned by the fact that Arbella, official appearances apart, 'is living very retired'. Perhaps she was not finding her new life easy.

For the first time in her life, at the age of twenty-seven, she was free – or bereft – of the tutelage of her family. Gilbert and Mary had sponsored her introduction at court, had done their best to ease her path, but now she was on her own. Her uncle was being sent back to an official post in the midlands, on a route which 'though it bend directly northward will not hinder you from thinking or looking to the south', as Arbella wrote to him on 14 August. For the next few years of her life, Arbella's correspondence with these two close kin offers our best source of information on her progress, until Mary Talbot comes to take a yet more direct part in her story.

Arbella's relatives were leaving her 'to take my fortune in an unknown climate, without either art or instruction but what I have from you'. Though, she wrote, 'I be very frail', yet her aunt and uncle would see in her the good effect of their prayers, 'to your great glory for reforming my untowardly resolutions and mirth'. She signed the letter 'Your disciple', mischievously. But, in all seriousness, she was indeed setting sail on an uncharted sea.

# 'Much spoken of'

THEY WERE STORMY WATERS THAT ARBELLA HAD TO NAVIGATE; AND almost simultaneously with her arrival at court had come a wave that could have swamped her completely. In the first fortnight of July the ever-vigilant Cecil – anxious to place his mark irrevocably on the new regime – unearthed two linked conspiracies against the new king. The lesser, the so-called 'Bye' Plot, the work of the Protestant George Brooke and the Catholic Griffin Markham, aimed to kidnap James and force him to extend a promise of greater religious toleration all around. Markham was an old neighbour of Hardwick days, a friend of Arbella's family. (His brother would enter Arbella's service, and be her first companion on that disguised escape abroad.) But she was not directly concerned in his plan.

The second plot, the 'Main' Plot, was more serious. A handful of conspirators – who included two Catholic priests, Lord Cobham (Brooke's brother, and Bess of Hardwick's godson), Lord Grey and, most notably, Sir Walter Ralegh – allegedly planned to kill James and his son Henry and, with Spanish assistance, to place Arbella on the throne.

Cobham was 'a most silly lord, but one degree from a fool'; and Ralegh's involvement is ambiguous. He later claimed with some plausibility that in discussing where a Spanish army might land, he hoped only to draw the plotters on. But Ralegh was visibly a fish out of water in the new regime. He had steered an erratic path through the politics of the 1590s, his bitter rivalry with Essex forcing him into Cecil's party. But now that enmity with Essex – 'my martyr', as James had taken to calling the earl – stood him in bad stead; even Cecil had found it politic to forget his quarrels with Essex and dwell instead on 'the mutual affections of our tender years'.

What is more, an adventurer like Ralegh was never a natural colleague for Cecil, and in the last years of the old queen's reign his had been one of the names blackened in the letters sent by Cecil and by Northampton to the Scottish king. Ralegh had greeted James with pamphlets promoting a war with Spain, had even offered to finance an attack out of his own purse; clearly he stood in the way of Cecil's long-sought peace with that country. There were certainly reasons why it was politic for Cecil to discredit Ralegh. No-one asked too loud or too insistently whether his lifelong hostility to Spain did not make his participation in the Main Plot unlikely.

Arbella's name, early in her new career, was thus once again dubious currency. 'Most of the conspirators belong to her faction,' the Venetians reported, adding that she was 'reputed a Catholic' – though once again there are enough details wrong to cast doubts on their accuracy. Cobham – so the evidence at his trial revealed – had sent to Arbella a deeply compromising letter. He suggested that she should write to Philip III of Spain, promising toleration for Catholics, the cessation of help to the Protestant Dutch and her agreement never to marry without his consent. She was also to write to those Spanish satellites, the archdukes of Austria (governors in the Netherlands) and the duke of Savoy. This document Arbella immediately turned over to the authorities. From the isolated heights of Hardwick it might have seemed possible to imagine herself queen. Now she was out alone in the wider world, she clearly saw things differently. But the bald facts of Arbella's role come too glib and easy. They need more illumination. There is here a sense of hidden wheels turning; of deals that we cannot see.

Later in her court career, Arbella would write to Gilbert of a miracle she saw: 'a pair of virginals make good music without help of any hand but of one that did nothing but warm (not move) a glass some five or six foot from them.' We do not know any details of this pseudo-scientific party piece, though it seems to have been a regular sight of the town: 'A dancing bear, a giant's bone/A foolish engine move alone.' But the image had a clear applicability. 'If I thought thus great folks invisibly and far off work in matters to tune them as they please, I pray your lordship forgive me . . .'

But the dozen epistles she sent to her aunt and uncle through the second half of 1603 make little direct mention of the treason. Instead, Arbella wrote about the other side of her new life; the all-important trivialities. She wrote of her upkeep – not the long-delayed pension this time, but the lesser, still useful, matter of a 'diet': a number of dishes which would be provided from the king's table to feed Arbella and her own retainers. She suspected that the king – who after all had made 'protestations of extra-ordinary affection' to a cousin still too inexperienced to doubt them – was having his kindly intentions diverted by 'evil counsel'. She wrote of new customs and manners that seemed to her bizarre. From isolated Hardwick, she had been pitchforked into a world where the normal preoccupations – somewhat in abeyance, during this extended progress – were gallants and games, 'embroiderers, jewellers, tire-women, sempsters, feathermen, perfumers'; a world where, in Ben Jonson's words, a lady might kiss a page, be a stateswoman, censure poets; 'answer in religion to one, in state to another, in bawdry to a third'. The change must have been extraordinary.

On the one hand, she could not resist bragging in a brief note north – so brief, because there is 'some company come to fetch me' to the royal presence – that 'I am as diligently expected, and as soon missed as they that perform the most acceptable service.' The lonely girl was enjoying the pleasures of company, although she clung to some of her old ways. 'Because I must return at an appointed time to go to my book,' she wrote, 'I must make the more haste thither.' On another occasion she was less enthusiastic, grumbling about the toothache, and of 'this everlasting hunting' – James's passion. Arbella did not exactly complain – how could she? – of her 'never intermitted attendance on the queen who daily extendeth her favours more and more towards me'. But her tone was weary.

Throughout that late summer and into the autumn the court, and Arbella with it, was travelling around the southern counties – Farnham, Basing, Fulston. As Cecil grumbled in a letter to Gilbert, the plague 'drives us up and down so round as I think we shall come to York'. Woodstock drew particular disfavour – a small and outmoded old palace whose excellent hunting recommended it to James, but which, Cecil complained to Gilbert, was unsavoury ('for there is no savour but of cows and pigs') and uneaseful, in that none of the English counsellors could so much as get a room. It was a rag-tailed procession that crammed into buildings too small for them, clad 'in ruinous suite of apparel' since no-one dared order new garments for fear infection would come with the cloth.

In London, the plague's death toll, counting 'the out parishes', reached 1,396 in the fourth week of July alone; then 1,922 the week after. (The overall population was something like 200,000.) Among their friends and relations, it was said, people were finding it quicker to number the living than the dead. The city, wrote Thomas Dekker, had become 'a vast silent charnel house', whose music was 'the loud groans of raving sick men; the struggling pang of souls departing; in each house grief striking up an alarum.' Stray dogs in the streets, believed to carry the infection, were rounded up and killed – more than five hundred of them in Westminster alone. The annual Bartholomew Fair was cancelled, and it was reported that 'a coach passed through London strangely and wonderfully dressed, for it was all hung with rue from the top to the toe of the boot to keep the very leather and nails from the infection, even the very nostrils of the horses being stopped with the herb grace.' Such were the only preventatives.

Outside the city, the royal party moved ever onwards, and the disease with them. 'The queen goes from hence tomorrow,' Arbella wrote from Woodstock. But 'The plague follows the court,' the Venetian envoy reported. 'Two of the Queen's household are dead. People are well and merry and dead and buried the same day.' On 18 September the queen's court arrived at Winchester, followed two days later by the king's. Sure enough, the plague came with them, but the city took strict – and fairly effective – precautions. So did the crown; by the end of September, the Venetian added that all who did not have urgent business were sent away from court, nor could anyone enter there without a signed ticket to prove they had not come from an infected area.

Winchester was where the trial of the conspirators would take place, but still Arbella makes no mention of it. It is as if two worlds exist side by side – the one open for discussion, the other impossible to mention. Her relatives seem to have spoken forcefully to her on the subject of discretion, and she was trying, though concealment never came naturally. In one letter she wrote to Gilbert, on 16 September, she curtailed a story of a Dutch visitor – of how the royal party had made 'merry at the Dutchkin' – lest her uncle should 'complain of me for telling tales out of the queen's coach'.

In the separate letter she wrote to Mary on the same day, the echoes of danger and reproof sound even more clearly. The last letter from her aunt had obviously warned Arbella to write more cautiously. 'I . . . interpret your postscript to be a caveat to me to write no more than how I do, and my desire to understand of your health.' She had been making some incautious remarks about the moralities of the new court. Perhaps even that could prove dangerous if her letter were intercepted; little would be forgiven in the woman the conspirators had intended should replace James on the throne.

The interception of letters was a serious concern. Over the next months we get to know the named and trusted messengers: old family allies and servants, preferred as couriers to the king's mails. There was repeated fear lest some letter should prove to have gone astray: at one point, Arbella offers to number hers for security, and a relative, Lord Pembroke, writes of 'the danger of mis-superscribing letters'. The post in the early seventeenth century, a regular subscription courier service, was not one to be trusted with any dangerous matter, since it was primarily a government convenience and anything it carried might be subject to scrutiny. 'I beseech you let us know if you received [the letters] safe,' wrote Arbella, at last awake to the risk: 'if I had thought they would have been sent by post I would have written more reservedly.'

As the date of the treason trials, set for November, got closer, Arbella's letters became shorter and more tense. One can sense the constraints of writing in such circumstances; how much she longed to pour out her heart through a secure channel but, missing such, could only yield to Mary's requests to write often, be it never so briefly. On 4 November she was waiting for her aunt's 'long expected trusty messenger', and that expectation 'shall keep me from troubling you with so plain and tedious a discourse as I could find in my heart to disburden my mind withall'.

Given how hard it was to get news, it is easy to imagine how the distant Talbots must have worried that Arbella would suddenly be implicated more seriously in this latest scandal – especially when the interrogations threw up the name of her uncle Henry Cavendish, who was summoned south for questioning. Arbella, in this state of tension, complained repeatedly of her health. On 27 October 'my bad eyes crave truce', and prevented her from writing longer; on 6 November, with the trials about to begin, 'my eyes are extremely swollen' again.

The trials took place at the bishop's palace, the prisoners being brought to Winchester from the Tower for the occasion. Above the ancient room, in symbolic authority, hung the great simulacrum of King Arthur's Round Table; Arthur, from whom the Tudors had claimed ancestry. But Arbella's interest must have been focused on one particular: how would her name come up in the debate? On the first days came the lesser-ranking figures; the priests, Markham, Brooke and their associates. On 17 November came the trial of Sir Walter Ralegh. Most of the court ladies were there, and in a 'standing' [gallery], seated beside the lord admiral, the earl of Nottingham, there was of course Arbella – who, as Sir Dudley Carleton pointedly remarked, 'heard herself much spoken of these days'.

A state trial in the seventeenth century was less an assessment of innocence than a public demonstration of guilt (which had already been decided in examination by the privy council). The accused was allowed no lawyer, and only the most restrictive opportunities to plead in his own defence, while the rhetoric of the official prosecutors could pound home the state's authority. The attorney-general, Sir Edward Coke, invoked Arbella's name in his first attack on Ralegh: 'I think you meant to make Arbella a titular queen, of whose title I will speak nothing: but sure you meant to make her a stale [dupe]. Ah! Good lady, you could mean her no good.' So far, so reassuring.

But the charismatic, arrogant Ralegh spoke brilliantly on his own behalf. 'My innocency is my own defence,' he said. Once, Ralegh had given damning evidence at Essex's trial. 'What booteth it to swear the fox?' the earl had sneered, proud of his own aristocratic disdain for dissimulation. Now it was Ralegh's turn to stand accused. But Sir Walter, the 'most hated man in England', rebutted the points against him with such clarity that one spectator declared that while before he would have gone a hundred miles to see him hanged, afterwards he would have gone a thousand to save his life.

Thrown on the defensive and casting around for someone to blame, the prosecutor Coke came perilously close to accusing Arbella – a softer target than the aggressive Ralegh. It was, ironically, Cecil himself who stood up to halt Coke, his nephew by marriage and his protégé:

Here hath been a touch of the Lady Arbella Stuart, the king's near kinswoman. Let us not scandal the innocent by confusion of speech. She is innocent of all these things as I, or any man here: only she received a letter from my Lord Cobham to prepare her, which she laughed at and immediately sent to the king. So far was she from discontentment that she laughed him to scorn.

From his seat beside Arbella, the earl of Nottingham stood up. 'The lady doth here protest upon her salvation that she never dealt in any of these things, and so she willed me to tell the court.' Even Ralegh added his unflattering mite. Arbella was, he said – forgetting or more gallantly ignoring that early encounter at Elizabeth's court – a lady of whom he knew little, and that little he never liked. In this practice, 'I never heard so much as the name of Arbella Stuart,' he said, rather oddly, 'but only the name Arbella.' 'I had been a slave, a villain, a fool, if I had endeavoured to set up Arbella, and refused so gracious a lord and sovereign [James].' Like the rest of the conspirators, Ralegh was sentenced to be hung, drawn and quartered – but Arbella walked from the court free.

And yet there was a sting in the tail of the proceedings, when she came to consider them afterwards. Serjeant Hale, opening the case for the prosecution, had said: 'As for the Lady Arbella she, upon my conscience, hath no more title to the crown than I have.' He gave a little pause – as if he had missed the expected titter – before adding that he for his own part did disclaim and renounce any such rights. He was proclaiming official belief in her innocence, but an innocence grounded in her irrelevance; suggesting she cannot have been trying for the crown because she had no plausible title to it, no more than a mere lawyer, a Serjeant Hale. Ralegh, indeed, had picked up the theme. 'What pawn had we to give the king of Spain?' he asked. 'What did we offer him? Or how could we invent to offer him the letter of an Arbella, whom he could not choose but know to be of no following; what a mockery is this!' But, as with so many of the events of 1603, perhaps the Main Plot needs to be considered more carefully.

Cobham was tried the day after Ralegh and, wrote Dudley Carleton: 'For anything that belonged to the Lady Arbella, he denied the whole accusation, only said she had sought his friendship and his brother Brooke had sought hers.' Cobham, who 'discredited the place to which he was called; never was seen so poor and abject a spirit', may not be the most convincing witness. Yet to discount his speech leaves a number of anomalies.

If, as is usually reported, Arbella passed on Cobham's letter unopened, how did she know the matter was treasonous? The Venetians stated flatly that she presented the letter to the king 'without even having broken the seal' (*sigillata senza haverla ne anco aperta*; a phrase which, if anything, could be translated yet more forcefully). It was this act of loyalty, they said, which 'has saved her life'. Perhaps they simply got it wrong; the usual report is only that Arbella did not 'entertain' the letter, which hardly precludes her having given its contents at least one horrified glance. But still there are discrepancies. The Venetians, in the late autumn, mentioned it as having been delivered 'this last August', by which time Cobham was already in prison and she would certainly have regarded dubiously any communication from him . . .

But why, at that time, would he have sent it? It was far too late in the day.

A document discovered only in the 1990s casts a new light on the mystery, and gives a far stronger suggestion of Arbella's complicity in the plot. 'The most comprehensive manuscript of its kind relating to the Main Treason' is how it was described by Mark Nicholls, who explored the document in a 1995 essay. It lays out the evidence, gained from the interrogations of the summer, that the government planned to use against Ralegh and Cobham, and Arbella's name appears repeatedly.

'19 July B: First, Brooke confesseth that Cobham wrote to Arbella and received answers and sent him to Arbella to persuade her to write severally to the king of Spain, the infanta, and the duke of Savoy.' The 'received answers' is crucial, obviously. And again, from another confession Cobham made on 13 August:

> Being asked what was the cause that moved him to have [conference] with Arbella, answereth, that Frances Kirton [noted by Nicholls as being Cobham's kinswoman, in service with Arbella] told him that Arbella was desirous to know why his lordship's brother was so busy to have intelligence with her, Cobham answered he knew not. Kirton replied that the lady was desirous to be acquainted with him and *to be advised by him*, pressing him earnestly to write to the lady . . .

And again: '17 July, D, F, G: Cobham confesseth he received and wrote letters to Arbella, but burnt the same.'

It's hard to see why Cobham should invent such letters. Indeed, since the letters were burnt, it's hard to see why he should mention such damning evidence at all – unless by now, a month into the interrogations, he was scared to the point where he was speaking the truth involuntarily.

Yet little of this came out in court (at least, not so far as we can judge, from evidence that is sometimes scanty). In the interval between August and November there appears instead to have emerged this famous unopened letter; the letter Arbella handed over to the crown, so very virtuously. She was declared ignorant, in the official story. 'For the Lady Arbella, the archduke and the king of Spain, they were merely ignorant of any such thing,' as Cecil wrote flatly to Sir Thomas Parry on 1 December.

Had she been, once again, conspiring for the crown? Once the plot was uncovered, did she agree to save her neck by providing documentary evidence for the government? It would explain why she escaped so lightly, when her recent offences, and those ahead, were treated so seriously.

It is true that everyone, thus early in the new reign, had an interest in not rocking the boat by allowing things to end too bloodily. 'The king's glory consists as much in freeing the innocent as condemning the guilty', Cecil proclaimed – or so Carleton reported to Chamberlain. The privy council put in a plea that the conspirators should be treated with mercy. But even had Arbella been completely innocent of the Main Plot, it is still worth remembering that Jane Grey had gone to the block for a plot to place her on the throne, although it had been none of her inventing. Elizabeth, too, had gone to the Tower for Wyatt's rebellion. Arbella, by contrast, got off scot free (unless, perhaps, you count a presumed black mark against her name, of the kind James did not forget easily). If Arbella were to any degree 'on the strength', it would certainly account for Cecil's support. As Arbella wrote to Mary later:

> I humbly thank you for your thanks to my Lord Cecil for me. I am a witness not only of the rare gift of speech which God hath given him, but of his excellent judgement in choosing most plausible and honourable themes, [such] as the defending of a wronged lady, the clearing of an innocent knight, etc

The 'knight', whom the investigation early exonerated, was the trouble-prone uncle Henry.

Whatever Arbella's involvement in the case, the following weeks saw her suffering from an understandable reaction. As the Venetians put it, Arbella, 'although now proved innocent, and held in much honour by the queen, is, by reason of these grave events, kept in a state of constant perturbation of mind'. On 28 November her letter to her uncle was only a few lines long, due to the 'extreme pain of my head'. The few lines to her aunt thanked Mary for the pills and hartshorn; she meant to sweat that day for her 'extreme cold'. Mary had obviously been worrying about Arbella's part in the affair. But her niece's next letter was quick to reassure her. 'When any great matter comes in question rest secure I beseech you that I am not interested in it as an actor, howsoever the vanity of wicked men's vain designs have made my name pass through a gross and subtle lawyer's lips of late.'

On the day after she wrote from Fulston outside Winchester, the two Catholic priests involved in the plot were executed in the city itself, with all brutality. Sometimes, when a prisoner was to be hung, drawn and quartered, a compassionate executioner would let the victim swing until he was beyond pain before he was disembowelled. Not this time: Clarke and Watson were 'very bloodily handled' by the executioner; Clarke both strove to help himself and spoke after he was cut down. On 5 December Brooke, too, was executed, though the sentence was commuted to beheading, as was usual for the aristocracy.

The executions did not cast a gloom over the court. The king's players were sent for; preparations for the seasonal festivities began, and on 8 December Arbella was recovered enough to write more lengthily to both aunt and uncle. Her letter to Gilbert has rather a rambling feel, with its allusions to the martyrdom of St Ursula with her thousand virgin handmaidens, and to the biblical prophecy that the rich man shall hardly enter into the kingdom of heaven. Such verbal oddities cannot but raise the spectre of her Hardwick days. But in this letter, Arbella recovered herself quickly and moved on to serious business: gifts, patronage and bribery.

Arbella added one last note on the conspiracy as the court moved at last to London (or at least, to Hampton Court, which James, the country-lover who called London a filthy town, tried to use as his urban base). 'I have reserved the best news for the last,' she wrote at the end of a long letter, 'and that is the king's pardon of life to the not-executed traitors. I dare not begin to tell of the royal and wise manner of the king's proceeding therein, lest I should find no end of extolling him for it till I had written out a pair of bad eyes.'

After the two priests and Brooke had died, the remaining conspirators, Ralegh apart, had, a few days later, been told to prepare themselves for death. They had said goodbye to their family and friends, been led to the very scaffold – and then (just at the moment, surely, when they finally cast the world away), taken back indoors on some pretext for an hour's delay. They were then each in turn brought back to the scaffold, and informed they were granted a reprieve. It is fortunate that Arbella described this 'royal and wise' manner of proceeding in such strong terms – terms no spy would dare to take for irony. Otherwise, one might call the manner in which the wretched men were treated the last refinement of cruelty.

# 'A confusion of imbassages'

THE LETTERS ARBELLA WROTE DURING HER FIRST MONTHS AT COURT may have omitted some important matters, but they give a wonderful taste of what her new life was to be: crowded, colourful and competitive. If anything, the first Christmas and New Year of the new reign were more packed than usual with official celebrations. Because of the extended peregrinations outside the capital, several of the ambassadors extraordinary sent to greet the new king had not yet had their official welcome, but were already in haste to depart.

It was, as Arbella wrote to Gilbert, a 'confusion of imbassages' (embassies). Spanish, French and Florentine; a knight from the Pope; a chalice from the Turk; two envoys from the Venetians; the duke of Savoy's envoy daily expected; and one poor unfortunate from Polonia (Poland) 'fain would . . . be gone again because of the freezing of their sea'. In the autumn, Arbella had told how the Spanish ambassador, Juan de Taxis, count of Villamediana, had brought 'great store of Spanish gloves, hawks' hoods, leather for jerkins and moreover a perfumer. These delicacies he bestows among our ladies and lords, I will not say with a hope to effeminate one sex but certainly with a hope to grow gracious with the other.' Now, at the New Year, gifts figured largely, in an exchange that was ritualized to an extraordinary degree. The earl of Huntingdon, handing over his gift of a purse (cash, neatly wrapped) on New Year's Day 1605,

was required to put his gift to the king of £20 in gold coins into a
purse worth about 5 shillings, and deliver it to the Lord
Chamberlain at 8am. Later in the day, he would be summoned to
the Jewel House for a ticket to receive 18 shillings and sixpence as
a gift for his pains, and to give sixpence there to the man in the box
for his ticket; he should then go to Sir William Veal's office, show
the clerk that ticket, and receive the 18 shillings and sixpence.
Then he must go back to the Jewel House again, to choose a piece
of plate of 30 ounces in weight, mark it, and in the afternoon he
can go and collect it . . .

Presents to lesser persons did not have to be cash-coded so carefully. Arbella prepared 'a trifle' to give to Cecil, in return for
which she received 'a fair pair of bracelets'. She had asked
another lady for advice on the gift both she and her aunt Mary
had to make to Queen Anna, and was told that 'the queen
regarded not the value but the device.' Arbella's adviser

neither liked gown nor petticoat so well as some little bunch of
rubies to hang in her ear, or some such daft toy. I mean to give her
Majesty 2 pair of silk stocking lined with plush and 2 pair of
gloves lined if London afford me not some daft toy I like better . . .
I am making the king a purse. And for all the world else I am
unprovided. This time will manifest my poverty more than all the
rest of the year, but why should I be ashamed of it when it is
others' fault and not mine? My quarter's allowance will not defray
this one charge I believe.

At least she was getting to grips with how it all worked. Arbella
had been promoting the Talbots' interests to the queen, and had
succeeded in obtaining for them two patents, for which a
reciprocal gift had to be given. (The whole arcane web of patents,
'imposts' and monopolies essentially gave a courtier the right to
skim a layer of profit off a stated industry, in the shape, often, of
an extra layer of taxation. Arbella herself would later petition for
the impost on oats; these rights, while bitterly resented by the
common people, were a major means of support for the high-
spending aristocracy.) The Talbots' thanks for these examples

'will come very unseasonably so near Newyearstide, especially those with which you send any gratuity,' she wrote to Mary. Rather than lose the thank-you in a large seasonal gift, better to get out of the way the compulsory New Year's gift, and then send thanks and another gift separately; blame her, Arbella, for the delay . . . She could be practical enough when she wanted to be.

Her pension had come through, but it was still proving woefully inadequate. The problems of showing sufficient seasonal open-handedness were eased when she received from Gilbert 'a large essay [sample] of your lordship's good cheer at Sheffield' – perhaps the much-prized 'red deer pies' which were to feature regularly in their correspondence. 'Your venison shall be most welcome to Hampton and right merrily eaten,' was a message she wrote to him regularly. (In return she would send cheese, or 'the sharpest salad that ever I ate . . . If you have of it in the country I pray you let me know, that I may laugh at myself for being so busy to get this.') But the court needed a lot of feeding. 'The king will feast all the ambassadors this Christmas,' Arbella wrote to Gilbert. 'It is said there shall be 30 plays.'

The King's Men performed several of them, probably including Ben Jonson's *Sejanus*, and it is likely Arbella here saw Shakespeare act. The *Robin Goodfellow* 'played before the prince [Henry]' may have been a version of *A Midsummer Night's Dream*. But there was a form of celebration that concerned courtiers more directly, one which was to become identified with the reign. As Arbella wrote to Gilbert:

> The queen intendeth to make a masque this Christmas, to which end my lady of Suffolk and my lady Walsingham have warrants to take of the late queen's best apparel out of the Tower at their discretion. Certain noblemen (whom I may not yet name to you because some of them have made me of their counsel) intend another. Certain gentlemen of good sort another.

There was indeed the expected masque of noblemen, led and arranged by Arbella's kinsman the duke of Lennox. But his masque of orient knights – supposedly come all the way from China and India to pay homage to the new King James – was not to be the chief attraction of the season. That position was reserved for the first masque presented by Queen Anna: the *Vision of the Twelve Goddesses* by the poet Samuel Daniel, in which – a major innovation – the queen herself was to appear as Pallas Athene. In the third stage of the masque, as was customary, each masquer invited an honoured spectator to the dance. None of James's Scottish lords was numbered in that first dozen, save alone the duke of Lennox. Anna had made a very clear statement: her favour was a prize to be won separately from that of her husband. As part of Anna's court, Arbella – besides being placed in the way of Catholic worship – was being drawn into a dissenting society; the French ambassador noted with horror that Anna went to the theatre when a satire was on 'in order to enjoy a laugh against her husband'. (A few years later the Venetian envoy would be explaining how, the king having withheld one of the prized invitations to a masque, Anna invited him to come incognito, while Arbella offered to host his train.)

The masque was an art form Anna was to make her own: superb, lavish and immensely costly spectacles built around a moral designed to hammer home the importance of the monarchy. Ambassadors clamoured for a seat in the audience, since the scale of the scenery meant that places in Hampton's great hall were limited. The Spaniard and the Pole bore off the prized invitations, though Dudley Carleton reported that the French ambassador made 'unmannerly expostulations with the king and for a few days troubled all the court'.

Given the significance of the masque, we have to ask why – this time at least – Arbella was not included as a dancer; nor named, indeed, as a partner of any of the orient knights. Absence may be the reason – the toothache, or her still-troublesome eyes? It is even possible that she simply couldn't pay for her costume. But one wonders if – in the structure Anna had framed – she was not also rather difficult to place. A lady of the very highest rank by birth, but one who was yet unmarried (and one, moreover, from whom that politically significant invitation to the dance might seem to be a shade *too* significant?). All through her life at court – as throughout her life before it – this confusion about Arbella's status was to dog her path.

Some rights could not be denied her. On 15 March she rode right behind the queen, 'in a richly furnished carriage . . . with certain maids of honour in attendance', backed by seventy splendid ladies on horseback, when the royal family made their triumphal progress through London, the ceremony postponed from the previous year because of the plague.

> First came the messengers of the chamber and the gentleman harbingers, the sergeant porters; the gentlemen and esquires, who were servants of the prince, the queen and the king; the clerks of the signet and privy seal, the privy council, the parliament and the council; the chaplains; the aldermen of London; the prince's counsel at law; the queen's counsel at law; the king's advocate and remembrancer, the attorney and solicitor; Sir Francis Bacon, the king's counsel at law; the sergeants at law; the masters of the chancellery, the secretaries of the Latin and French tongues, the sewers, carvers, cup-bearers; the masters of the tents, revels, armoury, ordnance . . .

. . . and many more. The cheering crowds who lined the streets – the three hundred children of Christ's Hospital, clustered on a specially built scaffold – must have waited all day for them to pass. The conduit of Fleet Street ran with claret. Seven great gates were erected to make formal stopping points for music and oration on the six-hour route from the Tower of London through the City to Westminster; one, near the Poultry, sounded Danish music to delight Queen Anna.

Anna has gone down in history as an incorrigibly vain and frivolous woman – a political nonentity – and Arbella's own comments have had something to do with this. But it is far from the whole truth. The new queen, rather improbably, had become Arbella's best ally. Indeed, the two women had something in common; enough to make them, when first they met, form a defensive alliance.

Like Arbella, Anna arrived at the English court fresh from something of an emotional crisis. The Danish princess had never become resigned to the Scottish custom whereby the heir to the throne was removed from his parents' orbit to be brought up

One of the seven triumphal arches erected
for James's entry into London in 1604

wholly by another noble. When James rode south, leaving her to follow, she used the interval to make an armed attempt to seize her son Prince Henry. Thwarted, at a time when she was four months pregnant, she violently 'beat her belly', and suffered a miscarriage. (In one of their previous quarrels, her husband had hurled at her the charge of insanity.) Like Arbella, Anna had a pride in her own royal lineage, which her husband was at pains to dismiss: 'king's daughter or cook's daughter, you must be alike to me being once my wife,' he had written to her in the midst of the battle for Prince Henry. Like Arbella, she was in her late twenties, twenty-nine to Arbella's twenty-seven. And the new queen, noted Anne Clifford, selected for her favour only such younger women, not the established elderly ladies the privy council had sent northwards to meet her.

Throughout her years in Scotland, report after report had mentioned Anna's political influence. 'The queen, as ever, knows all,' one envoy would write, after detailing a piece of intrigue. The queen, wrote the French king's ambassador extraordinary, 'was naturally bold and enterprising; she loved pomp and grandeur, tumult and intrigue. She was deeply engaged in all the civil factions, not only in Scotland, and in relation to the Catholics, whom she supported and even first encouraged, but also in England.' Anna had herself converted to Catholicism a couple of years before her arrival in England; a move accepted complacently enough by her husband, as long as she was discreet. He had even found it rather useful; a tantalizing carrot (would Anna convert him also?) with which to keep Catholic opinion supportive of his claim.

But in England, Anna found herself cut off from more active political engagement. When James headed south with certain of his nobles, they were those of his own faction; he left those of the queen's party behind. Anna arrived in England isolated – a woman disenfranchised. She had the popular knack, as Arbella wrote approvingly:

> if ever there were such a virtue as courtesy at the court I marvel
> what is become of it, for I protest I see little or none of it but in the
> queen, who ever since her coming into Newbury has spoken to

the people as she passeth and receiveth their prayers with thanks and thankful countenance.

The queen even showed herself about 'barefaced' – i.e. without the protective travelling mask ladies usually wore – to the 'great contentment' of the people. James, by contrast, was soon beginning to show his distaste for the carefully orchestrated accessibility by which Elizabeth had endeared herself to the populace. Told that his people loved to see the king's face, he replied impatiently: 'God's wounds, I will pull down my breeches and they shall also see my arse.'

To the end of Anna's life, her graceless husband would make a parade of submitting his choice of male favourites for her approval. It was a unique, an 'only James' solution to the problem of juggling bisexual urges and domestic harmony. But there were strongly marked limits to Anna's sphere, and probably Arbella did not well understand the compromises Anna was forced to make – any more than she enjoyed the solaces Anna found.

For a long time the queen remained a protector to Arbella, who in turn was believed to have some influence over her. But the two were never going to be a natural match on a day-to-day basis; nor were the daily pursuits of Anna's court congenial. Arbella's words have become the indictment of Anna, when she wrote to Gilbert wearily that:

> there were certain child's plays remembered by the fairs ladies. Viz. I pray my lord give me a course in your park. Rise pig and go. One penny follow me, etc., and when I came to court they were as highly in request as ever cracking of nuts was. So I was by the mistress of the revels compelled to play at I knew not what (for till that day I never heard of a play called Fier) but even persuaded by the princely example I saw to play the child again.

To this world of women and childish games she was relegated, for the coming of James to the English throne saw the reintroduction of the consort's court, in abeyance for half a century during the reigns of two women and a boy. The queen now had her own household, her own officials; and to this establishment (often, but by no means always, residing with the king's) Arbella as an unmarried woman would naturally be assigned. Anne Clifford wrote of waiting often on 'the queen and Lady Arbella' at Basingstoke. Indeed, Arbella's own references are to 'we on the queen's side', 'the queen's coach' and 'the queen came hither'. But 'we on the queen's side' were not those with whom Arbella would ever be in sympathy.

The ladies Anna took to her bosom were an experienced, worldly gang. Arbella had taken against them almost as soon as they met. 'Our great and gracious ladies leave no gesture or fault of the late queen unremembered,' she had written to Mary back in August, 'as they say who are partakers of their talk as I thank God I am not.' The past might have been a bond, since Anna's first intimates included the ladies Essex and Rich, widow and sister to the earl of Essex, and the countess of Bedford, Lucy Russell, whose husband had ridden in his rebellion. But the years Arbella had spent in lonely virtue at Hardwick had been used by the women who were now her companions to accrue a formidable history of sexual and political intrigue. Penelope Rich, for example, was well known to be the mistress of Lord Mountjoy, who fathered several of her children. Arbella wrote to Gilbert of how 'I daily see some even of the fairest amongst [our sex] misled and willingly and wittingly ensnared by the prince of darkness.'

As early as the autumn of 1603 Anne Clifford was writing (with all a teenager's self-righteousness) that 'all the ladies about the court had gotten such ill names that it was grown a scandalous place, & the queen herself was much fallen from her former greatness & reputation she had in the world.' And the old earl of Worcester wrote to Gilbert: 'I must a little touch the feminine commonwealth . . . The plotting and malice among them is such that I think envy and hatred hath tied an invisible snake about most of their necks, to sting one another to death.' As Arbella wrote to Gilbert again:

> I dare not write unto you how I do, for if I should say well I were greatly to blame, if ill I trust you would not believe me I am so merry. It is enough to change Heraclitus [the 'weeping philosopher'] into Democritus [the 'laughing philosopher'] to live

in this most ridiculous world, and enough to change Democritus into Heraclitus to live in this most wicked world.

Perhaps her secluded life had made her a little prudish, but her opinion was shared by many contemporaries. It is one with which history has found no reason to disagree. 'A nursery of lust and intemperance' was how Lucy Hutchinson described it decades later. (Lucy was the wife of John Hutchinson, a Puritan commander in the Civil War – and one whose mother-in-law Margaret Byron, significantly, had served devotedly in Arbella's household.) The holy state of matrimony, wrote the antiquary Simonds D'Ewes, 'was perfidiously broken, and amongst many made but a may-game ... even great persons prostituting their bodies to the intent to satisfy and consume their substance in lascivious appetites of all sorts.' The court was full – said Mrs Anne Turner, one who should know, at her trial for the poisoning of Sir Thomas Overbury – of 'malice, pride, whoredom, swearing and rejoicing in the fall of others ... so wicked a place as I wonder the earth did not open and swallow it up.' Webster began his *Duchess of Malfi* with mention of a court 'of flatt'ring sycophants, of dissolute / And infamous persons'. As the Duchess's virtuous suitor said:

> a prince's court
> Is like a common fountain, whence should flow
> Pure silver-drops in general. But if't chance
> Some curs'd example poison't near the head,
> Death and diseases through the whole land spread.

Of course, James's was hardly the first court to be accused of dubious morality. In 1540 Arbella's own grandmother Margaret Lennox had been sent away from Henry VIII's court for overmuch 'lightness' with an attractive courtier. Four years earlier, one observer had remarked that it would not be surprising if she had slept with Thomas Howard, 'seeing the number of domestic examples she has seen and sees daily'. But James – kissing his male favourites in 'so lascivious a manner' in public as to lead to the wildest speculations about his behaviour in private – went just that step too far.

This was only one breach of public decorum. Tales abound of public drunkenness; of banquets at which the tables were over-turned by the press of greedy courtiers. At the wedding of Philip Herbert (a favourite of the king's and soon to be a family connection), the guests were so rowdy that 'there was no small loss that night of chains and jewels, and many of the great ladies were made shorter by the skirts.' In the morning James, as was his prurient habit, visited the newly-weds in nightgown and cap to enquire how matters had gone, and spent an hour with them 'in or upon' the bed. Even the experienced Cecil complained to Sir John Harington: 'I wish I waited now in [Queen Elizabeth's] presence chamber with ease at my food and rest at my bed. I am pushed from the shore of comfort and know not where the winds and waves of a court will bear me.'

Cecil kept his high office. Queen Elizabeth's 'Pygmy' had become James's 'Little Beagle'. But lesser men had to share in-fluence with the Scots who had come in James's train. The new king carefully did not give too many of them formal power, in the shape of a seat on the privy council. But they packed his private household and thus controlled access to him to some degree, while the lavish gifts he gave them aroused universal jealousy. The distrust between the two nations made itself widely felt. 'We all saw a great change between the fashions of the court as it is now and that in the queen's time for we were all lousy by sitting in the chamber of Sir Thomas Erskine' – a prominent Scotsman – Anne Clifford wrote contemptuously.

Moreover, Arbella was not the only one to be quickly wearied by James's 'everlasting hunting'. The new king's passion for the chase (and for retiring to a hunting lodge with only his Scottish cronies) quickly became a problem of government. His ministers had little choice but to follow him as best they might, writing bitter little notes about the difficulties of trying to do their work without so much as access to a secretary.

The Venetian ambassador wrote early in the new reign that James 'seems to have almost forgotten that he is a king except in his kingly pursuit of stags, to which he is quite foolishly devoted, and leaves [his ministers] in such absolute authority that beyond a doubt they are far more powerful than ever they were before'. This was not quite right; James took the most active interest in his government, and was inclined to rate his own kingly powers and experience high. But, hating crowds and towns, convinced that constant outdoor exercise was essential to his health, he would let nothing stand in his way.

Still, his passion for outdoor life was only one side of his personality. James was the 'most learned king in Christendom', as well as the 'wisest fool'. In the first January of his reign he threw himself into the Hampton Court conference, at which he hoped once and for all to mediate a settlement among the different religious groups in England. Probably Arbella (reported as spending her time listening to sermons) would have enjoyed involvement in the discussion. Instead, she was struggling with a kind of domesticity. She had been made carver to Queen Anna, and feared she attacked the meat badly.

> After I had once carved the queen never dined out of her bedchamber nor was attended by any but her chamberers till my lady of Bedford's return. I doubted my unhandsome carving had been the cause thereof, but her Majesty took my endeavour in good part, and with better words than that beginning deserved put me out of that error.

Carving was an elaborate art in the seventeenth century, when each kind of flesh had its different technique, described with a different vocabulary, so that a goose was 'reared' and a swan 'lifted'. It was an aristocratic skill – but in any case, the proximity of majesty was held to gild any role it touched, and in performing this service for the queen Arbella was taking an elevated place in the ritual of the court; one which drew down on her some jealousy. (In the same letter to Gilbert, Arbella mentions Mary Talbot's prospects of being made cup-bearer, and even relays malicious gossip that Mary too had succumbed to envy of her niece.) Courtiers were frantic for seemingly menial offices. That very rising man Thomas Erskine (Viscount Fenton) was considered to have pulled out a major prize when he was appointed groom of the stool – literally, of the closed stool, or toilet. To

attend the king at such a moment was, after all, to have unparalleled intimacy ... Nor were Erskine's lavatorial duties
merely nominal. 'His Majesty has been a little loose since coming
to Royston,' he wrote to Cecil, 'but not to extremity.'

Despite (or because of?) the crudities of her new life, Arbella's
intellectual interests were as active as ever. Several books were
dedicated to her in her first court years. Hugh Holland's
*Pancharis* cast the presentation verses in a Latin he knew she, at
least, would be able to read; Richard Brett, in dedicating his
Hebrew and Latin *Ritus jejunii Judaici*, paid her a compliment
even more marked. David Hume's *Davidis Humii Theagrii Lusus
Poetici*, John Owen's Latin epigrams and John Wilbye's second set
of madrigals also bore her name. There was usually a compliment
to Arbella's own erudition in the dedication, as when George
Chapman, dedicating his translation of the *Iliad*, hailed her as
'our English Athenia, chaste arbitress of virtue and learning'.
Even her taste for sermons was an intellectual as much as a
theological interest, at a time when the argument might last so
long the preacher had to pause for refreshment, and 'puritan
preachings' were listed with masques and mad folks as entertainments of the day.

But James had no use for learned women. To teach women
Latin, he said, only made them more 'cunning'. And faced with a
girl who, he was told, was a prodigy of scholarly accomplishment, he asked sourly: 'But can she spin?' All those dedications
didn't count for much, in this new court, if Arbella wasn't up to
scratch with her carvery.

# 'My estate being so uncertain'

ARBELLA, AMID THE BUSTLE OF THE COURT, TOOK TIME TO THINK OF her family. She could now be useful; a conduit in the all-important game of patronage and favour. Even before the coronation, she had begged Gilbert to invite her uncle Henry and his wife to join them in town 'because I know my uncle hath some very great occasion to be about London for a little while and is not well able to bear his own charges'. ('They shall not long be troublesome to you, God willing,' she added. We all have relations about whom we feel that way.) She had pursued advantage for her uncle Charles and for the earl of Kent, her recent host. And her uncle William wrote home to old Bess that: 'His majesty, four days since hath been moved by my Lady Arbell for me.'

But neither Arbella's position nor her skills were reliable. Her currency was access to the king, and this was unpredictable. The great royal palaces resembled villages more than houses. Within one, Arbella would have had her own apartments. (The favourite Robert Carr, taking over the Whitehall apartments which had belonged to James's daughter before her marriage, found himself with forty-one rooms which he furnished with a serious collector's complement of pictures and tapestries.) By the same token, the king had his private chambers; a set of rooms where he could spend most of his time surrounded by male intimates and accessible only briefly to the clamorous masses.

A retainer of the Talbots', shrewd Thomas Coke, gives a vivid picture of Arbella almost literally clamouring at the king's door on some family errand: 'I observed that she wrestled extraordinarily with my lord duke [Lennox], Sir George Hume and Sir Richard Asheton for access to the king, and betwixt jest and earnest rather extorted the same from them by fear than obtained it by kindness.'

Coke clearly liked her: 'this lady permitteth me to treat her with much less awe than I find in myself when I attend some others.' But her rank still forbade of his casting doubt on her word or her judgement – which he would otherwise have done, evidently. Through Coke's long letter we picture Arbella promising more than she could perform, brazening her way through to the king's presence and promises with sheer beginner's luck; not something that would last, in an environment so competitive and so wary. 'What end this day's speech with her honour will sort, God knoweth, but surely she seemeth to have mastered them all that limited her before,' Coke concluded dubiously.

Before he left for the north Gilbert had asked another Talbot retainer, Sir William Stewart, to keep an eye on Arbella. Stewart was able to report back that 'although her virtue and knowledge has been envied of to me, yet her ladyship has acquired many favourers and sundry well-affected to her humour and good merits by her good behaviour'. She was, he said, 'considerate and wise'. But she had few natural allies.

She wrote to Gilbert about some piece of business which required 'certain conditions and promises as well on your Lordship's part as mine'; striving at the same time for some reassurance that she was not to be made a milch cow for the pressing needs of her family.

> I assure myself you are so honourable and I so dear unto you, that you will respect as well what is convenient to me as what you earnestly desire. Especially my estate being so uncertain and subject to injury as it is. Your lordship shall find me constantly persever[ing] in a desire to do that which may be acceptable to you and to my aunt, not altogether neglecting myself.

There is a note of sharpness here. On one occasion Arbella complains of being kept in the dark, and of having no answer for friends who enquired as to Gilbert and Mary's plans. 'These people do little know how circumspect my aunt and your lordship are with me.' Nevertheless, when she was stricken with the measles in the Christmas season of 1604–5, she may have stayed with the Talbots to recover.

From her strange new world, Arbella would beg her aunt to 'let me hear of my faults from you when you will have me mend them.' She needed a touchstone of moral reality. 'I neither think those faults which are thought so here, nor those qualities good which are most gracious here now.' Nostalgically, she commended herself to her uncle Charles and all her cousins. Distance from the family in Derbyshire had made her heart grow fonder. She wrote often in terms of jest: 'I shall as willingly play the fool for your recreation as ever.' On another occasion she wrote: 'I make it my end only to make you merry, and show my desire to please you even in playing the fool.' For, she added, 'no folly is greater (I trow) than to laugh when one smarteth.' But underneath her humour, there sounds always the same note of worry.

The spring of 1605 saw Arbella return to Hardwick after an absence of two years. The year before, she had been begging Gilbert for 'some Hardwick news'. Now it was was time to go back, on a visit of reconciliation to her aged grandmother, who had been unwell. A neighbour of Bess's wrote anxiously to Gilbert that he hoped her visit might help to mend 'such controversies and suits as yet depend unended betwixt your lordship and my old lady'.

Arbella had already been drawn in to Gilbert's dispute with Bess (who felt she was still owed four thousand pounds from the old earl's will) and had had to intervene with the king. She tried to mediate more directly, writing to her uncle of her hope for 'my grandmother's good inclination to a good and reasonable reconciliation between herself and her divided family':

> You know I have cause only to be partial on your side, so many kindnesses and favours have I received from you and so many unkindnesses and disgraces have I received from the other party;

MY ESTATE BEING SO UNCERTAIN

yet will I not be restrained from chiding you (as great a lord as you are), if I find you not willing to harken to this good motion, or to proceed in it as I shall think reasonable.

Now Arbella had something quite out of the common run to bring to Hardwick as a gift: the promise that she was on the verge of securing, finally, the barony that would translate William Cavendish to the ranks of the peerage. Even better – in that it put her in an even stronger position – the king promised her a patent of nobility with the name left blank, to bestow on whom she would. This was still most unusual for admission to a noble rank; knighthood was to be had more easily.

But Arbella also took the precaution of equipping herself with a letter from the king to Bess, urging the old lady to treat her granddaughter kindly, 'with her former bounty and love'. Bess was inclined to take this amiss. She sent southwards a tart letter to be read to the amused king. Bess found it very odd (she said) that Arbella should be taking such pains to return to Hardwick when last she 'had desired so earnestly to come away'. She wrote that 'for her part she thought she had sufficiently expressed her good meaning and kindness' by her old settlement of land which would bring in seven hundred pounds a year, and 'as much money as would buy a hundred pounds a year more'. Though Arbella would always be welcome to her, Bess added, 'she had divers grandchildren that stood more in need than she.'

She none the less gave Arbella 'a cup of gold worth a hundred pounds and three hundred pounds in money'. And James had at last increased Arbella's pension in December 1604. But when, a decade later, peerages came to be sold in an unofficial market-place, the going price for a barony was ten thousand pounds or more, not three hundred and a gold cup. Moreover, to push through William's barony was likely to cost Arbella herself considerable sums in sweeteners, and, increased pension or no, she still had little to spare.

William may have accompanied Arbella when she retired south again, perhaps to urge his niece on. A letter to Gilbert reported that:

239

Mr Ca[ve]ndish is at London, come to court, and waits hard on my Lady Arbella for his barony; but I am confidently assured that he will not prevail, for I understand that my Lady Arbella is nothing forward in his business, although we be certainly informed that my lady hath a promise of the king for one of her uncles to be a baron . . . It is not likely to be Mr William, for he is very sparing in his gratuity.

William (or his mother) was perhaps persuaded to be less clutch-fisted, for he got his barony. The queen that spring had borne another child, and Arbella was to be godmother to the new princess. William was among the eight barons who bore a canopy over the royal baby as she was carried to the font, and proclaimed to the sound of trumpets as 'the high and noble Lady Mary'. (She lived little more than two years, predeceased by a subsequent baby.)

Arbella was approaching her thirtieth birthday, but her own marriage was still the subject of many rumours. The accession of James had lowered her value in the market, but not wiped it out. She obviously relished the possibility, archly telling Gilbert that 'you may soon be dispatched of me for ever (as I am told) in more honourable sort.' There had been talk of Count Maurice of Nassau, leader of the Protestant Dutch, though that would have dealt a blow to James's cherished plan of peace with the Spanish. And in the spring of 1604 there had already been whispers that the Polish ambassador – he who had been so anxious to get home before the freezing of the seas – had carried a good report of Arbella with him. Later in the year, sure enough, Poland's King Sigismund III would formally ask for her hand.

William Fowler had written to Gilbert that 'The Lady Arbella spends her time in lecture, reading, hearing of service and preaching, and visiting all the princesses. She will not think of marriage.' It was about as convincing as saying she never wanted the throne. At the time she seemed a very sought-after match. Besides Nassau, besides the king of Poland, there was a Prince Anhalt who 'hath written to me . . . yet she nothing liketh his letters nor his Latin,' Fowler added.

Fowler was Queen Anna's secretary and master of requests; son to that Fowler who had served old Lady Lennox, he had already written fulsome praise of Arbella in some bad poetry. Certain words of his in this letter have been taken to suggest he would have gone further, had she not been such a great lady: 'I dare not attempt her,' he wrote. But 'attempt' could just mean 'approach' – and there is a suggestion one of Arbella's suitors may have paid him as an emissary.

Fowler believed the prize would fall to Sigismund. 'Poland will insist, for his marshal is upon his journey. God give her joy in her choice of destiny.' The prospect appealed to Arbella's connections, actual and potential. 'A great ambassador is coming from the king of Poland,' reported the earl of Pembroke (engaged to marry Arbella's cousin Mary) to his prospective father-in-law Gilbert Talbot. 'So may your princess of the blood grow to a great queen.' But by 1605, it was clear that this triumph was not to be realized.

The fact is that James was no more likely to let Arbella wed than Elizabeth had been. Any child of hers could still present a future threat to his dynasty. This reality dawned on Arbella only slowly. She must, by contrast, quickly have become aware that in the new court, forgetful of Elizabeth's example, there was less kudos than ever in her unmarried state; James knew well the political value of his own wife and thriving nursery and was fond of using an uxorious metaphor. 'I am the husband and the whole isle is my lawful wife,' he said, when urging the union of England and Scotland. And: 'By the law of nature the king becomes a natural father to all his lieges at his coronation.' But he was quick to clamp down on any sign of women stepping outside the role of home and hearth: John Chamberlain recounted how he even ordered the clergy to inveigh from the pulpit against 'the insolencie of our women'. (Their fashion for mannish dress – 'broad brimmed hats, pointed doublets, their hair cut short and shorn, and some of them [with] stilettos or poinards and such trinkets' – was especially condemned – lending Arbella's future disguise an especial poignancy.) In Elizabeth's day, the cult of the virgin queen had filled the gap left by Catholic worship of the Virgin Mary. But now? It was a depressing time to be a virgin lady.

In the summer of 1605, after all those proposals had vanished into smoke, James, with his wife and son and their courts, made a formal visit to Oxford. The timing gave rise to a curious co-incidence. Four days were crammed with entertainments and disputations, and while the elders lodged at Christ Church, Prince Henry stayed at Magdalen, being formally admitted as a member there. On his arrival, 'being conducted to his lodgings in the president's apartments, [he] was entertained there with disputations, in which Mr William Seymour . . . performed the part of respondent.' It is the first mention of Arbella's future husband in royal circles. With his companions, he 'gave his Highness so much satisfaction in the readiness of their wit that, in testimony of it, he gave them his hand to kiss'.

That October, weeks after the Oxford visit, Arbella was thanking Prince Henry, in terms which to our ears sit oddly with the fact he was still only eleven years old, for some 'late high favour and grace it hath pleased your Highness to do at my humble suit'. ('I both understand with what extraordinary respect suits are to be presented to your Highness; and withall that your goodness doth so temper your greatness as it encourageth both me and many others to hope that we may taste the fruits.') She used the prince's tutors Sir David Murray and Adam Newton for her intermediaries.

Henry, while always on good terms with Cecil, was growing up to gather around him a group linked to the old Elizabethan war party; Essex's party. He had indeed been brought up in close companionship with Essex's son. That, perhaps, was the mantle he aspired to wear – the flower of Protestant chivalry. He was interested in the visual arts and the moral debate, fond of the society of older people and notably unsympathetic to his father's foibles and favourites. A little bit of a prig, maybe . . . He had a certain amount in common with his kinswoman Arbella, and there is a received impression that she was close to him and to Elizabeth, the sister he adored, although evidence is scanty.

But something was always happening to cast Arbella in a dubious light. The first days of November saw the discovery of the Gunpowder Treason. Cecil may have learned of the ripening plot before 5 November. Once again there were rumours that, in

# MISCHEEFES
## MYSTERIE:
### OR,
Treaſons Maſter-peece.

The ſecond Part.

*Infernall* Fauks *with* Dæmoniacke *hart,*
*Being ready now to act his* Helliſh *part,*
Booted *and* ſpurr'd, *with* Lanthorne *in his hand,*
*And* match *in's* pocket, *at the* doore *doth ſtand ;*
But, *wiſe* Lord Kneuet *by* Diuine Direction
*Him apprehends : and findes the* Plots *detection.*

LONDON,
Printed by E. GRIFFIN, dwelling in the Little Olde
Bayly neerethe ſigne of the Kings-head. 1617.

A contemporary view of the Gunpowder plot

243

the later words of Bishop Goodman, Cecil had decided to 'first contrive and then discover a treason' to prove his own diligence and convince James of the Catholic threat.

The Catholic conspirators planned to install the young princess Elizabeth on the throne as a puppet ruler – one who would accept religious toleration – James 'and his cubs' having been blown away. But the Gunpowder Plot was never really the one-man act we celebrate on 5 November, Guy Fawkes' Day. Guido Fawkes was an obvious scapegoat for the whole conspiracy: the professional; the man with his hand on the fuse; and one of the few plotters, moreover, who survived long enough to be tried and vilified amid a blaze of useful publicity. The conspiracy really belonged to men like Robert Catesby; gentlemen who found their way to advancement blocked under James just as it had been under Elizabeth, and who had appeared as minor figures in the Essex rebellion of five years before.

Arbella was not directly implicated in this plot. (Indeed, had it succeeded in making James's daughter a papist puppet queen, Arbella might even have become figurehead for a rival Protestant party.) But her position could not but be made more vulnerable by this latest threat; the more so since Gilbert's name briefly arose in the investigations – probably due to the involvement of a remote Talbot connection with one of the plotters, coupled with his wife's known Catholic sympathies.

Arbella probably watched the trials; as, from hiding, did the king, queen and Prince Henry. Chief in rank among those who were brought low was the earl of Northumberland, whose relative Thomas Percy had taken active part in the plot. That and his religious sympathies ensured that Northumberland was sent to the Tower for the long stay. With Ralegh and Cobham already within its walls, he was the last of those against whom James in Scotland had been warned – the 'diabolical triplicity'.

# 'To live safe'

BY 1606, ARBELLA WAS EVER MORE DESPERATELY SHORT OF MONEY. AS the Venetian ambassador put it:

> The nearest relative the king has is Madame Arbella . . . She is not very rich, for the late queen was jealous of everyone, and especially of those who had a claim to the throne, and so she took from her the larger part of her income, and the poor lady cannot live as magnificently nor reward her attendants as liberally as she would . . .

It was the old, miserable story. In May she was petitioning Cecil for 'such fees as may arise out of his [Majesty's] seal which the bishops are to use . . . I am enforced to make some suit for my better support and maintenance.' She also asked Sir Walter Cope – chamberlain of the exchequer – to make an additional recommendation to Cecil, 'for that I thought his mediation would be less troublesome to you than if I solicited your Lordship myself'. It is a faintly desperate humility.

She didn't get her fees, on this occasion. There were so many gaping mouths to feed and Arbella was far from alone in her financial straits. James's court made a fetish from lack of economy; from consumption not only so conspicuous but so literal that more than one courtier was said to have pissed his revenues down the privy. It was the early seventeenth century that instituted the wasteful ostentation of presenting a splendid banquet, only to whip it away uneaten and serve one even more grandiose. The search for novelty (a pair of porpoises as side dish) was as notable as the sheer gluttony. Philip Massinger wrote of

> Their thirty-pound butter'd eggs, their pies of carps tongues,
> Their pheasants drench'd with ambergris, the carcases
> Of three fat wethers [sheep] bruised for gravy to
> Make sauce for a single peacock.

Consumption of alcohol was no less extraordinary. Sir John Harington left a memorable description of a sodden banquet provided in 1606 to honour Queen Anna's brother, the Danish king:

Ladies abandon their sobriety, and are seen to roll about in intoxication. One day a great feast was held, and after dinner the representation of Solomon in his temple . . . The lady who did play the queen [of Sheba]'s part did carry most precious gifts to both their Majesties, but forgetting the steps arising to the canopy, overset her casket into his Danish Majesty's lap and fell at his feet . . . Peace entered, but I grieve to tell how [she] most rudely made war with her olive branch . . . Hope and Faith were both sick and spewing in the lower hall . . .

'We are going on hereabouts', Harington wrote, 'as if the devil was contriving every man should blow himself up by wild riot, excess, devastations of time and temperance.'

It is not simply the amounts of money spent during the reign of James I that raise eyebrows. It is that it was spent so – in the puritan Lucy Hutchinson's word – intemperately, with a kind of crude and wilful recklessness that still sticks in the craw. The trouble was that, after poverty-stricken Scotland, the coffers of the English crown seemed bottomless to James. His expenditure rapidly doubled that of the old queen. In 1608, the clothing of thirteen-year-old Prince Henry alone cost more than Elizabeth spent yearly on her famous wardrobe, and the king bought a new pair of gloves every day.

James's gifts to his favourites were similarly enormous. In 1603 the crown paid out less than twelve thousand pounds in cash gifts. By 1612 the amount had multiplied by six. The king gave ten thousand pounds in jewels to Lady Frances Howard on her marriage to Robert Carr; handed out honours and offices with a prodigality that rebounded on his own head. ('You will never let me alone,' the king cried once. 'I would to God you had first my doublet and then my shirt, and when I were naked I think you would give me leave to be quiet.')

But the corollary to the amounts James gave was that he expected those around him to spend as freely. There was no mileage in quiet domestic economy. The aristocracy took their tone from a king ineradicably convinced that he had come to a land of milk and honey. The historian Lawrence Stone estimated that five thousand pounds a year was the smallest sum that could possibly support the establishment of an earl – and Arbella, who arguably ranked higher than an earl, had, at the highest computation, less than three thousand a year to support herself and perhaps ten servants. It was a great deal in the outside world where the rent of several manors might be less than three hundred pounds a year; but not much at court, where a presentation sword could cost the whole three thousand. And Cecil himself, with an income in 1608 of twenty-four thousand pounds, found (Stone writes) that his expenditure was almost fifty.

And yet you had to come to court – to 'the sun', in the words of a play that was later to be associated with Arbella, Beaumont and Fletcher's *The Noble Gentleman*, 'that draws men up from a coarse and earthly being'. Beyond the intoxicating prospect of a high-stakes game of favour and fortune there was increasingly a kind of intellectual (almost, in a roundabout sort of way, a moral) imperative; and plays like *The Noble Gentleman*, even while they set up the virtuous country-loving husband against his vain and courtly wife, perpetuated the dazzling mythology. 'Either come up now and see this bravery or close your eyes whilst you live,' was the challenge sent to Arbella's friend Anne Newdigate in 1603. If the world of court and city was wicked in comparison to the quiet country, it was also the place to be if you wanted to improve yourself and your family.

Soon after first coming south in 1603 Arbella had asked Gilbert for the use of a room in his house on Broad Street in the City: an occasional refuge from the incessant flattery and face-painting required of the court lady. But leaving the court permanently would not be so easy. Even had James allowed Arbella to dwell out of his sight – and courtiers needed specific permission to quit the court – what would she do, in a world where a woman of her rank had no career but matrimony? Better to try (however ill her upbringing might have fitted her for the task) to compete with those others who lay 'sucking at the breast of the state', in the disgusted phrase of one contemporary.

A courtier might manage to save money where it didn't show. The inveterate letter-writer Dudley Carleton described a drunken courtier who fell overboard into the Thames, whose breeches were 'but taffetta and old linings', so that when he was hauled up by the seat the first thing that appeared 'was his cue and his cullions'. But a more obvious way to make ends seem to meet was to borrow. Men of rank owed money, often to one another, in a mad merry-go-round of usury. Ben Jonson satirized the court as ablaze with jewels 'not paid for yet'. When Arbella finally performed in the queen's *Masque of Beauty*, John Chamberlain wrote that 'one lady and that under a baroness is said to be furnished [jeweled] for better than an hundred thousand pounds, and the Lady Arbella goes beyond her, and the queen must not come behind.' That Twelfth Night, Chamberlain continued, 'there was a great golden play at court. No gamester admitted that brought not £300, at least.' No wonder Arbella wrote of the 'even [ever?] greater mounds of my debtors', of a poor fortune which 'should supply nothing clearly'. Her problems should be seen in the context of the Jacobean aristocracy. But that didn't help her, day to day.

In this plight, she could use all she could get of power and influence. The visit of Anna's brother, King Christian of Denmark, in the summer of 1606 seemed to give her an opportunity. Arbella – besides her regular presence in attendance on the queen – seems to have been called in to mediate in a parting dispute between the jovial but loutish king and Arbella's kinswoman Margaret Stuart, coupled with her husband the old admiral, the earl of

Nottingham. The Danish king, it was said, had joked that in marrying a woman so much younger than himself, the earl risked becoming a cuckold. The occasion was a ceremonial review of the fleet, at which Arbella was present, and one version of the story has the king, who spoke no English, trying to tell the countess by sign language that it was time their party was away, and accidentally seeming to make the two-fingered horns . . . It sounds like a storm in an ale-cup, frankly. But since the countess had complained in writing, it was an embarrassment to King Christian as he set sail for home, and his secretary Sir Andrew Sinclair appealed for Arbella's defence. She gave it with a readiness that is painful to see. 'I shall think that breath of mine best bestowed which may add, if it be but a drop, to the sea of [his Majesty's] honour . . . I beseech his Majesty this indiscretion of my lady of Nottingham may not impair his good opinion of our sex or climate . . .'

The following year saw a brisk interchange of letters through which Arbella tried to maintain this important connection, sending gifts of 'handiwork' and similar 'womanish toys'. Those to the Danish king himself, or to his wife, were written in Latin as a common tongue, and the formal, not to say oleaginous, phrases contrast with her ardent and lively private style. She clung to the Danes, for 'by the patronage of so worthy a prince, so interested in them of whom my fortune depends [James and Anna] . . . I cannot doubt but at last to come to some such stay as shall give me perpetual cause to pray for his Majesty.' In the rough draft she had written, even more tellingly, that she could not doubt 'but to live safe'.

In the end, Arbella was to lose more than she gained by the Danish connection. In the spring of 1608 would come a demand – or rather, a series of them, since Christian had letters sent from his sister Queen Anna, his nephew Prince Henry and the courtier Sir John Elphinstone – that she should send to Denmark her lutenist Cutting, to fill the place lately vacated by John Dowland. She had no choice but to comply, 'although I know well how far more easy it is for so great a prince to command the best musicians of the world than for me recover one not inferior', and although she was losing 'the contentment of a good lute'. Cutting's feelings in the matter seem never to have been considered. But then, neither were Arbella's.

# 'Without mate and without estate'

ARBELLA'S LIFE WAS SOON TO BE AFFECTED BY EVENTS FAR FROM THE
English or the Danish courts. The first months of 1608 saw a
bitter cold. Above Westminster, John Chamberlain wrote, 'the
Thames is quite frozen over, and the archbishop came from
Lambeth on Twelfth Day over the ice to court. Many fantastical
experiments are daily put in practice as certain youths burnt
[mulled] a gallon of wine upon the ice,' and one honest woman
('they say') begged her husband to get her with child upon the
frozen water.

In windy Derbyshire, the cold was even worse. Bess of
Hardwick – so legend goes – had been told in a prophecy that she
would never die while she continued her life's great work of building. When her bricklayers at Oldcotes sent word they could not
work because the water to mix the mortar was frozen, she sent
word that they should use boiling ale. But even this expedient
failed.

More soberly, if less dramatically, Bess's close relations had
long known that, in her late eighties, the old lady's health was at
last failing. The messenger who took a New Year's gift from the
Shrewsburys reported (so Gilbert told Henry) that 'she looked
pretty well and spoke heartily.' But Gilbert himself found otherwise when he and Mary went to Hardwick on a visit of reconciliation: 'She did eat very little, and [was] not able to walk the
length of her chamber betwixt two, but grew so ill at it as you

might plainly discern it.' Soon, Bess's waiting woman sent a secret message that her mistress was so ill 'that she could not be from her day or night'.

On 13 February she died; died, moreover, as she had lived. She had long since taken careful precautions for the ordering of her tomb, but her family relations were in disarray. William, her favourite son, was even then driving away her herds of sheep and cattle before they could be seized by the other heirs. (He had won not only the two houses at Hardwick, and Oldcotes, and a London property, but even the contents of Chatsworth, though that house itself was entailed on Henry.) Sir George Chaworth (the chivalrous servitor of Hardwick days, now grown successful) did not hesitate to congratulate Gilbert openly on so 'great and good fortune to your lordship' as the old lady's demise. Mary Talbot, long estranged, was at the last minute bequeathed Bess's best pearl-embroidered bed.

Arbella did not manage the long journey north in time to be at Bess's bedside. Four days after her grandmother's death, Cecil was writing to Gilbert that 'my lady Arbella is gone towards you.' She arrived at Hardwick soon after, to find the rooms swathed in yards of black fabric, and stayed some weeks while her grandmother's body lay in state, perhaps saying a last goodbye to the house and servants and garnering her old possessions. (She was long gone before the funeral – but then, Bess did lie embalmed for three months before her burial, long even by the norm of the day.) In March Arbella made a visit to Gilbert and Mary at Sheffield, writing to her aunt from Hardwick again before her final return to the south. The money Mary had asked her to convey to her daughter 'shall be safely and soon delivered her'. But Arbella, Gilbert wrote in a letter, had seemed 'ill at ease'.

Arbella, like Henry, had been cut out of Bess's will in 1603, but the old lady had relented. The months ahead saw a burst of financial activity. She was popularly supposed to have negotiated the lucrative marriage between William's son and the red-headed Christian Bruce, the twelve-year-old daughter of the master of the rolls, Lord Kinloss. She certainly pursued her own money matters with new energy and perhaps increasing desperation. She petitioned James for the right to import Irish hides, and to nominate the sellers of wine in Ireland. She seems to have made some stir: Francis Bacon made a note to himself in July 1608 'To remember to be ready for argumentation in my lady Arbella's cause.' Most controversially, in October 1608 Chamberlain reported

> the muttering of a bill put into the exchequer or some other court concerning much land, that by reason of pretended bastardy in Queen Elizabeth should descend to divers persons. The chief actors named in it are Lady Arbella, St Leger of the west, and others. If there be any such thing, methinks the whole state should prevent such an indignity.

*If* Arbella did really try such a desperate measure, it is no surprise that she failed. But necessity was making her increasingly inventive.

She had been moved to take a hand in her own legal affairs. Litigation had become a regular occupation for the nobility, and a peer might not unusually have a dozen or more suits on the go; indeed, 'he that hath not some is out of fashion,' as the earl of Huntingdon told his son. Arbella found that her lawsuits kept her busy. 'I have found by experience this term [legal term] how much worse they thrive that say Go ye to the plough, than Go we to the plough,' she was writing grimly to Gilbert in the autumn, 'so that once more I am settling myself to follow the lawyers most diligently.' She begged of him the next two good clerical livings in his gift that should fall vacant; 'not that I mean to convert them to my own benefit, for I aspire to no degree of Pope Joan,' she joked; but they would be useful trading pieces in the relentless game of patronage.

In the welter of colossal court expenditure it took, by contrast, only a modest two hundred pounds for Arbella to purchase a town house in Blackfriars. 'For want of a nunnery I have for a while retired myself to the Friars,' she wrote to Gilbert that November. Five years before, in the first flush of freedom from Hardwick, she had described herself to him as pressed with 'the several cares of a householder'. Now she could say it seriously.

There is a lovely description of a London lady's home life in *The French Garden*. The fictitious Lady Ri-Melaine must, like Arbella, live within the City walls, since the great shopping centre of the Royal Exchange was 'not far hence'. Having dressed and spoken to her servants, she receives two morning callers. All three women decide to visit the shops, since it is barely eleven o'clock, and dinner still a little time away. They haggle for lawn cloth and a waistcoat, for silk stockings and fustian 'of good colour which will not stain', for cloth of gold and silver lace. They inspect velvet ('Raised velvet, pinked, wrought velvet, or tuff-taffeta?'), and hand over a hundred pounds in gold for enough pearls to make a necklace.

Returned to her house, the lady chides her butler to set every trencher with a knife, spoon and newfangled silver fork; to fill the copper tub with water to keep the drink cool; to check that the silver bottle is full of vinegar of rose, and that the drinking glasses are clean. The ladies will take their oysters before they wash; the peacock is well spiced and the turnips home grown. Her guests need not fear that the 'herne' [heron] will taste of the sea, 'for they are brought us alive and we feed them in the house.' The sheer number of comestibles mentioned – several pages' worth – reminds us that *The French Garden* was written as a language exercise to encompass many useful words, so we cannot take it as a realistic menu. But the picture is none the less of a London growing fast, full (for those who could afford it) of foreign luxury.

'Do you love cheese? There is Holland cheese, some Angelot, Auverne cheese, Parmesan. Will you have some grated cheese with sage and sugar?' No? Then out to the nearby fields, to admire the flowers and the birdsong, and perhaps 'fish with the line' before an evening party with games: London was still very near the country, and bugloss grew in the banks of what became Piccadilly.

This was a boom town, and expanding rapidly; so fast it seemed likely in sober earnest to fulfil the prophecy the epigrammist Thomas Freeman had made in jest:

> *London has got a great way from the streame;*
> *I think she means to go to Islington*
> *To eat a dish of strawberries and creame.*

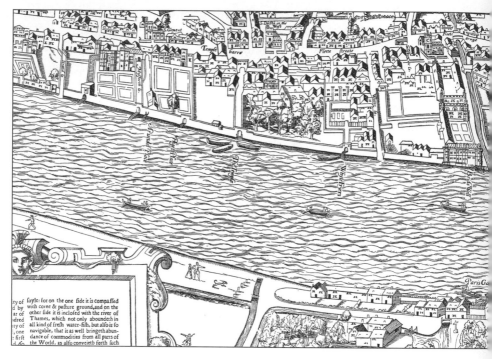

Blackfriars from the Agas map, mid sixteenth century

The rush to the decadent city was another social ill for which 'the pride of the women', in King James's words, was blamed, needless to say ('because the new fashion is to be had no where but in London: and here if they be unmarried, they mar their marriages, and if they be married they lose their reputations and rob their husband's purses'). But even in the 1590s when Fynes Moryson visited, he found the houses were built five or six stories high, due to the pressure of space, and so close together 'that opposite neighbours may shake hands without stirring from home'. At every corner, Thomas Dekker wrote, 'men, women and children meet in such shoals, that posts are set up of purpose to strengthen the house, lest with jostling one another they should shoulder them down.'

Under London Bridge the waters of the Thames, forced between the great stone piers, seethed and boiled into artificial

cataracts. For several hours a day the river here was impassable even by the boldest waterman, and for several more hours a dangerous gamble, in which lives could easily be lost. But above, the bridge was like another street; top-heavy with tall houses carved and gilded, bulging out into space in defiance of gravity. Two carts could hardly pass in between the press of humanity, and the drawbridge mechanism that once let tall ships through had long since fallen into disuse, so that the forest of high masts was penned downstream. The thriving City was bursting its traditional bounds. The Blackfriars to which Arbella came was just one newly fashionable sanctum within the walls; a riverside district carved out of land freed up when the friars had been dispossessed.

Arbella lived in a house previously inhabited by the earl of Hertford's brother, probably near to the south-western corner of the district, where the River Fleet ran into the Thames, London's artery, alive with traffic. Baynard's Castle, town home to her cousin Mary and her husband the earl of Pembroke, was a literal stone's throw away. And Blackfriars had other attractions, like the churches where you could hear the most controversial puritan preachers. Sermons and shopping . . . It was a recipe for heaven to a woman who loved both dress and doctrine. She was close to St Paul's, where gallants would show off their new suits before the noonday dinner, and close enough to Somerset House (renamed Denmark House in the queen's honour) where Anna, ceasing to cohabit with her husband, had set up court amid the Strand mansions of aristocrats like Arbella's cousin Alethea, now countess of Arundel.

The mansions were interspersed with luxury stores – like the 'china houses' that sold silk and porcelain imported from the orient, and served as places of assignation on the side. In 1609 the New Exchange, built on the site of the stables of Durham House, where Ralegh had lived, was launched under the auspices of no less a person than Robert Cecil. The New Exchange was a shopping centre filled with 'manufactures of the most beautiful description'. It was originally to have been called 'Armabell', in compliment to Arbella – but James had decreed differently.

Arbella herself, in Blackfriars, found herself among printers, guildsmen and actors as well as aristocrats. Ben Jonson and the miniaturist Isaac Oliver rubbed shoulders on the one hand with the great duke of Lennox, and on the other with a thriving Huguenot colony. She was also, in the cheek-by-jowl nature of the City, not far in any direction from a prison. The Tower to the east was less than a mile away; to the west were Bridewell and the Fleet, and also the Ludgate gaol, the old medieval gatehouse, where debtors stretched their hands through the bars, imploring money. You could never get far from suffering and violence in Jacobean London. The parboiled heads of executed traitors, left to rot for years on pikes above nearby London Bridge, must surely have jolted any woman whom their plots had touched so nearly. But Arbella was pleased with her new dwelling. She was allowing herself increasingly frequent absences from court.

Then, in December 1608, she was taken ill with the smallpox, as Sir John Harington reported. 'My lady Skinner attendeth her, and taketh great pains with her.' This, of course, was a serious matter. Many died of smallpox; Queen Elizabeth herself had almost succumbed half a century before, so badly taken, she later said, that 'Death possessed every joint of me.' Many who survived were left disfigured – but since no mention was ever made of it, we can hope that Arbella was spared the hideous scarring. Lady Skinner may have been sufficiently enlightened to avoid the bloodletting which was the more aggressive course of treatment, and to rely (as Queen Elizabeth's nurses had done) on rest and warmth, and herbal decoctions, with red cloth hung over the sufferer's window to block the sun's rays from damaged skin. The ailing Arbella missed the extravagant *Masque of Queens*, in which Queen Anna and her ladies, portraying the female rulers of history, celebrated women's power. But she survived the dangerous illness (just as she had survived the measles four years before). The following summer she was able to go north to recuperate with the Shrewsburys – taking, perhaps, the opportunity to pave the way for another journey.

In August 1609 Arbella set out from London on what can only be described as a progress; a winding tour northwards to the midlands which was marked by the same combination of hospitality and ceremony as any official royal journey. Even Gilbert seemed to be affected by the formality, writing to his steward that 'my lady Arbella will be at Sheffield some day this week . . . Fish enough must be watered, for there will be an extreme great multitude in the hall every day. Fat beef and fat muttons must be had, and the beef in time killed and powdered. Fat capons provided and reserved till then . . .'

Arbella's steward Hugh Crompton kept a detailed account of expenses along the way. (Also a list of all the sums he received over the following year, from one September to the next – £2,160, in total.) Overall, the trip cost her more than three hundred pounds. On the first night at St Albans: 'Supper £2 8s 6d; breakfast £2 11s 10d; horse meat for 20 horses £2 2s 6d; hostelers 2s 0d; musicians 10s; poor at the gates 10s.' Ten shillings for the bell ringers who signalled her arrival, two and six for a trumpeter. Ten shillings to a laundry woman; four shillings for cakes and ale at the alehouse in Nottingham; thirty shillings to a keeper who sent her a stag; three shillings to a farrier for 'blooding and

drenching Freake's nag sick of the staggers' – Arbella seems to
have brought her old embroiderer (another Derbyshire native)
northwards with her. The bulk of the sums are tips to the
servants of her hosts and the officers of the towns through which
she passed on her way: grooms, butlers, bakers, porters,
waiting women, kitchen boys, coachmen. Five shillings to a
gardener who brought her nosegays, six to a schoolmaster
who presented her with some verses; ten to the footman who
brought word her cousin Alethea was delivered of a boy; and
always those alms to the poor. It is a great picture of an
aristocratic journey.

   The way was often hard – all the harder, perhaps, once she had
reached the midlands, her old familiar territory. Past Sheffield,
where she stayed with Gilbert and Mary, the road at one point
was so bad that three men had to mend it before Arbella could
pass – and then the party found themselves lost in the falling
darkness. Time and again there are payments to a coachman sent
to guide the wanderers to their next lodging place; guides across
the moors to Chatsworth; guides again to lead her on from
Buxton. Buxton had first been developed as a spa by the old earl
of Shrewsbury, and the queen of Scots had praised its health-
giving 'milk-warm waters'; Arbella tried them too, and gave a
pound to 'him that kept the well'. She visited Wrest Park, where
she had stayed in 1603, now home to her cousin Elizabeth and
her husband; she visited Shrewsbury's old seat at Sheffield;
and with Mary Talbot she made a trip to Rufford, where her
parents had met and married. It was as if she were making some
kind of pilgrimage – as if, in a life that had been abruptly ruptured
by the events of 1603, she felt the need to reacquaint herself with
the places of her past.

   This was an interlude, but also something more than that.
Perhaps the best holidays do change you in some way, and the trip
into Derbyshire seems to have set the seal on Arbella's determination to break away from the wearing life of court. In her
home country she was not so alone as she must often have felt
down south, and this was the environment she sought. She stayed
with Isabel Bowes at Walton Hall near Hardwick. This was
obviously a friend, for a letter from Lady Bowes to Arbella in

London the following winter is warm in tone. ('I would be glad to know how your ladyship proceeds in your Irish suit: but I long more to hear how you keep your health this wet winter.') Arbella had obviously asked Lady Bowes and her brother Sir George St Paul to find her a house in the district. With Sir George, Arbella seems also to have made certain financial plans.

Back in London, she began negotiating to change the way in which she received her income. In the summer she had been desperately petitioning for the right to license the selling of wine (the suit was made out in the names of St Paul and another of her recent hosts). But in late December she was writing to Cecil offering to return the licence in exchange for the payment of her debts, and to trade in her diet – her allowance of dishes for herself and her servants – for another thousand pounds a year. She was probably wise to choose the bird in the hand rather than the flock in the bush; the grant of wine was potentially worth thousands, but she had come to realize the money might prove hard to collect. 'Some friends of mine, of good judgement and experience', had advised her to get the patent validated by the royal seal. But there is more here than normal caution. Arbella was liquidating her assets.

She hoped, with the aid of the extra money, to be able 'to live in such honour and countenance hereafter as may stand with his Majesty's honour and my own comfort'. She did not intend to do it in the expensive whirligig of society. Already her heart and mind – if not yet her heels – were carrying her away from the court. Many of her contemporaries saw it as a kind of death to withdraw from the centre of power and influence; to live retired and within their means. Some, like Essex, quite literally chose to risk their lives instead. But in this as in so much else, Arbella was out of her time. It is as if Bess's death had set something free; allowed her to consider other ways of living, to weigh up different possibilities.

The shrewd Venetian Correr had written in his report two years before that the king 'promised when he ascended the throne, that he would restore her property, but he has not done so yet, saying that she shall have it all and more on her marriage, but so far the husband has not been found, and she remains without mate and without estate.' Without mate and without estate ... It was all too neat a summary. But Arbella had decided that, whatever the risk, she was not prepared to stay that way.

The great crisis of Arbella Stuart's life was almost upon her. But it began in confusion, appropriately. There was a false dawn to the day that saw the long drama of her marriage. In December 1609 all her world knew that she was in disgrace; but no-one knew why, precisely. As John Chamberlain wrote on the thirtieth: 'I can learn no more of the lady Arbella but that she is committed to the lord Knyvet, and was yesterday again before the lords. Her gentleman-usher and her waiting woman are close prisoners since her first restraint.'

This was just the kind of story the Venetians sniffed out most expertly. 'His Majesty had a hint last week that [Arbella] intended to cross the sea with a Scot named Douglas, and had some idea of marrying him.' Arbella's Lennox grandmother had been born into the Douglas family. Arbella, Correr reported, was taken by the captain of the guard (Fenton) and his wife – Arbella's cousin, Bessie Pierrepont – from the house of one of the Seymour family, 'under pretext of friendship and an invitation to sup with them'. Instead, deceitfully, 'they conveyed her to the palace where she was placed under guard several days.' But Arbella, questioned, 'answered well' and was set at liberty.

A little later, the Venetian suggested a new and more colourful story. On 28 January 1610, Correr writes: 'Lady Arbella's troubles are caused by a consignment of money which her excellency made at Constantinople for a Moldavian prince ... The Moldavian was many months ago at the English court, and as I hear, with the king's consent negotiated about a marriage with the lady.'

The so-called prince was a pretender to that distant throne – an adventurer by the name of Stephen Bogdan (from 'Bugdania' or Moldavia, now Romania), who had come to England seeking James's backing, and gone on to Venice to boast that the king had promised him a royal bride. If, as Correr believed, James had acquiesced in Bogdan's marriage with Arbella – 'to depend on his making good his claim to his state' – James probably knew this was one prospective match to which he could consent in perfect safety. Given the improbability of Bogdan's ever taking his throne, it is even possible the king of England was enjoying a private black joke – albeit one unlikely to have struck his cousin as funny.

There seems at this time to have been yet more debate as to whether Arbella was not secretly inclining to Catholicism. As Chamberlain put it: 'she be not altogether free from the suspicion of being collapsed.' Many of her tastes and associations might more easily suggest a bent towards puritanism than papistry. But the plots of James's first months on the throne had shown how extreme opinions could wind up meeting on the far side of a circle: in practical terms, all that really mattered was whether Arbella was or was not outside the middle ground so beloved of authority. (As James had once written: 'I did ever alike hate both extremities.') Correr again:

> In reply to a question on religion Lady Arbella said that she had never any intention to become a Catholic but her troubles and worries have prevented her from attending church for some time. She complained loudly of the small account in which she is held, and recalled the frequent promises of the king. His Majesty has taken it all in good part and has ordered that she be repaid for the moneys remitted to Constantinople. Her pension will be increased. All the same she publicly declares she is not satisfied. She claims the restoration of her patrimony and asks to be married or at least to depart and choose a husband.

She would, he said, 'neither affirm nor deny that she had thought of leaving the kingdom; she merely said that ill-treated as she was by all, it was only natural that she should think of going.'

Arbella, by now, was making little attempt to hide her discontent. Indeed, her concern was all to have her wrongs heard and righted. She was past caring if she made a clamour. Perhaps it is not surprising that, with this seething volcano of rebellion on his doorstep, James made good his promise to give Arbella more money. If, as Chamberlain believed, 'the chiefest cause of her discontentment' was want, it must have seemed worth a little cash not to drive her, as the ambassador put it, 'to farther despair'. Two hundred pounds' worth of plate as a New Year gift, an increase in the annual pension, and a thousand marks to pay her debts: the sums she received were not so little, but they did come too late.

That winter Arbella kept much to her own rooms; 'nor is she visited except by intimates.' In February 1610 Correr was reporting that she 'is seldom seen outside her rooms and lives in greater dejection than ever. She complains that in a certain comedy the playwright introduced an allusion to her person and the part played by the prince of Moldavia. The play was suppressed.' The unnamed play is usually taken to have been Ben Jonson's *Epicoene* – an identification made the more readily since Jonson, at around the same time, was in trouble with Lady Bedford over a slanderous epigram, and came with a ready-made reputation for scurrility. The identification rests on one throwaway line about the prince of Moldavia and 'his mistress, mistress Epicoene' (with a crack about whether the boastful bachelor has 'found out her latitude'). But the anti-feminist satire about the emasculating Ladies Collegiate led by Lady Haughty (James's dislike of learned women was obviously filtering through) and the deceit of the eponymous Epicoene, set up as the one silent woman a noise-hating bachelor could bear to wed, offers more general grounds for dismay. It is, alternatively, possible that the offending piece was *The Knight of the Burning Pestle*, thought to be by Beaumont and Fletcher, a multi-layered satire where, in the crudely romantic 'play within a play', the knight disdains the prince of Moldavia's daughter. Too thin a ground for anger, surely – except that *The Knight of the Burning Pestle* is believed first to have been performed in the exclusive, private Blackfriars Theatre, on Arbella's very door, and for just the sort of sophisticated audience whose ridicule Arbella would feel keenly.

Arbella, Correr added, was 'very ill-pleased. She shows a determination to secure the punishment of certain persons.' The Venetians sometimes got facts wrong, but they handled temperament sensitively. Correr, who had bestowed on Arbella that dauntingly accurate tag 'without mate and without estate', added at the end of February that there remained 'much suspicion about'; partly because 'the malcontents may some day use her as a pretext for their schemes,' partly because she was 'a lady of high spirit and ability'. Was it likely such a one would indefinitely tolerate the situation he had already described so acutely?

That month of February, Arbella had her own reasons for remaining secluded. By the end of it, she was being examined as to her relations with a man much closer to home (and closer to the English throne) than the would-be ruler of Moldavia. Indeed, it is possible that when Arbella, according to Correr, confessed 'that fault of her womanish credulity in the matter of love with the prince of Moldavia', she was herself putting Stephen Bogdan forward as a stalking-horse to conceal her real lover's identity.

# V

1610–1615

## 'A pattern of misfortune'

'I shall think myself a pattern of misfortune in enjoying
so great a blessing as you so little a while.'

Arbella Stuart to William Seymour, 1610

# 'Affectations of marriage'

WE KNOW FRUSTRATINGLY LITTLE ABOUT THE BIRTH OF ARBELLA'S
romance with William Seymour – the earl of Hertford's second
grandson, and younger brother to the Edward Seymour of
Hardwick days. At this most sensitive moment in her story, it is
as if, temporarily, she steps away from us again – out of the direct
communication of her letters and into the mists of supposition.
But her first feelings for William, the nature of the negotiations
into which they entered together, were not something to be put
down on paper. And in the gossiping letters of James's courtiers it
was actions, not emotions, which held sway.

There is a theory that the two met as far back as 1605, on that
royal visit to Oxford when William spoke before Prince Henry at
Magdalen; or (again in Oxford) in 1606, when he offered Latin
verses to King Christian. There is another that they met only
when William quit the university, having taken his degree in
December 1607, and came to court. But the time and place of
their first encounter are not really the point. However acrimonious
relations had become in those strained last months of the old
queen's reign, Arbella never really lost contact with the Hertford
family. How could she, in the small world of the Jacobean
aristocracy? In her duties around Queen Anna, Arbella would
constantly have been in company with the countess of Hertford,
until the earl summoned his wife home from court; the two
women were much of an age, and the earl's young third wife was

less than a decade older than her step-grandson William. In 1606, a request made by the painter William Larkin to become a free-man of the Painter Stainer Company was sponsored by the earl and by Arbella, and it had been from a Seymour family home that Arbella had been brought in for questioning in December 1609.

The acquaintance between Arbella and William was public. Even their engagement seems hardly to have been a secret for long. On 2 February 1610, in the palace of Whitehall, William Seymour went to the chamber of Arbella Stuart and shared with her some sort of betrothal ceremony. Less than a fortnight later, on the fifteenth, the young secretary James Beaulieu was writing that

> The Lady Arbella who (as you know) was not long ago censured for having without the king's privity entertained a motion of marriage, was again within these few days apprehended in the like treaty with the Lord of Beauchamp's second son, and both were called and examined yesterday at the court about it. What the matter will prove I know not, but these affectations of marriage in her do give some advantage to the world of impairing the reputation of her constant and virtuous disposition.

Arbella was not just embarked upon a reckless adventure. In 1603 she had launched herself towards wedlock on a tide of desperation and naïve ignorance. Seven years later she had reason to know more about the ways of the world – but her nature had not changed profoundly. She seems still to have acted with the Duchess of Malfi's own misplaced rationality:

> *Why might I not marry?*
> *I have not gone about, in this, to create*
> *Any new world, or custom.*

But in the Duchess we have another royal lady who married without the permission of her relatives and who paid dearly. For Arbella as for Malfi, it could never be that easy.

In seeking an alliance with a fellow royal, Arbella may have had dynastic ambitions that yet fell far short of seeking here and now to usurp James's position. She may just have wanted to hold for her own children the place she herself had held in the succession, in case of any future vacancy. She may have seen that ambition as harmless enough. James would see it very differently.

Given that Arbella wanted desperately to marry (and, given the paucity of other options, it is hardly surprising that she should), the list of potential bridegrooms was very short. To negotiate, on her own responsibility, with any foreign prince would be at once impracticable and quite definitely treasonous. If she married a man from her own country, she could at least claim to believe she had the king's authority. But if she married a man of birth much lower than her own, she would in effect be negating, throwing away, that royal blood she had been reared to value highly. And she could immediately discount those of the nobility with whom her court life had no contact, and those who were contracted already. The list dwindled very rapidly.

Arbella of her own choice sought two husbands – two brothers – from the royal branch of the Seymour family. And in 1608 this family had been newly proved royal: the earl of Hertford finally, remarkably, succeeded in producing the clergyman who had married him to Catherine Grey half a century before, and the offspring of that marriage were officially recognized as legitimate (which, under the terms of Henry VIII's will, of course, would have meant that they should have inherited the Tudor crown – except that one of James's first acts had been to have parliament lay that will aside, providentially).

It may seem illogical thus to stress the political implications of Arbella's match, and then to propose it as a kind of love story. But we need to look at the individuals involved – and also at the concept of love as it was presented in the early seventeenth century. In the case of the match Arbella had once proposed with the unseen teenager Edward, there can be no question of personal affection. In the case of her match with William, by contrast, there is reason to believe that her emotions were engaged; and that at least one factor in her choice was the character of her betrothed.

William Seymour was a man whose tastes matched Arbella's own – one of the few at James's court of whom that could be said. As a student, he (unlike many of his fellow noblemen), had used his time at Oxford to take his BA. 'Loving his book above all other exercise,' said Clarendon after the Restoration, he would later take his MA and a DMed at Oxford, besides twice serving as chancellor of that university. But he also shared Arbella's value for the royal blood they had in common (and perhaps her flexibility in religion), and though he was at this time only in his early twenties and thus well over a decade the younger, her sequestered life had not allowed her to develop early. 'Love maketh no miracles in his subjects, of what degree or age whatsoever,' she had once (about the marriage of a connection) written aptly.

We have one letter Arbella wrote to William during their marriage; it is quoted briefly in the prologue and in full in a later chapter. From that, from the gifts she made him and from the risks she took to be with him, it seems clear that Arbella at least *came* – as was her duty – to love her husband deeply. That, after all, was the seventeenth-century ideal: not an unsanctioned Romeo and Juliet passion, but a growth into connubial affection. A few decades earlier Catherine Grey, told by her mother: 'I have provided a husband for you . . . if you are willing to frame your fancy and good will that way,' answered: 'I am very willing to love my lord of Hertford.' The proverb 'There belongeth more to marriage than two pair of bare legs' did not suggest that a wedding was a callously arranged bargain: marriage was indeed meant to be more – the meeting of spirits that alone could help 'increase unto Christ'. No battle was perceived between pure affection and practicality; quite the reverse, indeed. A few decades later Arbella's kinswoman Margaret Cavendish would boast simultaneously her devotion to her husband and her lifelong freedom from the romantic passion; the one being seen as the opposite of the other, rather than as a corollary.

About William's feelings it is far harder to be sure. We have no private letters from him to Arbella, nor was his personality, at this early stage of his career, analysed by contemporaries. His motives were probably practical, up to a point. He may have had his share of Seymour ambition. His later letters show that he knew his family's history. Sixty years earlier his ancestor Thomas Seymour had approached the young princess Elizabeth with a blend of passion and pragmatism. And William was, after all, like Thomas, that drug on the market, a younger son, whose usual portion would be 'that which the cat left on the malt heap', as another younger son, Thomas Wilson, wrote disgustedly. But if we jump forward, to a time when William had become a public personality, we do get the picture of a man who – even if he were making a political bargain – would surely have kept his part honourably.

The newly restored Charles II, recreating for William his great-grandfather's title of duke of Somerset, would tell his parliament that 'it is for an extraordinary person, who hath merited as much of the king, my father, and myself as a subject can do'. Certainly, in his relation to the later Stuart kings, William would show himself capable of self-sacrifice and loyalty. Having offered his life for that of the condemned Charles I, he was then summoned by Cromwell to consult on the future of the country; not, surely, a man to be dismissed as a nonentity. And though Arbella was the more eager of the pair, William did make repeated attempts to be allowed to live with his wife; did enjoy conjugal relations with her; did take her servants into his household after her death; did cherish her portrait for the rest of his life. Marrying again in later years, he named his eldest daughter after her. Having said all that, looking at the one early image we have of William – a dreaming curate, so different from the puffy-cheeked royalist commander of the mid-century – it is easy to imagine that he was just that brand of romantic who would idealize a dead wife (especially a dead *royal* wife?), but espouse a living one less successfully.

It was certainly Arbella who had to take the more active part in planning the practicalities of their union, their income and their eventual escape. (The Duchess of Malfi, too, would be called upon to orchestrate the same tasks.) Perhaps it was inevitable that she should be the promoter of their marriage; as the Duchess lamented, it was

*The misery of us, that are born great,*
*We are forc'd to woo because none dare woo us.*

And even the later tributes show William as someone in whom steadfastness of purpose combined with a curious passivity.

Certainly his behaviour in the weeks after his betrothal did not manifest any great ardour. On 20 February he sent a letter to the privy council, pleading 'the clearness of an unspotted conscience and a loyal heart to his Highness'. He urged his belief that the noble lady 'might, with his Majesty's good favour, and no just offence, make her choice of any subject within this kingdom, which conceit was begotten in me upon a general report after her ladyship last being called before your lordships'. He had therefore thought no wrong in seeking her in marriage, 'which is God's ordinance common to all'. He wrote that he sought Arbella,

> myself being a younger brother and sensible of mine own good, unknown to the world, of mean estate, not born to challenge any-thing by my birthright, and therefore my fortunes to be raised by mine own endeavours, and she a lady of great honour and virtue, and, as I thought, of great means.

If he really thought Arbella was of great wealth, he must have been the only one around the court who did. It seems unlikely. Practical motives, of course, would have been quite acceptable in William's own century. And if William's motives were mercenary, he none the less gallantly took the blame for the affair:

> I boldly intruded myself into her ladyship's chamber in the court on Candlemas Day [2 February] last, at what time I imparted my desire to her; which was entertained, but with this caution of either part, that both of us resolved not to proceed to any final conclusion without his Majesty's most gracious favour and liking first obtained.

They claimed to have had no doubt such 'favour' would be forthcoming. After the inquiry into her rumoured Moldavian match, Arbella seems to have believed she had won James's per-mission to make any *English* marriage – that he had, in the words of her later letter, 'given me your royal consent to bestow myself on any subject of your Majesty's'. This the king had done, she said, a few days before she became contracted to Willliam, and also 'long since'.

But there is another point of interest in William's words. That Candlemas meeting between himself and Arbella, he said, had been their first. Their first of any significance to the council? Or really the first time they had encountered one another? If the latter, it would suggest that their alliance was indeed conceived as one of policy. Either way, in the weeks that followed they had achieved only two meetings alone, away from the court in the comparative anonymity of the crowded London streets: at a Mr Bugg's house in Fleet Street and at a Mr Baynton's – 'at both of which we had the like conference and resolution as before'. Now William promised again that: 'there is neither promise of marriage, contract, or any other engagement whatsoever between the lady and myself, nor ever was any marriage by me or her intended, unless his Majesty's gracious favour and approbation might have been first gained therein.' These fulsome declarations probably reassured the council as to William's part. Arbella, typically, was less accommodating.

The king, reported the Venetian ambassador, having had the pair examined apart, summoned them both together before him, there being present also the lords of the council and Prince Henry. One can only imagine the scene. Arbella spoke at length, 'denying her guilt and insisting on her unhappy plight. She complained again that her patrimony had been conceded by the king to others. She had sold two rings he had given her.' Arbella was then required to beg the king's pardon, but replied that, seeing herself deserted, she had imagined she could not be accused if she sought a husband of her own condition in life; 'however, if she had erred in this assumption, she was ready most humbly to ask pardon.'

This did not satisfy the king, who demanded that she 'should confess directly that she was in fault, and ask frankly for forgiveness'. That ritual abasement was important; Elizabeth, in her day, always similarly insisted on an acknowledgement of wrongdoing. Arbella – said the ambassador – complied. She received fresh promises of money 'and leave to marry provided only that it should be someone to the taste [*gusto*] of his Majesty'. There seems to have been sufficient uncertainty in the wording that

Arbella could persuade herself that she had leave to marry, period – as long as she did not perpetrate the diplomatic outrage of looking outside the country. So she and William were both set at liberty. But the affair was not over so quickly.

After the council's stern warning, William sent Arbella a message – to be read out by a third party – that he

> hath seriously considered of the proceedings between your lady-ship and himself, and doth well perceive, if he should go on therein, it would not only prove exceedingly prejudicial to your contentment but extreme dangerous to him . . . He doth, therefore, humbly desire your ladyship . . . that you would be pleased to desist from your intended resolution concerning him, who likewise resolveth not to trouble you any more in this kind, not doubting but your ladyship may have one more fitting for your degree, and himself a meaner match with more security.

What could her feelings have been? It was an unforgivable thing to do . . . unless it was a feint, a matter of mutually agreed policy.

A Scottish lord wrote to Cecil on 31 March mentioning Arbella's intentions with William – 'we have much talk of her business here.' Talk was right. The relationship might be in abeyance, but it was not over. Still, for the moment, at least, James continued his wonted ways in happy ignorance. Arbella got the price of her seeming complaisance and received the rights to sell wine, whisky and aqua vitae in Ireland for twenty-one years, made out in her name with those of two Derbyshire gentlemen in whose houses she had stayed the previous summer. James also promised to pay her debts and increase her pension. In April, apparently back in highest favour, she sat with the royal family under a golden canopy to receive the prince of Württemberg.

But the appearance of normality was only that – an appearance. At the end of May, William was telling his friend and relation Edward Rodney of 'his resolution concerning his marriage'. Rodney quoted William as believing that Arbella had 'the king's consent to make her own choice without exception':

he never spake unto me of the means which he used in the reobtaining of her love, nor once mentioned unto me either letter, token, message or ought else which had passed between them, only that since it pleased her to entertain the matter . . . and since he found himself bound in conscience by reason of a former pledging of faith unto her, that he resolutely intended it.

It was a weird double world in which the couple must have been living: outward appearance, secret reality. Only a week or so after William's conversation with Rodney, Arbella was engaged on one of the most important (appropriately enough, since it was to be the last) ceremonies of her court career. The seventeen-year-old Prince Henry was to be invested as prince of Wales, the first prince of Wales in a century. The ceremony at Westminster, the festivities at Whitehall, were crowned on 5 June by a masque, *Tethys' Festival*, of even more than usual splendour.

Queen Anna represented Tethys, Queen of the Ocean, with the princess Elizabeth as the River Thames, followed by Arbella as the Derbyshire Trent. Her cousins Alethea and Elizabeth also took part. Their father Gilbert had been active in the investiture itself the day before, and the presence of her family at court may help to explain why Arbella committed so little to paper at this time. Thus we cannot be sure who knew of her plans – though it is always tempting, wherever rebellion lurks, to suspect the influence of Mary Talbot, countess of Shrewsbury.

As Tethys received the homage of the tributary rivers, Henry's younger brother Charles presented him with a diamond-studded sword, and frolicked charmingly with a flock of pre-pubescent noble maidens. Arbella was rigged out in a head-dress

composed of shells and coral, and from a great murex shell in the form of the crest of an helm hung a thin waving veil . . . The upper garments had the bodies of sky coloured taffeta, for lightness, all embroidered with maritime invention . . . Her long skirt was wrought with lace, waved round about like a river, and on the banks sedge and seaweed all of gold.

The spectacle finished only within half an hour of the rising sun,

A river nymph's costume for *Tethys' Festival*

and yet there was still a staggering banquet for the 'viewing and scrambling'. But Arbella's mind can hardly have been on the festivity. The ceremonies dispatched, the court moved downriver to Greenwich. James set off for a few days alone with his cronies, and perhaps his absence seemed to the couple like an opportunity.

On Thursday, 21 June William returned to London, to beg Rodney to be a witness at his wedding. The two men (with the gentleman servant Edward Kyrton) were rowed back to Greenwich, arriving about midnight. With Arbella they found Crompton and Edward Reeves, another of the gentleman servants, and her gentlewomen Mrs Biron and Mrs Bradshaw. The party (as William later confessed ) 'did sit up in the Lady Arbella her chamber all the night until they were married'. The ceremony was conducted by 'one Blagen [or Blagew]', son to the dean of Rochester, on the Friday morning, 'between four and five of the clock'.

They may have had to wait to find a priest who would perform this risky service. But the hour was not so unusual, astrology being as likely a reason as practicality. Old Bess had married William Cavendish at a similarly uninviting time of day. In one all-important matter things were done according to ceremony, and the presence of all those witnesses was duly noted down by Crompton in Arbella's account book. She had taken this much warning at least from history; it was the shortage of witnesses to Catherine Grey's marriage long ago that had made it possible for William's father to suffer the slur of illegitimacy.

There is no doubt that the marriage ceremony was in itself legal. While marriage in a church with banns or else a special licence was the favoured norm, a mere declaration was enough. When the Duchess of Malfi said she had heard that 'a contract in a chamber' – like Arbella's – would suffice, she was merely reflecting reality. *The Lawe's Resolution of Womens Rights*, in 1632, said specifically that 'There needs no stipulation or curious form of contract in wedlock making . . . It may be made by letters.' And the canons of 1603 had set twenty-one as the age at which consent of a parent or guardian was no longer legally necessary.

Social approval was a different matter. A father whose daughter married without his consent might well feel himself as aggrieved as if he had been robbed of a valuable piece of property. One pamphlet, indeed, declared that children were 'so much the goods, the possessions of their parent that they cannot, without a kind of theft, give away themselves'. Romantic love was still widely mistrusted as a basis for matrimony. Ralegh, expecting his execution in 1603, wrote a letter to his wife urging her to remarry 'not to please sense, but to avoid poverty, and to preserve thy child'.

But times were changing. James himself propounded the comparatively novel idea that parents, while entitled to 'forbid their children an unfit marriage', had no right to force them to a distasteful one. Whereas Elizabeth had imprisoned courtiers for an illicit match, James – who approved of matrimony – had several times sentimentally smoothed over a marriage made without parental consent. Lawrence Stone saw a dramatic shift in a woman's right to control her own marriage between 1560 and 1640. And can anyone believe the Jacobeans strangers to romance who has read a line of Shakespeare's poetry?

All parties agreed that once married, for better or worse, husband and wife had a duty to each other. William's father Lord Beauchamp, kept by his father the earl from going to his own wife, wrote angrily that Hertford was hoping 'in time to bring me not to care for my wife, whom I am bound in conscience, as well as by God, God and his law, to love as myself'. The injunction that no man should put asunder those whom God had joined was taken very seriously: Antonia Fraser has noted how recusant wives might be released from prison to bear their husband a child or cook the Christmas dinner. Once Arbella had married William, many contemporaries would have thought that (as she herself suggested) James was doing wrong to prevent him from enjoying her company. Perhaps Arbella was counting on James's bowing to the sanctity of the marriage vows she had made, and accepting a *fait accompli*.

> *Alas: your shears do come untimely now*
> *To clip the bird's wings, that's already flown.*
> *Will you see my husband?*

the Duchess of Malfi asked her brother briskly. But, as so often in Arbella's life, it was not a question of morality that would trip her up. It was political reality.

# 'Your faithful loving wife'

AS WORD OF THE MARRIAGE LEAKED OUT, THE COUPLE HAD ONLY
days in which to see each other freely. There is no reason to doubt
that in this time they enjoyed sexual relations; passion apart, they
would have had every reason to do so, since a marriage unconsummated could be more easily set aside. Contemporaries certainly had no doubts. Dudley Carleton – in a letter which reflects
the double standards of the day – sneered about 'the lady's hot
blood, which could not live without a husband'; by contrast, he
pitied 'the poor gentleman'.

But the time was short. The authorities acted quickly. On 8 July
William was summoned before the privy council and sent to the
Tower. On the next day, Arbella was committed into the custody
of Sir Thomas Parry, chancellor of the duchy of Lancaster, at
Lambeth: probably less a matter of leniency than of the fact that
there were not two prisons suitable for the incarceration of the
nobility. And heaven forbid that the couple should be placed in
any proximity. Though she might some day be granted liberty, she
would never have free access to her husband 'before she is too old
to bear him children', wrote the Venetian ambassador matter-of-
factly. The great fear was always that these two would found a
dynasty.

Towards the end of July, the chroniclers of court gossip had
much to report. 'The great couple', as Dudley Carleton called
them, had been summoned for interrogation. The Venetian

ambassador reported that 'The young man who was brought in first denied the fact; she however freely confessed it and excused the denial of her husband on the score of fear. She endeavoured to demonstrate that neither by laws divine nor human laws could she be prevented.' The council had reproached William with having, as they saw it, broken his promise not to rekindle the relationship. Arbella leapt to his defence. William, she said, had done no more than Abraham or Isaac, who both disclaimed their wives for a time. But the Venetian saw it gravely. 'A law forbidding under pain of "*loesa majestas*" and rebellion the descendants of blood royal to intermarry without leave is a serious injury to her case . . . rumour says she will not be so easily set free.'

As so often, Arbella's timing could hardly have been worse. In the summer of 1610, James already had every reason to feel both alarmed and touchy. The spring had seen a Catholic fanatic strike down the French king Henri IV, a former Protestant, and the shock waves that reverberated from the murder saw recusant Catholics in England stripped of their arms and forbidden to come within ten miles of the court. Barely weeks after Henri's death, Cecil had been busy trying to negotiate a happier arrangement between the king and his parliament, by which James would give up some of the more unpopular royal perks in exchange for relief from the massive royal debts. But the negotiations had not gone smoothly. The Commons had taken the king's tone as an infringement of their liberty. He for his part 'neither could nor would' submit to any questioning of his prerogative. These were ominous foreshadows of the years ahead.

Parliament had been prorogued for the investiture of the prince of Wales; but even here was another source of concern for a king becoming sensitive about his heir's popularity. James had given orders that the investiture ceremonies should be cut back to the bone, finding his son, in the words of the interregnum historian Arthur Wilson, 'too high mounted in the people's love' already. It was no time to be flouting James's authority.

Arbella's conditions of restraint were not so uncomfortable. Parry's was a pleasant house and garden, described by the topographical writer John Norden as 'a capital messuage, bounded by the Thames . . . a fair dwelling house, strongly built, of three

ILLUSTRISSIMI GENEROSISSIMIQUE PRI. HENRICI
MAGNÆ BRITANNIÆ ET HYBERNIÆ PRINCIPIS,
Vera Effigies.

Henry, prince of Wales

stories high'. The council's warrant to Parry granted her 'one or two of her women to attend her' – without, however, 'access of any other person until his Majesty's pleasure be further known'. Inevitably Arbella's state of mind was very far from easy; but this was far from being her darkest hour. She must by now have expected that she would be in trouble – briefly – and probably went to Lambeth in a spirit both combative and hopeful. Shortly, moreover, she had a very particular hope to keep her company.

Touchingly, her first concern is for her servants. Men like Freake and Dodderidge, who had been with Arbella at Hardwick, would remain in her service until the end of her life. The names of Kyrton and of Mrs Bradshaw, intimate attendants present at Arbella's recent marriage, are present in the accounts of that projected marriage seven years before. The destinies of several satellite families followed those of Arbella and William, and theirs is an important subtext to her story. A generation later, Lucy Hutchinson described the ardent attachment between Arbella and her waiting gentlewoman Margaret Byron, Lucy's mother-in-law, who had come to Arbella at nine years old and 'minded nothing but her lady'. When Arbella was taken away to prison, Sir John Byron (the same whom Brounker had described as being at Arbella's devotion) came to take his sister home. But even then, for many melancholy hours, Lucy related, Margaret Byron would sit and weep in remembrance of her 'unfortunate princess'.

'There are divers of my servants with whom I never thought to have parted whilst I lived,' Arbella herself wrote to Gilbert in the middle of July. They had been her second family. 'But since I am taken from them, and know not how to maintain either myself or them, being utterly ignorant how it will please his Majesty to deal with me, I were better to put them away now, than towards winter. Your lordship knows the greatness of my debts and my unableness to do [anything] for them.' As an afterthought, she mentions her horses: 'The bay gelding and the rest are at your lordship's commandment.' But her next letter returns to her domestics; Gilbert had obviously stepped into the breach, and she thanked him for his care of them.

Another letter that summer, to the privy council, asked that two of her imprisoned gentlemen servants, Hugh Crompton and

Edward Reeves, be moved away from the dangerous air of the Marshalsea, where there were prisoners dead 'and divers others sick of contagious and deadly diseases'. She gave what sounds to us like a curiously unfeeling reason for her care. 'Consider that they are servants, and accountable for diverse debts and reckonings, which if they should die would be a great prejudice to me and others.' 'If Crompton should die the poor lady would be infinitely distressed,' Gilbert wrote, 'he being the man in whom she most reposed trust touching her debts.' But in view of her other letters it is permissible, perhaps, to believe that Arbella was making the appeal she thought best suited to the council's hard-headed practicality, and that her real concern for her men was less mercenary.

Arbella signed her first letter to Gilbert: 'The poor prisoner your niece, Arbella Seymour'. There is pride in the new name – and there is hard reality. Her letters to the court were often, instead, signed with the tactfully ambiguous 'A.S.' When the king first saw a petition from his newly wed cousin he was so vexed that she had signed herself 'Arbella Seymour' that he could hardly be persuaded to listen to her plea. Indeed, the privy council had at first been unwilling to pass on Arbella's petition at all; but they agreed 'to oblige her', the Venetian ambassador reported. Arbella had taken pains over it – four versions of this letter survive. 'Restraint of liberty, comfort, and counsel of friends and all the effects of imprisonment are in themselves very grievous, and inflicted as due punishments for greater offences than mine,' she had written in a rough draft, but the bold words did not make it into either of the final copies. By the same token, in the rough drafts she had written 'we suffer' and 'our life' on behalf of herself and her husband – but subsequently changed the pronouns to the more tactful 'I' and 'my'.

The council was supportively effusive about the elegance of the petition's style. Cecil 'declared that he did not blush to admit that his style, for all that he was first secretary, could not rival that of a woman, for he thought it would tax all parliaments to draw up an answer which would correspond to the arguments and eloquence of the petition.' But James was not to be won, demanding 'whether it was well that a woman so closely allied to the

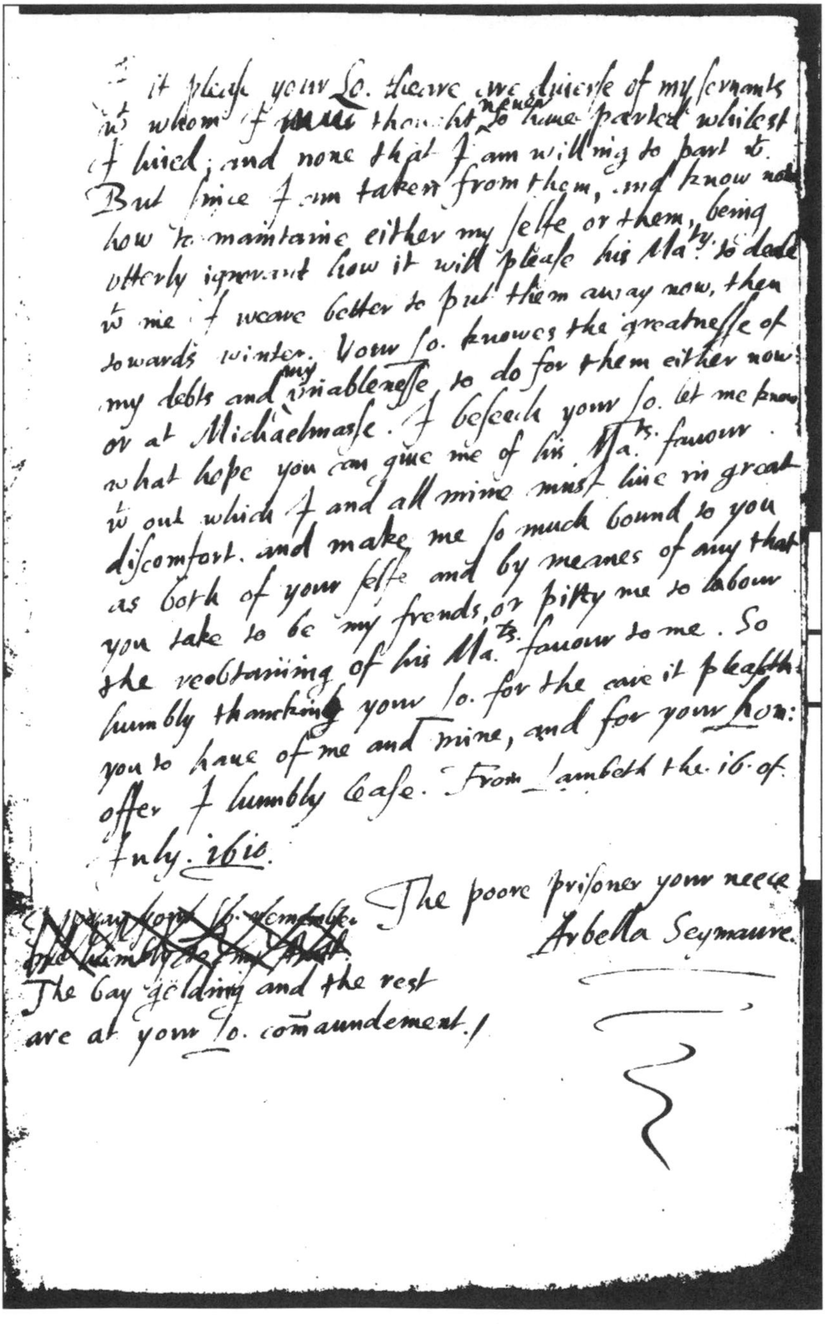

Letter from Arbella to Gilbert Talbot

blood royal should rule her life after her own humour'. He had spent much of his life under the shadow of a contested succession, and had indeed some reason to fear the bogey of a child from this union – a child who had the blood of both Margaret and Mary Tudor.

In September it looked as if those fears might prove well founded. The lady – said her woman Mrs Bradshaw, at an inquiry much later – was 'distempered'. Her body became so swollen that a gown had to be let out. Such swelling would correspond with the modern diagnosis of porphyria, but this was unknown in the seventeenth century. Arbella seems to have leaped to the more obvious conclusion: 'she her self let fall words that she thought she was with child.' And Arbella was 'apt enough to entertain that conceit', Mrs Bradshaw said, rather touchingly.

She began to swell, so Mrs Bradshaw said, within a month of her marriage (surely too soon – unless the betrothed couple had anticipated their wedding day?), and the distemper fell 'into an issue of blood which came from her', and which lasted several days. She showed the blood to her physician, Dr Moundford, and the matter should have ended there; though even at that, it would have frightened James badly. But the rumours proved so persistent that, three years after Arbella's death, it proved necessary to call an inquiry to confound the tale that Arbella had indeed borne a living child, who had been smuggled away to safety. Mary Talbot, Moundford, the servants and William himself all denied it – but the story, at the time, was hardly calculated to soften James's heart. Meanwhile, Arbella had to come to terms with the loss of the hope that had helped her face captivity bravely.

The queen, Prince Henry and Cecil all counselled that James should be lenient to Arbella, and many of 'the wisest men' at court expected it. First among Arbella's advocates was Queen Anna, 'on whose favour I will still chiefly rely'. Anna, out of her 'gracious commiseration', did all she could, but to no avail. As Arbella's correspondent reported: 'when [the queen] gave your ladyship's petition and letter to his Majesty he did take it well enough, but gave no other answer than that ye had eaten of the forbidden tree.'

That Christmastime Anna planned to stage a masque of *Love Freed from Ignorance and Folly*, in which the dancing ladies can free the captive Love only by throwing themselves on the king's generosity. Did others think of Arbella when they saw Anna's masque – a rather uncharacteristically placatory one? Did she think of Arbella when she commissioned it? Dudley Carleton, attributing the match to lust on the lady's part and folly on the man's, represented the viewpoint of the cynics among the court; but to sympathetic women it might not have seemed unreasonable to cast Arbella as an endangered heroine in one of the popular romance narratives of the day.

Certainly others understood Arbella's peril more clearly than she did herself. Arbella's route to the queen was through Jane (or Jean) Drummond, her own kinswoman and one of Anna's closest ladies, and when Jane was forced to report lack of success (albeit softened with promises of the queen's continuing favour) Arbella sent another indignant note expressing gratitude – and disbelief. 'I cannot rest satisfied till I may know what disaster of mine hindreth his Majesty's goodness towards me, having such a mediatrix to plead so just and honest a cause.'

Jane, hearing the court gossip, was less sanguine. 'The wisdom of this state, with the example [of] how some of your quality in the like case has been used, makes me fear that ye shall not find so easy [an] end to your troubles as ye expect, or I wish.' Arbella, still indignant, would reply that 'I never heard nor read of anybody's case that might be truly and justly compared to this of mine.' She was sweeping over the obvious similarities with Catherine Grey. But Jane Drummond's was to prove an accurate prophecy.

One letter in Arbella's handwriting was evidently meant to come from William, referring as it does to the liberties and the lieutenant of the Tower, where he was held. He begged the council's intercession in restoring him to James's 'most wished-for favour and my former liberty . . . I must confess I have offended his Majesty, which is my greatest sorrow, yet I hope not in that measure that it should deserve my utter ruination and destruction, since I protest my offence was committed before I knew it to be an offence.'

This, evidently, was the excuse the pair had agreed upon – that they had entered into a binding engagement at that meeting on 2 February, at a time when, in the wake of the Moldavian debacle, Arbella could reasonably claim to believe that the king had given her permission to marry any Englishman. ('Seeing herself deserted she had imagined that she could not be accused if she sought a husband of her own rank,' she had told the council hardily at that second inquiry.) It is an excuse that would have seemed reasonable to many contemporaries. The era knew two forms of betrothal, and depending on the exact form of words used (whether Arbella and William had promised to take each other in the future or the present tense) it may indeed have been a contract very nearly as binding as a marriage vow.

Of course, that argument is negated by the public message William sent to Arbella, specifically denying any such commitment. But once the theme had been chosen, the couple would embroider it enthusiastically – embroider it as Arbella did the gloves she sent this summer to the still supportive queen. Arbella also wrote to the king, pleading the 'great affliction to my mind' engendered by his severity:

> I most humbly beseech your Majesty ... to consider in what a miserable state I had been, if I had taken any other course than I did; for my own conscience witnessing before God that I was then the wife of him that now I am, I could never have matched with any other man but to have lived all the days of my life as an harlot.

At some point in the course of summer and autumn, Arbella seems to have despaired of attaining James's pardon through intercessors. It was always her taste to speak directly. She began pouring out letters to him, carefully worded to please his flattery-loving ear. His Majesty's 'handmaid', his 'most humble faithful subject and servant', claimed that 'the thought never yet entered into my heart, to do anything that might justly deserve any part of your indignation.' If any such thing had been done in-advertently, she begged, 'let it be covered with the shadow of your gracious benignity, and pardoned in that heroical mind of yours.' In exculpation for what she had done, she pleaded 'the necessity of my state and fortune, together with my weakness'. This would move him, surely; James liked to think of a woman's weakness. Arbella signed off her letter with her prayers for the 'most happy prosperity' of himself, his queen 'and your royal issue in all things for ever' – a protestation of loyalty to James's dynasty. But James was not swayed.

In December she wrote to James that 'your Majesty's neglect of me and my good liking of this gentleman that is my husband' had driven her to act independently. That was the final, the secretary's draft; in Arbella's own first draft she had written of her 'love to this gentleman'. But scaling down 'love' to 'liking' was a useless piece of tact, when she was openly accusing James of negligence. Indeed, Arbella offered James a blatantly backhanded compliment: that he, surely, would never do evil [separating a couple] that good [political security] might come of it – even though it were 'as convenient as malice may make it seem to separate us whom God has joined'. Such a consideration would be as impossible for so good a king 'as David's dealing with Uriah'. David, desiring Bathsheba, ordered her husband Uriah to be placed in the front line of battle . . . This was going very far. And yet Arbella seems still to have had hopes that the festive Christmas season, a traditional time for leniency, might bring pardon. She wrote to the queen, enclosing a copy of her petition to James 'at this time when . . . his Majesty forgiveth greater offences as freely as he desireth to be forgiven'. She asked Anna to consider 'how long I have lived a spectacle of his Majesty's displeasure'. Anna may well have been aware of it; but persuading James was another matter.

Arbella had already admitted, in a letter to William's brother Francis, that: 'I must confess I fear the destiny of your house and my own . . . Your brother's constancy notwithstanding, yet I bring him nothing but trouble.' To William himself, Arbella wrote encouragingly, and movingly – so movingly that it is painful to read at the letter's end that William has not written to her (not 'so much as how you do') for 'this good while'. Not that she reproaches him. Write 'when you please'. But her own letter is redolent of tenderness. It is worth quoting at length. 'Sir', she addresses him formally:

I am exceedingly sorry to hear you have not been well. I pray you let me know truly how you do and what was the cause of it, for I am not satisfied with the reason Smith [their messenger] gives. But if it be a cold I will impute it to some sympathy betwixt us having my self gotten a swollen cheek at the same time with a cold. For Gods sake let not your grief of mind work upon your body. You may see by me what inconveniences it will bring one to . . .

. . . we may by God's grace be happier than we look for in being suffered to enjoy ourselves with his Majesty's favour. But if we be not . . . I for my part shall think myself a pattern of misfortune in enjoying so great a blessing as you so little a while. No separation but that deprives me of the comfort of you, for wherever you be or in what state so ever you are, it sufficeth me you are mine. Rachel wept and would not be comforted because her children were no more, and that indeed is the remedy-less sorrow and none else . . . I assure you nothing the state can do with me can trouble me so much as this news of your being ill doth . . . Be well, and I shall account my self happy in being

your faithful loving wife.
Arb.S.

Just so, in 1563, Catherine Grey had lamented to William's grandfather: 'what a husband I have of [in] you, and my great hard fate to miss the viewing of so good a one.' Catherine's husband Hertford had once been betrothed to her sister Jane, just as Arbella had once sought William's brother Edward. And another Cecil, Lord Burghley, had had to enquire – just as his son Robert enquired about Arbella – whether Catherine's was a private match, or a political story. Both Cecils were inclined to the former theory, and to leniency. But one way and another, the echoes were beginning to sound ominous.

# 'A poor distressed gentlewoman'

INSTEAD OF RELEASE, THE FIRST DAYS OF 1611 BROUGHT WHISPERS OF a fresh controversy. It was a 'great secret' as yet, but the tongues were clacking. The Lady Arbella was 'called before the lords . . . she shall be sent to Durham . . . with intent that she and her husband shall not come together'. The story of the possible pregnancy had leaked out; and coupled with it there may have been the idea that William and Arbella had managed to meet during their imprisonment, due to the sympathy, laxity or sheer cupidity of their gaolers. It is notable that when the time came for their escape abroad, both prisoners told their attendants they were simply going to enjoy a brief conjugal visit, and had their excuse accepted, in a way that suggests this was no novelty. And the last thing the authorities wanted was a repeat of Catherine Grey's story, whereby an alternative line of succession would plague the crown for generations to come.

In January Arbella was informed that her husband was condemned to life imprisonment in the Tower, and that she herself was to be sent north, into the bishop of Durham's custody – 'clean out of this world', as she wrote despairingly. Things could be worse yet. The Venetians wrote that

> It is thought that the king will send her even further, and by putting her out of the kingdom [to Scotland] he will secure himself against disaffection settling round her. Her husband is confined to the

Tower for life and more closely guarded than heretofore; this has thrown him into extreme affliction nor are there wanting those who bewail his unhappiness.

Arbella, as she heard, was to experience the same distant captivity that had destroyed her royal aunt Mary.

She wrote to Sir Thomas Fleming, the lord chief justice, and Sir Edward Coke, lord chief justice of common pleas, protesting that she was to be removed 'far from these courts of justice where I ought to be examined, tried, and then condemned or cleared'. She wanted them 'to enquire by an *habeas corpus* or other usual form of law what is my fault and if upon examination by your lordships I shall thereof justly be convicted let me endure such punishment by your lordships' sentence as is due to such an offender.' If they could not offer her 'the ordinary relief of a distressed subject', then she asked them to intercede that she might still receive 'such benefit of justice . . . as both his Majesty by his oath hath promised and the laws of this realm afford to all others'. If no answer was made, then perhaps it is because no answer *could* be made – no answer that was at once logical and politic, anyway. Coke was later to recall that he had sworn, in his judge's oath, 'Ye shall not delay any person of common right for the letters of the king' – that is, you shall not keep anyone in custody merely on the king's instruction; ten years later, he even dared remind James of those words. The Magna Carta had stated clearly: 'No free man shall be seized or imprisoned . . . except by the lawful judgement of his equals or by the law of the land.' Four decades later the Leveller John Lilburne would believe so passionately in the universal applicability of the right to trial by jury that he, an ardent social revolutionary, none the less sent several imprisoned royalist noblemen law books for their defence. But in 1611 things simply did not work that way.

Over the next few weeks Arbella wrote letters with a frenzy that – like the ill-health she suffered – recalled her Hardwick days. She wrote to an unnamed knight (described by an earlier biographer as Sir Oliver Cromwell, wealthy uncle to the protector): 'Sir, though you be almost a stranger to me . . .' The letter, like all the others, begs that he will help 'a poor distressed gentlewoman . . . out of this great distress and misery and regain me his Majesty's favour which is my chiefest desire'. To a relative she described herself as 'the most penitent and sorrowful creature that breathes'. To Cecil she wrote of 'my soul overwhelmed with the extremity of grief'.

She wrote to Viscount Fenton in a slightly different tone. He, she had heard, had been speaking against her. Rather tartly, she pointed out that 'the fault cannot be uncommitted', and added an ominous rider: 'if you remember of old, I dare to die, so I be not guilty of my own death, and oppress others with my ruin too if there be no other way.'

In amid all this high emotion, she had to find the energy to deal with one of William's bills. An Italian jeweller called Prospero Gorges was demanding – if that is the word for a document so obsequious, so lavishly detailed about his own woes – £6 8s 6d for some silk and amber points he had made for Seymour. Arbella, desperate, forwarded the note to William's brother Francis, begging him to show it to Mary Talbot 'or any friend you think will lay out so much for me at this time when it seems everyone forsakes me but those that cannot help me'.

In the middle of March the journey north was to begin. On 13 March a warrant was sent to the bishop of Durham, which laid out in full what James felt to be his grievance. His cousin the Lady Arbella 'hath highly offended us in seeking to marry herself without our knowledge . . . and in proceeding afterwards to a full conclusion of a marriage with the self same person whom (for many just causes) we had expressly forbidden her to marry.' It went on to censure William's duplicity, after the 'solemn protestations' he had made to the council of intent to leave off the affair. But James's central point seems to have been the setting of a bad example:

> forasmuch as it is more necessary for us to make some such demonstration now of the just sense and feeling we have after so great an indignity offered unto us, as may make others know by her example that no respect of personal affection can make us neglect those considerations wherein both the honour and order of the state is interested.

None the less, he emphasized 'the difference between us and her. That whereas she has abounded towards us in disobedience and ingratitude, we are (on the contrary) still apt to temper the severity of justice with grace and favour,' as witnessed by his sending her to the bishop's virtuous care.

The bishop, Dr William James, presented himself in Lambeth at eight in the morning on 15 March. He described the scene to the privy council with vivid urgency. Arbella, he wrote, was so distressed that cold drops burst from her forehead. She demanded a sight of the king's warrant; he gave it, and 'used all the poor skill' he could muster to persuade her to go quietly. He told her tales of those less fortunate, of prisoners and martyrs: a strange way to soothe a fearful hysteric, surely. Arbella's host-cum-gaoler Parry and her own doctor Moundford added their pleas, but in vain. Whether through obstinacy or real incapacity, she could not be moved, and in the end the bishop's men were forced to carry her into the street on her mattress.

Dr Moundford had to administer cordials three times to his fainting patient on the way from Lambeth to Highgate where (since they were clearly never going to make the intended destination of Barnet) a house had hastily been commandeered for a one-night stop. She was lifted from the litter and carried into the house, where she remained half swooning but sleepless until midnight. The bishop, 'being somewhat distempered himself', could do little to soothe her (later, he claimed 'half a year's sickness and lameness' as legacy of his attendance on the lady). But the next morning he appeared at her bedside, urging 'the sweet day, and air, and duty of her journey'. Arbella was having none of it; nor, more to the point, was Moundford. He said she could not possibly travel that day. The bishop had urgently to send a letter to the privy council. The lists of official expenses for Arbella's enforced journey feature the cost of messengers with alarming regularity. The stay at Highgate grew from one day into six, but the rest did not help her. Moundford, in his determination of 'cherishing her to life', yet suspected shrewdly that no cordials could 'warrant either amendment of her health or continuance of life if some contentment of mind be not gained'.

On 21 March, the king's orders obliged the bishop to remove

his charge forcibly to Barnet. She was to be taken 'by the strength of men's hands', if necessary. Once again, she had to be carried to the litter in her bed: 'the means prescribed, which were employed with all decency and respect'. Gilbert wrote to Moundford thanking him for his care. 'For my part I can do her very small service more than by my prayers.' As a privy counsellor, he had had to sign the order for Arbella's remove; he had absented himself from more than enough council meetings already. He tried to speak to James on his niece's behalf. The king was unsympathetic: 'It was enough to make any sound man sick to be carried in a bed in that manner she is, much more for her whose impatient and unquiet spirits heapeth upon herself far greater indispositions of body.'

He may have had the vestige of a point about his cousin's 'unquiet spirits': suffering Arbella undoubtedly was, with violent pains in the head and bouts of sickness – but not so sick that she was not planning ahead. She and William had jointly signed a document relieving Crompton of any responsibility for their financial affairs: 'discharging him of all accounts, reckonings, receipts and demands whatsoever, whereby he may be charged by us or by either of us from the beginning of the world until the day of the date of this present'. Crompton would later confess to having acted as liaison between Arbella and her aunt Mary – to having handled 'the preparation of means, and the receipt of monies', with which to facilitate his mistress's plans, and this sounds as if something drastic – a flight abroad? – were planned already.

At Barnet the party ground to a halt again, and once more the doctors supported Arbella's determination to go no further. James, suspicious, sent his son's physician Dr Hammond to see her. He took her pulse and prescribed medicine – and agreed she could not travel immediately. Gilbert was present when Hammond made his report to the council, and reported that the doctor had found his niece

very weak, her pulse dull and melancholy for the most part, yet sometimes uncertain; her water bad, showing great obstructions; her countenance very heavy, pale and wan; nevertheless, she was free from any fever or any other actual sickness, but of his con-

science he protested that she was in no case to travel until God
restored her to some better strength both of body and mind.

Arbella herself wrote to Viscount Fenton that she had been 'sick
even unto the death'. And yet still she could not get 'those ordinary helps whereby most in my case, be they never so poor or
unfortunate soever, are preserved alive. I can get neither clothes
nor posset ale nor any thing but ordinary diet . . . not so much as
a glister [enema] when I call for it, saving your reverence.'

For what was intended to be a one-night stop at Barnet, Arbella
had been housed in an inn. This was clearly unsuitable for a
longer stay, so the home of a Mr Conyers at East Barnet was
requisitioned as a lodging. The bishop was (no doubt thankfully)
going ahead to Durham to pave the way for his fragile prisoner,
his place as chief custodian being taken by Sir James Croft. On
31 March Croft reported that on the day of the short remove
Arbella 'apparelled herself with what convenience she might by
reason of her weakness', but that when he galloped ahead as an
advance guard, he found the Conyers house far from ready. It was
just as well, perhaps, that the party had not already set out, since
sitting up for the half-hour's wait had already brought on Arbella's
faintness again. The doctor 'averreth that her la[dyship] was
afflicted at that time with a melancholy passion proceeding from
her heart and forming up to the brains which caused a dizziness in
her head with extreme pain, but that fit did not long endure'.

Arbella's eventual remove to East Barnet on 2 April was
attended by 'powerful' sickness on the way, and the next day she
was still exhausted from the mile-and-a-half journey. As a letter
of her own to the privy council put it:

I am in so weak case as I verily think it would be the cause of my
death to be removed . . . My late discomfortable journey (which I
have not yet recovered) had almost ended my days and I have
never since gone out of a few little and hot rooms, and am many
ways unfit to take the air. I trust your lordships will not look I
should be so unchristian as to be a cause of my own death, and
I leave it to your lordships wisdom to consider what the world
would conceive if I should be violently enforced to do it.

Proceeding north was clearly impracticable, and it was agreed Arbella should be allowed to stay at Barnet through April. She sent James a note of thanks for granting her the 'Halcyon days . . . since it hath pleased your Majesty to give this testimony of willingness to have me live a while'. The much-tried bishop stopped at Royston on his way north to give a report to the king in person, urging Arbella's grief, her 'hearty and zealous' prayers for the king and 'her willingness, if it might be so, to sweep his chamber', all of which pleased James so much that he called over Prince Henry to hear. The bishop afterwards sent back words of encouragement, via Croft, to Arbella herself. 'My poor opinion is that, if she wrong not herself, God in time will move his Majesty's heart to have compassion upon her.'

On 17 April Croft wrote that rest and physic had made Arbella 'somewhat better and lightsomer' than before, but that she had still not so much as walked the length of her bedchamber, nor did he ever find her other than upon her bed.

> She apprehendeth nothing but fear and danger in the most ugliest forms, conceiving always the worst and much worse than any way can happen to her . . . that his Majesty should dispose of her at his pleasure she does not gainsay, but the horrors of her utter ruin and end which hourly present themselves to her phantasy, occasioned . . . by the remoteness of the place whereunto she must go, driveth her to utter despair.

James was unmoved. He had been dropping hints that compliance on Arbella's part might be rewarded, that she might not have to make more than a short stay in the north – but she did have to comply, and to be seen to comply. On 28 April he sent fresh orders, swearing that if he were king she would leave for Durham on the Monday following. He was king. But for all that, Arbella was certainly to have a little longer. And longer again, maybe.

It took her four drafts to word a final petition, in which she begged for yet three weeks more, promising, if they were granted, then to make the journey without resistance (being assured on all sides that her cousin the king had no purpose 'to make my correction my ruin'). But the subservient tone is belied by the comments written in the margin: 'whereupon I must confess I bely myself extremely', she added beside her promise to make no future resistance, aware she might seem to be admitting she had been guilty of resistance in the past. In the main body of the text, she hopes to receive James's grace. In the margin: 'what man of grace this is I cannot guess.' Today, the comments sound like an alarm bell signalling the storms ahead. But at the time, the king heard no such warning. On reading Arbella's petition, James — after much hesitation, reported Moundford, who with Croft had gone to court in person to plead Arbella's cause — 'did yield that one other month should be employed in her perfect cure'. He 'used not one unkind or wrathful word of her, but mildly taxed her obstinacy', and the letter, 'penned by her in the best terms (as she can do right well) was commended'. Arbella would have until 5 June.

The journey from Lambeth to Barnet, originally scheduled for a day, was running at twelve weeks already, and by now, her residence at Mr Conyers' house had taken on an air of society. Prince Henry sent his chaplain Mathias Melwarde to her. She may have been soothed by evidence of sympathy from such as a Lady Chandos, staying nearby, who had written to Dr Moundford offering the best drink in her family's cellars and urging him that 'if you want for the honourable lady what is in this house, you will send for it.'

More to the point, for the first time Mary Talbot was allowed to visit Arbella. Mary had already pleaded with James's current favourite, the handsome young Scotsman Robert Carr, to intercede for her niece. He had rejected her with contempt: 'he would rather lose his life than deal in a matter so distasteful to his Majesty.' Perhaps Mary, like Arbella herself, had concluded that it was useless trying to move the king to pity. And hers was not a temperament to take opposition lightly.

Some time in those weeks of sickness, Arbella's goals had changed. While hiding any sign of improvement in her health, she and Mary, through Crompton's agency, set about amassing a sum of money. William had written rather grimly of his new aunt by marriage that 'I can expect no good from her, since I am credibly informed that she doth more harm than good.' But Mary could be a remarkably effective ally. Arbella and William proposed to start life on the continent with £2,800, of which at least half came from Mary – and £850 of that from a source freighted with significance for Arbella. Mary bought from her some embroideries done by the Scots queen – not worth a tenth of the price, as they were later described scornfully. The time for letters was past. It was, finally, time for action.

# 'To break prison and make escape'

TO ARRANGE THE ESCAPE OF ONE PRISONER WITH SO HIGH A PROFILE as Arbella Stuart was surely a coup. To arrange the simultaneous escape of her husband from the Tower of London sounds extra-ordinary. But while conditions of imprisonment in the seven-teenth century could be appalling, they could also resemble a kind of house arrest; even house arrest with occasional leaves of absence, to be won not by good behaviour but by bribery. The conditions in which Arbella and William were held, at this stage, were predicated on the assumption that they would not want to run away; that, being who they were and what they were – dependent on their public identity, unable to move without a retinue of servants – they had simply nowhere to go.

This was true – so long as they remained in the country; and to leave England without permission was against the law for any-body, never mind a prisoner. Such, however, was the ambitious plan. Eighteen months before, perhaps the couple had hoped to be allowed to retire quietly to the midlands together, but by June 1611 those days must have seemed a long time away. And Arbella had already, in 1603, shown herself capable of venturesome (if misguided) action – even without the support of Mary Talbot, the redoubtable countess of Shrewsbury.

Escape abroad had, after all, been achieved not so long before, in the love-match of Leicester's bastard son Sir Robert Dudley and the old queen's maid of honour Elizabeth Southwell. She had disguised herself as his page for the flight, and soon the pair would be living very successfully in Florence under the protection of the Medici. As Arbella lay in bed at Barnet she must have dreamed of another happy outcome: meeting William at Blackwall; heading out to sea with him; starting a new life in his company. They may have intended to settle in France; a letter in the Talbot papers proves that Mary Talbot had maintained contact with Mary Seton, once lady to Mary, queen of Scots and later abbess of a French convent. The letter mentions that Mary Seton had asked Arbella to present a petition for her – vainly, as she complained. But clearly the ladies of Arbella's family had their own contacts beyond the sea.

We know that Arbella's plan miscarried; that her great effort ended in disaster. On the Monday morning, she and William were both captive in England, in comparative proximity. By Friday evening, they were in different countries: he in freedom, she in closer custody. Where – in the course of a mere four days – did it go so wrong, precisely?

The Venetian ambassador, writing home some days after Monday, 3 June – after collecting all the news and rumours – gave a version of events rich in details slightly different from those recounted by Sir John More. On 'the evening' of Arbella's escape, her waiting woman slipped the porter some dishes from Arbella's table. A mild form of bribe, maybe? After slipping out through the gardens in her male costume, Arbella rode the thirteen miles to the river 'in little more than an hour, it is said'.

While Arbella could simply walk away from her lodgings in Barnet, William had to be freed from a more formal captivity. Still, escape from the Tower was far from unknown – and William had successfully negotiated a fairly comfortable existence there. In the first weeks of his confinement (as witnessed by his and Arbella's letters), William's health had declined. July, he later said, was the very worst month of all to be shut within such dank and airless chambers. But, as a result of his complaints, he had been granted 'the liberty of the Tower' – freedom, that is, to move around the extensive precincts: a crowded complex the size of a village, which also contained a royal palace, a mint, an armoury and a menagerie.

He had also been moved from the lieutenant's own quarters to rooms above Traitor's Gate. These he proceeded to furnish with goods either bought on credit (or with money loaned to him by the lieutenant, who later protested wildly that William had trimmed a tapestry to fit a fireplace, making it impossible to return) or sent to him from Arbella's house. Four decades later, during the Civil War, when William's own 25-year-old son was similarly imprisoned in the Tower by parliamentary forces, William wrote to him there: 'It seems it is a place entailed upon our family, for we have now held it five generations . . . I like not the place so well but could be very well contented the entail should be cut off, and settled upon some other family that better deserves it.' But now, he would make the most of such familiarity.

The Jesuit John Gerard, escaping a few years before, had simply lowered himself from a riverside window to a waiting boat below. William's room over Traitor's Gate likewise looked to the wharf and the river, but his windows were mere arrow-slits. He had to find another way. This was not as hard as one might think. William could walk around to enjoy fresh air and exercise; and, in his eleven-month stay, he had had ample time to become familiar with the routine of the Tower, including the comings and goings of the tradesmen who catered for its large community. Most days, a cart laden with hay and firewood trundled along the alley just within the Tower's southern walls, and pulled up beneath the arch just opposite St Thomas's Tower. The carter proved amenable to bribery.

Outside the Tower, William's friends had done a good deal of groundwork. The day before the escape itself, Edward Rodney had taken lodgings across the river from the Tower, at the house of his former landlady in Southwark, telling her he had been unwell, and wanted a change of air. Next, his servant appeared there with some bulky luggage: 'a cloak, a cap, a cabinet and a fardel [bundle], all lapped in a white sheet, to be laid in his chamber', followed the next day by a buckram bag 'full of stuff'.

Next came a gentleman (one of Arbella's gentleman servants) in a cloak lined with purple velvet, purple hose and a green doublet, who told the landlady a second version of the story. Rodney's illness, he said, was but a feint; the truth was, he had taken the lodging to meet a gentlewoman of fashion, 'by whom he hoped to receive much good'. This seemed to be borne out by his re-appearance in company with a lady (probably Mrs Bradshaw) with a wart under the eye. Early in the afternoon, she sent the goods off in the charge of a waterman, who was told to convey them to St Katherine's Stair. Gentleman and lady themselves departed at around three o'clock – just as Arbella in Barnet was starting her ride – having first peered into the street to make sure there were no watchers. The landlady, curiosity aroused, sent her servant to follow them, but could discover no more than that they had taken a boat, at Pickleherring by the Tower.

In twos and threes, inconspicuously, all the conspirators were making their way downriver: the attendants by water; Arbella and her party on horse. William was the last of all – and every-thing depended on careful timing. They had to meet at Blackwall, then take oar and set off away down to the sea before their absence was discovered – or before the tides of the Thames could put another problem in the way.

On the day of his escape (as Sir John More heard it), William had his servant give it out that he was sick with the toothache; an excuse for his not being seen in the usual way. The servant, appar-ently, had been told (and believed) that William 'was gone but to lie a night with his wife, and would surely return thither of him-self again'. The first stage of the plan at least went off without discovery. William had been provided with a disguise, 'a peruque and beard of black hair' and a tawny cloth suit. Thus clad, he slipped out of his room, and unobtrusively followed the cart as it trundled away. Again, the Venetian ambassador's report differs from More's in the details, though not in essentials. Foscarini (and the bill of those imprisoned later gives some credence to his version) says William had most help from his barber, who 'band-aged a leg, put on a false beard' and, thus disguised, came to the Tower and asked for himself.

He was told the barber was there. He went in and Seymour dis-guised himself in the barber's clothes and both went out together; nor did the guards raise any difficulty as they took him for the man who had just gone in; nor did they say anything to the barber, for he was accustomed to go in and out almost daily.

Either way, William had a nerve-wracking few minutes ahead of him. At a steady pace – not fast enough to attract attention – it was a long ten minutes from his own chamber to the first real taste of freedom. Along Water Lane and through the Byward Arch; past the menagerie, where the lions roared, and round the looping path; out by the Middle Tower, where the soldiers were on duty. It must have taken a steady nerve, under all those eyes. Then William was outside the Tower – but still his path, ironically, took him back against its walls and under the very rooms he had inhabited so recently, on to the Tower's south-eastern corner, just before the shallows of St Katherine's Dock. Here Rodney and the boat were waiting. So far, so good – but they were very late. There had been some kind of delay. It may have been as basic as the carter's late arrival. By the time William could embark on his escape, Arbella was already nearing the river.

William and Rodney knew it was too late to try to rendezvous at Blackwall as arranged, so they pressed straight on down the Thames to Leigh. There, the waters were by now too high for their little rowing boat, and so they hired a fisherman to take them out to an empty coal vessel, the *Charles*, that lay at anchor out to sea. The collier's captain was to remember Rodney's grand clothes – 'a full suit of satin with gold and silver lace' – and another younger man, William, 'in a suit of Murray coloured stuff', along with a servant and a Frenchman. He remembered still more vividly the enormous sum of forty pounds they offered him, saying that, because of a quarrel, Rodney had to flee the country. Forty pounds was a fortune to a working man. The captain agreed to postpone his trip to Newcastle, and take them to Calais. Like Arbella's party, William got successfully away.

Tuesday morning, and it looked as if the attempt might yet end well. But behind the fugitives, in London, an early discovery was almost upon them. Rodney had incautiously left a letter for William's brother Francis Seymour, with whom he himself usually shared lodgings. It was vaguely worded – apologies for not having shared some secret – but it was enough to send Francis rushing round to the Tower when it was given to him early on that Tuesday.

'Myself being come to his [William's] lodging,' Francis recounted to his grandfather the earl, 'I asked his man for him, who told me that he had not slept of all that night, and that he would not that morning be troubled.' Francis, 'not therewith satisfied', insisted that he 'must and would' speak with his brother. When the servant 'perceived he could not resist, he confessed the truth, which he had no sooner done, but at the very same instant comes the lieutenant, to whom I showed this letter of Edward Rodney'. By that time Arbella was only just reaching the open waves, and William only just leaving Leigh. It was not far enough away for safety.

Francis and the lieutenant hastened to see Cecil at Greenwich. The king was alerted, the council in London summoned. Francis was examined, as he wrote to his grandfather: '1st. How came he by the letter? 2nd. Why did he not instantly carry it to the Treasurer? 3rd. Whether Rodney had not slept with him the night before? 4th. What conference they had? 5th. Whether he knew where the fugitives were bound?' Ordered to hold himself ready for more questioning at Hertford House, Francis wrote another self-pitying letter, this time to his step-grandmother the countess, protesting that he was 'as clear of their escape or any of their practices as is the child that was but yesterday born'.

The old earl reacted to the news with his own burst of exculpatory letters, lamenting that 'I should in these my last days be grandfather of a child that, instead of patience and tarrying the Lord's leisure (lessons that I learned and prayed for when I was in the same place whereout lewdly he is now escaped), would not tarry for the good hour of favour to come from a gracious and merciful king'. William's 'foolish and boyish' action so shook his grandfather that the old man had to scrawl a postscript to Cecil explaining that his candle had set fire to the bottom of Francis's enclosed page. This fury seems rather unfair in view of the fact that all three of his own marriages had been made in secrecy, and without sanction. But Hertford's anger only reflected the reaction of the authorities.

When James heard of the escape on Tuesday morning

(according to an earlier, more urgent, dispatch by Foscarini), 'The council was summoned immediately and proclamations were issued and printed that same day.' By midnight the king's ship-wright, Phineas Pette, had received orders by messenger to take twenty musketeers out to sea to search all vessels. Admiral Monson had been dispatched to Blackwall to question the water-men there, and picked up some tale that among recent visitors to the tavern where Arbella had waited had been her cousin, Mary Talbot's daughter, Elizabeth Grey. Even as he questioned, men put ashore from a ship newly arrived, carrying another story of a strange party – Arbella's – taken by a French boat towards Calais.

But the winds that only slightly impeded Arbella's progress altered the whole course of William's journey. 'The wind standing cross to go for Calais' (as the bailiff of Ipswich later reported), William's ship instead put into Harwich on Tuesday night. There on the Suffolk coast it stayed – powerless to move, but safe from harassment, since there was no mass communication to give instant broadcast to James's fury – right through another long day. Behind Arbella, back in London, the pursuit gathered speed.

The royal proclamations demanded the fugitives' apprehension and return by anyone from whom they should ask help, declaring that they had 'by the wicked practices of divers lewd persons . . . found the means to break prison and make escape' after their committal 'for divers great and heinous offences'. (And that even after Cecil had persuaded the king to soften the wording con-siderably.) 'It is supposed', wrote the Venetian ambassador omi-nously, 'that those who fled with Arabella [*sic*] will pay the penalty of their act with their lives.'

'Couriers were sent in all directions, and especially to France . . . Today [Wednesday] the king returned to London, and the lords of the council have spent the whole day with his Majesty in secret consultation.' The countess of Shrewsbury was arrested; a house search through the city began weeding out papists; frantic letters were sent to ambassadors; a new order was sent out that Catholics and puritans alike should take the oath of allegiance. 'Both parliament and council thought this the sole way to pre-serve the king's life,' reported the Venetian ambassador. James always reacted with near-hysteria to the thought of any threat – a legacy of that youth of alarums, excursions and abductions, when the assassin's dagger was never far away. To his ever-fearful imagination, this was not a romantic escapade. It was a political threat – an enormity.

What the alarmists feared, of course, was that William and Arbella, once abroad, would throw themselves into the protection of a Catholic power and present an alternative, a Catholic, contention for the throne (though John More recorded an alternative speculation: that they might have been 'most pitied by the puritans' had they made their way to France). Such fears gained a certain weight from the involvement of Mary Talbot, that noted Catholic sympathizer, who was from the first recognized as a prime mover in the affair: 'an obstinate popish recusant', she would be called at the inquiry, who had 'perverted also the Lady Arbella'. From the start, it was 'generally affirmed', as the Venetian ambassador wrote, 'that this flight took place by the advice and help of some personage of weight' – and rumours of the involvement of some foreign power can only have been fostered by his report that Arbella's ship also carried a courier from the French ambassador, bearing dispatches to his king.

Meanwhile the culprits, the cause of all this consternation, had been borne apart by the water, unable to find each other across the expanses of the sea. It would have had the makings of farce, if it were not so patently brewing for tragedy. As Wednesday wore along, William still lay at Harwich – in an agony of frustration, no doubt, but in safety. For Arbella, disaster was imminent. The English ship that sighted her tiny bark in mid-Channel had received its orders to stop and search all vessels only a mere two hours before. So the Venetian reported, anyway. The guard ship 'ordered her to strike her sail and haul to'. Being disobeyed,

> the royal ship proceeded to compel obedience by firing, but finding this useless she dispatched her frigate and as the sea was calm and the wind had dropped, about a league off Calais she came up with the Lady Arabella's ship and instantly seized her without meeting the smallest resistance from her crew.

Foscarini recounted how, the king having returned from

'Hardwick Hall / More glass than wall'. The rooftops of Bess's great creation exalt her initials to the sky: ES (Elizabeth Shrewsbury).

# HARDWICK

James I (*left*) and
Robert Cecil (*below*),
his chief minister
and Burghley's son.

SERO. SED SERIO

Gilbert and Mary Talbot,
earl and countess of
Shrewsbury. Arbella's
uncle and aunt were
faithful correspondents
through her court years.

London in the early seventeenth century. Old St Paul's still dominates the skyline, and the Tower of London looms on the far right. The southern portal of London Bridge bristles with spikes bearing the severed heads of traitors.

Several versions of this portrait exist, all described as being
of Arbella, though there are no records of the date or
occasion of the painting. This one hangs above
the great staircase at Longleat.

London to Greenwich, 'Lord Salisbury [Cecil] had an express from Dover with news that Lady Arabella had been captured . . . Lord Salisbury went at once to the king, and the news was most welcome at court.'

The first news had come from Griffen Cockett, captain of the *Adventure*, the ship that captured Arbella. But by the Thursday morning Admiral Monson, Cockett's superior, was adding his might – anxious (to judge by his huffiness about the 'negligence of the postmasters' who delayed his first dispatch) not to miss his share of the glory. Under pretext of asking for orders about Arbella's treatment, 'unwilling she should go ashore until I have further authority', he recounted his own adventures. Having been becalmed off Gravesend in his first vessel, a 'light horseman', he had seized the chance of the first wind and 'the next ketch or fisherman I could meet withall', and set off towards Flanders in his commandeered craft. Meeting another ship at sea, he heard that the *Adventure* had already returned to the English Downs; guessed that she had made her capture; and at once turned around to follow.

William knew nothing of this. All that Wednesday his ship had still lain at Harwich, and it was not until Thursday morning that she finally set sail – by which time Arbella was being brought captive back to England.

Early on Friday morning – late, but peaceful – William finally reached Ostend. 'A little before the landing,' ran the report collated from Harwich by the bailiff of Ipswich, 'one of the ship asked the young gentleman what his name was. He said it was William Sea.' While 'William Sea' and his companions made their way from the shore up into the town in the fresh morning air, the ship's company, still ignorant of the dramatic part they had played, turned back for England: 'bound towards Newcastle', as the bailiff reported. 'Hearing at sea that inquisition was made for such persons as they transported, they have put into the harbour and repaired unto the town, whom we have made stay of until your lordship's pleasure be further known.' More fodder for the hungry maw of the official inquiry.

For William, all that now lay behind him as he took his first steps into a foreign country. While he was sending word to

Gravelines to scour the coast for news of his wife, Admiral Monson was receiving his instructions: Arbella was to be taken directly to the Tower. She had been their quarry; with Arbella secured, no-one bothered to pursue William further.

# 'A spectacle of his Majesty's displeasure'

ARBELLA ENTERED IMPRISONMENT WITH HER HEAD HELD HIGH, buoyed up by her captors' admission that William was still at liberty – less sorry that she should be taken, in John More's expressive words, than glad that Mr Seymour should have got away. To that unselfish relief there may well have been added, for the moment, a degree of nervous excitement; a febrile energy born of the action and drama of her escape. She may still have been on an adrenaline high. If Arbella was subject to fits of despair, she also had a capacity for quite unreasonable hope. It was yet another way in which she resembled her royal aunt, Mary. It would take not days, nor even months, but years for all hope to drain quite away.

But she could hardly fail to think of William's grandmother, Catherine Grey, whose case had so directly foreshadowed her own, and perhaps of Catherine's dwarfish sister Mary (and their sister Jane, who *had* lost her head ... but hers was a different story). Half a century before, Catherine had come to the Tower new-married, 'being great with child', and her captors must have hoped that both she and the baby would die. Perhaps that is why the furnishings for her rooms were chosen from the official stores with such callous economy: one damask coverlet 'all to-broken and not worth tenpence', as the then lieutenant of the Tower scrawled in the margin of the records contemptuously; a single chair, 'an old, cast thing'; and a quilt 'stark naught'. Now she,

Arbella, would have to contend all over again with the question of servants, and furniture, and the 'several cares of a householder' of which she had once written so joyfully.

Catherine had survived childbirth, and her baby, William's father, was christened in the Tower's own church. Her husband Hertford could visit her – 'passed through the doors of the prison standing open, to comfort her who mourned for the sentence pronounced, and pay my marriage debt', as he put it proudly, when their second child was born. But despite her blessings Catherine (and short Mary's gigantic husband Thomas Keyes, the court sergeant) had still died in captivity, and Mary herself been let out only to live a brief, ghost's life in poverty. Catherine's uncle had written pitifully of her 'miserable and most woeful state'; of how he never saw her 'but I found her either weeping or saw by her face that she had wept.' And yet Catherine had had hope to comfort her. Even while she sickened, while she refused food, she had thought of her babies. Arbella had no such distraction. Her husband was beyond the sea. The words of Chidiock Tichbourne might have been written for her; Tichbourne, the young Catholic who wrote them in the Tower, before he died for his part in the Babington conspiracy:

> My tale was heard and yet it was not told,
> My fruit is fallen and yet my leaves are green,
> My youth is spent and yet I am not old,
> I saw the world and yet I was not seen;
> My thread is cut and yet it is not spun,
> And now I live and now my life is done.

The bill of arrests made after Arbella's flight abroad was a long one, with suspects dispatched to the Fleet prison in the City, the Marshalsea in Southwark and the Gatehouse in Westminster.

La: Arbella
The ctess Shrewsbury

Fleet
Hugh Crompton, Gent

Marsh.
  William Markham, Gent
Gateh. Edward Reeves
  Mrs Bradshawe
Bonds
  Bullen, Mr Seymour's barber
  Mr Seymour's butler
Removed

| | |
|---|---|
|   Sir James Croft | In the Fleet |
|   Dr Moundford | |

Bonds

| | |
|---|---|
|   Adams, the minister's wife | Gatehouse |
|   Surson, the skipper of Ipswich | |

Loses his place

| | |
|---|---|
|   Edward Kirton, Gent | " |
|   Tassin Corvé, the French skipper, to be sent to the ambassador | In Newgate |
|   John Baisley, waterman | " |

To be delivered
  Balis, the earl of Shrewsbury's man, with the Bailiff of
  Westminster

And the man who had made Arbella's wig had already been released . . . But such a wholesale, panicky collection of prisoners could not be held for long. Some were quickly released: Sir James Croft, for example, guilty at the worst of a little slackness, and pathetically pleading his thirty-five years' loyal service to the crown. But not Markham, nor Crompton, nor indeed the countess of Shrewsbury.

The cooler heads among James's advisers were prepared to treat this as a marriage with only private implications; to assume, as John More wrote to Sir Ralph Winwood,

> that if this couple should have escaped, the danger was not likely to have been very great, in regard that their pretensions are so many degrees removed, and they ungraceful [i.e. out of favour] both in their persons and in their houses, so as a hot alarm taken

at the matter will make them more illustrious in the world's eye than now they are, or (being let alone) ever would have been.

By contrast, some, as More said contemptuously, 'aggravate the offence in so strange a manner, as that it might be compared to the [Gun]Powder Treason'. The earl of Nottingham, the lord admiral, who even in the first flush of alarm had advised James simply to let William and Arbella go off and live together, had found his cool voice drowned in a clamour of anti-Catholic feeling.

But by the end of June efforts were being made to put a good face on things, to play down the threat – for foreign consumption at least. Cecil's letters to ambassadors abroad stressed that the fugitives were to be presented as 'contemptible creatures' and James as concerned only with the affront to his authority. The Venetian ambassador had a meeting with the king, and came away with the impression that unless Arbella were found to have made a treasonable alliance with Catholics (in which case she too could face execution), nothing harsh was planned; 'for all may be attributed to her great love for the person she had chosen to be her husband'. James, no doubt furiously resenting the need to justify himself, protested that 'he had resolved to marry her suitably to her rank; he knew quite well what was right and proper.' The French ambassador, rushing on a round of exculpatory visits, protesting that neither his courier nor the captain of the French vessel had known the identity of the lady passenger, had his excuses accepted, diplomatically. The earl of Hertford, who had at first been summoned to London for questioning, was allowed to relapse into his quiet country life – chastened enough grovellingly to submit for the council's approval every chiding letter he wrote to William, his 'ingrate boy'. None the less, six weeks after the escape he was writing jokingly to Cecil about his wife's 'inveterate malice' against the rabbits of a warren belonging to Cecil. 'She went thither without me on Thursday last, with bows and arrows, making reckoning to murther many.' But far into July, while the countess of Hertford practised field sports, Arbella in the Tower was still being interrogated regularly.

There were, as one diplomatic dispatch put it, 'many in this city of London who heartily deplore her unhappy case'. The Florentine secretary noted that 'from the least to the greatest, every one rejoiced over this escape and showed so great an affection to the Lady Arabella that it nearly surpassed convenience'. One Captain Flick, who grumbled over the dinner table about the king's iniquities, was himself briefly sent to the Tower. Popular opinion was reflected in a stage success of that year, *The Second Maiden's Tragedy* (speculatively identified as the lost *Cardenio* of Shakespeare and Fletcher). Two lovers, 'the Lady' and 'Govianus' – described as 'the rightful king' – are imprisoned for their love by 'the Tyrant'. Though kept apart, they are allowed by their gaolers to meet until Govianus is forced to leave the land. The specific parallels to Arbella and William were made in slips of paper pasted into the original text, either to circumvent the censor or to cash in on public opinion, which was evidently running in the lovers' favour. (Fletcher's *The Noble Gentleman* makes more significant allusion; so much so, however, that it has been argued that the play could not have appeared in this form until some years after the event.) James was being touched in his most sensitive part: his dignity. The wound was hardly likely to make him regard Arbella kindly.

Henry Howard, earl of Northampton, was placed in charge of the inquiry. Member of a powerful clan, Northampton had seen his father executed by Henry VIII and his brother (the duke of Norfolk) by Elizabeth, so that his own career had been blighted by 'contempt, oblivion and secret nips'. He was sixty when his far-sighted support for James's claim brought him the prospect of power at last, and he had no intention of letting it get away. A crypto-Catholic, and yet regarded with suspicion even by Spain's ambassador, he beguiled James with displays of scholarship and sycophantic flattery. His report to his 'most excellent most gracious and most redoubted and dear sovereign' certainly makes awkward reading. But his conclusion was that 'the mystery hath been involved in one crafty pate [Mary's] to which the principal herself [Arbella] will appear in a sort to be but an accessory ... Your Majesty hath been advertised before that my La. of Shrewsb. was the only worker and contriver of the lady's bedlam opposition against your Majesty's direction ...

'Lady Arbella dares not clear her [Mary] by oath, though she clears all foreign princes.' Mary's purse, he added, was the 'only instrument' of the escape, but 'this mystery was managed with so great art' that it was unlikely they would ever be able to prove 'more than that my La. of Shrewsbury had by her traffic for a penny some kind of pennyworth'. Even though 'by confession we can prove that of that £1800 which [Arbella] brought together, £1400 at the least came out of her aunt's purse . . . yet the matter will be drowned in obscurity.' Arbella and her aunt would die rather than denounce one another, he said.

Northampton further wrote that Mary, 'intending to work her own haughty ends out of the passion of one that was pliant to advise [Arbella], hath kept within her breast the poison that was to break out.' Thus the investigators, he complains, were left 'to work upon acts intermediate, that in the first appearance only regard the satisfaction of a young lady's instant humours'. But Arbella being once abroad – the bird, as Northampton colourfully put it, being 'freed of her cage' – no-one could doubt but that she would be 'a fit scholar to receive some deeper infusion when time should serve, distance secure and combination encourage'. A fit subject for Catholic indoctrination . . . Mary herself provided ample evidence to support this theory.

More relates that the biggest charge against the countess was having put together a large sum of money for the fleeing couple. 'She is said to have amassed a great sum of money to some ill use, £20,000 are said to be in her cash [account] . . . And though the Lady Arbella hath not as yet been found inclinable to popery,' More added significantly, 'yet her aunt made account that being beyond the seas in the hands of the Jesuits and priests, either the stroke of their argument or the pinch of poverty might force her to the other side.'

Arbella answered the committee of inquiry 'with good judgement and discretion', to the effect that she had sought only freedom to live with her husband. Mary Talbot, by contrast, 'is said to be utterly without reason, crying out that all is but tricks and jigs; that she will answer nothing in private, and if she have offended the law she will answer it in public.' Ironically, of the two, it was Arbella who was within weeks reported ill. Mary, like a true daughter of doughty old Bess, gives the impression of having thrived upon a life full of drama and controversy.

Her husband Gilbert, who had correctly removed himself from the council table while the inquiry was carried out, seems to have been given the impression that Mary's captivity would not be of long duration; perhaps even short enough to spare him the embarrassment of its being known outside court circles. Charles Cavendish wrote to a friend on 19 June: 'my lord putteth me in hope that her abode [in the Tower] will not be long . . . I understand she had not gone thither if she had answered to lords, so for that contempt she suffereth.' But the family reckoned without James's nervous terror of any potential threat – and perhaps without Mary's own intransigence.

In one sense her protests were entirely justifiable. Both Mary and Arbella were 'without reason' only if you take respect for the letter of the law to be a proof of insanity. Arbella clearly believed that, while it may have broken the social code, her marriage had not broken the law of the land. It is hard to say if she was right or wrong. One can prowl through the statute books; track the passage of Henry VIII's old act; ponder the Venetian ambassador's idea of *loesa majestas* . . . but the fact is that English law in the early seventeenth century was as much a matter of custom as statute; and custom came down heavily in favour of royal authority.

Arbella, with her scholar's respect for a written code, her imperfect understanding of other personalities and her pronounced sense of right and wrong, relied on the fact that there was no clear reason why she should ever have been imprisoned. But there were a plethora of reasons why it was unrealistic to claim she could not be. King James had demonstrated his disregard for English law when, on his journey south from Scotland, he ordered a thief hanged without trial or ceremony. Only the marriage that was itself the chief of her offences, moreover, had removed Arbella, as an unmarried woman, from James's familial authority.

And Arbella had now committed a definable offence. As Bishop Goodman put it, in the *History of His Own Times* he wrote soon after the end of James's reign: 'be the crime what it will, yet the breaking of prison is punishable.' She had attempted, without papers or permission, to leave England for the dominions of a foreign power: 'a great offence against the law', thundered the bishop sanctimoniously.

Yet Goodman's very apologia for James reflects the unease with which many viewed Arbella's case. It is true, he admits, that the king might seem to have behaved tyrannously. 'To be imprisoned for the honourable estate of marriage was against God's law and the law of nature: yet I confess it hath been frequent and usual with princes, especially with Queen Elizabeth.' Let us hear what King James said in his own defence, the bishop suggested, hopefully.

'First, that the Lady Arabella was his nearest kinswoman, and therefore both in duty and respect unto him he should not have been neglected in a business of that high nature. Secondly that she was his ward, and therefore in the course of common law she ought not to have disposed of herself.' He adds, thirdly, that James 'did often proffer marriages' to Arbella, which she turned down: a statement for which there is no independent authority. But the real point is 'Fourthly, that she did match with one of the blood royal who was descended from Henry the Seventh, so that by this match there was a combination of titles, which princes have ever been jealous of.' It is an appeal not to legality, but to practicality.

# 'A bird in a cage'

THE TOWER WAS PERMEATED WITH ARBELLA'S FAMILY'S HISTORY, AND the portents surely made her sojourn there more gloomy. Half a century before, the great fortress had been home simultaneously to William's grandmother Catherine Grey; to Catherine's husband Hertford; and, by a curious coincidence, to Matthew Lennox, the grandfather Arbella never knew. Later, Arbella's grandmother Lennox and her ladies scratched into the walls the time and place of their imprisonment, when the queen of Scots married Darnley. Later yet – on the marriage of Arbella's parents, indeed – Lady Lennox, captive again, had here embroidered for the queen of Scots gifts made with grey hairs from her own head.

The walls of the Tower were laced with carved graffiti. What time – where time had no value – it must take to carve a name, a message, even in this soft sandstone. What useless determination, what a torment of wasted energy. It would be the boredom, in the end, that killed you slowly here. The young Leicester and his brothers carved a verse, and the ornate Dudley crest. Even Guildford Dudley – not the most industrious of youths – scratched out Jane Grey's forename with painstaking exactitude. On the walls of the Salt Tower, the carving of an elaborate sphere – detailed enough to be used to tell a horoscope – is the legacy of one Hew Draper, accused of practising sorcery against Bess of Hardwick in 1560. (The old story that Bess had herself been held here, unwilling confidante to Catherine Grey, is now discredited –

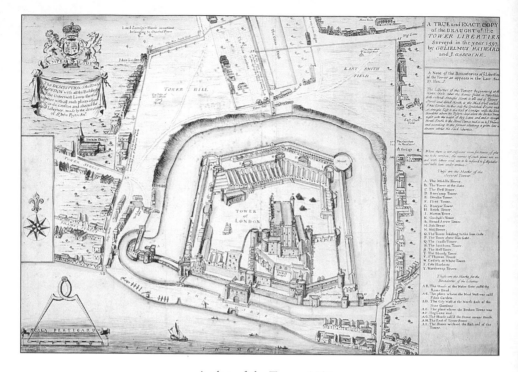

A plan of the Tower, 1597

but hers was still a presence from which it was hard to get away.) In the Beauchamp Tower, in 1585, the Thomas Bawden who piously inscribed that 'it is virtue maketh life, so sin causeth death' was an agent of the earl of Shrewsbury, accused of carrying letters for the queen of Scots.

No such markings survive to spell out the exact site of Arbella's imprisonment, or even the conditions in which she was first held. The best source of information about prisoners in the Tower are the acts of the privy council which regulated any change in their state – but the acts from 1605 to the end of 1612 are missing, destroyed in a small Whitehall fire soon after they were set down. In this vacuum, a legend grew up – recounted by subsequent biographers – that Arbella (like the young princess Elizabeth) was taken to the Bell Tower, an isolated apartment on the south-west corner of the inner fortress, in the oldest part of the Tower and thus perhaps the gloomiest: a place reserved for top-security prisoners, since it was accessible only through the lieutenant of the Tower's own quarters.

In the reign of Henry VIII, the Catholic martyr John Fisher had been held in this circular, vaulted chamber. 'I decay forthwith, and fall into coughs and diseases of my body, and cannot keep myself in health,' Fisher had complained. The Bell Tower, redolent of hardship and of mystery, makes a good backdrop for a heroine; and the Victorians – who loved a persecuted princess – had a passion for placing prominent prisoners in a definite (and still conveniently extant) locality. But it is now established that the princess Elizabeth was held, instead, in the royal lodgings decked out for her mother Anne Boleyn. A wealth of new information has emerged in the last few decades suggesting that Arbella, too, was held here in the old palace, close to her aunt Mary Talbot.

The royal lodgings were situated in the south-east corner of the Tower precincts. They were dismantled in stages through the eighteenth century, and a lawn stands there today. They had, indeed, fallen into disrepair when James and Anna, as custom dictated, spent the night before their coronation there. (Elizabeth, unsurprisingly, had disliked the place and rarely used it.) Within a year or two of James's accession, work was put in train to convert these apartments into a state prison for high-ranking offenders, though Gilbert Talbot still complained that rain came in through a hole feet wide above Mary's head. But his complaints were heeded, and Mary wound up with 'three or four fair rooms' in the old palace, as her brother Charles reported with satisfaction. Arbella certainly – since the bill of work describes the pipes – had a kitchen where her own servant could prepare her food. But that does not mean her conditions were easy.

There were essentially two kinds of imprisonment in the Tower, though within those broad categories there were many anomalies. A prisoner who (as William had done) had 'the liberty of the Tower' might move comparatively freely around the bustling precincts, and enjoy a measure of communication with the outside world. Mary, who for much of her time there did have this liberty, conducted her financial affairs almost normally.

Thus Sir Walter Ralegh, a prisoner for thirteen years in all, could not only have beer brought to him by his own boatman and see his steward to give orders about his estate; he also had the company of his wife and young son Wat as well as two personal servants. (Prisoners often had company. The earl of Southampton famously had his cat, which climbed down the chimney to find him.) While in the Tower, Ralegh fathered a second baby, and there are further records of 'a preacher and three boys in ordinary', and a tutor-cum-personal-secretary. An extra floor was built into the Bloody Tower to accommodate them.

Ralegh had a room kitted out as a study in which to write his *History of the World*, and a garden where he could plant the exotic specimens he had brought back from his travels. In a converted chicken shed outside he could cure tobacco, experiment with turning salt water to sweet, try vainly to extract ore from the minerals he had brought back from Guiana in the New World, and brew his famous Great Cordial: a concoction of pearl, musk, hartshorn, bezoar stone (found in the stomachs of ruminants), herbs and spirits. From the Tower he sent long and welcome letters of advice to the young prince of Wales. 'None but my father', the prince exclaimed, 'would keep such a bird in a cage.' Perhaps his conditions changed with the ebb and flow of security, for Ralegh complained to Queen Anna that he could get neither rest by night nor breath by day; that he had become so unaccustomed to exercise as no longer to be able to walk up the lawn in the Tower a few yards away; that his son slept next to the room where a child had died of plague. But Robert Cecil was wont to say that Ralegh had not been so well housed or attended upon in his liberty.

The rich 'wizard earl' of Northumberland, a prisoner for sixteen years, made even more arrangements for his comfort than did Ralegh. He paid to take over the whole extensive Martin Tower, and took rooms on Tower Hill to accommodate the rest of his retinue. He had a canvas-roofed bowling alley installed alongside Martin Tower; paid for the walls where he walked to be gravelled for his greater convenience in wet weather; and imported two hundred books from his own library. In his still room, he tried to distil beer and wine into whisky.

But even for such as Northumberland or Ralegh, the Tower was still a prison, and isolated enough. During his first confinement there Ralegh had vainly besought the then lieutenant to have him rowed out onto the river when the queen was due to pass by, in the hope of attracting the royal attention. Letters reflect how easily a prisoner could come to feel forgotten by the outside world – and how completely news from the outside world could be kept from them. Arbella would need, like Hamlet, to be content in a nutshell to accept such surroundings, such a situation, with equanimity. But in fact she seems not to have belonged to this comfortable company.

Arbella does seem to have been treated with (for her rank) most unusual severity – treated, in fact, less as a princess than as a proven escapee. Later in her incarceration she was described as being kept 'close prisoner', and this – the second category of imprisonment – meant that you were not allowed out of your lodgings (however well or badly furnished those might be). It was unusual to keep anyone close prisoner for long, let alone a royal lady. It was widely recognized that the lack of fresh air told on the health, especially in view of the primitive sanitation facilities. Noblemen sent to the Tower seemed always to die there, the Venetian ambassador had written home, inaccurately but prophetically.

But much was unusual about Arbella's captivity. At one point, Mary Talbot accused her doctor of having told tales of Arbella to the king, saying that as close prisoner Arbella could not have communicated any other way. Was even the right to send letters denied to her? If so, that – almost as much as shortage of air and exercise – must have taken its toll. It was not only physical hardship she had to fear, but a life of grinding emotional poverty.

She entered the Tower, moreover, at a time when conditions there had suddenly become less easy. In 1606 a new lieutenant had taken over, one Sir William Waad (or Wade). 'That beast Waad', was how Ralegh described him bitterly. Waad was a man, said the Jesuit Father Garnet, 'very kindly in his usage and familiarity, but most violent in speeches when he entereth matters of religion.' He had taken part in the torture of the Gunpowder Plotters, and been sent to ransack the rooms of the captive Queen

*The lively Portraiture of the worthy Knight Sir William Wadd late Lieutenant of the Tower &c.*

Sir William Wade (also spelt Waad or Wadd)

Mary. He was, in other words, a man likely to be prejudiced against Arbella by her presumed Catholic sympathies.

Waad had begun to revive and enforce regulations that had been allowed to lapse, and to introduce new ones. From the time the curfew bell rang at five o'clock, prisoners would be confined to their own chambers. The ladies Northumberland and Ralegh would no longer be allowed to have their coaches driven in and out of the gates. On his arrival at the Tower, Waad had complained that the warders 'have no care, many of them, to execute their office but perform their [duties] by deputy and seldom come to give attendance . . . some bankrupts, some given to drunkenness and disorder . . . also selling their places to unfit persons'. But a warder was expected to be a prisoner's conduit to the outside world, his channel for obtaining essential goods and money. He expected then to be paid for his trouble, which opened the way for corruption. A few years before Waad's arrival Bennett, warder to John Gerard, had let Gerard visit his friend Arden (from whose chamber Gerard eventually escaped), and carried messages between them. Gerard felt warmly enough towards his gaoler that he carefully left behind him a letter for Bennett, clearing him of complicity.

The autobiography of John Gerard highlights the anomalies of imprisonment in the Tower. Bennett had been told to check over Gerard's letters, but proved unable to read, and Bennett's wife prayed for the Jesuit while he was put to the torture. The gaoler afterwards brought him the luxury of an orange for his supper; Gerard carved the peel into the shapes of the cross, though his swollen hands meant he could not do so easily. Gerard had the rank of gentleman, and had the means to buy comforts, like the kind of mattress he preferred. None the less, his story makes eerie reading. At one moment he gave an account of the pain inflicted by the manacles. 'I thought that blood was oozing out from the ends of my fingers . . . but it was only a sensation caused by my flesh swelling above the irons holding them.' At the next, he described the five or six bread rolls he is brought for dinner, diet being graded according to a prisoner's status. 'Very good bread rolls,' he wrote approvingly.

Captives were certainly expected to contribute towards their own keep. (As Chief Justice Montague had put it, half a century before: 'The prisoner ought to live on his own good. And if he have no goods he shall live on the charity of others, and if others will give him nothing then let him die in the name of God . . . for his own presumption and ill-behaviour brought him to that punishment.') The allowance given to the lieutenant of the Tower to cover the basic maintenance of each state prisoner was drawn from that prisoner's own confiscated estates. (The aged Bishop Fisher wrote to Henry VIII's minister Thomas Cromwell: 'I have neither shirt, nor suit, nor yet other clothes that are necessary for me to wear, but that they be ragged and rent so shamefully. Notwithstanding, I might easily suffer that, if they would keep my body warm. But my diet also, God knows how slender it is at many times . . . I have nothing left unto me for to provide any better, but as my brother of his own purse layeth out.') Moreover, it was expected that the lieutenant's probity in passing the money on would be guaranteed by some gratuity. This system may have contributed towards the fact that Arbella was kept in conditions of some stringency; even if she were allowed to purchase comforts, she could hardly afford many. In her first days in the Tower, Arbella was supported by Mary Talbot. But Mary (having prudently handed over most of her funds to her husband, to prevent possible confiscation) was herself none too flush of cash, and her servants had to send for funds from Gilbert when Mary herself had no means of paying for her keep.

Of the £2,800 that had been raised for the escape, all that her captors found with Arbella was £868, some gold and her jewels. The Venetian ambassador heard that she had, when she saw her captors' ship approaching, given the rest of her money away, rewarding especially the gallant Corvé. But such wealth as she still had was confiscated, and handed over to the exchequer. James's instructions to the council were 'That they cause all such sums of money as are to be defrayed by his Majesty for the charges of apprehension of the Lady Arbella and her company, and her bringing up, to be paid out of such gold as hath been found upon her or in her company'. She had to pay for her own pursuit. It was both insult and injury.

The jewels were delivered to one Sir William Bowyer, who was instructed to 'take them to the Tower, and there, in the company and presence of the Lieutenant, show the said gold and jewels to the Lady Arbella, and to inform yourself from her ladyship to whom all the said gold and jewels belong'. If Arbella said they were hers, Bowyer was to 'detain them to her use' – that is, keep them to provide her income – 'issuing and delivering no part therof upon any warrant from her ladyship unless you first acquaint the chancellor of the exchequer'. This was another blow to her rights, her identity.

Arbella claimed that several of the jewels had gone missing since being taken from her, and the descriptions noted down sound a frivolous note that is oddly touching in the gloomy context.

*Item* – A poignard diamond ring. *Item* – A flower de luce set with diamonds, which she thinketh is in a little box of wood, and left amongst her jewels. *Item* – In the same box was a ring wherein was set a little sea-water green stone called an emeryn [aquamarine]. *Item* – A little jewel like a horn, with a great yellow stone called a jacynth, with opals and rubies.

Bowyer was later instructed to sell the jewels 'at the cost price', and to use the money to pay 'such of her creditors as she shall nominate'. Though stripped of her pleasures, Arbella, in the Tower, was not free from the dreary pains and problems she had known in liberty.

Attendance was another issue. Her aunt Mary had her own servants about her. Charles Cavendish wrote to a friend on 28 June: 'The king hath granted six of my lady's servants to repair to her at all convenient time, and Mistress Anne to attend her continually there.' Arbella requested a similar favour, less successfully. Memo:

The Lady Arbella desireth that her servants that are now in the Tower, or so many of them as shall be thought fit, to be allowed to her. That Peter, who attended Mr Seymour, an ancient servant of hers, may be her bottleman. To have herewith another servant, an embroiderer, whose name is Roger Fretwell. For a woman, she desireth the Lady Chaworth. Her desire is that Mr Yelvertone may receive her money and jewels. That Smyth, her servant, may have access unto her. There must of necessity be linen bought, both for her wearing [and] for sheets and table linen, whereof there is not any amongst her stuff. She hath *xxxij* [32] servants, for which some order would be taken.

But few of her own familiar servants seem to have been allowed to her immediately. It was two years later that the above-named Samuel Smyth, 'being employed by her ladyship in the managing of her private estate', was finally allowed access to his mistress. Even then, the council's orders were that he was to speak to Arbella only in the lieutenant's 'presence and hearing'.

Arbella's rank meant that she was never going to be treated

brutally; the foul and stinking cells also found in the Tower were not for such as she. What she probably lacked most acutely was society. The Tower, after all, held some dangerous associates; people with whom Arbella might easily join forces. This may be why she was kept so stringently. Besides Mary Talbot, who had planned Arbella's escape, it was still home to Ralegh and Cobham, who had allegedly plotted to place her on the throne; to Lord Grey, to whom, it was said, the plotters had planned to marry her; and to Northumberland, another potential bridegroom. And oddly enough, the Tower also held Scotsman Patrick Ruthven, younger brother to the earl of Gowrie. It was a Ruthven who, in Scotland, had conspired against Mary; a Ruthven who had abducted the king in boyhood; a Ruthven – the earl himself – who had once again seized and bound him in 1600. A contemporary rumour declared that that same earl, on an early visit to England, once fell in love with the young Arbella . . . The Tower seemed to be over-full of her putative suitors or their near relations. Except, of course, for the successful suitor, who had got away.

# 'The most wretched and unfortunate creature'

FROM OSTEND, WHERE HIS SHIP FINALLY LANDED, WILLIAM HAD MADE his way to Bruges. At first the authorities in London were in some doubt where to find him; ten days after the escape the English ambassador in Brussels, William Trumball, had been told that 'we have no news of Seymour but suppose him harboured in some of your towns under the charitable shadow of the Spanish wing.'

In fact, with Arbella safely under lock and key, William's whereabouts were (or were presented as being) 'a thing of no such consequence', as Cecil told Trumball dismissively. Or, as another of the ambassador's London acquaintances put it only a few weeks later: 'Our tongues and ears have been so long busy about the Lady Arbella and your wandering esquire that now we care no more about the subject. His wandering into Germany is here little regarded, for the greatest harm he can do is to slip in again from whence he went.'

A little of the unconcern may have been faked. Cecil did order Trumball to 'carry always a watchful eye to observe what entertainment [William] doth find there; how he is respected, to whom he most applies himself; who especially resort unto him, and what course he purposeth to take either for his stay or his remove'. As for William's own petition, as soon as he learnt of Arbella's capture, that he and his wife should be allowed to live privately abroad together, that was treated with contempt. Indeed, as Cecil put it in his reply, he himself was 'now neither willing to remember that I have done [William] any courtesies, nor mean to entertain any [ac]knowledgement of them to me'.

Quite what poor William was supposed to do with himself – where he should go – was far from obvious. Trumball was told to warn him away from all Spanish territories, so from the Netherlands towns of Liège and Spa he crossed into France, giving out that he did so 'out of respect to his Majesty, being advised by friends that his stay there increased his Majesty's indignation'. But in October 1611 James was telling the Venetian ambassador 'with considerable indignation' that William was 'seen openly at Paris' – having already demanded that the Venetian doge should show 'readiness to declare himself an ally in time of danger' by packing Seymour off home to England if he showed up in that city. 'The king is much concerned about the flight,' noted the ambassador shrewdly, 'more perhaps than he shows. It is commonly held that Seymour will go either to the states of the Pope or of his Catholic Majesty.'

William had persuaded the archdukes, the Spanish governors of the Netherlands, to send an ambassador to James on his behalf. John More reported that the ambassador 'hath brought a letter from the archduke in favour of Mr Seymour, no less strange than the rest, that his Majesty would be pleased to pardon so small a fault as a clandestine marriage, and to suffer him and his wife to live together.' To William's credit, he was not giving up on Arbella.

William, unlike his wife, was at liberty; but his life had difficulties enough. In the first place, he was roaming the continent without money. 'I think young Seymour will quickly wish himself back in the Tower where he was well provided for,' Dudley Carleton had written to Trumball, grimly. The deal tacitly offered to William by the English government was that he would be let alone as long as he refrained from allying himself directly with the Catholics. They no doubt felt he should think himself grateful for small mercies. But unless he sought Catholic protection, the exile had no means of support. William himself wrote of how he had to leave Paris to be free of 'those parts where I might be liable to the action of creditors . . . My only desire is to avoid disgrace in the country I left and repair unto merchants with whom I have yet some credit, to support my necessary expenses, and to be near England from whence only I seek and hope relief.'

There was a very real fear that 'some Jesuit or other ill-affected Englishman should seize upon Seymour and by his enchantments lead him blindfold to his perdition,' as Trumball put it. 'I wish', wrote one mediator to the ambassador, William 'had such supply from home as might enable him to return to his former and safer station.' For this reason James eventually instructed the old earl of Hertford that he should make his grandson an allowance of four hundred pounds a year – adding, as a proviso, instructions to stay away from known Catholic strongholds. In addition to this income, throughout the period of her imprisonment he received sums of money from Arbella, drawn from funds that were already skimpy. But William protested his inability to live on such an amount; and reports state that he did indeed make at least a token conversion to Catholicism, perhaps not coincidentally.

An article written in 1951 by B. Fitzgibbon SJ for the journal of the Catholic Record Society gives as a fact that William was 'received into the Church at St Omer in the late months of 1611', the source being a set of dispatches by Guido Bentivoglio, the papal nuncio in Flanders. Bentivoglio was happy to report that Seymour had the firm intention of living and dying in the Catholic faith – this fact to be kept secret, the nuncio noted, for fear lest Seymour should suffer repercussions from the angry English. Fitzgibbon added that William's second wife almost certainly had a Catholic upbringing since her mother (previously Sidney's wife and Essex's wife) had been received into that church, and married another convert as her third husband. But, scrupulously, Fitzgibbon also relayed the comments from the unknown Jesuit noted earlier about William's 'great ignorance' of religion as a whole and his tendency rather towards atheism than Protestantism – the very comments, in other words, that suggest any conversion might have been motivated less by conviction than by expediency.

Paris, Luxembourg, Paris, Liège. A word picture of William's party describes how three young men, accompanied by an older one who acted as guide and interpreter, arrived in Luxembourg rather sketchily disguised. 'They all called themselves merchants trading by sea and land,' one of Trumball's correspondents wrote, 'but I could easily judge them from their physiognomy and their way of doing things that they were other than they said.' The husband of the lady (Arbella), the writer added, 'is about 28 with a black beard, a very fair skin, and of quite medium height'.

It was no fun trailing back and forth over northern Europe, belaboured all the way by letters from a grandfather terrified lest William should indeed become 'corrupted in your religion' and so irate, old Hertford threateningly wrote, as almost to come to hate William's memory. ('The loss of the most gracious child, by God's visitation,' Hertford wrote, 'is less grief to parents than the daily vexation of him that lives untowardly.') But all in all, William had got off lightly. He was accurate as well as diplomatic in writing to the lords of the council, albeit rather grovellingly:

> It is no small comfort unto me in my hard misfortunes that I have now opportunity whereby I may show obedience unto his sacred Majesty and the state . . . I acknowledge myself beyond measure bound to your lordships for the very mild proceedings which through your honourable mediations I have found.

In December 1611, William was secure enough – or cheeky enough – to request that the lieutenant of the Tower send on to him the clothes and furnishings he had left behind when he made his escape. Sir William Waad replied in a long and indignant letter to Cecil. If William had died in the Tower, 'or been by order discharged out of his place', his property there would have fallen to the lieutenant as a legitimate perk – 'and I hope it is not meant his escape shall be construed to his benefit or my disadvantage'. In any case, Waad protested, nothing of William's was really his own, but 'either from the Lady Arbella, or bought by me, or yet unpaid for'. Nothing William had left behind was of value enough to compensate him, Waad, for the sums he himself had paid out already, since 'no penny since Christmas last' had been paid towards William's 'diet'. The apothecary's bill alone had come to £32 16s – 'whereof there are divers cordials, almond milks, juleps, electuaries and other things very costly'. But William's challenge, and Waad's horrified response, offer a light interlude in a story which otherwise becomes ever more gloomy.

Several events of 1612 contributed to making Arbella's situation more precarious. In May, Robert Cecil died of stomach cancer, unaided by the 'scorbut' [scurvy] grass Gilbert Talbot had him sent fresh from the Peak District every fourth day, or by Mary Talbot's prescription of quintessence of honey. Thus Arbella lost a man who might still have been of help to her in the future. Cecil's letters of the summer before showed that he felt she really had gone a step too far. But he was a humane man; one who (despite his rejection of William) had often proved his right to boast that 'my manner is not to fly [from] men in difficulties.' He had been, what is more, a long-time friend to the Shrewsburys. But Cecil himself was out of tune with James's court, as the king gave more and more power into the hands of his male favourites. Some claim that the 'Great Little Secretary' had already begun to look like yesterday's man even before he died, in agony of mind and body, still only in his forties.

Coincidentally or otherwise, it was in the month after Robert Cecil's death that Mary Talbot's case was finally heard, on 30 June, by a 'select council' including the three chief justices and the master of the rolls. We have a record of the prosecution's speech on this occasion; it is traditionally attributed to Francis Bacon, though there remains some uncertainty about this. The case was certainly a tricky one, worthy of all Bacon's ingenuity.

Lady Shrewsbury – 'a lady wise, that ought to know what duty requireth' – was charged with contempt in refusing to answer questions eleven months before. But this was obviously a subsidiary issue. Mary's true offence was her alleged part in Arbella's escape, which had thus to be proved to be contrary to national security. However, if it were, this would only highlight the fact that Arbella herself should logically be on trial. But Arbella was not – in 1612 or at any subsequent time – brought to trial or charged with any offence; for any attempt to do so might have shown all too clearly that there were no grounds upon which she could be held with propriety. From the start, Francis Bacon (if it were he) took his stand upon what sound more like social or moral than legal grounds.

> My lady [Arbella] transacted the most weighty and binding part and action of her life, which is her marriage, without acquainting his Majesty, which had been neglect even to a mean parent; but being to our sovereign, and standing so near his Majesty as she doth, and she then choosing [a man of] such a condition as it pleased her to choose, all parties laid together, how dangerous it was, my lady might have read it in the fortune of that house where-with she is matched; for it is not unlike to the case of Mr Seymour's grandmother [Catherine Grey].

She had been 'extremely ill-advised', he said, excusingly. The repeated attempts of the authorities tacitly to dismiss Arbella as a puppet – a child, or an idiot, void of legal standing – seem meant to justify their holding her thus, without the chance to prove either guilt or the contrary.

> But now did my lady accumulate and heap up the offence with a far greater than the former, by seeking to withdraw herself out of the king's power into foreign parts. That this flight or escape into foreign parts might have been a seed of trouble to this state, is a matter whereof the conceit of a vulgar person is not incapable.

Even if Arbella had 'put on a mind to continue her loyalty, as nature and duty did bind her, yet, when she was in another sphere, she must have moved in the motion of that orb, and not of the planet [James] itself.' It had always been the practice of the wisest princes 'to hold for matters pregnant of peril to have any near them in blood to fly into foreign parts'. The sum total of accusation made sounds rather anti-climactic for the 'great and heinous offences' proclaimed so dramatically after Arbella's escape, and the convoluted prose of the prosecutor's long speech makes it sound as though he is labouring rather consciously. Being neglectful to her 'parent', picking an inappropriate hus-band, attempting to flee her sovereign's power . . . only the last sounds like a political offence, surely? Perhaps the charges might have rung differently when rank and grandeur carried moral weight. But perhaps not.

The woman whose case was supposed to be at issue here – not

Arbella, but Mary Talbot – refused to answer any questions, on the double grounds, first, that as a peeress she had the right to be heard by her peers, and second, that she had made a solemn vow not to speak upon this subject. Her stubbornness did not help her. As Chamberlain described it, the council found themselves – understandably – 'much aggravated'. The prosecutor addressed Mary directly. 'This fact of conspiring in the flight of this lady [Arbella] may bear a hard and gentler construction. If upon over-much affection to your kinswoman, gentler; if upon practice [conspiracy] or other end, harder.' As for her obstinate silence: 'Nay, you may learn duty of the Lady Arbella herself, a lady of the blood, of a higher rank than yourself, who declining ... to declare of your fact [refusing to admit your fault], yieldeth ingenuously to be examined of her own.'

Mary was fined the enormous sum of twenty thousand pounds: a penalty so large it was never likely to be collected in full, though the threat could always be held in reserve, and was indeed later used against her. She was returned to the Tower to be held at the king's pleasure. Perhaps Arbella was glad to have her aunt still near, but that can at best have been cold comfort. She must certainly have been daunted by this fresh evidence of how seriously the authorities still regarded her escape.

Arbella suffered another blow immediately after Cecil's death: her allowance from the exchequer was halved, from sixteen hundred pounds a year to a mere eight hundred. The events of 1612 were piling up. In July, Lord Beauchamp, William Seymour's father, died, bringing William a generation nearer to the throne. In November, tragedy struck the royal family when Prince Henry died very suddenly, from what later generations have diagnosed as typhoid, though there were rumours of poison. Not even the last-minute dose of Ralegh's famous cordial, sent from the Tower, could save him. James's posterity now rested on Elizabeth and Charles: a young girl and a sickly boy.

Henry's death must have hurt Arbella. The prince had lost any youthful sympathy for her – the Scots, said More in that earlier letter, had filled the king with fearful imaginings after her escape, 'and with him the prince, who cannot easily be removed from any settled opinion' – but he was another former well-wisher whose influence might yet one day have moderated her punishment. One by one, her possible friends were being taken away.

Throughout her imprisonment in the Tower, there is no record of her uncles trying to help Arbella; nor indeed her cousins, though the Talbot daughters were becoming women of influence. (Elizabeth and Alethea between them would successfully win Lady Anne Clifford the right to sue to the king about her lands.) To be fair to Arbella's relatives, their first efforts would probably have gone into the more realistic attempt to free Mary. But Arbella must have felt quite forgotten. Looking at the documentary evidence – the acts of the privy council, when the interrupted records begin again – it strikes one unpleasantly that her name is mentioned only in the context of some sort of trouble. When nothing goes wrong, when she makes no stir, it seems as if king, court and council forgot her all too happily.

None among the collection of Arbella Stuart's own letters can authoritatively be said to date from her time in the Tower. Most of the appeals she wrote have since been reallocated to the time of her earlier imprisonment in Lambeth. But one fragment may be the exception. The paper is torn in half across a sentence, and there is no evidence as to whether the missive was ever finished or sent. It is up to each reader to decide whether the tone of self-abasement goes beyond even the most extravagant rhetoric Arbella had used in her earlier custody.

'In all humility, the most wretched and unfortunate creature that ever lived prostrates its self at the feet of the most merciful king that ever was desiring nothing but mercy and favour . . . Mercy it is I desire, and that for God's sake.' In this letter, and this letter alone, Arbella says that 'if it were to do again', she would not adventure the loss of the king's favour 'for any other worldly comfort'. Thus to regret her marriage, in Arbella's terms, was to have fallen low indeed. But it seems possible the letter was never sent. Could Arbella not bear, even at this desperate juncture, to humiliate herself so completely?

# 'Far out of frame'

THE SPRING OF 1613 SAW THE COURT IN CELEBRATION, OF A MUTED
form. The princess Elizabeth, James's only surviving daughter,
was to be a Valentine's Day bride. Her marriage to Frederick,
elector Palatine – the same marriage that, a war later, would make
her Bohemia's tragically exiled Winter Queen – was not to be
delayed by the recent death of Elizabeth's beloved brother Henry.

The bride wore white and silver tissue, jewelled 'like the Milky
Way'. Poignantly, blindly, Arbella seems to have thought that she
would be allowed out of her prison to take some part in the
festivities. She ordered four costly new dresses. She had several
hundred pounds' worth of pearls embroidered on a single gown.
(Only three days after her death the jeweller, still unpaid, would
be suing for it, and the lieutenant of the Tower ordered to take the
'said gown as [well as] all other her ladyship's apparel' into his
safe custody.) James, it is true, wore six hundred thousand
pounds' worth of jewels, and a mere Lady Wotton wore a gown
so embroidered it cost fifty pounds a yard. But for a prisoner, and
an impecunious one at that, Arbella's still seems a fantastical gesture, often taken as proof that her wits were awry.

Perhaps Arbella thought James might use the occasion for one
of his famous displays of mercy. Perhaps she thought that the
bride would request the presence of the cousin to whom she had
always been close. Elizabeth may instead have nudged her
prospective bridegroom into pleading for Lord Grey, still

languishing in prison for his part in the plots of 1603. But whatever requests Frederick made were greeted coldly. 'Son, when I come into Germany, I will promise you not to importune you for any of your prisoners,' James promised his prospective son-in-law sourly. If Judas were alive again, and condemned for betraying Christ, some courtier would be found to beg his pardon, the king said angrily.

So Lord Grey died, still in prison, a few years later. And the closest Arbella got to Elizabeth's wedding celebrations was to see from her window the glow of fireworks on the Thames; to be deafened by the ordnance fired from the Tower as the bridegroom-elect passed by; and perhaps to hear whisper of the bustle as he was brought, by way of a wedding treat, to see the lions in the royal menagerie. When Elizabeth set sail across the Channel, it was yet one friend more gone away. Queen Anna had now lost two children in as many months: one dead, one gone to live abroad. She and her husband even enjoyed a 'pacification', under the influence of their common misery. James gave to Anna the palace of Greenwich, where she began building in the new Palladian style. Any chance of her continued championship of Arbella must have gone with Elizabeth and Henry.

But there were more powerful reasons why Arbella was not released for Elizabeth's nuptials; why there was never a chance she would be. In the months before the wedding, Waad had garnered suggestions of a fresh conspiracy – one declared by Arbella herself and fostered, if we are to believe her niece's extraordinary words, by Mary Talbot.

The previous autumn, Arbella falling ill, Waad had sought permission for her own physician Dr Moundford to attend her, and Arbella claimed that her revelations now were made to requite this 'kind tenderness'. Moundford's report of Arbella's allegation – 'here is a fine piece of work, that aunt of mine will never be quiet' – at first sounds almost cosy. But from the authorities' viewpoint, there was nothing comfortable about the plan she revealed (or pretended to reveal) of escape and bloodshed, plot and papistry.

At Lambeth (so Arbella now said), her aunt 'among others' would have delivered her into the hands of the papists. To this

Arbella ('not knowing . . . how it should be done, nor to whom I should be delivered') would not consent – 'and in full resolution never to change my religion shortly after did take the sacrament', she added, virtuously. But long-ago Lambeth, it seems, had not seen the end of the conspiracy. When Waad (in the presence of Moundford and of a divine, Dr Palmer) taxed her with the continuance of the plan, 'we could not say that her lady[ship] did deny it, but rather put it off by her sudden rising,' Moundford reported. She had initiated the interview 'at the time appointed' by her; she could end it. She was still royalty. But her mood was not always autocratic. On 12 January, visiting Arbella in the afternoon, Moundford found her asleep, and so spoke to her gentlewoman, who said her mistress could take neither food nor rest. Waking, Arbella answered his salutation 'drowsily and heavily'. He asked her how she did. 'Not well,' she answered. 'I know not how I should do better. I am every day so troubled with my aunt.'

Throughout these months Arbella spoke of Mary Talbot – this 'thorn' in her side – with unremitting hostility, 'terming her the most wicked woman in the world, enemy to the state etc', as Waad reported alarmedly. Arbella knew, she said, that all the world 'will condemn me to undo my aunt that endures for me', but said that she could not stay silent when the security of the whole state was imperilled by that aunt's folly. She refused her aunt's repeated attempts to see her; insisted Mary should be removed to lodgings further off; and even used items Mary had given her with 'strange incivility'. As for Mary, Waad describes her clamouring at the staircase of Arbella's rooms. How did the relationship between the two women, once so close, come to such a pitch?

This sudden estrangement, and Arbella's recent dangerous illness, had been triggered by a conversation held between Mary and Arbella the autumn before; the one from her chamber window, the other from the gallery of the lieutenant's lodgings (proof that they were not allowed to associate freely). The root of the trouble, said Arbella, was: 'I will not be of her religion. I had rather that all aunts should perish than that I should alter my religion.' But, ardent Catholic though Mary was, her niece may have been speaking disingenuously.

Arbella's allegations were surrounded with the kind of verbal smokescreen that had cloaked her gambits in Hardwick days: her assertion that this was a truth that torture could not have obtained, but one she was admitting now because of Waad's kindness; that no-one would suffer for their part in uncovering it, for 'there is not the meanest gentleman in England, if I bring him into a business, he shall be cleared and suffer no wrong'; that her aunt, of course, would deny all this, but surely 'the meanest word I speak shall be of more credit than all the oaths she can swear.' Phrase for phrase, Arbella's rhetoric – the hyperbole, the self-aggrandizement – was becoming more and more like that she had used in 1603. And, as in 1603, one has to juggle the questions of intent and insanity. Was she delusional? Was she reporting sober fact? Or (the least attractive option) was she – to a greater or lesser degree, consciously or unconsciously – sacrificing the name and safety of those who loved her in the hopes of herself climbing a few steps higher into the favour of the authorities? Or was it a cocktail of all three?

Once again, there is the possibility that Arbella may have been trying to win the king's attention by herself 'exposing' plots, in a way which had worked, albeit drastically, ten years ago. Once again she seems – divide and conquer – to have been trying to ally herself with one official against the rest. Once again, her attempt was timed to tie in with a significant event; in this case, the royal wedding. Was this planned exposure the reason she had felt sure enough to order her dresses so confidently?

At the beginning of February, questioned further (just as the royal wedding preparations were nearing their final stage), Arbella finally went so far as to declare that Mary Talbot did still have a plan to free her from the Tower and help her into the protection of the Catholics. To this Arbella had given scant assent: 'The Lady Arbella doth not deny but of her self she would be delivered into the hands of the papists, Turks, Jews or infidels so she might be quit out of their hands. But she doth not like her aunt's projects, though her aunt and she do both aim at one end.' Arbella told Dr Palmer that she was now revealing the plot only for Waad's sake; Mary Talbot had said the lieutenant's throat would have to be cut. The men hastened to assure her that a project so dangerous would indeed require 'force and bloodshed'; that 'If the lord mayor would go about to deliver her from hence, he would not be able to prevail.' But they may not really have felt so confident. The problem for their investigation was that the accusations against Mary Talbot 'come all from one root, namely the only [unsupported] relation of the Lady Arbella', so that the charge might yet 'fail in the groundwork and foundation. Therefore it is to be advisedly considered how credit may be given to these accusations, and how they may be upheld by other concurring matter or circumstances.' In trying to assess the situation, they were debating the very questions that trouble us today.

Arbella, to be sure, was threatening wildly – but when she talked as wildly in her Hardwick days, inventing a presumably fictitious plot to claim the attention of the court, Henry Cavendish had arrived with forty men, which suggests at least a nugget of hard reality. By the same token, it is worth noting that Waad, like Brounker before him, was inclined to believe the basis of Arbella's story: 'Now, that there was a plot for the Lady Arbella's escape, it is out of question.' Arbella's devoted gentlewoman Mistress Bradshaw, he said, had left her service rather than be party to it, riding north on a carrier's horse – though later evidence suggests it was in fact ill-health that drove Mrs Bradshaw away. He weighed the evidence, including the demeanour of the two women. 'Therefore I note these contrary courses of these two ladies; the lady Arbella charging, imputing and discovering her aunt in this sort, and the countess will not take knowledge of these offences, but seeketh all means of reconciliation.'

Shrewdly, Waad noted that when Mary was told her niece wanted her 'removed', she did not demand the cause of it ('which in reason she should have done for her own clearing'). The implication is that she knew already; that Arbella's allegations were justified. But when Waad told the countess that Arbella's words had been reported at court, she turned upon him, 'cursing and banning most impiously'. Was she trying to protect herself – and perhaps also her niece? Mary said that Arbella would be sorry when she 'came to her self'. Arbella, she said, was in 'some melancholy humour', caused by distress at her husband's 'deboshed carriage'. (His debts? His conversion? Or the *modus vivendi* which, in tacit rejection of their relationship, he seemed by now to have agreed with the authorities?)

But Arbella may indeed have been sick. She certainly had been so the previous autumn: she herself referred to her 'late dangerous illness', and the mentions of 'fits of distemper and convulsions', of the 'dangerous distemper' Waad said 'could be no fiction', come often enough to suggest that this was no single event, quickly over. Mary Talbot, frantically and repeatedly trying to reach her niece, claimed she needed to 'minister physic' to her. Mary even threatened herself to write to the king, demanding access to Arbella: strange behaviour in one concerned only that she was herself about to be caught out in a major felony.

Arbella may have been at once ill and actively scheming: just because they are after you doesn't mean you aren't paranoid. But, again, Arbella may have been ill and, through her illness, deluded to a greater or a lesser degree. (And Mary may have failed to press for Arbella's words only because she knew how unlikely they were to relate to reality.) Several earlier biographers have pointed out that any easy diagnosis of insanity, with its dismissive implications, should be treated very cautiously, simply because it is unlikely anyone would have tried to free a lunatic. But episodes of porphyria can come and go quickly; when Mary said that Arbella would soon regret her words, she may have known from experience that it would be so. We are left with only one comparative certainty: that the same war was raging in Arbella's mind as in her body. This was the idea towards which Moundford was reaching when, exasperatingly, he prescribed her 'my old cordial of patience and humility'. 'Good madame, said I: remember one rule which I have often repeated. I did learn it of a wiseman. If thou be crossed, cross not thyself.' She was suffering, he suggested, from *Agritudo* (sickness) rather than *Morbus* (disease), and the cure lay in her own hands.

On 10 March Chamberlain was writing that 'the Lady Arbella hath been dangerously sick of convulsions, and is now said to be distracted'; on 26 April, that Arbella was under restraint, though she 'continues crackt in her brain'. (He added that the countess of Shrewsbury was under extra restraint 'upon good cause as the voice goes'; clearly, contemporaries did not insist on a one-dimensional reading of the story.)

The affair dragged on. Soon afterwards Lord Grey was made close prisoner for what turned out to be no more than a matter of 'love and dalliance' with Arbella's gentlewoman. (Chamberlain thought it was with Arbella herself, a more dangerous possibility.) Another prisoner, Thomas Bull, whose relationship with Arbella's kinswoman Mistress Pierrepont was revealed by 'some speech of my Lady Arbella's in some of her distempers', complained they were all kept so close in consequence that for twelve weeks they did not leave their lodging.

Then, on 6 May 1613, Sir William Waad was discharged from his position as lieutenant – 'removed suddenly from his place, to the great contentment of the prisoners,' wrote Sir Thomas Lake. Arbella's part in this is difficult to assess. On the one hand, she was apparently his victim. Waad was dismissed not only because of the 'continual complaints' as to his general comportment, but on the specific charge of 'certain gold embezzled from the Lady Arbella, whereof either he or his lady or his daughter cannot so clearly acquit themselves'. On the other hand, Arbella may have set Waad up; have used him to position herself in a favourable light, in a manner as deliberate as the measure of a masque, or the composition of the *tableaux vivants* of a later century. Here the evidence comes from Viscount Fenton, who wrote to a relation on 20 May that Arbella had obtained a duplicate key to her prison. She had persuaded Waad's daughter to lend her a key, from which she took a wax impression. But she did not plan to use it in the obvious way. Instead, she asked Fenton to present her duplicate to the king, in a dramatic gesture designed to show that with the means of escape in her hands, she none the less chose instead to submit herself to James's mercy.

By her stroke with the keys, of course, Arbella also rid herself of a lieutenant she probably had every reason to dislike. It was said that Waad was accused of being too lax with other prisoners, and too strict with Arbella herself. It was, moreover, he who had first set in motion the train of events that led to her recapture, after his early alarm when William had got away. But if Arbella's theatricals were aimed at impressing James she had, as usual, misjudged her psychology. Evidence of her continued ability to behave autonomously, even in the Tower, is more likely to have thrown the king into fresh anger and alarm than to have convinced him of her loyalty.

Arbella's actions in these months are confirmed by other sources: some words of Carr's, and the fact that Waad's daughter and a servant of the Talbots were themselves committed to the Tower at this time. But where Waad's removal was concerned, it may be that all Arbella said and did does not represent the whole story. The plot around her, indeed, could even have been a pretext or an opportunity stage-managed by a third party – for there was a third party which, in these months, urgently needed a way to get rid of Waad, and a way to keep the Tower's prisoners isolated from each other while pursuing their own plan. And that third party included persons powerful enough to make Waad's dismissal a certainty.

At the end of April 1613, one Sir Thomas Overbury was committed to the Tower. The nominal reason for his imprisonment (the discourtesy of his having refused an appointment abroad) was even shakier than the grounds for Arbella's incarceration. But the fact was that Overbury, a long-time friend and mentor of the king's favourite Carr, had dared oppose Carr's marriage to Frances Howard, niece to Henry Howard, that earl of Northampton who had been so unpleasantly busy about Arbella and Mary's affairs.

For Frances, perhaps with the connivance of her lover and her uncle, the incarceration of Overbury on a pretext was only the precursor to a darker plan: his murder. For this, she and her conspirators needed to get rid of Waad. Venal in his own way though the lieutenant may have been, he was active, observant and no fit man for their plan. So Waad was fired; and if the Overbury murder were the real reason he was got rid of, one still notes with interest that one of the instruments of his fall – one of the two noblemen Northampton arranged should call for Waad's removal – was none other than Gilbert Talbot, earl of Shrewsbury.

Waad was replaced by Sir Gervase Helwys, 'a somewhat unknown man', who was profoundly grateful for this new promotion – grateful enough to keep his eyes tight shut, maybe, as a stream of poisoned tarts and jellies from Frances Howard made their way to the unfortunate Overbury, topped off by a poisoned enema from a bribed apothecary. By the autumn Overbury was dead. A few years later, his death was to rebound dramatically upon everyone involved. But then, in 1613, it passed off quietly. Carr married Frances Howard, very soon after Overbury's putrid corpse had been buried with excessive haste in the Tower precincts. And in the Tower that autumn, attention was focused once again upon Arbella, and another possible escape.

In November, Northampton was writing again to Carr – a letter which, while itself vague enough to apply to anyone, is endorsed with the single word 'Arbella'. It began with some suggestive words which seem to expand on the fact that Mary Talbot, who had just been allowed out on leave to visit her ailing husband, had suddenly been recalled to the Tower again. 'Though a letter was in drawing with an humble suit for longer leave,' Northampton wrote, 'yet upon better advertisement my lord [Shrewsbury] resolves to send her back to Mr Lieutenant.' Northampton went on to explain the details of the newly uncovered plan.

> With much ado, and withal by good fortune, we have hit upon the place destined to the escape. It falls out to be under a study of Mr Revenes but of these things I shall have occasion before it be long to deal more thoroughly. In the meantime his Majesty will be pleased to reserve this secret from all the world but yourself, till we sound the bottom, for it hath thus far been carried with a great deal of art.

Much, of course, hinges on the identity of 'Mr Revenes', and Northampton's handwriting has been variously interpreted; Reeves (Arbella's faithful servant) has been offered as one possibility. But it is suggestive that, shortly after this letter was written, a Mr 'Ruthen' (also 'Riothen') – presumed to be Patrick Ruthven, the earl of Gowrie's brother mentioned earlier – was committed close prisoner. Ruthven's servant was also examined, and asked whether he had ever heard the noise of hammering coming from his master's study. (He had; but had put it down to some experiment being carried on with one of Ruthven's regular visitors, an alchemist. Experimentation seems to have been a popular Tower hobby.)

The link between the two prisoners was given more definite form in the spring of 1614. Arbella had been selling jewellery – some of the pearls she had bought for princess Elizabeth's wedding. (She seems – predictably – to have been cheated by her agent.) But the point was that the errand man claimed, when questioned, that he had not known they were Arbella's. 'He answered that Master Ruthen both delivered the pearls and gave him warrant [to sell them].' And to whom did he hand the money? Why, to Master Ruthen. It is enough to make the least suspicious wonder if Ruthven were not helping Arbella to collect money for yet another escape attempt.

Once again, it would seem, Arbella was conspiring with a man who not only was a distant connection through her grandmother Lady Lennox, but who also felt he had his own claim to the Scottish throne, through a disputed marriage some way back on the family tree. Smyth, Arbella's servant, and Dr Palmer, the divine Arbella had asked to oversee the sale, were both imprisoned that summer; 'for my Lady Arabellay's escape out of the Tower', in the words of one contemporary. (It was only recently that Smyth had finally been allowed to speak with his mistress, and it is tempting to wonder whether the authorities did not permit the chaperoned meeting in the hopes of overhearing something compromising.) On 7 July Chamberlain recounted that 'Dr Palmer, a divine, and Crompton, a gentleman usher were committed to the Tower last week for some business about the Lady Arbella.' On 6 August her servant Reeves, too, was described by the Reverend Thomas Larkin as having been returned to imprisonment in the Tower about a fortnight ago for 'some new complot for her [Arbella's] escape and delivery'.

But if there were such a plot – and that seems fairly certain – it was now over. King Christian of Denmark visited England again this year, but where was the 'holy friendship' he had boasted when she needed it? Chamberlain's letter went on to say that Arbella was 'far out of frame this midsummer moon'. This was not just a repeat of the ambiguous rumours that had spread in 1603. There was indeed grave reason to fear for Arbella's health, in mind as well as body.

# 'I dare to die'

EVEN WILLIAM, ABROAD, HAD LONG BEEN HEARING REPORTS DIRE enough to convince him that his wife had become 'distracted of mind whereby he knew that she could not live long'. Knowing that King James had no plan 'to let him and his lady come together', he was resolute to show that he was neither 'beast nor fool; but that he hath courage enough to anger the best of them'. He was now openly called 'a prince of England' by some of his companions. (Maddeningly, the edges of this document have been burnt so that the subsequent mention of how William's ancestor, the conquering Henry VII, had once sailed from Brittany into Wales with a thousand men stands alone in menacing uncertainty.)

William's concern must have been partly on his own account. He had once again been venting his regular complaint, that he couldn't live on four hundred pounds, and was threatening to travel to Rome – and with a known Catholic, the poet Henry Constable, who 'persuaded him to ill courses'. But Arbella was indeed reaching the end of her tether; 'sad', as Bosola said of the Duchess of Malfi,

> as one long us'd to't: and she seems
> Rather to welcome the end of misery
> Than shun it.

The Duchess counted this world, she said 'a tedious theatre, / For I do play a part in't 'gainst my will.' But she (little knowing that her murder was planned) none the less believed she had found her own way out of her misery. 'The Church enjoins fasting: I'll starve myself to death.' Arbella's imagination was tending the same way.

There is something both moving and disturbing about the shortage of information we have for the last year of Arbella's life. It may be just the chance of some lost documents; but it feels more like a conspiracy of silence; as if at the last she gave in, and colluded with her oppressors. As if she – the protester, the writer – turned her back and retreated, finally, into muteness. If she had ever seemed histrionic – self-pitying, a spoiled little rich girl – now, surely, she had cause. And yet she seems at this juncture to have chosen the route of stoic suffering.

We know she was subject to depression, to the 'dumps'. At the start of her captivity in the Tower she had done everything she could to keep herself in spirits; asked for her lady companion and her embroiderer. But surely by now, without hope or stimuli, in whatever exercise she was allowed the black dog must have shadowed her footsteps every inch of the way.

There is one particularly telling glimpse of Arbella in these last years, with the most frightening implications for her sanity. Imagine a July day, and Arbella (secretive? mocking? distraught?) stopping an unknown interlocutor on his way through the Tower and asking if he could maintain a confidence in order to prevent a civil war. No descriptive details come down through the bare statement given to the lieutenant. Indeed, the witness stressed that he lent Arbella an ear only to discover her plan.

That plan was improbable in the last degree. It would be rumoured – Arbella said – that her husband William had died. He would seem to be buried, but in fact smuggled into the Tower, known only to a few. Her auditor protested that William would eventually be seen; Arbella said the windows to the garden would be boarded up. He told her how dangerous her project was; she countered that she was protected by foreign and domestic supporters. Asked if Mary Talbot were involved, she said 'by no means'.

Questions have been asked about the date of this document –

1613 or 1614? But what strikes home to the ordinary reader is its poignancy.

Just as in the last months at Hardwick, Arbella could have been either delusional or trying to delude; fantasizing for bitter amusement, or else to create a smokescreen to cover some more realistic plan. But, just as at Hardwick, one is inclined less to juggle with the medical possibilities – was she clinically certifiable, and if so for causes emotional, genetic, or biochemical? – than to pity the form her fantasy took.

In her restricted life in the Tower, so short of other pleasures or distractions, her affection for William was never going to dwindle. More likely, she fanned the flames with brooding. But she must by now, and with the failure of the latest escape attempt, have despaired of ever seeing him again. A garbled story spread in the autumn of 1613 that William had died abroad; 'should be dead at Dunkirk', as Chamberlain told it. He had, indeed, by his own account, been sick of smallpox and 'in great danger'. If Arbella heard the tale of his death – if it were not just a Chinese whisper originating with her own fantasy – it can only have added to her agony, just as the waxwork effigy of her husband's corpse tormented the Duchess of Malfi.

In the summer of 1614, after the failure of her last escape attempt, the conditions of Arbella's imprisonment seemed to be set for the long haul. Crompton was allowed to organize her accounts, and pawn some more of her jewels. But such evidence of preparations for an indefinite stay can hardly have cheered her. She knew (she may have been deluded; she was never stupid) that her career had been a series of mistakes. She was helpless to herself and dangerous to her family – her 'guiltless friends', as she had written from Hardwick, that easy captivity. Every night, the sound of the keys turning in the locks forced home the lesson of how futile her schemes must be. With the dwindling light, as summer slipped into autumn, Arbella's will to live faded away.

As we already know, ill-health was nothing new to her. The earl of Northampton wrote mockingly about it in letters that, while undated, seem likely from internal evidence to date from that spring of 1613, when Arbella herself referred to her 'late dangerous sickness'. She was, he wrote, in very great danger:

of no special disease but of a wasting with an extreme debility. She hath neither taken broth nor any drink more than once these three days which excess of fasting breeds idleness. She will admit no doctor either for the body or the soul at this present, but commands her women to read sometimes a psalm, out of which she sometimes picks a verse to raise her meditation with a show of great repentance for her sins, and resolves touching her own state that she cannot continue. Nothing puts her so much out of patience as the proffer of the doctors either of physic or the other kind of divinity to draw near, for then she storms with extremity.

The day before, he wrote, she had been in 'a kind of trance' until roused by the shrieks of her women. Then she laughed, and told them that the hour was not yet come. Clearly those around her thought death could not be far away.

Northampton, however, saw her situation differently. He wrote with the most extreme lack of sympathy of his incredulity in anything that concerned Arbella, based 'upon my former knowledge and experience of more giddy parts played formerly by her than any man or woman that I never know'. Perhaps it was a kind of tribute, in a way. 'She pretends to fast from meat and drink, but God knows what supplies are brought in when the curtains are drawn.' The rapid recovery characteristic of porphyria, Sara Jayne Steen points out, often led to accusations of duplicity. 'She prays, she rails, she cries, she laughs and talks idly. Her mind runs only upon Devonshire by whom she affirms that she had a child and at this instance that he nightly lies withall.' The earl of Devonshire, until his death in 1606, had been that great Elizabethan courtier Lord Mountjoy: Essex's friend, devoted lover to Essex's sister Penelope Rich, and one of those with whom Arbella's name had implausibly been linked in 1603. (Mountjoy's illegitimate children by Penelope Rich could not inherit his title, which was subsequently purchased by Arbella's uncle William in 1618.) In the absence of other evidence, one can only assume Mountjoy was the subject of her fantasy. 'When they cannot make [Arbella] drink by any instance or persuasion, the only trick is to persuade her to drink to Devonshire's health. Thereupon she never suffers the pot to be taken from her hand so long as there is one drop in the bottom.' This 'experiment' Northampton recounted to make his friend 'merry'.

From this extremity of weakness and delusion, Arbella had clearly recovered, to some degree. But on 8 September 1614 the council, hearing that 'The Lady Arbella, prisoner in the Tower, is of late fallen into some indisposition of body and mind,' sent a clergyman to her, a 'person of gravity and learning . . . to give her that comfort as is expedient for a Christian in cases of weakness and infirmity'. He was 'to visit her from time to time, as in your judgement shall be thought fit', and to 'give her spiritual comfort and advice'. They asked that his first visit should be 'speedy and undelayed'. The matter obviously had some urgency.

In the autumn of 1614 Arbella took to her bed; and if it is probably exaggerating in literal terms to say that she would never rise again, it is certainly true metaphorically. For a year, as the physicians complained after her death, Arbella would not allow doctors to feel her pulse or inspect her urine; she did not, apparently, want to be cured.

She may have been constrained to take to her bed by illness, mental or physical; the Tower had broken stronger constitutions than hers. She may conceivably have been making a play for sympathy. The tactic had a good pedigree in the seventeenth century; Arbella had used it herself at Barnet and perhaps at Hardwick. It had been a favourite of her girlhood friend the earl of Essex; and Thomas Overbury had paved the way for his own murder when he asked his supposed friend Carr to provide him with drugs that would give him symptoms convincing enough to move James to mercy.

But when Arbella refused medical attention, it is possible that she was responding to a different lesson learned from the death of Overbury. In *Unnatural Murder*, her analysis of the Overbury case, Anne Somerset horrifyingly described the medical practices of the day, and posits a theory that Overbury (however many people were trying to poison him) may in fact have died from septicaemia from the wound his doctor had made to bleed him. This doctor's usual practice was to keep such a wound open by the insertion of 'five to seven peas', and daily to anoint it with balsam of earthworm or bats. If this is a reasonable sample of the remedies on offer, Arbella might have refused them with the greatest rationality.

Even at the time, voices were raised in query as to whether the physicians did not hurt more than they healed. If Arbella were a porphyriac – if her belief that William was coming to join her was indeed the delusion born of illness – she would be especially well advised to avoid the 'cordials' she had previously been prescribed, a combination of laudanum and red wine, often stored in lead vessels. She may have learned as much from experience. But nothing here is cut and dried. Nothing was cut and dried even in the case of Sir Thomas Overbury, so much more extensively documented after the murder inquiry. Even Overbury's apothecary opined that he died 'of a consumption proceeding of melancholy by reason of his imprisonment', and Overbury himself had written that if he were kept any longer in gaol his mind would 'overthrow my body forever'.

However one interprets the words, Arbella's mind probably did overthrow her body – or perhaps it might be better to say overrule it. It is possible she had resolved on her own destruction. 'I dare to die, so I be not guilty of my own death,' she had written earlier in her captivity. To refuse medical attention – just as Queen Elizabeth had done in her last illness – did not, to seventeenth-century thinking, constitute the mortal sin of suicide. Even to refuse food did not put one in that dreadful category. And Arbella had, after all, very little reason to go on living; there was no chance she would ever be let out, ever know anything more than this constricted existence. As Ralegh wrote from the Tower:

> Despair bolts up my doors, and I alone
> Speak to dead walls: but these hear not my moan.

If ever Arbella looked back to the days when she called Hardwick her prison, wrote of captivity and her grandmother's custody, she must have remembered them wryly. By comparison, the Arbella of Hardwick days had been lucky. As she had written all too prophetically in 1603, 'Daily more and more, to my unceasing grief, I am and hereafter shall be more unfortunate than I lately thought I could possibly have been.'

She had written, too, that death alone could make her absolutely and eternally happy. Almost half a century before, the Fugger newsletters had reported the death of Spain's mad crown prince, Don Carlos, King Philip's son:

> The prince of Spain during his imprisonment, apart from a few times, has not wished to touch food. Nevertheless he had been persuaded to give up such a whim. But when the hot days began he waxed impatient on account of his incarceration and behaved in unseemly fashion. It is said that he caused his room to be deluged with water and oft walked barefoot in it. About ten days ago, for several days – some have it as many as six – he would partake of nothing but fruit and drink great quantities of cold water. By means of this he caused his digestion and his whole body to become greatly discomforted. When after this he wished to take food once more, he was no longer able to retain it and was taken so ill in the forenoon that he passed away last night at one . . . It is said that the king has neither seen him in his illness nor wished to go to him, neither has the queen nor the princess.

Nothing more lonely can be imagined – unless it were from Arbella's story.

The chronicle of Arbella's imprisonment is silent through her last illness. No reports survive (were any written?) from one September to the next. But it cannot have been pretty. As a winter so harsh England saw 'the greatest snow which ever fell upon the earth, within man's memory' was followed by a summer of unusual heat, Arbella's state declined.

The post mortem suggests she died more or less of starvation, and that is something that happens very slowly. First the deprived body consumes fat, then muscle tissue. Then it starts to cannibalize tissues – such as the optical nerves – that are not essential to survival. However her last illness started, it must have come as a relief to her when, on 25 September 1615, Arbella Stuart finally died.

Arbella's actual death, the Venetian ambassador reported afterwards, was 'almost instantaneous, accompanied by a sudden tremor and loss of power in the lower limbs'. But earlier, he had written that her aunt Mary, a short while before (days? weeks?), had found her 'almost entirely unconscious and moribund'. Mary wrote of her shock at this 'heavy loss' in a December letter to the countess of Cumberland, Anne Clifford's mother. Her niece's state had not been made known to her until two days before Arbella's death, when she was 'in all men's opinions that were about her' considered likely to die that very night; the next morning Mary had misleadingly been told that Arbella was, instead much better. Hoping that Arbella died 'a saint' – which for her surely meant a Catholic – Mary apologized for being unfit to write of any other matter when her heart was 'possessed' with this.

Of course, poison had to be considered as a possibility. The day after Arbella's death Sir Ralph Winwood, the secretary of state, ordered Dr Moundford and a panel of physicians to view the corpse: 'according to former custom upon like occasions, when prisoners of great quality die in that place, her body should be viewed by persons of skill and trust, and thereupon certificate be made of what disease she died, as their judgement might appear.' A post mortem was ordered – as it would have been even without the rumblings of a delayed scandal about the death of Overbury. The doctors, on opening her body, found the organs to be sound, her death being caused by

a chronic and long sickness; the species of disease was *illam jamdiu producem in cachexiam* [one that after a long time resulted in ill-health and malnutrition], which, increasing as well by her negligence as by refusal of remedies . . . by long lying in bed she got bedsores, and a confirmed unhealthiness of liver, and extreme leanness, and so died.

The liver – the unhealthy liver – was considered to be the seat of love, appropriately.

Arbella's body went through the usual processes – the de-humanizing ritual of embalming: '*By order dated 12th of October, 1615. –* To Duncan Primrose, one of his Majesty's Surgeons, the sum of £6 13s and 4d, for charges disbursed about the embalming of the late Lady Arbella.' It seems to have been the end of the next July before the unfortunate Dr Primrose was paid. But all the other business was transacted quickly. The government clearly feared a popular outcry – needlessly, as it turned out.

Arbella's corpse was taken to Westminster Abbey. A near contemporary – and many biographers since – describes how it was 'brought at midnight by the dark river' and buried 'with no solemnity' in the tomb James had recently erected for his mother Mary. But the Venetian envoy Foscarini recorded, instead, how sixty coaches followed her coffin to the grave, and perhaps it is fitting that her life ended in confusion, as it had begun. Queen Anna wanted the court to put on mourning, but James refused. 'They decided that as she had died in some respects contumacious, the court should not put on mourning, and that she should be buried wherever her people desired,' wrote Foscarini on 16 October. 'Her death is deplored by a great number of the chief of the people. The king has not said a word about it.'

There was no official epitaph, but the bishop of Norwich composed these lines privately:

> How do I thank thee, Death, and bless thy power
> That I have passed the guard and 'scaped the Tower!
> And now my pardon is my epitaph
> And a small coffin my poor carcase hath;
> For at thy charge both soul and body were
> Enlarged at last, secure from hope and fear
> That among saints, this amongst kings is laid,
> And what my birth did claim my death has paid.

Arbella was scarcely cold, and the myth-making had begun already.

# Epilogue

ARBELLA STUART'S LIFE SEEMED TO HAVE ENDED NOT WITH A BANG
but with a whimper – and that is no finish for a story. It is true
she left no obvious legacy: in the most direct sense, her few goods
were immediately seized on the privy council's authority. In the
broader sense, her contribution (*Malfi* apart; and perhaps that is
enough) is an elusive matter. And yet, almost four hundred years
after her death, she does live in posterity.

Several chains of action and event – genealogical, historical,
ideological – make it hard to end her tale in 1615. They are
tenuous, amorphous; so much so that to overemphasize any one
is to perform the conjurer's trick of misdirection. To proclaim that
this, *this*, is why she mattered, is to evoke a strong aroma of
sawn-up lady. But together the fragments of the kaleidoscope
make Arbella Stuart a curiously ubiquitous ghost; one whose
presence cannot easily be dismissed, though she may haunt only
the fringes of history.

Shortly after Arbella's death, the Tower became a more crowded
place – crowded, ironically, with some of the people she would
have known at court, and as a result of just the kind of morality
that caused her to hate court life so passionately. At the beginning
of September 1615 – while Arbella was still alive, but probably in
no condition to take much of an interest – King James belatedly
ordered an investigation into the death, two years before, of Sir

Thomas Overbury. In the middle of September Overbury's gaoler, Richard Weston, was arrested and given into the charge of Arbella's old Lambeth custodian, Sir Thomas Parry.

It was the start of a landslide. The snowballing investigation ended not only with the wholesale execution of the lesser functionaries (among them the Tower's lieutenant Sir Gervase Helwys, guilty of having turned a blind eye to murder) but with the trial of the king's erstwhile favourite Carr and his wife, the court beauty Frances Howard – and, perhaps, with a widespread disgust at the court's laxity. The whole scandalous story – how the two chief culprits followed Arbella into the Tower; how Frances sensationally pleaded guilty at her trial; how the king was moved to clemency – is well known. Less well known is the fact that the whistleblower, who finally won for Overbury his long-delayed justice, was probably none other than Mary Talbot, whose husband Gilbert first put the investigation into motion. Carr had, after all, contemptuously refused Mary's request that he should intercede for Arbella with the king. Frances's uncle the earl of Northampton (Pandarus in her affair with Carr) had hounded Mary herself after Arbella's escape. And it was never wise to cross a countess of Shrewsbury.

While Robert Carr and Frances Howard moved towards a lifetime of disgrace, Mary Talbot herself was released from the Tower just before Christmas 1615, to nurse Gilbert. Long plagued by ill health, he died the year after. But in 1618 Mary was recalled to face questioning by the committee set up to investigate rumours that Arbella had borne a child. Once again, her refusal to answer saw her condemned to imprisonment in the Tower – this time for life, it was said, though in fact she was released in 1623. She lived there in some style and the best lodgings; Anne Clifford wrote of visiting her and Frances Howard there on the same day. She maintained her business and charitable interests; subscribed to the Virginia Company, and underwrote the building of the second court at St John's College, Cambridge – even though the crown had reimposed the old fine of twenty thousand pounds, and taken her property of Worksop Manor in lieu of the money. She was almost seventy when she was released; nine years later, in 1632, she died.

Of Arbella's cousins and near contemporaries, the daughters of Gilbert and Mary Talbot, Mary had a fate as bleak as Arbella's own; tied to a barren marriage, she was compelled to raise her husband's children by another woman, his cousin the writer Lady Mary Wroth. But Elizabeth, the countess of Kent, became famous for her medical skill and the scale of her charity – and also the focus of a good deal of scandal. The lawyer and historian John Selden was employed as steward at the family seat, Wrest Park, and that great gossip John Aubrey claimed that the countess, 'being an ingenious woman and loving men, would let him lie with her and her husband knew it. After the earl's death he married her ... Mr Selden had got more by his prick than he had done by his practice.' It is a fine, smacking, Restoration story.

Alethea, scientific interests apart, travelled widely in pursuit of her own and her husband's artistic interests. Taking her children abroad in the 1620s, she had herself portrayed by Rubens with child, dog, dwarf, English ambassador and the painter himself all in attendance, before installing herself in the Palazzo Mocenigo on the Grand Canal and making some stir in Venetian society. She returned home with a velvet litter drawn by donkeys, a gondola to use on the Thames and a quantity of 'prodigious edible' snails. Her life was not easy; the Civil War saw Alethea and her husband living apart in exile on the continent, ruined and estranged from their children and each other. But all the same, her travels sound more luscious fun than poor Arbella's Derbyshire journey; just as her dramas have a different hue from Arbella's stark black-and-white tragedy.

Most of the characters close to Arbella – with one notable exception – did not very long survive her. Queen Anna died in 1619 of congestive heart failure, her funeral (which the king did not attend) twice postponed until money could be found to pay for it. James himself died in 1625, at Theobalds, having long taken an ever more passive part in affairs. Sir Walter Ralegh was released from the Tower in 1616 that he might once again go seeking that fabled land of El Dorado, from which to replenish the king's bare coffers. Returning empty-handed, he was re-arrested on the old charge of having tried to place Arbella on the throne. He was executed in October 1618, in Old Palace Yard,

Westminster; his death (like Arbella's own) was soon to become a symbol of royal tyranny.

But William Seymour, alone amid the leading players of her life, survived Arbella by almost fifty years; a half-century which saw him develop from the rather shadowy figure of his first marriage to one of the most prominent peers of the day. Within a few months of Arbella's death, he was petitioning to be allowed home. He wrote to James on New Year's Day 1616: 'Vouchsafe dread Sovereign to cast your merciful eyes upon the most humble and penitent wretch that youth and ignorance have thrown into transgression . . .' A favourable answer came back very quickly – as it probably would have done even had he written a degree less humbly. When Arbella was alive, the authorities preferred William should be as far away from her as possible. With her dead, to have him back in the realm and beyond the influence of any foreign power just saw a satisfactory line drawn under the whole sorry situation.

The day after William arrived back, in February, the king gave him an audience and a pardon; in November he was created a knight of the bath in company with Charles, prince of Wales. Four months after that, he married again. It was not quick, by the standards of the day, and one has to remember that if it was only eighteen months since Arbella's death it was more than five years since he had lived with her, and that only briefly.

His choice of bride seems significant: Frances Devereux, eldest daughter of the great earl of Essex Arbella had known (and sister to the incumbent). 'Dear Lamb', he would address her warmly in letters, signing himself 'Your most faithful and affectionate husband'. But this Frances is revealed in her later dealings as yet another formidable lady. A portrait shows her long-nosed and tight-lipped, a lock of her father Essex's hair welded into a macabre earring. If she tried to rule her husband, it was a pattern repeated in their children; their son John ('the mad duke') cited as reason for separating from his wife 'her endeavour to govern him'. During the difficult years ahead, no matter how kindly William and Frances wrote, it is noticeable that they did not seem to be often together. But perhaps the times were to try them rather high.

In 1620 William was elected a member of parliament, but on his grandfather's death a year later (his father and elder brother Edward being dead already) he was translated to the House of Lords as earl of Hertford. Arbella's steward Hugh Crompton and his fellow gentleman servant Edward Kirton both became MPs under his patronage. Much of William's life at this stage seems to have been lived far from court, at Netley on Southampton Water, a former Cistercian abbey, and in the mansion Inigo Jones had built for him on the site of another abbey at Amesbury.

The earl of Clarendon wrote later that William had been 'so wholly given up to a country life, where he lived in splendour, that he had an aversion, and even an unaptness, for business'; that he 'loved and was even wedded so much to his ease that he loved his book above all exercises; and had even contracted such a laziness of mind, that he had no delight in an open and liberal conversation, and cared not to discourse and argue upon those points that he understood very well, only for the trouble of contending'. This, mind you, was to be set against his 'honour so unblemished' and 'notable steadiness', and perhaps this cocktail of qualities itself helped to make him significant in the noisy, divisive years ahead. As England began to split into factions, William was repeatedly spoken of as someone whose own choice would draw many others to either the royalist or the parliamentarian side. 'It was thought his example would either keep out or draw in many with him.'

Perhaps his enforced wanderings in France (where noblemen more easily placed went to learn swordsmanship and the handling of the 'great horses') had toughened him in some way. Found in a duel some years later, 'the earl closed with [his opponent] and had him down at his mercy'. 'It seems my lord of Hertford was infinitely abused and provoked,' the raconteur added excusingly.

In the Civil War, he was to play a part first political, and then military. As early as 1628 he was one of the justices urging Charles I to think better of a proposed taxation. This time, the advice was successful: but in 1640 he was one of the twelve English peers whose petition, 'in all humility', failed to steer the king away from his collision course with parliament. Besides the new monopolies and the Scottish wars, the peers lamented 'sundry innovations in matters of religion [and] . . . The great increase of popery'. If William had made a conversion on the continent, it was not of any great depth or durability. He subsequently waded into a debate between whether *jure divino*, divine right, lay with the bishops or the presbytery, declaring that 'For my part I think that neither the one nor the other, nor any government whatsoever, is *jure divino*' – a sentiment, for a committed royalist, surely revolutionary enough in its own way.

The crisis of the country seemed to be dragging William out of his quiet life. He was one of the commissioners who negotiated the treaty of Ripon with the Scots; he was made a privy counsellor, 'to the public joy'. His earldom was upgraded to a marquisate in thanks for his good work and good advice, and in the spring of 1641 the marquis of Hertford reluctantly accepted the appointment of governor to the prince of Wales (succeeding, at the latter's suggestion, Arbella's cousin William, Charles Cavendish's son, now duke of Newcastle).

At this delicate, but not yet openly divided, stage, his importance lay in the fact that he was clearly trusted in some measure by both king and Commons; the latter stipulating that William should be present when anyone came to talk to Prince Charles 'lest any evil counsels might be given him'. But when, a year later, open conflict finally came, he seems to have made his choice unhesitatingly, 'notwithstanding', as Clarendon wrote, 'all his allies, and those with whom he had the greatest familiarity and friendship, were of the opposite party'. One should perhaps remember that, after all, he would still have been the best contender for the throne himself had their enemies successfully eliminated the Stuart dynasty.

The marquis of Hertford was appointed the royalist lieutenant-general of the west. He was on the same side as the duke of Newcastle, who held Yorkshire for the king until the defeat at Marston Moor. (A defeat, some said, triggered by the fact that Newcastle, in the artistic traditions of his family, was said to be too busy 'fornicating with the Nine Muses' to be an effective commander.) But William was set against his brother-in-law the earl of Essex, a commander of the parliamentary forces, and his sympathies must have been divided quite agonizingly.

William was now in his fifties, and never an obvious choice for a military commander. His abilities in the field seem to have been mixed, and increasingly he came into conflict with his second-in-command, King Charles's nephew, the young professional soldier Prince Maurice. (Especially they clashed over William's reluctance to let his troops sack the countryside, while Maurice saw no reason not to give the soldiery their head.) William was eventually withdrawn from his military role – nominally, so that he should be closer to the king. Ironically, his brother-in-law Essex, on the other side, was himself being sidelined in much the same way. They were not natural place-winners in that family.

But, as the tides of war turned against the royalists, William remained close to Charles I. He was with the king when Charles negotiated with parliament from his prison/refuge on the Isle of Wight, and by his side at the time of the king's trial. William was one of the four noblemen who (so established legend has it) begged that they, as Charles's advisers, should be executed in his place. This refused, they asked at least that they might be allowed to give his body burial and perform 'their last duty to their dead master'. They were allowed to take the corpse from London to Windsor; but there, the new governor of the castle refused to allow the bishop of London to carry out the burial rite according to the discredited Book of Common Prayer. The lords, moreover, found the church so altered by despoilers that they could not find an appropriate burial place until a friendly resident showed them where Henry VIII lay, so that Charles might be interred in some royal company.

William was now out of the war, allowed (on twenty thousand pounds' security) to retire to Netley. From there in 1650 he wrote to his wife, about a planned visit: 'I am confident you will find it neither unpleasant nor unsafe if any place in England be safe, for all are now alike, but this has something the advantage being out of all roads.' But he was still keeping the exiled Charles II supplied with money (one source says as much as five thousand pounds a year, besides what he had provided for his father Charles I). And in 1651 the council of state was ordering the marquis to move on again, to Amesbury. 'We are informed that many dangerous and disaffected persons resort to your house.'

Not far away, in parliamentarian Marlborough, William's brother Francis Seymour's house had been commandeered by hostile forces, and his wife and daughter held prisoner, while William's eldest son, Lord Beauchamp, was sent to the Tower for his efforts in the royal cause.

As far back as 1644, indeed, sent abroad for his health (his uncle's influence helping him through the parliamentary lines), the eighteen-year-old Beauchamp had carried a letter from Charles I to the earl of Essex, asking if they could not try to settle the dispute between them. The health troubles were serious ones; five of the eight children of William Seymour would predecease him, his eldest daughter Arbella among them. Sick with what was probably tuberculosis, Beauchamp was allowed out of the Tower to take the waters at Epsom, but in vain. In 1654 he died. 'An unspeakable loss in England', wrote Clarendon from abroad. By Beauchamp's loss, wrote another royalist, 'the west will be much unprovided. But I am confident the marquis of Hertford, tho' he be old, would not be idle.' Oliver Cromwell, himself ageing, sent a messenger to William to commiserate on his loss, and later invited him to an extraordinary meeting.

'Cromwell received him with all imaginable respect; and after dinner took him by the hand and led him into his withdrawing room, where they two being alone, he told the marquis he had desired his company that he might have his advice what to do. "For", said he, "I am not able to bear the weight of the business that is upon me."' William advised him to recall Charles II from exile, and to restore the monarchy.

Cromwell died in 1658, leaving the protectorate in the unsafe hands of his eldest son. When the Restoration of the monarchy did indeed come in 1660, William was among the party who travelled to Canterbury to greet the king, and later that year Charles II re-created for him his great-grandfather's title of duke of Somerset. But he did not live long to enjoy it. On 14 October his son-in-law, the earl of Winchilsea, was writing: 'I doubt he cannot hold out long, the king was this afternoon to see him.' William died at Essex House in London on 24 October 1660, of 'a general decay of nature'. 'A man of great honour, interest and estate,' Clarendon called him, 'of an universal esteem over the whole kingdom.'

The bishop of Salisbury added that William, in times of distress, claimed to have found comfort in repeating Psalm 57 – and one sentence particularly: 'Under the shadow of thy wings shall be my refuge, till this tyranny is overpast.' To the bishop, as to the ageing William, the tyranny was presumably parliamentarian rule, which kept from England its rightful monarchy. And yet, how differently could the sentiment have been used earlier in William's (and Arbella's) story.

But there is another 'wrap' to the story: one that would have pleased old Bess, and Lady Lennox – and Arbella and William too, probably. As the Talbot lands were broken up and the Seymour titles passed sideways, the Cavendish family rose ever higher in the seventeenth century. From Bess's son William came the dukes of Devonshire, from Charles the dukes of Newcastle (and from her daughter Frances the dukes of Kingston) until, in the nineteenth century, marriage brought them into the Bowes-Lyon family. By then, William Seymour's line (through his daughter Frances) had joined the Cavendish family tree. The house of Windsor came originally from James I's daughter Elizabeth; so the blood of both Arbella's grandmothers, and of her husband (along with that of the earl of Essex) is united in Britain's present royal family.

There is, alas, no reason to give credence to the rumours that Arbella bore William a living child. Mary Talbot was finally brought to admit she thought it unlikely, and William denied it. There is certainly no reason to put faith in the theory (issuing from America's south in the 1940s) that her daughter was the New England Quaker Mary Barratt who, after marrying a William Dyer in London, went on to become America's only female religious martyr. This was floated as a purely speculative possibility and carries with it not the faintest shred of proof, nor even of probability. And yet, the new world does have a share in Arbella's legacy.

In the years immediately after her death, the name Arbella crops up in other prominent north country families. Probably some of its bearers were named in compliment to our Lady Arbella: George Chaworth's daughter, for example, and Lady

Arbella Clinton, sister to the fourth earl of Lincoln (himself imprisoned in the Tower, not long before, for his opposition to the forced loan raised by Charles I). The Clinton family (through the maternal line, the Knyvets) were tied by a web of connections, social and political, to Arbella's family. (Lady Chandos of Barnet had been a Clinton.) Even by comparison with that of Arbella Stuart, Arbella Clinton's is a dramatic story.

At the end of March 1630, eleven ships set sail from Southampton, bound for the Americas – not the aristocratic trading posts of Virginia, but the northern coast of Massachusetts. It was the desire for religious freedom that had sent them on this dangerous passage across the sea. On board the small fleet were Sir Richard Saltonstall (whose family were close friends to Captain John Smith), the wealthy Isaac Johnson (grandson to the puritan bishop of Lincoln) and his well-born wife – and another puritan, John Winthrop, whose name would go down in history. The ship named rear-admiral of the fleet was the *Ambassador*; the vice-admiral was the *Talbot*. The admiral, the flagship on which the prominent settlers sailed, had been renamed in honour of her 'illustrious passenger', Johnson's wife. The old *Eagle* – a ship of 350 tons, with fifty-two seamen and twenty-eight pieces of ordnance – had become the *Arbella* before she put out to sea.

John Winthrop's diary chronicled the voyage. The Channel winds at first served them little better than they had Arbella Stuart twenty years earlier. April had begun, and still the party lay near English shores; so near that 'the Lady Arbella and the gentlewomen, and Mr Isaac Johnson and some of the others went on shore to refresh themselves.' They finally weighed anchor and got through the Needles, only to be becalmed again as they waited for the rest of the fleet. They saw eight sail astern 'and feared they might be Dunkirkers' – the ships of England's Spanish enemy, clustered around Dunkirk. The hammocks were taken down, guns were loaded, inflammable bedding thrown overboard. 'The Lady Arbella and the other women and children remained in the lower decks that they might be out of danger.' But 'It was much to see how cheerful and comfortable all the company appeared, not a woman or child that showed fear,' Winthrop wrote admiringly.

The ships proved to be their own friends. Fear and danger 'turned into mirth and friendly entertainment'. For the next two months Winthrop's diary records their life at sea – the catching of cod, the coldness of the weather, the punishment of young men caught fighting and of a servant cheating at rations; the winds, the sighting of a whale, the birth of a child and the death of a cow; a storm in which few were sick 'except the women, who kept under hatches'; days when they fasted, since it was too rough to prepare food; a day when they feasted the masters of the other ships in the roundhouse, 'the lady and the gentlewomen' being fed in the great cabin, out of the way.

It was early June, on the Lord's Day, when 'we sounded (as we had so often before) and had ground at about 80 fathoms, and the mist thus breaking up we saw the shore.' A week later they came at last to port and anchor, and landed at Salem (as it was later known) 'where we supped with a good venison pasty and good beer, and at night we returned to our ship, but some of the women stayed behind.' At Cape Ann, they gathered 'a good store of fine strawberries', and 'American Indians came about us and laid there all night.'

The *Arbella* had got through her journey well, though other ships of the fleet had suffered more severely. The men went looking for new ground to settle – to what became Charlestown, on Massachusetts Bay. But tragedy was waiting for Winthrop in the new land, and the death of his son in an accident broke the flow of his diary. It is from different records that we know the fate of others. A letter the next year to the countess of Lincoln in England from her former steward, the settler Thomas Dudley, tells how many died 'for want of warm lodging and good diet, and in the sudden increase of heat that they endure who are landed here in summer – especially after the salt meat at sea'. Every household, he said, had lost someone: two hundred of the original thousand had died, and some of the others had returned home. Isaac Johnson died early, on 30 September 1630, 'his wife having died a month before'. She was buried at Salem, in an unmarked grave; she had spent little more than six weeks in the promised land.

But just as the colony eventually prospered, as other settlers survived, so the name Arbella lived on, linked with a speech that became part of America's mythology. It was during his voyage on board the *Arbella* that Winthrop (later the first governor of Massachusetts) wrote memorably of the settlers' mission: 'to do justly, to love mercy, to walk humbly with our God'; to keep 'the unity of the spirit in the bond of peace . . . For we must consider that we shall be as a City upon a hill. The eyes of all people are upon us.'

Even in England, after her death, Arbella Stuart's name was associated with ideas of liberty and democracy. It is interesting today to read contemporary speculation that England, after Elizabeth's death, might have been governed as a republic or commonwealth, with Arbella as titular queen – the kind of monarchy with which we are now familiar, though it may have looked less convincing in 1603. The years of her troubles saw Sir Edward Coke (himself sent to the Tower in 1621, for his opposition to the crown) develop his ideas of civil liberties; the Civil War soon set out to institute the freedoms for lack of which she had suffered. In one ballad from the eighteenth century, Arbella's enemies represent the 'tyranny' that would 'strive to chain the free-born mind'. Verses that appeared soon after her death, entitled 'The True Lovers' Knot Untied', put the theme more clearly:

> 'I never raised Rent', said she,
> 'Nor yet oppressed the tenant poor.
> I never took no bribes for fines
> For why I had enough before.
>
> 'I would I had a milkmaid been,
> Or born of some more low degree
> Then I might have loved where I liked
> And no man could have hindered me.'

Of course, it is by no means clear that Arbella would have shared the sentiment of the 'True Lovers' Knot' (any more than it is clear that, had she and hers succeeded to the throne instead of James and his son Charles, the seventeenth century would have unrolled less bloodily). She has attracted many writers; Shakespeare himself may have pleaded her cause in *Cymbeline*, with its virtuous cross-dressing princess, forbidden marriage and banished husband. But since then, successive generations have reflected upon her the preoccupations of their own age – usually by amputating some inconvenient part of her personality.

The ballads that proclaimed her an innocent victim of royal tyranny disregarded her own immense pride in her royalty. The Victorians, in their determination to see her as a romantic heroine, ignored any trace of ambition in her. By contrast I, as a writer of the twenty-first century, am strongly drawn to the idea of Arbella as a contender; her ambition, her activity. But perhaps this, too, is a perception that will be challenged by later generations.

The historians who wrote of her in the middle of the twentieth century seemed to regard her with disapproval as a woman who wanted too much, and who behaved foolishly as she set about achieving it – if not insane then unbalanced, certainly; and perhaps that is a clue to the latest revival of interest. It is only recently that we have been able to acknowledge all her problems, her 'distraction' – to dwell on the agonized pages of evidence – and still to admire her.

Even Arbella's defenders have felt the need in some sense to excuse her, to explain her away – 'an eccentric even the Jacobeans failed to explain', as her recent biographer David Durant put it. More often, she has been dismissed with a kind of casual cruelty. Her life, wrote the not untypical David Mathew, who in 1963 devoted to her one chapter in his book on King James, 'had been a very sad adventure. Old Lady Shrewsbury made a mistake in arranging her conception.' This is an extraordinary dismissal of a woman who lived, loved and wrote memorable letters; who enjoyed red deer pies and lute music, and may have inspired one of the greatest works of English literature – even if she failed either to rule a nation or to change the course of history.

After several decades of neglect, Arbella Stuart benefited from the rise of feminist criticism, which triggered a resurgence of interest in her through the 1990s. She has received fresh recognition as a writer and a rebel; 'Arbella Stuart and the Rhetoric of

Disguise and Defiance', read the title of one American essay. Yet she fits only uneasily into the original, the simple, feminist model. Arbella did not eschew the 'normal' woman's destiny of marriage. She sought it desperately. Although the choices open to her would undoubtedly have been more varied had she been born a boy, her painful youth saw her dominated not by a man or men, but by more powerful women. This seems to me a field of conflict which we, today, have not yet explored to any great degree. Is it a co-incidence (as Sara Jayne Steen first asked) that the periods of greatest interest in Arbella Stuart have been those which have also seen us making delicate adjustments to our ideas about women and society – the dawn of the twentieth century; the years around the 1960s; the present day?

But Arbella's true appeal is more fundamental. There is a temptation to feel that any life deemed worth of a biography must exemplify something; must be, in some sense, exemplary. The life of Arbella Stuart has been variously taken to epitomize martyr-dom (sexual, religious or political), rebellion and romance. She seems to me rather to represent how far the human spirit can fall into frustration and despair without ever giving up completely. 'I am the Duchess of Malfi still,' declared Webster's heroine, abandoned and imprisoned. Whatever the failings of Arbella Stuart, she fought the same fight for her identity.

# Appendix A
## 'One Morley'

IT WAS A LETTER IN THE TIMES LITERARY SUPPLEMENT ON 27 February 1937 that speculatively identified Arbella's tutor Morley with that other spy, the playwright Christopher Marlowe; and indeed the two men appear to show a number of personal and biographical similarities.

About the Hardwick Morley, Morley-the-tutor, all our information comes from that one letter cited from Bess to Burghley in the 1590s. But there are assumptions we can make based on this. For instance, it is fair to assume that Morley came to Hardwick more or less straight from university – Oxford or Cambridge – perhaps recommended by the university itself, since it sounds a little as if there had been some pressure on him to leave to fill this post.

Marlowe-the-playwright came out of Cambridge in 1587, not long before Morley appeared at Hardwick; and Morley was one of the variants of his name Kit Marlowe used at Cambridge (along with Marley – the version both he and his father favoured – Merling, Marlen, Marlyn, Marle, and more). Like the Morley of whom Bess writes, Kit Marlowe was said to have had questionable religious views – was indeed, at the time of his death, under investigation on suspicion of atheism. Like Morley, he was given to shooting his mouth off, whether inadvertently or on purpose; Bess says twice over that Morley had shown himself to be 'much discontented' – had been advertising himself as such

369

around the household. While his discontent may well have been genuine, this was also a favourite technique of the Elizabethan spy. Advertise yourself as a malcontent, and wait for approaches; it was the technique Polonius would advocate in *Hamlet* while instructing his servant in surveillance.

The first suggestion that Marlowe was a government spy comes at Cambridge. When he received his MA in 1587, it was due only to the intervention of no less a body than the privy council. The university complained that he had mysteriously been absent from Cambridge for substantial periods; worse, that he had gone 'beyond the seas to Reames [Rheims, home of the Catholic seminary] there to remain'. In other words, he appeared to be a papist, as Bess came close to suggesting of Morley. The privy council instructed Cambridge that this breach of rules should be ignored, and no questions asked. They did so, moreover, in the strongest terms. Marlowe's absences were due to 'good service' and 'faithful dealing' done 'in matters touching the benefit of his country', and it was not her Majesty's pleasure that anyone thus employed 'should be defamed by those that are ignorant of th'affairs he went about'. Throughout his latter years at Cambridge, moreover, the shoemaker's son from Canterbury seems to have been drawing an income from somewhere, as his expenditures regularly exceed his scholarship money. It is worth noting that the chancellor of Cambridge University at that time was none other than Burghley.

Essentially, the Marlowe-for-Morley theory as advanced in 1937 runs thus. Soon after leaving Cambridge, this eminently suitable agent was placed at Hardwick as an all-purpose informer by either Burghley (though Bess writes to him of Morley as someone he doesn't know) or Walsingham. Like Burghley, Sir Francis Walsingham was a member of the privy council that secured Marlowe his MA.

Writer after writer – George Gascoigne, Samuel Daniel and Ben Jonson in Arbella's day – doubled the profession with that of spy. Several, in Marlowe's day, also doubled the roles of spy and tutor. A tutor to the Talbot children had been accused of acting for the queen of Scots. If Marlowe were Morley, then he would not be unique in literary history. And the identification takes a little colour from literary sources: in Marlowe's *Edward II* (II:ii) the scholar Baldock hopes to be 'preferred' through the agency of a lady, cousin to the king, 'Having read unto her since she was a child'.

The case *against* the identification of Marlowe with Morley first appeared in the *Times Literary Supplement* the week after the original suggestion. In brief, the counter-argument runs that Marlowe could not have been Morley since we 'know' that Marlowe was elsewhere at various points during the time we assume Morley was at Hardwick. But when you look at these instances from the perspective of Arbella's movements, the rebuttal is not so conclusive.

To take a general point first: there is no reason why Morley-the-tutor – whoever he was – should have been uninterruptedly present in Hardwick for all of those three and a half years. Not only did Bess and her entourage spend much time away, but James Starkey, the chaplain who later read with Arbella, certainly took a winter out in London. More specifically, each of the Marlowe 'sightings' during these years (and they are few) can be contested. It is worth examining them individually.

(1) On 18 September 1589, Marlowe got into a fight in London, in the course of which his friend and fellow poet Thomas Watson killed one William Bradley. Both men were arrested and spent some time in Newgate. The record reports that the men taken up were Watson and 'Christoferus Marlowe nuper de Norton Fowlgate yoman' – in other words, Marlowe was (or was claiming to be) a resident of London at this time.

*But*: Some at least of Bess's household were known to have been in the capital that week. Her agent opened her account ledger in London the next day.

(2) Marlowe was again arrested in London in May 1592, and 'entered into a recognizance to keep the peace towards two Holywell constables'.

*But*: This falls into the period when Bess and Arbella were definitely down south, making that extended visit to London in connection with the proposed Farnese marriage.

*And*: That same visit covers the month of January 1592 when 'Christofer Marley scholar' was shipped back to Burghley from Flanders – site of Arbella's marriage negotiations – apparently for trying to issue forged gold coins. (The absence of any apparent punishment for this very serious offence is one of the more convincing pieces of evidence that he was indeed still on government service.) Arbella was with the court that month, so her tutor would probably have been given leave.

(3) The last fact that is offered to prove that Marlowe could not have been Morley is a claim made in 1593 by the dramatist Thomas Kyd, that in 1591 he and Marlowe had shared a room in London where they both wrote.

*But*: Not only does Kyd not specify exactly when, how often or for how long they shared lodgings, his reason for making the claim was suspect. An 'atheist treatise' had been found in Kyd's rooms. Shifting the blame onto his now-dead friend, and claiming the treatise must have been 'shuffled' with his own papers, made sense – whether true or false.

There are, in fact, no certain records of Marlowe being in the south when Bess and her family *weren't* in town – circumstantial evidence for the Marlowe-is-Morley theory.

The best circumstantial evidence *against* Marlowe's being Morley must surely be Bess's manner of describing the tutor. *Tamburlaine* had appeared in 1589 and caused a furore. Would Bess, so soon thereafter, have referred to him thus baldly, as someone of whom Burghley would have no reason ever to have heard? And if Marlowe were that infamous, would he ever have been employed – as tutor, of all things! – in a respectable household? Then again, a well-known name in London theatrical circles may not have meant anything in Derbyshire ... or even Chelsea. Nor, at a time when playwrights were not distinguished from the mass of entertainers, rogues and vagabonds, would a very grand old lady necessarily have deemed stage news worthy of her notice. There is, after all, no reference to Marlowe's writing in any of the court or inquest papers that concern him. He managed to split the different sides of his life completely.

\*

Christopher Marlowe died young; fatally stabbed in Deptford on 30 May 1593. The reason given at the time was an altercation with one Ingram Frizer, a man in the service of Thomas Walsingham, over the settling of a 'reckoning' – the bar bill for four men who had spent the day together. Charles Nicholl, in his study of Marlowe's death *The Reckoning,* persuasively argues that there was more to it than this. He takes a microscope to the events of that room in Deptford, and argues convincingly that the meeting was a professional meeting of spies. His research also provides some suggestions why Marlowe could indeed be Morley.

Robert Poley and Nicholas Skeres, the two other men present at Marlowe's death, had both been involved in the unmasking of the Babington plot to free Mary Stuart. Poley had been the undercover agent at the very centre of the story. He had also been involved in plans for Arbella's marriage, through his agent Michael Moody, one of those who had been clamouring for Arbella's portrait in pursuit of the Farnese match.

Skeres, meanwhile, was later noted as an associate of (i.e. probably a spy upon) two Williamson brothers – one of them the former servant of the Talbots who had been questioned in the 1590s. In 1589 and again in 1591, Nicholas Skeres is recorded as being the earl of Essex's man, employed in carrying confidential mail. Was Marlowe engaged in the same line of work? If Essex and Arbella were in communication, as has been suggested, they would have needed a conduit for messages, a secure and private postal service being an innovation of the next century.

Before death intervened, Marlowe was planning, according to Kyd, 'to go unto the K. of Scots' and 'persuade with men of quality' . . . But on whose behalf would he have been dabbling in – presumably – the question of the succession?

Thus far, any putative connections traced would seem to place Marlowe/Morley in what you might call the government camp. But that is not the only possibility.

Kit Marlowe was closely connected to ('very well known to'

was his own term) Henry Percy, earl of Northumberland, and had 'read the atheist lecture', it was said, to Sir Walter Ralegh and others. Ralegh and Northumberland (with Cobham) were members of the 'diabolical triplicity' accused of trying to keep James from the English succession; Ralegh was later even accused of trying to place Arbella on the throne. The 'wizard earl' Northumberland had once been rumoured to be her husband. Marlowe/Morley could have found work to do here, either as go-between or as spy.

But possibilities are not proof. Pending any further evidence, Charles Nicholl described the possibility of Kit Marlowe's being Arbella's tutor as the most fascinating of all the false trails in researching *The Reckoning*. But he concluded regretfully that Marlowe cannot be Morley simply 'because I want him to be'. It is an eminently reasonable position, with which, on balance, one has to agree.

We want the anonymous Morley to be the exciting Marlowe, just as we want Marlowe's death to have been more than a tavern brawl; to have been significant in some way. And, of course, one would love to think of Arbella companioned by that 'pure elemental wit'.

But Marlow/Marlowe/Marley/Morley was not an uncommon name. We know of five people called Christopher Marlowe or Morley (never mind the other variants of the name) in London alone at this period, and the passage of time gives undue prominence to the few individuals the record of whose existence still survives, masking the fact that these were only a few pebbles on a vast seashore.

The most one can say is that the theory that Christopher Marlowe spent some time in Arbella's service does read pretty easily. But pleasant reading is not proof. It is not even probability. The identification is a possibility; no more than that. Among the many theories surrounding the elusive Marlowe, this must go down as just another tantalizing uncertainty.

# Appendix B
## Arbella and porphyria

THE QUESTION OF WHETHER ARBELLA STUART DID OR DID NOT SUFFER from porphyria cannot be answered with complete certainty. But the question obviously has far-reaching implications for any understanding of her writings, and indeed of her very identity. The physical symptoms she suffered could be attributed to many different causes, but when combined with mental disturbance – with extensive evidence of the disease throughout her family tree – they are suggestive in the extreme.

The family member who has been diagnosed with most certainty is James I, thanks to the detailed notes made in 1613 by his doctor, Sir Theodore Turquet de Mayerne, who compared the colour of his urine to the dark red colour of Alicante wine. But Ida Macalpine, Richard Hunter and C. Rimington – who did the first vital work on porphyria in the royal line in the British Medical Association's 1968 collection of articles on the disease, entitled *Porphyria – A Royal Malady* – trace the disease right back to Margaret Tudor (great-grandmother to both James and Arbella). They observed symptoms in Mary, queen of Scots, and in James's granddaughter Henrietta Anne, duchess of Orleans, and suggest that this disease – rather than typhoid – was responsible for the early death of James's son Henry. More recently, John C. G. Rohl, Martin Warren and David Hunt, in their book *Purple Secret: Genes, 'Madness' and the Royal Houses of Europe*, noted Antonia Fraser's suggestion as to the 'mysterious hysterical manner of the death of James V', father to the queen of Scots. Indeed, I noted with interest a letter from Eleanor Brandon – James V's first cousin, daughter of Henry VIII's younger sister Mary – in which she laments to her husband that 'I have been very sick and at this present my water is very red . . . I have [no appetite for] meat and I have such pains in my side and towards my back as I had at Brougham' (quoted in Ashdown, *Tudor Cousins*). Steen, in Daybell's *Early Modern Women's Letter Writing*, states that symptoms observed also in Arbella's father support the idea that she suffered from acute intermittent porphyria (AIP).

In their return to the subject, *George III and the Mad Business*, Macalpine and Hunter dealt with Arbella specifically. While stopping short of a categorical affirmative ('if' she also suffered from porphyria), their opinion is plain to see:

> Arabella [*sic*] had three attacks of serious illness and during each her mind became deranged. Some speak of her as insane during most of her life – a falsification she shared with George III. She suffered from nervous symptoms very similar to those of her relations: she had pain and weakness, headaches and colic. Like her aunt, Mary queen of Scots, she was thought to feign illness under pressure of adversity, and like her cousin James's her urine was discoloured.

(This important symptom had long been obscured. A letter written by Gilbert Talbot to Arbella's physician at the end of March 1611 was reproduced at length by, for example, Hardy. But Hardy, with other of Arbella's earlier biographers, while dutifully recording Arbella's dull pulse and wan countenance, decorously omitted Gilbert's report of 'her water bad, showing great obstructions'.)

'It may seem odd that her illnesses occurred when circumstances put her in a corner, but perhaps we should look at it the other way round. Only when there was political commotion was the state of her health noteworthy. Other attacks may well have gone unrecorded.' As Macalpine and Hunter further note, 'Information about her medical history is so mixed in with political events that they cannot be separated.' That is indeed a problem of her biography.

But a concrete diagnosis of porphyria in Arbella might present its own problems for a biography written out of the intellectual climate of the late twentieth century. If Arbella's agonies and rebellions were the result not of social or psychological pressures but of a biochemical imbalance, what then becomes of a feminist or a psychological reading of her story? It is interesting to see how two very different writers of the last decade tackle 'the porphyria theory'. Sara Jayne Steen, introducing the *Letters*, collates valuable evidence to show not only that Arbella may indeed have suffered from porphyria, but why her attacks were particularly acute at certain times. She none the less concludes: 'That Stuart had porphyria cannot be proved at this distance . . . But even if Stuart had the disease, as seems probable, that diagnosis should not be understood to imply that Stuart was not in control of her actions or striving to rule her own life. Until porphyria is advanced, the higher functions of reason remain intact between and sometimes during episodes.'

Rather than dismissing Arbella's struggles because of her supposed disease, Steen is inclined to honour a courage that could go on fighting even in the throes of an ailment so excruciatingly painful. By contrast Ruth Norrington, whose recent biography, dedicated to Macalpine and Hunter, had as one of its main objects to place Arbella in the porphyriac line, has no doubts about the fact she was a sufferer. Norrington interestingly suggests that other bouts of ill-health Arbella experienced may be attributed to the disease. But unfortunately she makes no reference to the new evidence brought forward by Steen (explored in Part V).

The medical theories both of Arbella's day and of our own do offer other possibilities. Jeffrey Boss, who wrote a paper on the hysteric affection, pointed out to me that, to a contemporary physician, Arbella's symptoms, in 1603 and later, might have seemed to fit that diagnosis just as neatly.

Previously regarded as being caused by the condition of the womb, after 1600 the hysteric affection came increasingly to be regarded as a problem of the brain. The physician Thomas Sydenham, writing at the end of the century, noted the symptoms (in Dr Boss's words): 'Sometimes there are spasms like those of epilepsy, perhaps with distension of the belly . . .' Arbella's death was preceded by fits, and at one point the swelling of her body led to rumours of pregnancy. 'There may be the *clavus hystericus*, a severe headache sharply localized to a small area.' Arbella often complained of pain in her eyes (one of Burton's symptoms of melancholy) and in her head. Sydenham also lists abdominal pain, 'incurable despair . . . fear, anger, jealousy, suspicion . . . caprice and no moderation'.

Long-standing hysteria, Sydenham noted, may lead to anorexia and cachexia – the state of self-induced debility and malnutrition that was to be specifically noted in the report of Arbella's post mortem. 'This fully developed mental state is found only in those who have had a long and hard struggle with the disease and have finally given in, and is most likely to have developed when, to the impaired bodily diathesis, has been added change of fortune, a grieving mind, anxiety, over-study or excessive exertion.' Modern medicine may give different names to the conditions of the mind, but Sydenham's description fits the Arbella of later years almost perfectly.

On the other hand, the mention of anorexia invites consideration of another condition: one with particular resonance for our own century. A 'slimmer's disease' has indeed no relevance for Arbella's world. But a recent book, *Hungry Hell*, written by former sufferer Kate Chisholm, shows that anorexia nervosa has a broader applicability. (And describes how the philosopher Thomas Hobbes, who tutored the children of Arbella's cousin William, rode over from Chatsworth to see one of the 'Derbyshire Damosells' who starved themselves in the name of holiness later in the seventeenth century.)

'Not-eating is only the symptom, the outward expression, of an inward dis-ease,' Chisholm writes. Victim of painfully high expectation and ambition, of isolation and what one authority described as 'fatal impotence', the anorexic refuses to eat in order, paradoxically, to preserve her identity. Susie Orbach (the author of *Fat Is a Feminist Issue* and of *Hunger Strike: The Anorectic's Struggle as a Metaphor for our Age*) described it as a dramatic expression of women's attempt 'to negotiate their passions and desires in a time of extreme confusion'. That, surely, describes the quest on which Arbella Stuart was so painfully embarked in the spring of 1603. The balance of probability must be that she did indeed suffer from porphyria. But other diagnoses cannot be dismissed entirely.

# Appendix C
## Places and portraits

WHEN THE SIXTH DUKE OF DEVONSHIRE SHOWED VISITORS AROUND Hardwick Hall, it was always the great Gallery that drew gasps of admiration. Those early Victorian tourists, he said, 'begin to get weary and to want their luncheon, but they are awakened when the tapestry over the north door is lifted up, and they find themselves in this stupendous and original apartment.' It was the sixth duke who installed in a then all but empty Hardwick many of the present furnishings in a conscious recreation of the sixteenth century, often simply returning pieces which had been scattered elsewhere around the family properties. To the structure of the house, to the basic decoration, he needed to do almost nothing. Though most of the other Elizabethan prodigy houses are long since gone, Hardwick has remained comparatively unchanged from Bess's day. Ironically, it owes its survival to its unimportant position within the massed properties of the Cavendish family. When William Cavendish also inherited Chatsworth (through the death without heir of his elder brother Henry), the latter became the family's principal seat. It was Chatsworth, therefore, that was completely remodelled in the late seventeenth and eighteenth centuries, while Hardwick was left to moulder intact – as a dower house or, when the fashion for the historic and the picturesque set in, a romantic novelty.

The serendipitous result of this neglect is that anyone interested in Arbella Stuart's life can trace her history here with unusual clarity. Trace the route Brounker must have trodden, through the

claustrophobic Hall – relict of the style of Bess's distant youth, a
hangover from the medieval day – up the oddly modern stairs and
into the Gallery, furnished much as it would then have been, still
as chilly today. Or walk out into the courtyard – still as elegantly,
implacably, walled in golden stone – and to the gatehouse where
Arbella's flight was arrested in 1603. The great symbolic set-
pieces of décor are the same – the enigmatic plaster frieze of
Diana in the High Great Chamber; the tapestries of the womanly
virtues; the Hardwick arms with their wild roses and rearing
stags. And – although she herself was never there – the house still
boasts the needlework of Mary, queen of Scots, treasures even in
Arbella's day. The extraordinary textiles of Hardwick owe much
to the house's last private inhabitant, the Dowager Duchess
Evelyn, who lived there until it was taken over by the National
Trust in 1956. It seems appropriate that her special care should
have echoed that of the needlewoman Bess – and that Hardwick's
treasures were preserved through female energy.

Today the M1 roars right below the hill upon which Hardwick
stands, but you can hear it only from the Old Hall, the house
where Bess and Arbella lived for a decade. If Hardwick Hall
stands foursquare and impressive as when Bess entered it, Old
Hardwick next door is a roofless ruin, belying the fact that the
two houses were built within a decade of one another, and
occupied simultaneously. But sufficient fragments of decoration
survive – like the huge plaster Gog and Magog above the chimney
in the Hill Great Chamber (or 'Giant's Chamber') – to give some
idea of what it would have been in Arbella's day. And quite a
small circle inscribed around Hardwick Hall brings within its
radius a cluster of other places closely associated with Arbella.
Rufford Abbey well repays a visit, though today it is perhaps
evocative more of its monastic origins than of the half-hearted
conversion that made it possible for Arbella's parents to meet and
marry there. Wingfield is another splendid ruin, its huge walls
rearing broken out of placid farmland, open by the goodwill of
the farmer and under the auspices of English Heritage. Owlcotes/
Oldcotes exists now only as a fragment of garden wall,
unrecorded even by the Ordnance Survey. But however little
remains, these sights have something to teach even in their
mere topography. Bolsover, the house Charles Cavendish built,

slightly postdates Arbella's day. But Bolsover, like Hardwick, Wingfield and Tutbury, is built on a hill. The views over the dwarfed fields and dwellings below – the sense of literal eminence – is extraordinary. To live in such settings must teach a sense of grandeur. To walk from one view to another attended always by bowing retainers must be to feel oneself an earthly divinity.

The restructuring of Chatsworth in the late seventeenth century was a comprehensive job. All that is left from the sixteenth century is the walled enclosure in the grounds, 'Queen Mary's Bower' – along with a tower up on a hill, used for the hunt, and a painting and a tapestry picture showing Bess's Chatsworth as it used to be. The entire village of Edensor on the Chatsworth estate, including the church where Arbella may have been christened, was swept away to clear the view when the grounds were landscaped, to be rebuilt a few miles off. But in the Victorian parish church there stands the transplanted double monument of Henry and William Cavendish, where the brothers – the one depicted as a skeleton, the other as a prosperous burgher – lie in eternal disharmony.

Bess herself was buried not here but in All Saints' church in Derby. She had herself overseen designs for her tomb, created by the architect of Hardwick, Robert Smythson. But the elegant black and marble edifice, topped by the ubiquitous Hardwick stags, now sits uneasily amid the sparse cream-coloured surroundings of the classical church that replaced the original construction in the eighteenth century. It is as if Bess's motto, 'safe by taking care', had let her down, finally.

Moving south, if Hardwick is the first site on an Arbella trail, then the Tower of London must certainly be the second. The upper room of the Bell Tower, where she was once thought to have been held, is now used for storage space. The old palace which is a more probable location has now disappeared, the site devoted to grass and gift shop. (A model reconstruction is promised shortly.) But traces remain. The hook to which the carter's horse was tethered when William Seymour escaped is still nailed in the wall; the walls themselves still boast their graffiti; and the Bloody Tower has been fitted out as it was for Sir Walter Ralegh.

From the Tower, it is possible to travel eastwards along the river towards Greenwich and Blackwall and on to Leigh, where the great open wastes of the waters can hardly have changed, and a small heritage centre, showing the town's shipbuilding past, nestles among the boards offering a 'seafood tea'. Westwards from the Tower, heading upriver, you can follow the route along the Thames which carried Arbella's body from prison to grave. She is buried in the cramped south aisle of the Lady Chapel of Westminster Abbey.

Here the queen of Scots lies, immortalized in a profusion of white marble petticoats. It was the great Victorian ghoul Dean Stanley who, in 1867, penetrated through Mary's tomb into the vault below. Night after night during his tenure at the abbey Stanley – 'that body snatcher' as Queen Victoria called him – would prowl with macabre fascination through the royal graves. The historian J. A. Froude accompanied him on one occasion. 'It was the weirdest scheme – the flaming torches, the banners waving from the draught of air, and the Dean's keen eager face seen in profile had the very strangest effect. He asked me to return with him the next night, but my nerves had had quite enough of it.' The dean was made of sterner stuff. But having hacked away the flags from beside Mary's tomb, and crept down the flight of stone stairs which led beneath the very monument, Stanley found what even he described as 'a startling, it may almost be said an awful, scene'; a 'chaos of royal mortality'.

There, in a brick vault claustrophobic as the heart of an Egyptian pyramid, 'a vast pile of leaden coffins rose from the floor; some of full stature, the larger number varying in form from that of the full-grown child to the merest infant, confusedly heaped upon the others.' James's son, Prince Henry, was here, along with Rupert of the Rhine and Elizabeth of Bohemia. (The chapel Henry VII had built as chantry for the Tudors was already being taken over by another dynasty – even before Queen Anne's eighteen stillborn children were added in the next century.) But the eighteenth-century historian Crull, on his own explorations, had noted two particular coffins which stood together – 'much compressed and distorted', Stanley noted, 'by the superincumbent weight of four or five lesser coffins heaped upon them'. The lowest, 'of a more solid and stately character', was that of Mary, queen of Scots; the beheaded body moved south from

Peterborough Cathedral when she had already been dead for a quarter of a century. The uppermost, a 'frail and ill-constructed receptacle' – so frail, indeed, that the skull peeped through – was that of Arbella Stuart.

Her presence is commemorated only by a name carved inconspicuously on a plaque with dozens of others – but perhaps it is not an unfitting resting place. The south aisle of the Lady Chapel holds three central tombs. In the middle is the one Arbella shares with her aunt Mary; to one end of it is the austere tomb Torrigiano designed for Margaret Beaufort, Henry VII's mother and founder of the Tudor dynasty; to the other end is the gaudy tomb of Margaret Lennox, Arbella's grandmother, with the sons who predeceased her carved kneeling on its side – Charles Stuart, and a crowned Lord Darnley. The south aisle, intentionally or not, is a monument to the distaff side of history.

Most of the royal palaces Arbella knew have changed beyond all recognition. Greenwich and Whitehall look quite different today – as, of course, does the Seymours' Somerset House, though work is continuing to explore its Tudor archaeology. The City and Blackfriars are full of Elizabethan echoes for those who know where to look, but the site of Shrewsbury House – today's Cheyne Walk – is covered by modern Chelsea. Further upriver, Hampton Court is the only one of the royal palaces still to boast much that belonged to Arbella's day. The chapel, the great Tudor kitchens, the apartments laid out for Henry VIII and used by James all show much about how things actually worked in the sixteenth and seventeenth centuries; how difficult, for example, was access to the monarch. A courtier writes of Arbella once, clamouring at the door of the king's own chamber; here, in wood and stone, you have mapped out the very face of this *lèse-majesté*.

Of the other sites in the south of England, Burghley's Theobalds is long since gone, seriously damaged in the Civil War and subsequently taken down in pieces – its staircase all the way to Herstmonceux in Sussex. That it left its name and site to a country park seems unlikely to have consoled Burghley. To feel some measure of Theobalds' grandeur, it is better to go to Hatfield, the house Robert Cecil built when King James took Theobalds away from him; or perhaps to the contemporary Audley End – though there the visitor should be aware that, impressive and seemingly complete though the standing structure is, it represents less than a third of the house's size in its heyday.

The few remaining objects associated with Arbella are spread around the country, and indeed beyond it. The Lennox Jewel is on display in James's old home, the palace of Holyrood House in Edinburgh. The Book of Hours bequeathed to Arbella by Mary, queen of Scots, made its way to the Hermitage museum in Russia. Arbella sent the book, as a souvenir and a valuable piece of property, to her husband in France, who seems to have sold it there; during the French Revolution it was repurchased, by one Peter Dubrowsky, on behalf of the tsar.

No-one has ever traced for sure the embroideries by the Scots queen which Arbella sold to her aunt Mary Talbot in order to finance her escape abroad. But they may not be that far away. In Oxburgh Hall in Norfolk are preserved the 'Marian Hangings' – three great green velvet curtains set with myriad embroidered panels (many of allegorical significance) worked and signed by Bess of Hardwick and her prisoner the queen of Scots. The panels are believed to have been gathered together and set onto the curtains by Alethea Talbot, Arbella's cousin and Mary Talbot's daughter, coming to Oxburgh when a descendant of hers married the son and heir of the Norfolk family. It is most likely that some of the embroideries came to Alethea through her mother-in-law, the Catholic countess of Arundel, to whom Queen Mary bequeathed her rosary and the white veil she wore at her execution. But even if some embroideries went along with the bequest, they can hardly have been so numerous as to encompass all the panels of the extraordinary Marian Hangings. The assumption is that Alethea (heiress to her parents' mansion of Worksop) must have added other panels she found in the Talbot property. It seems probable that some of these were the embroideries Arbella sold to Mary Talbot.

Like her property, the images of Arbella, too, are scattered. The National Portrait Gallery in London, of course, has portraits of many of Arbella's contemporaries, but only a crudely reproduced sketch from a contemporary pamphlet to show Arbella herself. The portraiture of Arbella Stuart is contentious territory.

The two pictures that hang and have always hung at Hardwick

– of the toddler and the teenager – are the only two which can be called Arbella with complete safety. There are many other possible Arbella pictures in the huge box file in the archives of the National Portrait Gallery. But these dubiously identified portraits can only be graded on a sliding scale of probability.

Thus the charming face by John de Critz hanging in a gallery in Raleigh, North Carolina, and once described as Arbella, is more probably Elizabeth of Bohemia, as is the child with parakeets and monkeys in the collection of Woburn Abbey. The youthful picture at Glamis Castle, on the other hand, with its screaming red hair and air of determination, carries a measure of conviction. Of course, the pretty Isaac Oliver miniature does paint 'Arbella' with her hair blonde; but Glamis was the childhood home of Queen Elizabeth the Queen Mother, and this family connection makes the identification more likely.

One image turns up in several different versions, belonging to Longleat, to Berkeley Castle and to the Government Picture Collection, and is variously attributed to Robert Peake the Elder, to Marcus Gheeraerts the Younger, and to Paul van Somer. (And Longleat, at least, has some reason to claim Arbella's portrait; William's widow left to her granddaughter a picture of 'my dear lord's first wife' which had been hanging in the Dining Room, and this granddaughter had married into the neighbouring Thynne family, Longleat's owners.) This is an older, or at least a more sober, Arbella; dark clad under the long rope of pearls. The posture and the pearls are always the same, but the expression – isolated from its heavy Jacobean background – varies considerably. In one version (and one stage of restoration), it is an alert, wary, questing face. In another, it is simply melancholy. This is not the way one wishes to see Arbella; but when you consider the marks life may have written on her face, it does have an air of authenticity.

It is a relief to turn to another picture, sold privately at Christie's in 1981 and tentatively attributed to William Larkin, a painter whom Arbella sponsored professionally. Larkin kept few records, and the picture is untitled, but the features were said (in the nineteenth century, before restoration work on both pictures alike destroyed all certainty) to resemble those of Arbella in the adolescent Hardwick portrait. Certainly features, pose and demeanour closely resemble the portrait of Arbella's aunt Grace, which hangs nearby.

This picture is an extraordinary visual game, a puzzle as deliberate as the famous Hardwick plasterwork. A young girl – finger to her lip, an expression of quizzical relish on her face – stands poised precariously on the back of a tortoise (used as a symbol by Darnley). A small bird perches on her other wrist, and her white dress juts out stiffly. At the bottom are the words *Haec talis fugit* – 'such as she does not linger' – suggesting the sitter may have died before her time.

The girl in the picture has been variously identified as Arbella, as Elizabeth of Bohemia, as Queen Elizabeth and as an allegory of wifely virtue. Plutarch described a statue of Aphrodite standing on a tortoise 'as a symbol that women should stay at home and be silent'. The moral doesn't really fit Arbella as a sitter, nor the peripatetic Winter Queen. But surely Queen Elizabeth is even less likely.

Only three images of William Seymour survive: the armoured Cavalier general of middle years; the elderly statesman, bewigged and bejowled; and an ethereal young man, with long pale hair and a goatee beard, looking like a romantic curate. It is presumably the last of the three with whom Arbella fell in love.

The Seymours have left their stamp on the south-west less clearly than the Cavendish family on the midlands. The Seymours' importance in Amesbury passed to another family, and the great house William built there has long since been replaced; the building now on the site, converted to a nursing home, dates from the nineteenth century. Only a few older traces remain: a cave in the grounds where it is said John Gay wrote *The Beggar's Opera*; two Tudor lodges which predate even William's occupancy. But still, of course, the river Avon in its upper reaches flows almost by the very door; and still Stonehenge stands no further than a pleasant ride away.

William's other wartime home of Netley is yet another of those gaping arched ruins; but beautiful even above the usual run, maybe. (Leave Southampton by water and you see it from the ship. You have to say this for William – he knew how to pick a locality.) But Netley is something of an outlier; the other 'Seymour sites' are grouped around the borders of Wiltshire and

Somerset, closer to Amesbury. Here too is Longleat, which holds one of the three main collections of Arbella's letters; the shirt Charles I wore on the block, supposedly preserved by William; and two 'Arbella' portraits: an attractive head and shoulders as well as the huge full-length image that looms above the main stairway. Little survives just a few miles from Longleat in the Seymours' ancient seat of Maiden Bradley.

Salisbury Cathedral holds the splendid tomb of the earl of Hertford and Catherine Grey, their two sons kneeling at either side in almost life-sized red and gold effigy. (Just across the aisle, curiously, lies the marchioness of Northampton, Arbella's hostess in 1603.) But William himself is buried in the parish church of Great Bedwyn, some ten miles to the north of Amesbury and hard by Wulfhall, seat of the Seymours in the sixteenth century. The walls of the church hold a brass plaque to William's father Lord Beauchamp, and a window to the memory of Henry VIII's third wife, the Seymour queen Jane. A marble bust – stripped by thieves of its supporting cherubs – commemorates Frances, William's second wife, with the information that he lies nearby. His own grave is unmarked, curiously. But restoration work in 1853 found his body beneath the chancel. The tale is that he was buried beside his daughter, Arbella, at his own request.

In the summer of 2003, a few months after the first English publication of *Arbella,* an extraordinary discovery was made at Hardwick Hall. During restoration work, panelling was removed from what is now the dining room – in a recess where the sixth duke, as a boy, once kept his menagerie – and in the cavity between wood and wall workmen found, among other items, a book bound in red leather and gold, *L'ABC des Chrestiens,* a manual of basic Protestant doctrine and French grammar, its title page dated 1583. How did it get there, by accident or design? The little cache, which included a few toys, looked almost like the hiding place of a recalcitrant child, naughtily tucking the hated schoolbook away.

Almost at once there was speculation that the book might have been connected to Arbella – and of course this is just the kind of romantic story about which every biographer dreams. There is always a huge temptation to link a new find to a known personality. Most such hopeful connections fade in the cold light of day, but this one is a little different.

For a start, the book must have had an aristocratic owner: with its special Turkey binding, it would never have belonged to the child of a servant, and not many children of the working classes would have had access to this private room – the low great chamber of Arbella's day, meant for the leisure hours of the family. And the book's publication date, 1583, was almost a decade and a half before Hardwick Hall was built, so we must look either for two unconnected owners or perhaps for someone who had occasion to return to a childhood book.

We know that Arbella was at Hardwick ('old' Hardwick) in the summer of 1583 – "about seven years old and learned," in the words of Sir Walter Mildmay. We know she spoke French by 1588, when she wrote a note in that language to Lord Burghley. We also know that she was in the new Hardwick Hall during and after the period (around 1597) when the panelling must have been installed.

By then Arbella herself was an erudite and multilingual twenty-two-year-old, past the stage of grammar books and secret cubby-holes. But we know that there were children of a suitable age present in the Hardwick household – Arbella's cousins, the offspring of her uncle William Cavendish – and we know that Arbella got roped into the little boys' schooling, speaking Latin with eleven-year-old Will. The children's tutor, James Starkey, was the very same who would help Arbella in her intrigues of 1603.

Expensive books might well have been passed down in the family, especially since William Cavendish was notoriously tight with his money. If Arbella did indeed hunt out her own old schoolbook for the benefit of her cousins, we know, too, that young Will (the future duke of Devonshire) was less studious than she had been. The little boy who had to be bribed to speak Latin grew up to be a likeable 'waster' (in the words of John Aubrey), who eventually died from what was described as excessive indulgence in good living.

Of course, we are in the realm of 'Possibly . . .' and 'One can imagine that . . .' We can never speak with certainty. But I, for one, can imagine this scenario easily. Arbella apart, there are simply not many other individuals whose ownership fits so neatly.

# Family Trees

# THE
# STUART/LENNOX
## LINE

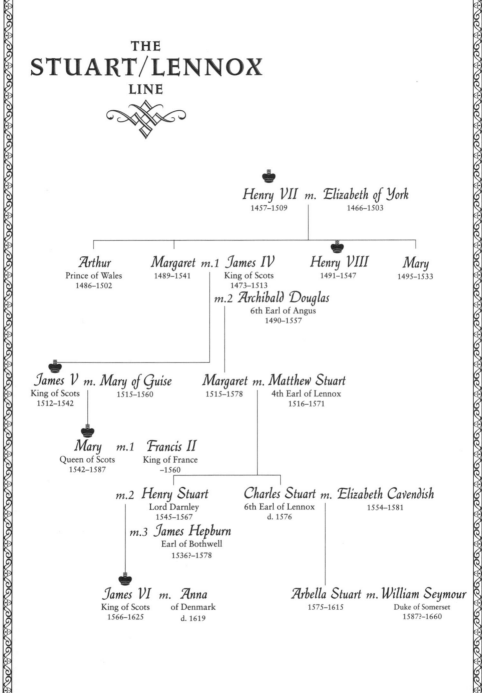

Henry VII *m.* Elizabeth of York
1457–1509    1466–1503

Arthur
Prince of Wales
1486–1502

Margaret *m.1* James IV
1489–1541    King of Scots
1473–1513

Henry VIII
1491–1547

Mary
1495–1533

*m.2* Archibald Douglas
6th Earl of Angus
1490–1557

James V *m.* Mary of Guise
King of Scots    1515–1560
1512–1542

Margaret *m.* Matthew Stuart
1515–1578    4th Earl of Lennox
1516–1571

Mary    *m.1* Francis II
Queen of Scots    King of France
1542–1587    –1560

*m.2* Henry Stuart
Lord Darnley
1545–1567

Charles Stuart *m.* Elizabeth Cavendish
6th Earl of Lennox    1554–1581
d. 1576

*m.3* James Hepburn
Earl of Bothwell
1536?–1578

James VI *m.* Anna
King of Scots    of Denmark
1566–1625    d. 1619

Arbella Stuart *m.* William Seymour
1575–1615    Duke of Somerset
1587?–1660

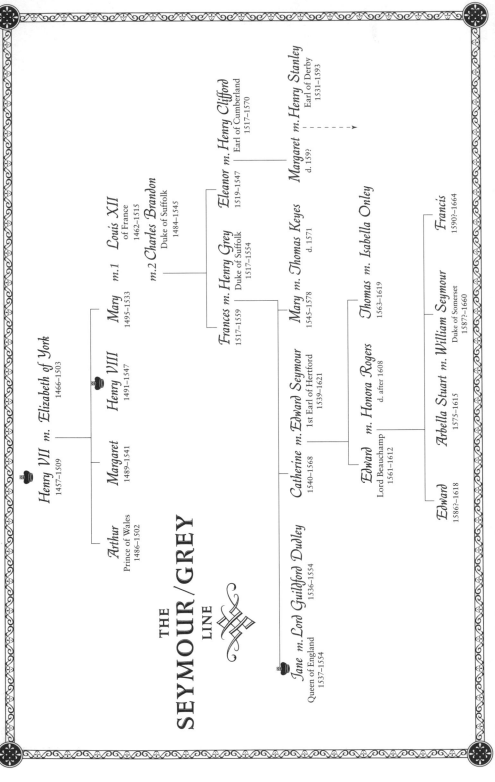

THE
SEYMOUR/GREY
LINE

Henry VII *m.* Elizabeth of York
1457–1509                    1466–1503

Arthur
Prince of Wales
1486–1502

Margaret
1489–1541

Henry VIII
1491–1547

Mary    *m.1*    Louis XII
1495–1533            of France
                              1462–1515

                              *m.2* Charles Brandon
                              Duke of Suffolk
                              1484–1545

Frances *m.* Henry Grey
1517–1559    Duke of Suffolk
                    1517–1554

Eleanor *m.* Henry Clifford
1519–1547    Earl of Cumberland
                    1517–1570

Margaret *m.* Henry Stanley
d. 159?              Earl of Derby
                          1531–1593

Mary *m.* Thomas Keyes
1545–1578    d. 1571

Jane *m.* Lord Guildford Dudley
1537–1554    1536–1554
Queen of England

Catherine *m.* Edward Seymour
1540–1568    1st Earl of Hertford
                    1539–1621

Thomas *m.* Isabella Onley
1563–1619

Edward *m.* Honora Rogers
Lord Beauchamp    d. after 1608
1561–1612

Arbella Stuart *m.* William Seymour
1575–1615              Duke of Somerset
                              1587?–1660

Edward
1586?–1618

Francis
1590?–1664

# THE CAVENDISH LINE

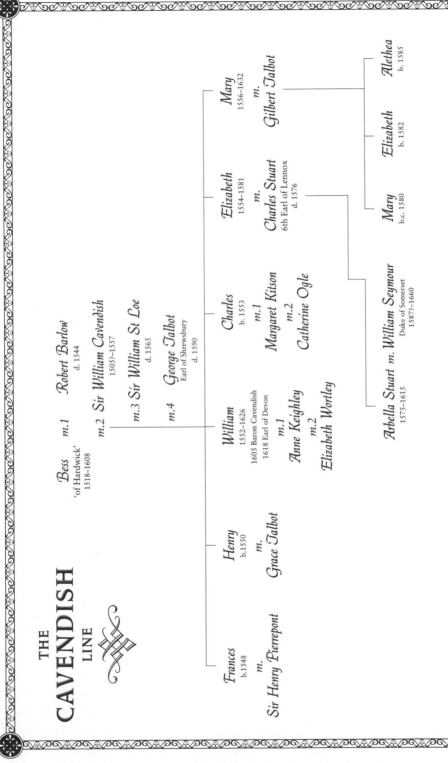

Bess 'of Hardwick' 1518–1608

m.1 Robert Barlow d. 1544

m.2 Sir William Cavendish 1505?–1557

m.3 Sir William St Loe d. 1565

m.4 George Talbot Earl of Shrewsbury d. 1590

Frances b.1548
m.
Sir Henry Pierrepont

Henry b.1550
m.
Grace Talbot

William 1552–1626
1605 Baron Cavendish
1618 Earl of Devon
m.1 Anne Keighley
m.2 Elizabeth Wortley

Charles b.1553
m.1 Margaret Kitson
m.2 Catherine Ogle

Elizabeth 1554–1581
m.
Charles Stuart 6th Earl of Lennox d. 1576

Mary 1556–1632
m.
Gilbert Talbot

Arbella Stuart m. William Seymour 1575–1615          Duke of Somerset 1587?–1660

Mary b.c. 1580

Elizabeth b. 1582

Alethea b. 1585

# Source notes

SELECTIVE SOURCE NOTES FOLLOW THE BRIEF BIBLIOGRAPHICAL ESSAY GIVEN below for each section of this book; since these are far from comprehensive, I have favoured those references which relate to Arbella Stuart's own story.

## List of abbreviations used

| | |
|---|---|
| Acts | Acts of the Privy Council |
| Batho | G. R. Batho, calendar* of Talbot Papers in the College of Arms |
| | (This is a collection quite distinct from – and less relevant to Arbella than – the Talbot at Longleat, to which I refer by the name Talbot [see below].) |
| BL | British Library Manuscripts Room |
| | (These documents may be further described under the name of the particular manuscript collection in which the paper is held: e.g. Sloane, Harleian ['Harl.']; Lansdowne or Additional ['Add.'].) |
| CSP Dom | Calendar of State Papers, Domestic |
| | (Some of these documents, transcribed after the compilation of the main calendar, are located in a supplementary volume, given as CSP Dom Add.) |

*A calendar, in this context, is one of the typed and indexed catalogues of many manuscript collections commissioned by the HMSO from the second half of the nineteenth century onwards. They range from summaries to complete texts, from modern to original orthography. Roman numerals signify the volume; Arabic numerals the page.

| CSP Scottish | Calendar of State Papers Relating to Scotland and Mary, Queen of Scots (or Calendar of Scottish Papers) |
|---|---|
| CSP Ven | Calendar of State Papers and Manuscripts relating to English Affairs. Preserved in the Archives of Venice |
| Cecil Papers | Papers compiled for Robert Cecil and his father, now held at Hatfield House, the property of the Marquess of Salisbury. (These citations refer to the original documents, as opposed to those in the calendar; see 'Hatfield'.) |
| Folger | Folger Shakespeare Library, Washington DC |
| Hatfield | Calendar of the Cecil Papers (see 'Cecil Papers'): Calendar of the Manuscripts of the Most Hon. The Marquess of Salisbury preserved at Hatfield House, Hertfordshire) |
| HMC | Historical Manuscripts Commission |
| PRO | Public Record Office, Kew |
| SP | State Papers (the reference given being that of the document, rather than the calendar page) |
| Talbot | Talbot Papers at Longleat, the property of the Marquess of Bath |

# Note on Previous Biographies

Any new biography builds on the work that has gone before. In the case of Arbella Stuart, that has accrued into a considerable body since the middle of the nineteenth century. Agnes Strickland devoted to her one section in her well-known *Lives of the Tudor and Stuart Princesses*. Even before that, however, Elizabeth Cooper had in 1866 published her two-volume *The Life and Letters of Lady Arabella Stuart* which – living up to the boast contained in its subtitle, *Including Numerous Original and Unpublished Documents* – remains a valuable resource today. Miss Cooper, however, complained that her researches had been hampered by the number of manuscripts then in private hands and inaccessible to historians. Twenty-three years later, in 1889, Emily Tennyson Bradley (later Mrs Murray Smith) was luckier. Her *Life of the Lady Arabella Stuart* also printed a substantial body of documents – including, this time, almost all Arbella's own letters, reprinted in full though with modernized spelling and punctuation.

In the next century, 1913 saw not one but two biographies: Blanche Christabel Hardy's *Arbella Stuart: A Biography* and M. Lefuse's less well-known *The Life and Times of Arabella Stuart*. Although by now normal practice was to incorporate documents into the text, rather than printing them separately as Cooper and Bradley had done, both Hardy and Lefuse offer much original material at length or in its entirety. They thus remain (despite the virtual absence of source notes) a useful tool; and to this category one should add *Lives of the Friends and Contemporaries of Lord Chancellor Clarendon* by Maria Theresa Lewis (later Villiers; 1852), in which the lengthy section on William Seymour, straddling volumes 2 and 3, includes some otherwise elusive documentation of the couple's flight.

Three biographies of Arbella Stuart were published in the second half of the twentieth century, of which the last was David Durant's *Arbella Stuart: A Rival to the Queen* (1978). This may perhaps best be seen as a companion volume to his authoritative and detailed *Bess of Hardwick*, first printed in 1977 and reissued in 1999. Ian McInnes's *Arabella: The Life and Times of Arabella Seymour, 1575–1615* tells her life as a ripping yarn. But the biography to which I personally feel most indebted is P. M. Handover's enormously well-documented *Arbella Stuart, Royal Lady of Hardwick* (1957). With this I would couple in gratitude *The Letters of Lady Arbella Stuart*, edited by Sara Jayne Steen (1994) which, while not a biography as such, adds a hundred-page biographical and critical essay to its invaluable transcript (footnoted, and with the original orthography) of virtually all the extant letters written by Arbella Stuart, and some she received. Most recently, Ruth Norrington published *In the Shadow of the Throne: The Lady Arbella Stuart* (2002), a comparatively brief survey of Arbella's life which places particular emphasis on her medical history.

# Prologue

The main source of information about Arbella's flight, right down to the ostler's words and the clothes Arbella wore, is the letter written by courtier Sir John More to Sir Ralph Winwood, then ambassador to the Hague. This is to be found in the third volume of Winwood's *Memorials of the Affairs of State in the Reigns of Queen Elizabeth and King James the First* (1725).

p. 2   'We may by God's grace': The letter Arbella wrote to her husband is to be found in BL Harl. MS 7003 ff. 150–1; others of her letters used here will be referenced later, when quoted at more length.

p. 5   Bright's account to the privy council: SP lxvi no. 30.

p. 6   brought in for questioning: Lists of arrests made are quoted in Cooper ii 190, 195.

p. 6   The admiral of the fleet: The report of Admiral Monson is in BL Harl. MSS 7003 f. 130.

p. 6   Griffen Cockett: The captain's report is in BL Harl. MSS 7003 f. 128.

# Part I

Arbella Stuart's early life is well-trodden ground. The sources for this first part of the book, therefore, are largely secondary. Inevitably the patterns of Arbella's early childhood were those laid down by others, notably Bess of Hardwick, of whom David Durant wrote an invaluable biography. (I should like here to acknowledge his generosity in making his notes for the book available to future research at the University of Nottingham Library; also to thank Peter Day, then librarian/archivist at Chatsworth, for informing me that he had done so.) At the time of writing there is no biography of Lady Lennox, though there is a good deal of information about her in Dulcie M. Ashdown's *Tudor Cousins*, which, fascinatingly, traces all the possible lines of claim through the sixteenth century. Ashdown is also a good source on information on Lady Catherine Grey whose romance, however, is chronicled in many places – notably as one of the *Two Tudor Portraits* in Hester Chapman's dual biography, and on pages 163–240 of the first volume of Cooper's *Life and Letters*.

p. 15   'was dealt in suddenly': CSP Scottish v 68.

p. 15   'Now my Lord': Lefuse 12–13; Durant *Bess* 85. Lady Lennox – like the earl of Shrewsbury – wrote several letters on this subject; for more of the correspondence see also Lefuse 2–4, 11–13, 15–16.

p. 18   The Lennox or 'Darnley' jewel: The jewel is described in Scarisbrick 84.

p. 19   The queen's spymaster: For Walsingham's interrogation of Fowler see CSP Scottish v 30; cited by Handover *Arbella Stuart*, who describes it (p. 304) as being erroneously calendared 1574.

p. 19   Back in London, she found herself committed to the Tower: It used to be said that Bess, too, was imprisoned; later opinion has tended to disagree. (Just as, by the same token, it was once believed that Bess was the Lady St Loe sent to the Tower after having been made the confidante of Catherine Grey; this is now identified, instead, as Bess's sister-in-law. See addendum to the 1999 reissue of Durant *Bess*.)

p. 19    precise date and place of Arbella's birth: the anomalies of the record are described in Cooper i 37; her godparents (p. 17) in Bradley i 33 who, however, gives no reference. Both these authorities accept as accurate the information given (in a pedigree of Lady Lennox's descendants, found in BL Harl. MSS, f. 588) that Arbella was *nata 1575 apud Chatsworth in Anglia*, while noting certain inaccuracies in the record, and that Chatsworth is written in a different hand. By the time Handover came to write, this was agreed to be insufficient evidence, and Durant in *Arbella Stuart* 212n, speculates that she was instead baptized from (and born in?) Hackney.

p. 19    'I yield your Majesty': CSP Scottish v 202.

p. 21    the convoluted web of debated rights: The issue of the succession as it appeared at the time of Arbella's birth is chronicled in much more detail in Ashdown: see esp. 33; 39ff for Lady Lennox's early history; 55 and 68 for the succession as laid down by Henry VIII; and 117ff for the marriage of Catherine Grey. For Henry VIII's will see also Nenner 13, 16, 38, 58, 272n.

p. 22    But as a Catholic, a foreigner and a prisoner: Nenner 57–8 has described how, by an act of parliament in 1351, no alien was permitted to inherit land in England – this covering, presumably, the right to inherit England itself. See also Ashworth 33.

p. 26    'greatest dolour': For Lady Lennox on Charles Lennox see Bradley i 21.

p. 26    'gives great promise for the future': Bradley i 22.

p. 26    'How the dower can be avoided': For Lady Lennox on the Lennox lands, see Lefuse 22. See also Elizabeth Lennox's letters on the same subject quoted in Bradley i 43, Hardy 27–8. 'Dower' may mean 'dowager's portion', i.e. Elizabeth Lennox's inheritance from her husband.

p. 27    A message was sent off: BL Harl. MSS 289, 198; quoted in Lefuse 22.

p. 27    In a draft will: Labanoff iv 356; quoted (in the original French) in Handover *Arbella Stuart* 54, Hardy 26.

p. 28    On 9 March she died: The circumstances of Lady Lennox's death are described in Ashdown 173–4.

p. 28    Wardship of the infant: The death of her father, the head of the household, had by the standards of the day made Arbella technically an orphan, although her mother was still alive. It is also worth noting that generational relationships were not described in the sixteenth century in such rigid terms as today: Bess refers to

Arbella as her daughter; Arbella to Bess as her parent; and the earl of Hertford refers to William Seymour as his nephew and his grandson within a single letter.

p. 30    Lady Lennox's will ordained the jewels: Lefuse 27, Hardy 24–5, Cooper i 49.

p. 30    'Be it known': CSP Scottish v 350.

p. 30    'She endured very well': Durant *Arbella Stuart* 21.

p. 31    'I have not so evil deserved': Steen *Letters* 15.

p. 31    'My mother hearing of the infection': Bradley i 44, Lefuse 24–5.

p. 31    The young countess left: Durant *Arbella Stuart* 29.

p. 32    'O my little heart!': Erondell *French Garden* 7–8.

p. 32    Shrewsbury wrote to Walsingham: CSP Dom 1581–90 42–3, quoted in Cooper i 57–62.

p. 32    Seven days later: For Bess's letters to Burghley see Bradley i 52–3; also Hardy 29–33, Lefuse 30–1, 35–7.

p. 32    four hundred pounds' pension: Charles Nicholl (*The Reckoning*) suggested multiplying by 500 to get a rough equivalent of modern value.

p. 33    'drinketh every day': Durant *Bess* 100.

p. 33    'I doubt not': Durant *Bess* 100.

p. 35    'The matter of the Lady Arbella's remaining': Durant *Arbella Stuart* 34.

p. 35    'Four times': Walpole's rhyme is quoted in Bickley 34.

p. 35    Bess was indeed: My picture of Bess's early history, and of the Shrewsbury marriage, was influenced by that given by Durant in *Bess*, chs 6–9.

p. 41    'Firstly that one': Labanoff vi 51–7; quoted (in English) in Durant *Bess* 130–1, Lefuse 47; see also Plowden 44–53.

p. 43    'First I assayed': Cooper i 68; Hardy 52. For Bess's schemes with Leicester, see also Bradley i 56, Durant *Arbella Stuart* 33.

p. 44    A few years on: For Shrewsbury on Arbella, see Hardy 57–8, Bradley i 72–3.

p. 46    one in three among the country's older peers: This is Lawrence Stone's estimate; see *Crisis* 66.

p. 46    'as near a free woman': Lambeth Palace Library, MS 3201 ff. 124–5, transcribed in Steen *Letters* 183.

p. 47    'Sir – After the closing': Hardy 34–5.

p. 49    Lady Jane had told Roger Ascham: Chapman *Lady Jane Grey* 46–8.

p. 49    'virtuous disposition': Harington *Tract on the Succession* 45.

p. 49    'Great learned lady': Steen *Letters* 56–7.

p. 51  'I may well say': For Lady Lennox's verses, see Ashdown 43–4.

p. 51  All three: Information on the Talbot daughters is drawn from Hunter and Hutton.

p. 53  'patching up every idle word': Cecil Papers 135 ff. 130–8.

p. 54  'pleasant quasi-maternal relationship': Fraser *Mary Queen of Scots* 575; the evidence she adduces, however – Mary's will, for example – suggests familial support, but leaves dark the question of daily contact. James Mackay, in his biography of Mary, asserts (272) that the hostility between Bess and Mary was further complicated by their rivalry for Arbella's affection, and that Bess 'sought, by her vile slanders, to deny Mary access to the little girl'.

p. 56  'Let me lose': Cecil Papers 135 ff. 130–8.

p. 56  Mary left to Arbella her *Book of Hours*: Bradley i 11–12, Hardy 44–5.

# Part II

The best single secondary source for the plotting and political machinations which dominated Arbella's life during the 1590s is P. M. Handover's *Arbella Stuart, Royal Lady of Hardwick*. Handover is by far the most politically oriented of Arbella's earlier biographers; and her book is particularly interesting in this context since she also wrote an important biography of Robert Cecil (*The Second Cecil*). More recently, Robert Lacey (*Robert, Earl of Essex*) has written of the earl of Essex, albeit concentrating largely upon his flamboyant personality and his relationship with the ageing queen. A different perspective may be found in several later academic studies, like that of Paul Hammer (*The Polarisation of Elizabethan Politics*), which paints the picture of an earl more complex and more astute than the conventional image allows. In more general terms John Guy, in *The Reign of Elizabeth I*, postulates the post-Armada years as a separate and distinct phase in the queen's long reign.

There is a substantial body of what one might call succession literature, to which the best guide I found was Howard Nenner's *The Right to be King*. A number of the contemporary texts are available in comparatively modern editions, most notably Sir John Harington's *A Tract on the Succession to the Crown* and Cecil's secret correspondence with James. My picture of Elizabeth's court was much influenced by Alison Weir's *Elizabeth the Queen* and also by *The English Court*, edited by David Starkey.

David N. Durant's biography *Bess of Hardwick* is invaluable for the background to Bess's building work – as for her household's expenses during the London trip of 1591–2. His work apart, the best secondary sources for Arbella's life at Hardwick Hall are those published by the National Trust, which administers the building today. Beyond the detailed guide book written by Mark Girouard, they are: *A Very Goodly Prospect* by Gillian White and *Of Household Stuff: The 1601 Inventories of Bess of Hardwick*, along with *Oldcotes* by Pamela Kettle and the English Heritage guide book to *Hardwick Old Hall* by Lucy Worsley. Mowl, *Elizabethan and Jacobean Style*, and Watkins, *In Public and in Private*, help to place Hardwick in a contemporary context.

Finally, this may be an appropriate place to mention the literature of a burgeoning field of study; the political interactions of women in the late sixteenth and early seventeenth century. This was not, of course, a game Arbella herself was at this point free to play. She was, however, ably represented by her aunt Mary Talbot – of whom I only wish I had been able to find a biography. Mary Talbot, however, does feature in Violet Wilson's 1924 precursor to the field, *Society Women of Shakespeare's Time*; I was also gripped (although the timescale tends to be slightly later) by Antonia Fraser's groundbreaking *The Weaker Vessel*. But in this area it is to recent academic publications that one must also look: such works as Frye and Robertson's *Maids and Mistresses, Cousins and Queens*; or *Early Modern Women's Letter Writing, 1450–1700*, edited by James Daybell. The former has a particularly interesting essay on 'Sewing Connections: Elizabeth Tudor, Mary Stuart, Elizabeth Talbot, and Seventeenth Century Anonymous Needleworkers' (Frye); the latter an essay on Arbella's letters by Sara Jayne Steen, to be discussed more fully under Part V below. Papers by James Daybell and Sara Jayne Steen on, respectively, Bess of Hardwick's information networks and the political interests of the Cavendish–Talbot women are published in a volume of essays edited by Daybell, *Women and Politics in Early Modern England, 1450–1700* (Ashgate, 2004).

p. 59  'Lady Cobham does not advise': Folger X d 428 (131). While the letter is dated 8 December, there is no year; the estimate of 1585 is approximate.

p. 60  The time was approaching: This is usually taken to be Arbella's first formal court appearance. But cf. *Fugger News-Letters, 2nd series 56–7*:

Antwerp April 29 1581: Letters from England of April 22 announce the arrival of the French Embassy to the Queen. It was received in audience the very next day. We are told that the Queen had with her a young lady who was called by every one her cousin and next heiress to the English throne after the Queen's death. But now it is said to be evident she is a daughter of the Queen whom she had by N.N. So a marriage is to be arranged between this young lady and the Duke of Alencon. This cannot long be kept secret.

This passage is endorsed by the editor, Victor von Klarwill, 'Presumably Arabella Stuart'. The theory of Elizabeth having had a daughter by the unidentified NN does, however, rather discredit anything else this reporter might have to say.

p. 63    Arbella would be the 'lawful inheritress': Handover *Arbella Stuart* 77, citing Strickland. Bradley i 64–5 usefully gives the French phrases.

p. 64    An entranced visitor: Frederick, later duke of Württemberg, who visited England in 1592. His narrative was compiled by his secretary Jacob Rothgeb and published at Tübingen in 1602.

p. 65    Charles Cavendish reported: HMC Devonshire Papers at Hardwick 3rd Report ii 42, quoted in Lefuse 49, Hardy 47, Bradley i 62–4.

p. 69    'my housekeeping doth stand me': Cooper i 93, Hardy 49–50.

p. 69    'Look to her well': De Chateauneuf to Henri IV, Handover *Arbella Stuart* 77, citing Strickland.

p. 70    a notorious smuggler: Ashworth 187.

p. 71    She was staying with Gilbert: for Arbella's note to Burghley, see Steen *Letters* 120.

p. 71    'My cousin Mary': Huntingdon Library, MS HM 803, quoted in Steen *Letters* 119.

p. 72    'displayed such haughtiness': CSP Ven ix 541 (and see introduction to Part III below).

p. 74    'then in highest favour': Cecil Papers 135 ff. 130–8.

p. 75    It is tempting to speculate: From earliest days, biographers have speculated on Arbella's relationship with Essex. Agnes Strickland wrote that she nursed 'a brief and hopeless passion' for the earl: a comparatively restrained romanticism for which (since she offered no proofs) she was nonetheless censured by both Handover and Durant. Hardy, however (83–5 and 96), went a good deal further, writing that in 1602 'her heart lay buried in the grave of Essex.' It is interesting to note that the old ideas, in a different form, have come around again: Norrington (50) perceives the same kind of emotional attachment I too see. She postulates 'clandestine meetings', and speculates that Arbella's 'wayward' behaviour in 1603 may have been due to her grief.

p. 75   'was wont to have the upper hand': CSP Dom 1581–90, 689.

p. 76   Heavy restoration in the early part: The latest restoration work was carried out for the National Trust in 2000. It was then discovered that earlier operations had virtually destroyed the original painting of the face, and what appears now is essentially a reconstruction, with features modelled upon those of other family members.

p. 81   'As the strict band': CSP Scottish 605. For commentary on the different drafts, see Steen *Letters* 276–7.

p. 82   'Given 27th of July': for Bess's accounts and details of the London sojourn, see Durant *Bess* 167–74.

p. 85   few records of Arbella leaving Derbyshire: This is not, of course, to say that she did not spend any time with relatives in London or elsewhere – though had she been much present at court, the fact (given the intense interest in all Elizabeth's possible heirs) would surely have been noted. Strickland envisages her as being at court in the 1590s, and McInnes (103–4) says she was there in 1597; neither, however, gives any source. A document in the Folger collection (X d 428 (24)) from Arbella's uncle William Cavendish to Bess mentions her being at Edmonton (and 'very well'); it has been provisionally dated as *c*.1600. Other papers, alas, lack even the most speculative date (or place of writing) – like the letter at Longleat (Talbot ii f. 294) from Elizabeth Wingfield to an unnamed recipient, possibly Bess of Hardwick. The writer had unexpectedly met Arbella, come to church to collect her 'sweet cousin', whereupon Arbella 'looked very strangely'. Arbella begged Mistress Wingfield to ask [Bess] not to be offended, since she had only come there by chance, a Mrs Humfreson swore she knew not of Arbella's coming . . . One would give much to know the locality of this incident, and still more the date, though some point between Arbella's adolescence and her liberation from Hardwick in 1603 would seem to explain the tone most readily. On the one hand, the letter seems to show Arbella as out and about, at a time when she still felt the need to explain her actions (to Bess); on the other, it reinforces the impression that her social contacts were monitored very carefully.

p. 85   'all the old holidays': Trease 25–6.

p. 88   'I have little': BL Lansdowne lxxi; cited by Handover *Arbella Stuart* 98; quoted in full by Hardy 65–7, Cooper i 119–23, Lefuse 52.

p. 89   'It is Arbella': CSP Dom 1591–4 259–60. (Handover *Arbella Stuart* 91–2, also cites Strype iii 142.

p. 89   'one young lady': Cooper i 115–6; Handover *Arbella Stuart* 92 (citing Strype iii 148).

p. 90   'simply no contemporary agreement': Nenner 13.

p. 90   James, by contrast: as James himself feared, there was also the danger that he could have been debarred by the Act of Attainder, which ruled that the connections of a traitor could not succeed to the throne.

p. 91   Soon after the old earl's death: For the letters concerning the Talbots' religion, see Batho H 463, 469, 813; M 342, 410.

p. 92   'In 1580 there were 66 English peers': Stone *Crisis* 741.

p. 92   One Catholic commentator: R. Doleman (or Parsons), author of *A Conference about the Next Succession to the Crown of England*.

p. 93   William Seymour: For more on William's religion, see notes to Part V below.

p. 93   'all platforms fell to the ground': CSP Dom Add. 1580–1625, 269.

p. 93   'one Morley': BL Lansdowne lxxi; cited by Handover *Arbella Stuart* 98; quoted in full by Hardy 65–7, Cooper i 119–23, Lefuse 52.

p. 94   A Catholic letter: CSP Dom 1591–4 106.

p. 96   If he really were the model: The identification of Essex as the subject of Hilliard's picture was made by Roy Strong in *The Cult of Elizabeth*.

p. 97   Arbella herself: For Arbella on Essex, see Cecil Papers 135 ff. 130–8.

p. 99   Sara Jayne Steen: Steen 'Crime of Marriage' cites a considerable body of earlier work establishing the connection between Arbella and Malfi.

p. 100   'No simple word': Ben Jonson, 'Inviting a Friend to Supper', *Epigrams* (1616).

p. 101   In 1589: For Barnes, see CSP Dom. Add. 1580–1625 270, 272, 275.

p. 101   'at the rate of Arbella': Hatfield iv 626.

p. 102   'England is gone': Hatfield iv 335.

p. 102   'the traffic of Arbella': Hatfield iv 625.

p. 102 'small account made': Hatfield xiii 494; quoted in Handover *Arbella Stuart* 101.

p. 102 'in the briars': CSP Dom 1598–1601, 460; quoted by Hurstfield in Bindoff et al. 378.

p. 102 In years to come: The letter from the anonymous observer is quoted in full in Handover's notes: *Arbella Stuart* 309–13.

p. 102 'The queen here daily': Handover *Arbella Stuart* 113.

p. 103 'all the plagues': Calendar of Talbot Papers at Longleat 119.

p. 103 'My Lady Arbella': Harington *Tract on the Succession* 42.

p. 104 one John Brystone reported: Hatfield iv 551.

p. 106 Thus, against Arbella: Doleman ii 126; see also 124–9 on Arbella's claim.

p. 106 'in that she is a young lady': Doleman ii 249.

p. 107 'hath only the Cavendishes': Doleman ii 129.

p. 107 'time, survival and delay': Lacey Baldwin Smith *Elizabeth Tudor: Portrait of a Queen* (Boston 1975) 218, quoted in Nenner 17.

p. 107 Amid the mass of documents: For Williamson's declaration see Hatfield v 251–4 (also other correspondence through the volume; and Williamson also in CSP Dom 1595–7).

p. 108 One Edward Thurland: Batho I 212.

p. 112 'how beautiful': Hatfield xiv 18.

p. 112 James in Scotland was said to suspect: CSP Scottish xii 267; quoted in Handover *Arbella Stuart* 115.

p. 112 'I should have no objection': Handover *Arbella Stuart* 115, Cooper i 127.

p. 115 It is a pleasant room: For the contents of Bess's and Arbella's chambers, see *Of Household Stuff* 53–5.

p. 118 'the marriage treaty': CSP Dom 1598–1601, 327–8; quoted in Handover *Arbella Stuart* 124.

p. 118 'a goodly young lady': Harington *Tract on the Succession* 43.

p. 119 At that time, a gentleman: For David Owen Tudor's letter, see Hatfield xii 605.

p. 119 Still, James in Scotland told: Nenner 24–5; also ibid. 17, 22, 24 for other contemporary speculations.

p. 123 Essex was brought to trial: For the trial and execution, CSP Dom 1598–1601, 545–9.

p. 124 But a later letter: For Arbella on Essex, see Cecil Papers 135 ff. 130–8.

p. 124 Cecil suffered a fresh wave: For Sir John Byron's report, Guy 59.

p. 127   Father Parsons had been told: Hurstfield in Bindoff et al. 377, Thomas Wilson quoted ibid. 373.

p. 127   In the summer of 1601: For Wilson's list of candidates, see CSP Dom 1601–3 60. Wilson calls Lord Beauchamp's brother 'Henry' (instead of Thomas). Henry Seymour was in fact brother to the earl of Hertford.

p. 128   'It is least likely': Harington *Tract on the Succession* 43–4.

p. 128   An anonymous letter from 1600: CSP Dom Add. 1580–1625 406–7.

p. 128   'Sir R. Cecil intends to be king': CSP Dom 1601–3, 37.

p. 128   One Captain North: Bradley i 90, Hardy 73.

p. 128   'higher by as many steps': Cooper i 158.

p. 128   In 1600 the Fugger newsletters: *Fugger News-Letters, 2nd series* 324, 325.

p. 129   'His Highness perceives': Cooper i 131–45.

p. 129   Another observer: Handover 309.

p. 130   an English *king*: the Catholic letter is quoted by Hurstfield in Bindoff et al. 378.

p. 130   'Lady Arbella is a notable puritan': CSP Dom 1601–3, 180; quoted in Handover 133, Bradley i 95.

p. 130   In the spring of 1602: For a report of the duke of Nevers' visit, see Handover 132.

p. 130   *Arbella Stuarta: tu rara es et bella*: Manningham 69.

p. 131   'Why should my muse': Handover 135, Bradley i 96.

p. 132   'of great beauty': CSP Ven ix 541. It is only fair to point out that the Venetian envoy had not at this time seen Arbella. The French ambassador, who had, described her as only 'sufficiently' handsome.

p. 132   She gave several gifts: For Bess's gifts to Arbella, see Durant *Arbella Stuart* 77–80.

p. 133   In 1601 Bess the provident: For Bess's will, see ibid. 90.

p. 133   'thought of all means': For Starkey's confession, see Hatfield xiv 258.

p. 134   Anne Newdigate: Newdigate-Newdegate 4–5. This is the only known letter written by Arbella which does not appear in Steen's edition, and was brought to my attention by James Daybell. In a brief note Arbella thanks 'sweet Mrs Newdigate', as Anne Fitton had become, for 'your fine cuffs and kind remembrance of me, hoping this our acquaintance newly begun shall continue, and grow greater hereafter'. Undated, it has at one point been annotated as 1615 but this is clearly impossible, since Arbella signs it from 'Chessey' – presumably Chelsea. Lady Newdigate-Newdegate's estimate of the early 1590s seems more likely.

# Part III

The sources for this section are concentrated to an unusual degree, since almost all the essential documents are held in the Cecil Papers at Hatfield House. Almost all Arbella's own letters from these months are there, in volume 135; the sole exception being her letter to Edward Talbot, referred to on page 170 – and even then, Robert Cecil kept a secretary's copy, along with Talbot's comments.

The Cecil Papers, moreover, also include the letters sent from Hardwick by Bess and by Brounker; the statements of Dodderidge, Starkey and Owen Tudor; statements relevant to the escape attempt of 10 March; notes on intercepted letters; and Chaworth's intercepted letter to Arbella. These are all reproduced in full, though in modern orthography, in the Calendar (described below as 'Hatfield'). Unusually, the bulk of Arbella's letters are not included in the Calendar, which merely referred the reader to Bradley, with a list of corrections (Hatfield xii 683). Today, of course, one would turn instead to Sara Jayne Steen's 1994 edition of Arbella's letters.

The single other most interesting source for these months of Arbella's life is the gossipy reports of the Venetian envoy. Having kept no representative in England for most of Queen Elizabeth's reign, towards its end the doge dispatched Giovanni Scaramelli, who arrived – to complain about the piratical behaviour of English seamen – in the last weeks of the queen's life. From this point onwards, a succession of Venetians (Scaramelli – technically a secretary rather than an ambassador, but I keep the more usual appellation – being succeeded in November 1603 by two ambassadors extraordinary, Duodo and Molin, and they, in due course, by Correr, Contarini and Foscarini) provide an invaluable commentary upon the crises of Arbella's career. The obvious reference point is the Calendar of State Papers and Manuscripts relating to English Affairs Preserved in the Archives of Venice (cited here as CSP Ven), but the necessity of translation (and the fact that large passages were also in cipher) inevitably opens up questions of interpretation; also, the translations sometimes vary from those in Art. X of the *Edinburgh Review* 1896 ('Lady Arabella Stuart and the Venetian Archives'). The difference is usually one of adjective and emphasis: I note specifically any observed discrepancy as to fact.

p. 144 'She told me I must go a hundred miles': For Dodderidge's confession, see Hatfield xii 583–6.

p. 144 Old Sir John Byron: It is possible that these were the Byrons whose kin – a family called Starkey – saw their children cursed by a warlock in a famous witchcraft trial a few years before; and also possible that this was the background of Arbella's Starkey. But either would be hard to prove at this distance of time.

p. 145 Dodderidge, Arbella wrote: For Arbella's instructions to Dodderidge, see Cecil Papers 135, f. 107.

p. 146 'my entertainment here': Cecil Papers 135 f. 108.

p. 146 Brounker's report: Hatfield xii 593–7.

p. 148 'May it please': Cecil Papers 135 f. 146.

p. 149 'A feigned answer': Hatfield xii 609.

p. 150 'seeing she hath been content': Ibid. 593.

p. 151 'the incongruity of his grandchild's years': Ibid. 626.

p. 151 'most gracious interpretation': Cecil Papers 135 ff. 144–5.

p. 152 'the bad persuasions': Ibid. 624.

p. 154 This first of her self-explanatory letters: Cecil Papers 135 ff. 139–41.

p. 158 'whether it be her Majesty's pleasure': Cecil Papers 135 ff. 147–9.

p. 160 'I know not how': Hatfield xii 658. James's undated letter to (Henry Howard for) Cecil, expressing concern about Arbella's supposed conversion, was dated May 1602 by Lord Hailes, who edited the *Secret Correspondence* in 1766; but scholars have since taken liberty to question this, since James's reference to Arbella's mishaps then appear to make no sense.

p. 161 'For my own part': Hatfield xv 253–5.

p. 161 'being sorry': Hatfield xv 252–3.

p. 162 'the real claimants': CSP Ven ix 541–2.

p. 163 Few documents: For the 'Exposition', see Cecil Papers 135 ff. 153–5 (version in Brounker's and Arbella's hand), 156–8 (secretary's copy).

p. 165 'It is not unknown to you': Bradley ii 135.

p. 165 'Soon after Sir H. Brounker's departure': Ibid. 136; also Hardy 116–17.

p. 166 'Writing was a mechanism': Steen *Letters* 42.

p. 168 'What I have written': Cooper i 244.

p. 169 'At last wounded to the heart': Cecil Papers 135 ff. 159–60 (Arbella's own hand), 161–3 (secretary's copy).

p. 170 'I went up to the great chamber': Cecil Papers 135 ff. 159–60.

p. 170   'I protest to Almighty God': Edward Talbot to Cecil, Hatfield xii 685.

p. 171   'And although they say': CSP Ven ix 554.

p. 171   'Whether Madame Arbella': Hardy 135, Cooper i 248.

p. 173   'In the context': Steen *Letters* 37.

p. 174   'I take Almighty God to witness': Cecil Papers 135 ff. 142–3.

p. 174   'and come attended with 500': Cecil Papers 135 ff. 159–60.

p. 175   'First I will never': Cecil Papers 135 ff. 142–3.

p. 175   *Damnata iam luce ferox*: The translation and interpretation are from Steen *Letters* 155.

p. 175   'this my prison': Ash Wednesday letter, Cecil Papers 135 ff. 130–8.

p. 177   'that my troubled wits': Cecil Papers 135 ff. 130–8.

p. 177   'transported by some Archimedes': Cecil Papers 135 ff. 159–60 and 161–3 (secretary's copy).

p. 178   'I have conquered': Ibid.

p. 180   'one Harrison': For Bess's letter of 1592, see Cooper i 119–23, Lefuse 52.

p. 181   John and Matthew Slack: The statements of the Slacks, Dove and the vicar are given in Bradley ii 172–5.

p. 182   'For that Arbell': Hatfield xii 689.

p. 183   'I presently departed': Hatfield xii 694–6.

p. 185   He carried a letter: Hatfield xii 690–2.

p. 185   'There is no fear': Hatfield xii 692–3.

p. 186   'Every man's mouth': Hatfield xii 693–4.

p. 186   'I am verily persuaded': Ibid.

p. 186   'as the situation is growing more serious': CSP Ven ix 552.

p. 187   'The report': Dekker 33.

p. 188   'All agree that she is worse': Hardy 136, Cooper i 250.

p. 188   Perhaps James needed: the official in Berwick was Sir John Carey; see Hatfield xii 699.

p. 190   Lord Beauchamp: for the rumour that Arbella was betrothed to Beauchamp, see CSP Ven ix 564.

p. 190   'a false alarm': CSP Dom 1603–10 1.

p. 191   'sayeth that all things': Handover *Arbella Stuart* 167.

p. 191   But not that feeble: Manningham 217.

p. 191   'in the west': CSP Ven ix 566.

p. 191   'The younger': CSP Ven x 3.

p. 193   'we are not like': Harington *Tract on the Succession* 51.

p. 193   'feigns herself to be' half mad: CSP Ven ix 557.

p. 194   'they give out' that Arbella is mad: Handover *Arbella Stuart* 161.

p. 194   The Venetians added: For Scaramelli's reports on Scottish machinations, see CSP Ven ix 559. This letter, however, was (like a number of the others) written in cipher – which may be why the other available translation, that in Art. X (490–1) differs quite significantly, spelling out the Scottish aims far more directly.

# Part IV

The first source of information about Arbella's years at court is obviously her own numerous letters. Those she wrote to Gilbert and Mary Talbot in this period – that is, the great majority of the letters quoted in this section – are all in the Talbot Papers at Longleat. The exceptions are: her notes to Cecil at the beginning and end of the section (quoted on pages 207 and 259); the letter to Gilbert quoted on pages 215 and 230; that to Gilbert quoted on pages 212–13 and 252; that to Prince Henry quoted on page 242; and her formal correspondence with the Danish court, quoted on page 249.

There are, however, a handful of other individuals whose correspondence is particularly relevant here – whose names figure repeatedly in the text, not because of any particular relationship with Arbella, but because the lengthy correspondence in which they exchanged court news with friends and contacts has been preserved and in several cases published. Thus the Ralph Winwood who received the report of Arbella's flight given in the prologue was a career diplomat then doing service in the Netherlands, where John More wrote regularly to him. Dudley Carleton was another career diplomat, who wrote to his friend (and Winwood's) John Chamberlain, first from the court and then from Venice, where he was posted in 1610 – receiving in return a flood of information from Chamberlain; a man whose letters were most likely his source of income, and certainly his posterity.

There is obviously no shortage of information about James's court, or about life in the city around it. (Contemporary dramatists found both a particularly luscious target.) Lawrence Stone is only one among many modern historians vividly to delineate the court's chaos and consumption. Some of his conclusions have inevitably been challenged in the thirty-five years or more since he wrote, but his books are still a rich source of information and analysis. None the less, the Jacobean era remains ground less familiar than the Elizabethan – often lost (as Linda Levy Peck points out in *The Mental World of the Jacobean Court*) between its Elizabethan predecessor and the Carolean years which preceded the Civil War. The traditional view is of a court David Starkey described as being one of the least attractive in history; a court Anne Somerset's *Unnatural Murder* paints all too clearly. This view has to some extent been modified in recent years, with Peck's book a leading example of the school of thought which points out the many intellectual and artistic advances which grew out of this world; a world which, in its very chaos, provided a fertile nursery for change.

p. 199   She described how: Lefuse 97. Bradley (i 166–7) gives Strickland as the original authority.

p. 199   'Lady Arbella has been released': CSP Ven x 18.

p. 200   'There is a foolish rhyme': Manningham 235.

p. 201   'to free our cousin': Hatfield xv 65.

p. 201   Arbella had by this time: It has also been suggested (leaving aside the Venetian's report that Arbella had been sent to a palace where Elizabeth had been imprisoned) that Arbella was initially sent to Sheriff Hutton: Cooper i 248.

p. 202   'The Lady Arbella Stuart, being of the royal blood': BL Sloane MS 718 f. 39; cited in Steen *Letters* 43, Lefuse 88, Cooper i 256. The original source is usually described as being an old servant of Lord Burghley's; Scaramelli (CSP Ven x 10) also reports the suggestion (he says, James's suggestion) that Arbella should attend the funeral, though not her refusal.

p. 203   'the duty of every good Catholic': CSP Ven x 48.

p. 203   'We have been informed': Hatfield xv 65.

p. 204   'Lady Arbella, who is a regular termagent': CSP Ven x 42. (Art. X 492 says 'virago'.)

p. 206   'from wherein she came' and 'to deal tenderly': Cooper i 263.

p. 207   'to remember the kiing's Majesty of my maintenance': all five letters transcribed in Steen *Letters* 176–9.

p. 209   James's very coronation: the ceremony is described by Nichols in his *Progresses . . . of King James I* 229–34.

p. 209   'in her appointments': CSP Ven x 82.

p. 210   'though it bend directly northward': Talbot ii ff. 188–9.

p. 212   'Most of the conspirators': CSP Ven x 70.

p. 212   'a pair of virginals': Arundel Castle MSS Autograph Letters 1585–1617 no. 167, transcribed in Steen *Letters* 230–2.

p. 213   'embroiderers, jewellers, tire-women': Ben Jonson *Epicoene* III i.

p. 213   'some company come to fetch me': Talbot ii ff. 194–5.

p. 213   'never intermitted attendance': Talbot ii ff. 257–8.

p. 215   'merry at the Dutchkin': Lambeth Palace Library MS 3201 ff. 124–5, transcribed in Steen *Letters* 182–3.

p. 215   'I . . . interpret your postscript': Talbot ii ff. 192–3.

p. 215   'the danger of missuperscribing letters': Talbot ii f. 224.

p. 215   'I beseech you': Talbot ii ff. 212–13.

p. 216   'long expected trusty messenger': Talbot ii ff. 198–9.

p. 216   'my bad eyes': Talbot ii ff. 196–7.

p. 216   'my eyes are extremely swollen': Talbot ii ff. 200–1.

p. 216   On 17 November: The trial of Sir Walter Ralegh (with, to a lesser degree, his fellow accused) is widely reported: for example, in Birch i 10–32, who prints descriptive letters from Cecil and Carleton. Cobbett ii 1–70 gives an extensive rendition of speeches, with correspondence. Hele's dismissal of Arbella is on 5, Coke's description of her as 'a stale' on 8, the interjections of Nottingham and Cecil on 23.

p. 218   The Venetians stated flatly: CSP Ven x 117.

p. 219   'The most comprehensive manuscript': Mark Nicholls, 'Sir Walter Ralegh's Treason', English Historical Review 110, Sept. 1995. The evidence concerning Arbella appears on p. 910. See also Nicholls, 'Two Winchester Trials: Lord Cobham and Lord Grey, 1603', Historical Research 68, Feb. 1995, and 'Treason's Reward: The Punishment of Conspirators in the Bye Plot of 1603', Historical Journal 38, 1995. I am grateful to Pauline Croft for bringing these articles to my attention.

p. 219   'Frances Kirton': It was an Edward Kirton (or Kyrton) who in 1610 assisted Arbella's escape – and Kyrton or Kirton was the name of the lawyer, employed by the earl of Hertford, who was instrumental in the 1590s proposal for a marriage between Arbella and one of the Seymour family. Arbella (Hatfield xii 584) states that he was also married to a stepdaughter of Bess's.

p. 219   'For the Lady Arbella': Birch i 18.

p. 220   'I humbly thank you': Talbot ii ff. 210–11.

p. 220   'although now proved innocent': CSP Ven x 117.

p. 221   'extreme pain of my head': Talbot ii ff. 202–3.

p. 221   'extreme cold': Talbot ii ff. 204–5.

p. 221   'When any great matter': Talbot ii ff. 206–7.

p. 221   Her letter to Gilbert: Talbot ii ff. 208–9.

p. 221   'I have reserved the best news': Talbot ii ff. 210–11.

p. 223   'confusion of imbassages': Talbot ii ff. 208–9.

p. 224   'was required to put his gift': Glashen 53.

p. 224   'a trifle': Talbot ii ff. 218–19.

p. 224   'the queen regarded not the value': Talbot ii ff. 206–7.

p. 225   'will come very unseasonably': Talbot ii ff. 208–9.

p. 225   'a large essay': Talbot ii ff. 214–15.

p. 225   'Your venison': Talbot ii ff. 210–11.

p. 225   'the sharpest salad': Talbot ii f. 254.

p. 225   The King's Men: It is also possible that Arbella saw *As You Like It* earlier in December, and that it was to this performance that she made slighting reference in a letter to Mary Talbot (Talbot ii ff. 208–9): 'There was an interlude but not so ridiculous (as ridiculous it was) as my letter.' Handover (212) suggests that in her years at court Arbella came to share the puritan disapproval of all plays.

p. 225   'The queen intendeth': Talbot ii ff. 210–11.

p. 226   the *Vision of the Twelve Goddesses*: Information on, and interpretation of, the significance of the masques is from Barroll.

p. 227   'First came the messengers': Nichols, *Progresses . . . of King James I* i 324–423. The Venetian Molin noted Arbella's presence: CSP Ven x 139.

p. 229   'if ever there were such a virtue': Lambeth Palace Library MS 3201 ff.124–5, transcribed in Steen *Letters* 182.

p. 230   'there were certain child's plays': Talbot ii ff. 208–9.

p. 231   'Our great and gracious ladies': Talbot ii ff. 190–1.

p. 231   'I daily see': Talbot ii ff. 208–9.

p. 231   'I must a little touch': Lodge iii 227–8; quoted in Handover *Arbella Stuart* 198, Bradley i 209.

p. 231   I dare not write': Talbot ii ff. 210–11.

p. 232   'a prince's court': John Webster *The Duchess of Malfi* I i.

p. 233   'I wish I waited now': Starkey ed. *The English Court* 196.

p. 234   'After I had once carved': Talbot ii ff. 232–3.

p. 235   Several books were dedicated: Steen *Letters* 56.

p. 236   'because I know my uncle': Talbot ii ff. 222–3.

p. 237   'I observed': Cooper ii 23–9, Hardy 176–8.

p. 237   'although her virtue': Cooper i 281.

p. 237   'I assure myself': Talbot ii ff. 228–9.

p. 238   'These people': Talbot ii ff. 232–3.

p. 238   Nevertheless, when she was stricken with the measles: Norrington (87, 94–5) suggests that on this occasion (as when she was later described as having smallpox) Arbella may instead have been exhibiting the rash of variegate porphyria, but Gilbert's reference – in the letter where he informs Cecil of Arbella's recovery – to that of all the other 'fair ladies' (Handover *Arbella Stuart* 211) would surely seem to suggest the presence of an infectious disease.

p. 238   'I neither think': Talbot ii ff. 190–1.

p. 238 'I shall as willingly play the fool': Talbot ii ff. 232–3.

p. 238 'I make it my end': Arundel Castle MSS Autograph Letters 1585–1617 no. 167, transcribed in Steen *Letters* 230–2.

p. 238 'You know I have cause': Talbot ii ff. 222–3.

p. 239 'had desired so earnestly': Rawson 343.

p. 240 'Mr Ca[ve]ndish is at London': Lefuse 178.

p. 240 'you may soon be dispatched': Talbot ii ff. 222–3.

p. 240 'The Lady Arbella spends her time': Batho M 260; see also Batho K 121 (incorporating 120), 124, 163. Fowler wrote of Arbella as the eighth wonder of the world and the 'phoenix of her sex' – 'more fairer than fair, more beautiful than beauteous, truer than truth itself' – and sent to Gilbert some verses in her honour, quoted in Hardy 166, Lefuse 117, Bradley 175–6:

> Thou godly nymph, possest with heavenly fear,
> Divine in soul, devout in life and grave,
> Rapt from thy sense and sex, thy spirits doth steer
> Toys to avoid which reason doth bereave.

p. 241 'A great ambassador': Talbot ii f. 224.

p. 242 'being conducted to his lodgings': Lefuse 184.

p. 242 'late high favour and grace': BL Harl. MS 6986 ff. 71–2.

p. 242 Henry, while always on good terms: My picture of Henry and his circle was informed by Roy Strong's biography *Henry, Prince of Wales*. An instance of the 'received impression' of his affection for Arbella is Hardy 193.

p. 244 Indeed, had it succeeded: the suggestion was made by Pauline Croft in a website set up to support Channel Four's programme on the Gunpowder Plot in the 'Plague, Fire, War and Treason' series, November 2001.

p. 245 'The nearest relative': CSP Ven x 514.

p. 245 'such fees as may arise': Cecil Papers 134 f. 94.

p. 245 'for that I thought': Ibid.

p. 246 'Their thirty-pound butter'd eggs': Stone *Crisis* 559.

p. 246 'Ladies abandon': Harington *Nugae Antiquae* ii 126.

p. 248 'one lady and that under a baroness': Chamberlain i 252–3.

p. 248 'even greater mounds of my debtors': translated from the Latin original and transcribed in Steen *Letters* 223–4.

p. 249 'The Danish king, it was said': Hardy 197 supplies this possibly rather bowdlerized version of the incident.

p. 249 'I shall think that breath': BL Harl. MS 7003 f. 42.

p. 249   'by the patronage': Ibid. f. 48.

p. 249   'although I know': Ibid. f. 37 (Latin version); f. 38 is translator's copy.

p. 250   'the Thames is quite frozen': Chamberlain i 253.

p. 251   'my lady Arbella is gone towards you': Batho L 141.

p. 251   The months ahead: For Bess's will, see Durant *Arbella Stuart* 161 (also 165 for more on Arbella's finances).

p. 251   She was popularly supposed: Lefuse 198, Batho L 155.

p. 251   She petitioned James: CSP Dom lxi Feb; also Lefuse 208, Bradley i 229 (for her grant of the impost on oats, see Batho L 158).

p. 252   'To remember to be ready': Jardine and Stewart 300.

p. 252   'the muttering of a bill': Chamberlain i 266–7.

p. 252   'I have found by experience': Talbot ii f. 254.

p. 252   'For want of a nunnery': Ibid.

p. 253   There is a lovely description: Erondell 86–104.

p. 253   'London has got a great way': Wilson *Society Women* 209.

p. 257   'My lady Skinner': Hardy 215.

p. 257   'my Lady Arbella will be at Sheffield': Lefuse 212, Cooper ii 89.

p. 257   Arbella's steward: Crompton's detailed account of expenses is quoted in full in Bradley ii 227–37; see also Hardy 218: The original document is at Longleat.

p. 259   'I would be glad to know': BL Harl. MS 7003 f. 55.

p. 259   'Some friends of mine': SP Dom James 50 f. 136, transcribed in Steen *Letters* 233.

p. 259   'promised when he ascended': CSP Ven x 514.

p. 260   'I can learn no more': Chamberlain i 292.

p. 260   'His Majesty had a hint': CSP Ven xi 405. (Art. X. 497 says Arbella was trying 'to escape over sea in company of a certain Scotchman called Douglas, with intent to marry abroad' – i.e. not to marry Douglas, necessarily.)

p. 260   'Lady Arbella's troubles': CSP Ven xi 414.

p. 261   'In reply to a question on religion': Ibid.

p. 261   'neither affirm nor deny': CSP Ven xi 410.

p. 262   'is seldom seen': CSP Ven xi 427.

p. 262   The unnamed play: Steen *Letters* 62n. For discussion see Handover 261.

p. 262   'much suspicion about': CSP Ven xi 433–4.

# Part V

The documents which deal with Arbella's imprisonment at Lambeth and abortive journey towards the north – including her own letters and petitions – are concentrated in the British Library (Harl. MS 7003). The Acts of the Privy Council for 1611 (38–44) provide a kind of diary of the week of her escape, with Winwood's *Memorials* also providing much useful material. Many of these documents have been widely reproduced in earlier biographies but Maria Theresa Lewis, looking at that time from the perspective of William, rather than of Arbella, offers a rather different selection, and the report of the Venetian envoy provides a refreshing alternative to the much-quoted tale told by Sir John More. The chief difficulty here, however, is in marrying up the different accounts.

Things are very different when Arbella reaches the Tower. It proved surprisingly difficult to build up a picture of Arbella's life in the Tower – and only partly becase of the destruction of important records. To get a feel for her daily life, one may turn to the biographies of other prisoners; but the attempts of writers before Durant to reconstruct her own experience are damaged by the assumption that she was held predominantly in the Bell Tower, which now seems unlikely to have been the case. It was Anna Keay, than a curator at the Tower, who suggested searching the exchequer records in the Public Record Office for evidence of Arbella's location, and she who first confirmed that the document found there (combined with other evidence, available only in recent years) placed Arbella rather in the old royal palace. Sara Jayne Steen, in her introduction to the *Letters* (98–100) and in her subsequent essay for *Early Modern Women's Letter Writing*, ' "How Subject to Interpretation": Lady Arbella Stuart and the Reading of Illness', first publicized the documents (most notably BL Add. MS 63543 ff. 1–25) I cite on pages 336–49.

p. 268   In 1606, a request made by the painter William Larkin: Strong *William Larkin* 21.

p. 268   'The Lady Arbella who': Winwood iii 119.

p. 268   'If all my royal kindred': *The Duchess of Malfi* I ii.

p. 269   'Why might I not marry?': Ibid. III ii.

p. 270   William Seymour: sources for Seymour's later life and character are more fully discussed under the Epilogue below.

p. 270   in his early twenties: The year of William's birth is a matter of dispute. Both *Burke's Peerage* and the *Dictionary of National*

*Biography* give it as 1588. The only precise evidence, however, comes from a document relating to the inheritance of his grandfather's titles and property. This states that when his grandfather died on 6 April 1621 William was 'aged 33 years, 7 months and 5 days' – and marks the year of his birth as 1587: *Wilts. Inq. p.m., Charles I*, Brit. Rec. Soc., p. 31, quoted in G. E. C., *The Complete Peerage of England, Scotland, Ireland, Great Britain and the United Kingdom, Extant, Extinct, or Dormant*, 13 vols (St Catherine's Press, 1910–40), vol. 12, part 1, p. 70.

p. 270  'Love maketh no miracles': Lambeth Palace Library MS 3201 ff. 124–5; Steen *Letters* 182–4.

p. 272  'The misery of us': *The Duchess of Malfi* I. ii.

p. 272  'myself being a younger brother': Lewis *Lives* ii 290–2, Lefuse 221–3, Hardy 232–3, Cooper ii 104–6.

p. 272  'I boldly intruded': Lewis *Lives* ii 290–2, Lefuse 221–3, Hardy 232–3, Cooper ii 104–6.

p. 273  'given me your royal consent': BL Harl. MS 7003 f. 82.

p. 273  'there is neither promise': Lewis *Lives* ii 290–2, Lefuse 221–3, Hardy 232–3, Cooper ii 104–6.

p. 273  'denying her guilt': CSP Ven xi 439. Art. X 500 says rather that Arbella was forced to return William's rings.

p. 273  'should confess directly': CSP Ven xi 439.

p. 274  'hath seriously considered': Seymour Papers (at Longleat) 6 ff. 1–3, transcribed in Steen *Letters* 290–1. Bradley i 247, Hardy 235.

p. 274  Arbella got the price: on her rights to sell wine, see Cooper ii 107, Hardy 236.

p. 274  'he never spake': Lewis ii 295, Hardy 238.

p. 275  'composed of shells': Cooper ii 111, Hardy 240–1.

p. 277  'did sit up in the Lady Arbella her chamber': Hardy 241–2, Lefuse 229. The Mrs Biron mentioned here may well be Arbella's devoted waiting gentlewoman Margaret Byron.

p. 277  'a contract in a chamber': *The Duchess of Malfi* I ii.

p. 277  *The Lawe's Resolution of Womens Rights*: Picard, *Restoration London* 224–31.

p. 277  'so much the goods': Somerset *Unnatural Murder* 9.

p. 278  'in time to bring me': Lewis *Lives* ii 285–6, Ashdown 189.

p. 278  Antonia Fraser has noted: in *The Gunpowder Plot* 28.

p. 278  'Alas: your shears': *The Duchess of Malfi* III ii.

p. 279  'the lady's hot blood': Birch i 124.

p. 279  'before she is too old to bear him children': CSP Ven xii 49.

p. 280  'A law forbidding': CSP Ven xii 19.

p. 280   'a capital messuage': Cooper ii 111–12.

p. 282   'one or two of her women': Ibid. 112, Bradley ii 241.

p. 282   'minded nothing but her lady': Lucy Hutchinson, *Memoirs of the Life of Colonel Hutchinson Written by his Widow Lucy* (George Bell & Sons, 1905) 44, quoted in Hardy 257.

p. 282   'There are divers': BL Harl. MS 7003 f. 71.

p. 282   But her next letter: Ibid. f. 74.

p. 282   Another letter that summer: Ibid. f. 92.

p. 283   'If Crompton should die': Cooper ii 113.

p. 283   'Restraint of liberty': Three drafts in BL Harl. MS 7003 ff. 90, 91. For comparison of the versions, see Steen *Letters* 239–41.

p. 283   'declared that he did not blush': CSP Ven xii 49.

p. 285   'distempered': The inquiry into the rumours of Arbella's pregnancy can be found in Acts 1616–17 133–5 for the answers of Mrs Bradshaw, William, Dr Moundford and the attendants; 183–4 for Mary Talbot. See also PRO SP 14/97 item 126, ff. 290–292. Steen, in her article in *Early Modern Women's Letter Writing*, ' "How Subject to Interpretation": Lady Arbella Stuart and the Reading of Illness', suggests (with reference to Macalpine) that such swelling could also be symptomatic of porphyria.

p. 285   'when [the queen] gave': BL Harl. MS 7003, ff. 64–5.

p. 286   'I cannot rest satisfied': Ibid. f. 70.

p. 286   'The wisdom of this state': Ibid. f. 65.

p. 286   'most wished-for favour': BL Harl. MS 7003 f. 113.

p. 287   'I most humbly beseech your Majesty': Ibid. ff. 87–8.

p. 287   'let it be covered': Ibid. f. 85.

p. 288   'your Majesty's neglect of me': Ibid. f. 57 (secretary's draft).

p. 288   Arbella's own first draft: Ibid. f. 82.

p. 288   'at this time': Ibid. f. 78.

p. 288   'I must confess I fear': Steen *Letters* 250.

p. 289   'I am exceedingly sorry': BL Harl. MS 7003, f. 150.

p. 290   'called before the lords': HMC Belvoir Papers i 427, cited by Handover *Arbella Stuart* 270. To make an interesting comparison with Arbella's imprisonment, see Somerset *Unnatural Murder* 134, on the arrest of Sir Thomas Overbury. Ironically, Sir Edward Coke – to whom, as lord chief justice, Arbella appealed in vain – was to be the jurist who did most to define the law. Coke had savagely prosecuted Essex, Ralegh and the Gunpowder Plotters as traitors to the king, but later in his life – perhaps, even, as a result of those trials? – he was to be the great defender of the common law against royal and ecclesiastical privilege.

p. 290 'It is thought that': CSP Ven xii 110.

p. 291 'to enquire by an *habeas corpus*': BL Harl. MS 7003 f. 152.

p. 291 'Sir, though you be': Steen *Letters* 261–2 (transcript and discussion of correspondent's identity).

p. 292 'the most penitent and sorrowful creature': BL Harl. MS 7003 f. 149.

p. 292 'my soul overwhelmed': Ibid. f. 104.

p. 292 'the fault cannot be uncommitted': Ibid. ff. 153–5.

p. 292 An Italian jeweller: for letter and discussion of source see Steen *Letters* 292–3.

p. 292 'hath highly offended us': BL Harl. MS 7003 ff. 94, 96.

p. 292 'forasmuch as it is more necessary': Ibid.

p. 293 Arbella, he wrote: The bishop's letter is in SP Dom lxii f. 30; quoted in Cooper ii 146–7.

p. 293 The lists of official expenses: given in full Cooper ii 158–67.

p. 293 'cherishing her to life': Cooper ii 149.

p. 294 'the means prescribed': CSP Dom. 1611–18, 17.

p. 294 'For my part': Cooper ii 150, Hardy 270.

p. 294 'It was enough to make any sound man': BL Harl. MS 7003 f. 114.

p. 294 She and William had jointly signed a document: Steen *Letters* 67, citing the Seymour Papers (at Longleat) 6 f. 5. Hardy (268–9) describes it in detail: 'sealed by Arbella with the Lennox crest, a wolf rampant; the witnesses to it were Rodney and Kirton . . . The date given on it is 21st March 1610, evidently an error for 1611, since the pair were not married the year before.'

p. 294 'very weak, her pulse dull': BL Harl. MS 7003 f. 116. Bradley (ii 5–6) and Hardy (271–2) both quote at length – omitting, however, the important (for a diagnosis of porphyria) mention of her 'water'. See Appendix B.

p. 295 'those ordinary helps': BL Harl. MS 7003 ff. 153–5.

p. 295 On 31 March Croft reported: Lefuse 248.

p. 295 'I am in so weak case': BL Harl. MS 7003 f. 147.

p. 296 'Halcyon days': BL Harl. MS 7003, f. 89.

p. 296 'her willingness': Lefuse 252, Bradley ii 12–13.

p. 296 'My poor opinion': BL Sloane MS 4161 59; quoted in Handover *Arbella Stuart* 272.

p. 296 'She apprehendeth nothing': CSP Dom 1611–18, 24.

p. 296 It took her four drafts: BL Harl. MS 7003 ff. 79, 80, 83; the last is the one with her own comments. For full texts and discussion, see Steen *Letters* 263–6.

p. 297 'used not one unkind or wrathful word': BL Harl. MS 7003 f. 107.

p. 297 'if you want for the honourable lady': BL Harl. MS 7003 f. 109.

p. 297 More to the point: CSP Ven xii 153.

p. 297 'he would rather lose his life': Cooper ii 170.

p. 297 'I can expect no good from her': Hardy 258.

p. 298 as they were later described: by Northampton; see Lefuse 283–6.

p. 300 Mary Seton: Talbot ii 250. In this letter, which I have not seen mentioned in other Arbella texts, Mary Seton (Marie de Seton) evokes the memory of the queen of Scots, and makes reference to the religion she and Mary Talbot shared.

p. 300 The Venetian ambassador: Foscarini's lengthy report to the doge and senate (CSP Ven xii 166–8) is the main source for this chapter. All references to the Venetians are from this document unless otherwise stated.

p. 300 After slipping out: contemporary references abound (Shakespeare's plays apart!) to women donning male attire. Besides Elizabeth Southwell and the habitual cross-dresser Moll Cutpurse, Queen Elizabeth's maid Mary Fitton used to 'put off her head tire and tuck up her clothes and take a large white cloak and march as though she had been a man' when she went to meet her lover William Herbert (he who subsequently married Arbella's cousin Mary). See Somerset *Ladies-in-Waiting*, 90–3.

p. 301 'It seems it is a place entailed': Briscoe 89.

p. 301 'a cloak, a cap': BL Harl. MS 7003 f. 126.

p. 302 On the day of his escape: Sir John More to Sir Ralph Winwood, *Memorials* iii 279–81.

p. 303 The collier's captain: Report in BL Harl. MS 7003 f. 132.

p. 304 'Myself being come': BL Harl. MS 7003 f. 122.

p. 304 Francis wrote another self-pitying letter: SP Dom lxiv item 8, quoted in Cooper ii 183, Lefuse 279, Bradley ii 38.

p. 304 'foolish and boyish': BL Harl. MS 7003 f. 124.

p. 305 'Council was summoned immediately': CSP Ven xii 164.

p. 305 By midnight the king's shipwright: Cooper ii 188, Hardy 294 (who also suggests the involvement of Elizabeth Grey).

p. 305 'The wind standing cross': Lewis *Lives* ii 322–4 (also for the further progress of William's journey, described on page 307).

p. 305 The royal proclamations: CSP Dom 1611–18, 38, quoted Cooper ii 188–9, 275–6. (For Cecil's letters to ambassadors abroad, see also Cooper ii 191–200.)

p. 305    'Couriers were sent': CSP Ven xii 164.

p. 305    'Both parliament and council thought': Ibid.

p. 306    'most pitied by the puritans': Winwood iii 280, quoted in Handover 279.

p. 306    'generally affirmed': Ibid.

p. 307    While he was sending word: For Admiral Monson's report, see BL Harl. 7003 f. 130.

p. 310    Chidiock Tichbourne's poem quoted in Rowse, *Tower*, 87.

p. 310    The bill of arrests: BL Harl. MS 7003 f. 143; also ibid. 140 for an earlier list.

p. 311    But not Markham: Hardy 298 says Crompton and Markham were tortured, but offers no source; a privy council warrant was necessary to authorize torture, but this was the period for which privy council records were destroyed.

p. 311    'that if this couple': Winwood iii 281.

p. 312    'for all may be attributed': CSP Ven xii 167. In the same letter Foscarini describes the embarrassment of the French ambassador.

p. 312    None the less, six weeks after: For Hertford's letters to Cecil see Cooper ii 204–14.

p. 313    The Florentine secretary: Steen *Crime of Marriage* 73.

p. 313    Fletcher's *The Noble Gentleman*: A sub-plot to *The Noble Gentleman* tells of mad Shattillion, who claims that his lady love is kept 'too close in prison': a lady who had taken to her bed; a lady the king had forbidden him to marry – since she was 'right heir general' after him to the crown of France – thus forcing them to try to flee the land.

> *He is strong opinion'd that the wench he loved*
> *Remaines close prisoner by the Kings command*
> *Fearing her title. (I ii)*

And 'There is no jesting with a Princes title,' Shattillion all too aptly said. Indeed, L. A. Beaurline, in his introduction to the play in *The Dramatic Works in the Beaumont and Fletcher Canon* iii (Cambridge University Press, 1976) wrote that, since audiences 'could not fail' to recognize the allusion, 'It seems unlikely that this would have been tolerated on the stage between 1610 and Arabella's death in the Tower in 1615.' Beaurline's point is that the play must have been written later; other authorities suggest it could have appeared during Arabella's lifetime, albeit in a modified form. See also Steen *Letters* 95–6.

p. 313  'most excellent most gracious and most redoubted': quoted in full Lefuse 283–6.

p. 314  'She is said to have amassed': Lefuse 282, Cooper ii 196.

p. 314  'is said to be utterly without reason': Winwood iii 281.

p. 315  'my lord putteth me in hope': Lefuse 298, Hardy 298.

p. 315  track the passage: Ashworth (118) states that the act passed by Henry VIII, forbidding the unlicensed marriage of his relatives, had been rescinded. Cooper (i 5–10) gives the full provisions which might in any case have made it irrelevant.

p. 315  'be the crime what it will': Goodman 209–11.

p. 319  But his complaints: Cooper ii 228–9, Hardy 297.

p. 319  'three or four fair rooms': Batho M 588, quoted in Lefuse 298, Hardy 298.

p. 319  But it is now established: Starkey *Elizabeth* 142.

p. 319  A wealth of new information: The first suggestions that Arbella was held in the old palace come from the documents in BL Add. MS 63543. Mentions are made of Mary Talbot's proximity to Arbella, and of their meeting repeatedly; and Charles Cavendish's letter (cited above) specifically says that Mary's 'fair rooms' are in 'the Queen's lodging'; that is, the palace. By the same token, mentions in the same BL folder of walks in a gallery and views of a garden fit better with the palace than the Bell Tower. Further evidence comes from the bill of work, PRO E351/3245 (membrane 4), which reads: 'To John Taylour for paving with ragstone 50 square yards in Coleharborowe over the pipe that was laid to convey water to the Lady Arbella her kitching.' 'Coleharborowe' (Coldharbour) was the term used for the area between Coldharbour Gate and the old palace, and makes the identification almost a certainty.

p. 321  Later in her incarceration: the phrase 'close prisoner' is used in BL Add. MS 63543 f. 11, where Mary Talbot blames Arbella's doctor for having passed a message on to court, alleging that since she was kept close prisoner the news could have spread in no other way – suggesting that her contacts really were monitored with unusual stringency. Acts May 1613–Dec. 1614 606 refers to Samuel Smyth 'servant to the Lady Arbella, now close prisoner', but it is hard to know whether the mistress of the man is so described.

p. 323  The autobiography of John Gerard: See 109 for the account of torture, 117 for the diet.

p. 324  In her first days in the Tower: In 1613 (Hardy 317) Crompton's accounts still show Arbella receiving money 'on a warrant from my lady [Mary Talbot]'. Arbella was also using some of the old goods that William had left behind (see Waad's letter in Cooper ii 216–21).

p. 324  'That they cause all such sums of money': CSP Dom 1611–18, 51.

p. 324  'take them to the Tower': CSP Dom 1611–18, 75.

p. 325  '*Item* – A poignard diamond ring': BL Harl. MS 7003 f. 141.

p. 325  'at the cost price': Cooper ii 226–7.

p. 325  'The king hath granted': Batho O 153.

p. 325  'The Lady Arbella desireth': BL Harl. MS 7003 f. 72.

p. 325  'being employed by her ladyship': Acts  May 1613–Dec. 1614 423 (29 April 1614), and a similar permission (implying that it had not simply been taken for granted in the interval) fourteen months later on 30 June 1615.

p. 326  The Tower, after all, held: CSP Dom 1611–18, 148, names of prisoners in the Tower; further evidence of who was there in PRO E351/3247.

p. 327  'we have no news': Briscoe 66.

p. 327  'a thing of no such consequence': Winwood iii 282.

p. 327  'Our tongues and ears': Briscoe 67.

p. 327  'now neither willing': Winwood iii 283.

p. 328  'out of respect to his Majesty': Briscoe 68.

p. 328  'The king is much concerned': CSP Ven xii 174.

p. 328  'hath brought a letter from the archduke': Winwood iii 301–2.

p. 328  'those parts where I might be liable': Briscoe 69–70.

p. 329  'some Jesuit': Briscoe 66.

p. 329  'had such supply from home': Briscoe 70.

p. 329  For this reason James: The allowance is described in BL Add. MS 63543 f. 20. This collection of papers will be discussed below. It is largely concerned with Arbella's illness and imprisonment, but ff. 17–20 are letters between William and his grandfather.

p. 329  An article written in 1951: *Biographical Studies 1534–1829* [a.k.a. *Recusant History*] i (1951–2) 117–19.

p. 329  'They all called themselves merchants': Briscoe 69.

p. 330  It was no fun: For Hertford's letters, see BL Add. MS 63543; on the point that he might 'hate William's memory,' f. 19.

p. 330  'is less grief to parents': ibid. f. 20.

p. 330  'It is no small comfort': Hardy 310, Lefuse 294.

p. 330  Sir William Waad replied: the letter is quoted in full, Cooper ii 216–21.

p. 331 Coincidentally or otherwise: On Mary Talbot's case, see Spedding iv 297–301, Cobbett ii 770–8. Spedding writes that 'A speech evidently made for this occasion is printed in the Cabala (iv 369) and though the name of the speaker is not mentioned, I suppose every body will agree with Robert Stephens that Bacon must have been the author. I have not met with any manuscript of it, or any independent copy.' Lisa Jardine and Alan Stewart, in their recent biography of Francis Bacon, briefly mention it as among his cases, though the turn of words might seem to suggest a confusion between Arbella and Mary.

Spedding seems (300) to make a distinction between a full Star Chamber trial and the hearing given to Mary – one she clearly thought inadequate; but Alan Cromartie points out to me that this might well be thought little more than a linguistic quibble. More interesting is the point Spedding makes (301) that his information here 'come[s] from the posthumous portion of [Sir Edward] Coke's reports, not prepared for publication by himself; and from some short comments and queries in the margin of the paragraph in which he states the substance of the charge, I gather that at some later time he would perhaps have been disposed to question the soundness of this judgement.'

It is exciting to see the repercussion of Arbella's tale affecting the progress of Coke's thought in any way. Coke, of course, was the man to whom Arbella had appealed for the right of *habeas corpus* – and the man who did most to ensure that, twenty years later, her pleas could not have gone unheard so easily.

p. 333 Her allowance from the exchequer: Durant *Arbella* 203–4.

p. 334 Most of the appeals she wrote have since been reallocated: by Steen, whose dating I have followed except in the case immediately below, 'In all humility' (BL Harl. MS 7003 f. 146). This Steen describes (*Letters* 260) as being 'perhaps' written in spring 1611. More commonly, she describes the dating as 'likely'.

p. 335 Elizabeth may instead: Hardy 315 states that Frederick also pleaded for Arbella, but as usual gives no source.

p. 336 'kind tenderness': BL Add. MS 63543 f. 6.

p. 336 'here is a fine piece of work': Ibid. f. 1.

p. 337 'not knowing how it should be done': Ibid. f. 3.

p. 337 'we could not say': Ibid.

p. 337 'Not well': Ibid. f. 5.

p. 337 'thorn' in her side: Ibid.

p. 337 'will condemn me': Ibid. f. 1.

p. 337  This sudden estrangement: Ibid. f. 9.

p. 337  'I will not be of her religion': Ibid. f. 5.

p. 338  'there is not the meanest gentleman': Ibid. f. 1.

p. 338  'the meanest word I speak': Ibid.

p. 338  'The Lady Arbella doth not deny': Ibid. f. 7.

p. 339  Mary Talbot had said the lieutenant's throat: Ibid f. 9.

p. 339  'force and bloodshed': Ibid. f. 7.

p. 339  'come all from one root': Ibid. f. 11.

p. 339  'Now, that there was a plot': Ibid. f. 12.

p. 340  'deboshed carriage': Ibid.

p. 340  'fits of distemper': Ibid. f. 11.

p. 340  'minister physic': Ibid.

p. 340  'the Lady Arbella hath been dangerously sick': Chamberlain i 437. (Also 434 to Winwood in much the same words; since Chamberlain's letters were in a sense news bulletins, he did not hesitate to replicate phraseology.)

p. 341  'continues crackt': Chamberlain i 443; also 449 to Winwood.

p. 341  'love and dalliance': Ibid.

p. 341  'certain gold embezzled': Chamberlain i 452.

p. 341  Here the evidence comes from Viscount Fenton: Steen *Letters* 90, 94.

p. 342  At the end of April 1913: On Sir Thomas Overbury, see Somerset, *Unnatural Murder*.

p. 343  'With much ado': SP James Dom lxxv f. 7; quoted in Cooper ii 241, with the name given as 'Revenes [Ruthven?]'. Lefuse 313 quotes in full, giving Ruthven. Hardy 319 offers Revenes interpreted as Ruithven or Reeves.

p. 344  'He answered that Master Ruthen': BL Add. MS 63543 f. 25.

p. 344  'Dr Palmer, a divine': Chamberlain i 546–7.

p. 345  'far out of frame': Ibid.

p. 346  'to let him and his lady': BL Cotton MS Caligula E X1.

p. 346  'as one long us'd to't': *The Duchess of Malfi* IV i.

p. 347  There is one particularly telling glimpse: BL Add. MS 63543 f. 15. See Steen *Letters* 93n for a discussion of the dating.

p. 348  'should be dead at Dunkirk': Chamberlain i 476.

p. 348  The earl of Northampton wrote mockingly: Northampton's letters (in BL Cotton MS Titus C VI) were discussed by Steen in ' "How Subject to Interpretation": Lady Arbella Stuart and the Reading of Illness'.

p. 348  seem likely from internal evidence: BL Cotton MS Titus C VI f. 89, for example, goes on (after recounting how Lady Waad had held Arbella 'in one of her fits') to discuss arrangements for 'her grace's transport' in terms which seem to link it to the wedding of the Princess Elizabeth in spring 1613.

p. 349    'of no special disease': ibid. f. 94.

p. 349    'upon my former knowledge': ibid. f. 99.

p. 349    'pretends to fast': Ibid.

p. 349    'She prays, she rails': Ibid.

p. 350    'The Lady Arbella, prisoner in the Tower': Acts May 1613–Dec. 1614 (12 Sept 1614).

p. 351    the 'cordials' she had previously been prescribed: Steen *Letters* 99.

p. 351    'I dare to die': BL Harl. MS 7003 ff. 153–5. David Durant voiced the idea that Arbella might have starved herself to death; Norrington attributes her end to porphyria. Steen (*Letters* 99–100) incorporates both explanations, postulating 'a complex set of interactions that may have included her inability or refusal to eat, with porphyria as the underlying disease that brought about her natural death'.

p. 351    'Despair bolts up my doors': Williams *Sir Walter Ralegh* 112.

p. 352    'The prince of Spain': *Fugger News-Letters* 6.

p. 353    'almost entirely unconscious and moribund': CSP Ven xiv 38. Art. X says 'voiceless and almost entirely senseless'.

p. 353    Of course, poison had to be considered: A rumour that Arbella was poisoned was clearly still extant a century and a half later, for in describing the debate in parliament that saw the passage of the Royal Marriage Bill in March 1772 Horace Walpole wrote: 'On the 24th the Bill was reported to the House, and opposed with vehemence by T. Townshend. The Lady Arabella Stuart, he said, was poisoned in the reign of James I. He wondered why the precedent had not been put in the preamble: it would have made as good a figure as prerogative.' *Journal of the Reign of George III* i 71, quoted in Art. X 512n.

p. 353    'according to former custom': Lewis *Lives* ii 340n.

p. 353    'a chronic and long sickness': HMC Appendix to Eighth Report, MSS of the College of Physicians, 229.

p. 353    To Duncan Primrose: Cooper ii 298.

p. 354    'brought at midnight': Cooper ii 245–6 says the body was brought 'silently at night by the black river', but gives no source. A letter of Carleton's (Dudley Carleton to Alice Carleton, 16 Feb 1615, Carleton 131), describes the night-time burial of Lady Cheke and adds that it 'is of late come much into fashion'.

p. 354   But the Venetian envoy: CSP Ven xiv, 38.

p. 354   'They decided that': CSP Ven xiv 45.

p. 354   'How do I thank thee, Death': Handover *Arbella Stuart* 295.
Also quoted by Bradley, Hardy and Norrington.

# *Epilogue*

The Overbury case has been extensively chronicled; most recently, of course, in Anne Somerset's *Unnatural Murder*. Mary Talbot's later brushes with the authorities can be traced through the Acts of the Privy Council and the letters of John Chamberlain. Her daughters' achievements are described in Hunter and Hutton's *Women, Science and Medicine*; for the personal aspect of Alethea's life see David Howarth's *Lord Arundel and his Circle*. For Elizabeth, one of the most fruitful (albeit unexpected) sources was a 1979 essay by Elizabeth David in *Petit Propos Culinaires*.

Lewis's *Lives of the Friends and Contemporaries of Lord Chancellor Clarendon* is the first source for William's career, from his marriage to Arbella right through the difficult years of debate, war and interregnum. His public career, indeed, gets honourable mention in all histories of the Civil War; little, however (even in the Seymour family histories) seems to have been written about him in a domestic capacity. An unexpected resource here was *A Stuart Benefactress: Sarah, Duchess of Somerset*, by A(rnold) Daly Briscoe: a biography of William's descendant which yet incorporates an extensive section on William, the author having scoured the Seymour family archives to come up with the letters to his wife and son here quoted. I found considerable help also in the researches of the Bedwyn History Society; Great Bedwyn is the village in which William is buried, close to the ancestral home of his family.

The public writings of John Winthrop are widely available – for example, in *Early American Writing* (Penguin 1994; the 'city on a hill' speech is on 112). His journal was published as *A Journal of the transactions and occurrences in the Settlement of Massachusetts, and the New England Colonies, from the year 1630–1644: written by J. W. first Governor of Massachusetts* (Boston, 2 vols, 1825–6). Other basic information about the voyage of the *Arbella*, and the new colony, comes from E. Keble Chatterton's *English Seamen and the Colonisation of America* (Arrowsmith, 1930). James Savage's *Genealogical Dictionary of the First Settlers in New England* ii 552–3 (Little, Brown [Boston], 1860) bears witness to the fate of Isaac Johnson and his wife, the former Arbella Clinton.

'The True Lovers' Knot Untied' appears in many of the older Arbella Stuart biographies (notably Bradley ii 275–8, Cooper ii 249–53). Cooper also prints in full the anonymous ballad supposed by Disraeli to be from Mickle (ii 254–9) and Felicia Hemans' poem (ii 260–71). It may be appropriate to end on a brief note about other fictional, dramatic or poetic works in which the legend of Arbella is perpetuated; Steen (1, 104) gives a summary of them (notably, for British readers, Doris Leslie's novel of 1949); to this I would add Ross Neil's play *Arabella Stuart* (Ellis and White, 1879), and mention of the eighteenth-century writer Elizabeth Hamilton, who began a novel about her.

# Select bibliography

Arnold, Janet, *Queen Elizabeth's Wardrobe Unlock'd* (Maney, 1988)

Art. X, 'Lady Arabella Stuart and the Venetian Archives', *Edinburgh Review*, October 1896

Ashdown, Dulcie M., *Tudor Cousins: Rivals for the Throne* (Sutton, 2000)

Ashelford, Jane, *The Art of Dress* (National Trust, 1996)

Ashelford, Jane, *Dress in the Age of Elizabeth I* (Batsford, 1988)

Ashton, Robert, *James I by his Contemporaries* (Hutchinson, 1969)

Aubrey, John, *Brief Lives*, ed. Oliver Lawson Dick (Secker & Warburg, 1960)

Axton, Marie, *The Queen's Two Bodies: Drama and the Elizabethan Succession* (Royal Historical Society, 1977)

Barroll, Leeds, *Anna of Denmark, Queen of England: A Cultural Biography* (University of Pennsylvania Press, 2001)

Bickley, Francis, *The Cavendish Family* (Constable, 1911)

Bindoff, S. T., Hurstfield, J. and Williams, C.H. (eds), *Elizabethan Government and Society* (University of London/Athlone Press, 1961)

Birch, Thomas, *The Court and Times of James the First*, 2 vols (1848)

Bowen, Catherine Drinker, *The Lion and the Throne: Sir E. Coke* (Hamish Hamilton, 1957)

Bradley, E. T., *Life of the Lady Arabella Stuart* (Richard Bentley & Son, 1889)

Brigden, Susan, *New Worlds, Lost Worlds: The Rule of the Tudors 1485–1603* (Allen Lane/Penguin Press, 2000)

Briscoe, A. D., *A Stuart Benefactress: Sarah, Duchess of Somerset* (Terence Dalton, 1973)

Bruce, J. (ed.), *Correspondence of King James VI with Sir Robert Cecil and Others in England* (Camden Society, 1861)

Carleton, Dudley, *Dudley Carleton to John Chamberlain 1603–1624: Jacobean*

*Letters*, ed. Maurice Lee, Jr (Rutgers University Press, 1972)

Cecil, David, *The Cecils of Hatfield House* (Constable, 1973)

[Cecil, Robert,] S*ecret Correspondence of Sir Robert Cecil with James VI King of Scotland*, ed. David Dalrymple (Lord Hailes) (Edinburgh, 1766)

Chamberlain, John, *Letters*, ed. N. E. Mclure (American Philosophical Society, 1939)

Chapman, Hester W., *Lady Jane Grey* (Jonathan Cape, 1962)

Chapman, Hester W., *Two Tudor Portraits* (Jonathan Cape, 1960)

Cheney, C. R. (ed.), *Handbook of Dates for Students of English History* (Royal Historical Society, 1961)

Chisholm, Kate, *Hungry Hell* (Short Books, 2002)

Clarendon, Lord [Edward Hyde], *History of the Great Rebellion* (Oxford University Press, 1967)

Clifford, Lady Anne, *The Diaries of Lady Anne Clifford*, ed. D. J. H. Clifford (Sutton, 1990)

Cobbett, *Complete Collection of State Trials*, vol. 2 (R. Bagshaw, 1809)

Cooper, Elizabeth, *The Life and Letters of Lady Arabella Stuart, Including Numerous Original and Unpublished Documents* (Hurst & Blackett, 1866)

Croft, Pauline (ed.), *Patronage, Culture and Power: The Early Cecils 1558–1612*, Studies in British Art 8 (Yale University Press, 2002)

Cuddy, Neil, 'The Revival of Entourage: The Bedchamber of James I 1603–1625', in David Starkey (ed.), *The English Court: From the Wars of the Roses to the Civil War* (Longman, 1988)

Daybell, James (ed.), *Early Modern Women's Letter Writing, 1450–1700* (Palgrave, 2001)

Dekker, Thomas, *Selected Prose Writings*, ed. E. D. Pendry (Edward Arnold, 1967)

Devereux, W. B., *Lives and Letters of the Devereux, 1540–1646* (1853)

Doleman, R., *A Conference about the Next Succession to the Crown of England* (Antwerp, 1594)

Durant, David N., *Arbella Stuart: A Rival to the Queen* (Weidenfeld & Nicolson, 1978)

Durant, David N., *Bess of Hardwick* (first publ. Weidenfeld & Nicolson, 1977; reissued by Peter Owen 1999)

Elizabeth I, *Collected Works*, ed. Leah S. Marcus, Janel Mueller and Mary Beth Rose (University of Chicago Press, 2000)

Erondell, Peter, *The French Garden*: one of two 'dialogues' published under the title of *The Elizabethan Home*, ed. M. St. Clare Byrne (Cobden-Sanderson, 1930)

Forman, Simon, *Casebooks of Simon Forman: Sex and Society in Shakespeare's Age*, ed. A. L. Rowse (Weidenfeld & Nicolson, 1974)

Fraser, Antonia, *The Gunpowder Plot: Terror and Faith in 1605* (Mandarin, 1997)

Fraser, Antonia, *King James VI of Scotland I of England* (Weidenfeld & Nicolson, 1974)

Fraser, Antonia, *Mary, Queen of Scots* (Phoenix, 2002)

Fraser, Antonia, *The Weaker Vessel: Women's Lot in Seventeenth-Century England* (Weidenfeld & Nicolson, 1984)

Freedman, Sylvia, *Poor Penelope: Lady Penelope Rich, an Elizabethan Woman* (Kensal Press, 1983)

Frye, Susan and Robertson, Karen (eds), *Maids and Mistresses, Cousins and Queens: Women's Alliances in Early Modern England* (Oxford University Press, 1999)

*The Fugger News-Letters 1568–1605*, ed. Victor von Klarwill (Bodley Head, 1924)

*The Fugger News-Letters 1568–1605, 2nd series (Elizabeth)*, ed. Victor von Klarwill (Bodley Head, 1926)

Gerard, John, *John Gerard: The Autobiography of an Elizabethan*, trans. from the Latin by Philip Caraman and with an introduction by Graham Greene (Longmans, 1951)

Girouard, Mark, *Hardwick Hall* (National Trust, 1998)

Glashen, Joan, *The Secret People of the Palaces* (Batsford, 1998)

Goodman, Godfrey, Bishop of Gloucester, *The Court of James I*, 2 vols. (1839)

Guy, John (ed.), *The Reign of Elizabeth I* (Cambridge, 1995)

Haile, Martin, *An Elizabethan Cardinal: William Allen* (Sir Isaac Pitman & Sons, 1914)

Hammer, Paul E. J., *The Polarisation of Elizabethan Politics: The Political Career of Robert Devereux, 2nd Earl of Essex, 1585–1597* (Cambridge University Press, 1999)

Handover, P. M., *Arbella Stuart, Royal Lady of Hardwick* (Eyre & Spottiswoode, 1957)

Handover P. M., *The Second Cecil: The Rise to Power 1563–1604 of Sir Robert Cecil, later First Earl of Salisbury* (Eyre & Spottiswoode, 1959)

Hardy, B. C., *Arbella Stuart: A Biography* (Constable, 1913)

Harington, Sir John, *Nugae Antiquae* (1838)

Harington, Sir John, *A Tract on the Succession to the Crown*, ed. C. R. and E. C. Markham (Roxburghe Club, 1880)

Haynes, Alan, *The Elizabethan Secret Service* (Sutton, 1992)

Haynes, Alan, *Sex in Elizabethan England* (Sutton, 1997)

Hibbert, Christopher, *The Virgin Queen: The Personal History of Elizabeth* (Viking, 1990)

SELECT BIBLIOGRAPHY

Hoby, Lady Margaret, *Private Life of an Elizabethan Lady: The Diary of Lady Margaret Hoby 1599–1605* (Sutton, 2001)

*Of Household Stuff: The 1601 Inventories of Bess of Hardwick* (National Trust 2001)

Howarth, David, *Lord Arundel and his Circle* (Yale University Press, 1985)

Hubbard, Kate, *A Material Girl: Bess of Hardwick 1527–1608* (Short Books, 2001)

Hunter, Lynette and Hutton, Sarah, *Women, Science and Medicine 1500–1700* (Sutton, 1997)

Laurence, Anne, *Women in England 1500–1760* (Weidenfeld & Nicolson, 1994)

Jardine, Lisa and Stewart, Alan, *Hostage to Fortune: The Troubled Life of Francis Bacon 1561–1626* (Victor Gollancz, 1998)

Jones, Kathleen, *A Glorious Fame: The Life of Margaret Cavendish, Duchess of Newcastle 1623–1673* (Bloomsbury, 1988)

Kettle, Pamela, *Oldcotes* (Merton Priory Press, 2001)

Labanoff, Prince Alexander, *Lettres, instructions et mémoires de Marie Stuart,* 7 vols (1844)

Lacey, Robert, *Robert, Earl of Essex: An Elizabethan Icarus* (Weidenfeld & Nicolson, 1971)

Lacey, Robert, *Sir Walter Ralegh* (Weidenfeld & Nicolson, 1973)

Lefuse, M., *The Life and Times of Arabella Stuart* (Mills & Boon, 1913)

Levey, Santina M., *An Elizabethan Inheritance: The Hardwick Hall Textiles* (National Trust, 1998)

Lewalski, Barbara Kiefer, *Writing Women in Jacobean England* (Harvard University Press, 1993)

Lewis, Jayne Elizabeth, *Mary Queen of Scots: Romance and Nation* (Routledge, 1998)

Lewis, Maria Theresa, *Lives of the Friends and Contemporaries of Lord Chancellor Clarendon* (John Murray, 1852)

Locke, Audrey, *The Seymour Family* (Constable, 1911)

Lodge, Edmund, *Illustrations of British History*, 3 vols. (1791, 1838)

Macalpine, Ida, Hunter, Richard and Rimington, C., *Porphyria – A Royal Malady*, articles published in or commissioned by the *British Medical Journal* (British Medical Association, 1968)

Macalpine, Ida and Hunter, Richard, *George III and the Mad Business* (Pimlico, 1969)

McInnes, Ian, *Arabella: The Life and Times of Arabella Seymour, 1575–1615* (W. H. Allen, 1968)

Mackay, James, *In My End Is My Beginning* (Mainstream, 2002)

Manningham, John, *Diary of John Manningham of the Middle Temple 1602–3,* ed. Robert Parker Sorliem (University Press of New England, 1976)

435

Mathew, David, *King James I* (Eyre & Spottiswoode, 1967)

Mattingly, Garrett, *The Defeat of the Spanish Armada* (Jonathan Cape, 1959)

Mowl, Timothy, *Elizabethan and Jacobean Style* (Phaidon, 1993)

Neale, J. E., *Queen Elizabeth* (Jonathan Cape, 1934)

Nenner, Howard, *The Right to be King* (Macmillan, 1995)

Newdigate-Newdegate, Lady, *Gossip From a Muniment Room (Being Passages in the Lives of Anne and Mary Fytton 1574–1618)*, transcribed and edited by Lady Newdigate-Newdegate, (Robert Nutt, 1897)

Nicholl, Charles, *The Reckoning: The Murder of Christopher Marlowe* (Jonathan Cape, 1992)

Nicholls, Mark, 'Sir Walter Ralegh's Treason', *English Historical Review* 110 (Sept. 1995)

Nicholls, Mark, 'Treason's Reward: The Punishment of Conspirators in the Bye Plot of 1603', *Historical Journey* 38 (1995)

Nicholls, Mark, 'Two Winchester Trials: Lord Cobham and Lord Grey, 1603', *Historical Research* 68 (Feb. 1995)

Nichols, J. G., *The Progresses, Processions and Festivities of King James I* (1828)

Nichols, J. G., *The Progresses and Public Processions of Queen Elizabeth* (1788–1821)

Norrington, Ruth, *In the Shadow of the Throne: The Lady Arbella Stuart* (Peter Owen, 2002)

Pearson, John, *Stags and Serpents: The Story of the House of Cavendish and the Dukes of Devonshire* (Macmillan, 1983)

Peck, Linda Levy (ed.), *The Mental World of the Jacobean Court* (Cambridge University Press, 1991)

Peck, Linda Levy, *Northampton: Patronage and Policy at the Court of James I* (Allen & Unwin, 1982)

Percy, Henry, Ninth Earl of Northumberland, *Advice to his Son*, ed. G. B. Harrison (Ernest Benn, 1930)

Picard, Liza, *Restoration London* (Weidenfeld & Nicolson, 1997)

Plowden, Alison, *Mistress of Hardwick* (BBC Publications, 1972)

Rawson, Maud Stepney, *Bess of Hardwick and her Circle* (Hutchinson, 1910)

Rohl, John C. G., Warren, Martin and Hunt, David, *Purple Secret: Genes, 'Madness' and the Royal Houses of Europe* (Bantam, 1998)

Rowse, A. L., *The Tower of London in the History of the Nation* (Cardinal, 1972)

Scarisbrick, Diana, *Tudor and Jacobean Jewellery* (Tate Publishing, 1995)

Seymour, William, *Ordeal by Ambition: An English Family in the Shadow of the Tudors* (Sidgwick & Jackson, 1972)

Sim, Alison, *Pleasures and Pastimes in Tudor England* (Sutton, 1999)

Somerset, Anne, *Ladies-in-Waiting: From the Tudors to the Present Day* (Weidenfeld & Nicolson, 1984)

Somerset, Anne, *Unnatural Murder: Poison at the Court of James I* (Weidenfeld & Nicolson, 1997)

Spedding, James, *The Letters and Life of Francis Bacon*, 14 vols (1857)

Starkey, David, *Elizabeth* (Chatto & Windus, 2000)

Starkey, David (ed.), *The English Court: From the Wars of the Roses to the Civil War* (Longman, 1988)

Starkey, David (ed.), *Rivals in Power: Lives and Letters of the Great Tudor Dynasties* (Macmillan, 1990)

Steen, Sara Jayne, 'The Crime of Marriage: Arbella Stuart and The Duchess of Malfi', *Sixteenth Century Journal* 22 (1991)

Steen, Sara Jayne, 'Fashioning an Acceptable Self: Arbella Stuart', *English Literary Renaissance* 18 (1988)

Steen, Sara Jayne, ' "How Subject to Interpretation": Lady Arbella Stuart and the Reading of Illness', in James Daybell, ed., *Early Modern Women's Letter Writing, 1450–1700* (Palgrave, 2001)

Steen, Sara Jayne (ed.), *The Letters of Lady Arbella Stuart* (Oxford University Press, 1994)

Stone, Lawrence, *The Crisis of the Aristocracy 1558–1641* (Clarendon Press, 1965)

Stone, Lawrence, *The Family, Sex and Marriage in England 1500–1800* (Weidenfeld & Nicolson, 1977)

Strickland, Agnes, *Lives of the Tudor and Stuart Princesses* (1888)

Strong, Roy, *The Cult of Elizabeth: Elizabethan Portraiture and Pageantry* (Thames & Hudson, 1997)

Strong, Roy, *Henry, Prince of Wales, and England's Lost Renaissance* (Pimlico, 2000)

Strong, Roy, *Tudor and Jacobean Portraits*, 2 vols (HMSO, 1969)

Strong, Roy, *William Larkin* (Franco Maria Ricci, 1995)

Strong, Roy and Trevelyan Oman, Julia, *Mary, Queen of Scots* (Secker & Warburg, 1972)

Strype, J., *Annales of the Reformation* (Oxford University Press, 1824; first publ. 1709)

Trease, Geoffrey, *Portrait of a Cavalier: William Cavendish, First Duke of Newcastle* (Macmillan, 1979)

Watkins, Susan, *In Public and in Private: Elizabeth I and her World* (Thames & Hudson, 1998)

Weinreb, Ben and Christopher Hibbert (ed.), *The London Encyclopaedia* (Macmillan, 1983)

Weir, Alison, *Children of England* (Jonathan Cape, 1996)

Weir, Alison, *Elizabeth the Queen* (Jonathan Cape, 1998)

White, Gillian, *A Very Goodly Prospect* (National Trust, 1997)

Williams, E. Carleton, *Bess of Hardwick* (Longmans, Green & Co., 1959)

Williams, Neville, *All the Queen's Men* (Weidenfeld & Nicolson, 1972)

Williams, Norman Lloyd, *Sir Walter Raleigh* (Cassell, 1988; first publ. Eyre & Spottiswoode, 1962)

Willson, D. H., *King James VI and I* (Jonathan Cape, 1955)

Wilson, D., *Sweet Robin: A Biography of Robert Dudley, Earl of Leicester, 1533–1588* (Hamish Hamilton, 1981)

Wilson, T., *The State of England AD 1600*, ed. F. J. Fisher (Camden Society Miscellany, vol. IV, 1936)

Wilson, Violet A., *Society Women of Shakespeare's Time* (1924)

Winwood, Sir Ralph, *Memorials of the Affairs of State in the Reigns of Queen Elizabeth and King James I* (1725)

Worsley, Lucy, *Hardwick Old Hall* (English Heritage, 1998)

# Picture acknowledgments

*Colour plates between pages 146 and 147*

*Lady Arbella Stuart at the Age of 23 Months*, 1577. Hardwick Hall. National Trust Photograph Library/R. A. Wilsher. Background: detail of a man's semi-circular cloak, slashed, pinked and embroidered, Italian, 1600–1620. V&A Picture Library.

*Lady Margaret Douglas, Countess of Lennox*, British School, 1572.The Royal Collection © 2002, HM Queen Elizabeth II; *Henry Stuart, Lord Darnley and his Brother, Charles Stuart, Earl of Lennox*, 1563. Holyrood House.The Royal Collection © 2002, HM Queen Elizabeth II.

*Chatsworth House*, after an Elizabethan original, by Richard Wilson (1713/4–82). Devonshire Collection, Chatsworth. By permission of the Duke of Devonshire and the Chatsworth Settlement Trustees; *Elizabeth Hardwick, Countess of Shrewsbury, c.*1590, attributed to Rowland Lockey. Hardwick Hall. National Trust Photographic Library/John Bethell; *Mary, Queen of Scots*, possibly by Rowland Lockey, 1578. Hardwick Hall. National Trust Photographic Library/Hawkley Studios; Gog and Magog, plasterwork overmantel at Hardwick Old Hall. English Heritage Photographic Library; the west staircase, Hardwick Old Hall. © English Heritage Photographic Library/Jonathan Bailey; needlework panel with 'MA' cypher and a cat by Mary, Queen of Scots. The Royal Collection © 2002, HM Queen Elizabeth II.

*Queen Elizabeth Receiving the Dutch Ambassadors, c.* 1585. Staatliche Museen, Kassel; *Queen Elizabeth I* by Marcus Gheeraerts the Younger,

1595. Burghley House Collection, Lincolnshire. © The Bridgeman Art Library; *William Cecil, 1st Baron Burghley* attributed to Marcus Gheeraerts the Younger, after 1585. © The National Portrait Gallery Picture Library; *Young Man Amongst Roses* (thought to be Robert Devereux, 2nd Earl of Essex) by Nicholas Hilliard, *c.* 1587. V&A Picture Library; *Sir Walter Ralegh* by Nicholas Hilliard, *c.* 1585. © The National Portrait Gallery Picture Library; *Sir Francis Walsingham* by John de Critz the Elder. © The National Portrait Gallery Picture Library.

*Arbella Stuart*, English school, 1589. Hardwick Hall. National Trust Photographic Library/John Hammond.

*Colour plates between pages 290 and 291*

Front view of Hardwick Hall. National Trust Photographic Library/ Nick Meers.

Long Gallery, Hardwick Hall. National Trust Photographic Library/ Andreas von Einseidel; Hardwick Hall, entrance gate. © Arcaid/Richard Bryant; view of the Withdrawing Chamber, with the sea dog table in the foreground. Hardwick Hall. © Arcaid/ Richard Bryant.

*James VI of Scotland and I of England* by Paul van Somer, *c.*1618. Yale Center for British Art, Paul Mellon Fund/Bridgeman Art Library. *Sir Robert Cecil, 1st Earl of Salisbury* by John de Critz the Elder, 1602. The National Portrait Gallery Picture Library; *Gilbert Talbot, 7th Earl of Shrewsbury*, attributed to William Segar, 1596. Christie's Images. © Bridgeman Art Library; *Mary Talbot, The Countess of Shrewsbury*, English School, 17th century. By permission of the Master and Fellows of St John's College, Cambridge; *London From Southwark*, Dutch School, *c.*1630. Museum of London.

*Arbella Stuart (?)*, circle of Paul van Somer, by permission of the Marquess of Bath, Longleat House, Warminster, Wilts.

Except where otherwise stated the textile used as a background to some of these illustrations is a detail of a satin cushion cover embroidered with silk, metal thread and metal strip, English, *c.*1600. © V&A Picture Library.

*Black and white text illustrations*

© **Bridgeman Art Library**: xvi: from *The Panorama of London* by Anthonis van den Wyngaerde, *c.* 1544. Ashmolean Museum, Oxford;

14: from the *Book of Kings* by Renold Elstrack, 1618. Private Collection; 38: Private Collection; 73: Private Collection; 243: Private Collection; © **The British Library**: 52 (778.c.3); © **British Library, Department of Manuscripts (MS Harl. 7003 f. 71)**: 284; © **British Museum, Department of Prints and Drawings**: 42: drawing by Federico Zuccaro, 1574; 121, 208, 281; **The Trustees of the Chatsworth Settlement/Photo © The Courtauld Institute of Art**: 276: Design for a naiad's costume for 'Tethys' Festival' by Inigo Jones; **Crown Copyright/NMR**: 86/7; **Sir John Soane's Museum/Photo © The Courtauld Institute of Art (B64/511A)**: 64; **The Society of Antiquaries of London**: 318: A True and Exact Copy of the Draught of the Tower Liberties Surveyd in the year 1597 by Hayward and Gascoyne; **V&A Picture Library**: engraving, 1604, designed and published by Stephen Harrison, engraved by William Kip.

Endpapers: Undated letter from Arbella to William Seymour © British Library, Department of Manuscripts (MS Harl. 150 f. & 151v.).

# INDEX

Abrahall, Mrs (waiting gentlewoman), 78
Adams, Mrs (attendant on A), 3, 6, 311
Allen, William, cardinal, 102
Anna of Denmark, queen consort:
  character, 227; in Scotland, 199, 206,
  229; children, 227, 229, 240, 336; relationship with husband, 229, 230, 336;
  religion, 229; arrival in England, 199,
  207, 227; relationship with A, 199,
  213–14, 227, 230–1, 234, 267, 285–6,
  288; coronation, 209, 319; in
  Winchester, 214; gifts for, 224; masques,
  225–6, 248, 257, 275, 286; progress,
  227; popularity, 229–30; household,
  230–1; brother's visit, 248; court at
  Somerset House, 256; Ralegh's appeal,
  320; Greenwich palace, 336; death, 357
Anne Boleyn, queen of Henry VIII, 17, 32,
  56, 319
Anna Cathrine, queen of Christian IV of
  Denmark, 249
Arbella Stuart: birth, 19, 21; christening,
  24; childhood, 25–6, 30–3, 34, 44, 45–6,
  47–51; father's death, 26; mother's
  death, 31–2; education, 32–3, 48–50,
  53, 67, 85, 107, 132, 235; marriage
  possibilities, 43–4, 66, 67–8, 71, 72,
  76–7, 78, 83, 112–13, 118–19, 128,
  130, 141, 240–2, 260–3; presentation at
  court, 63–7; Greenwich court visit, 71,
  72; sent away from court, 72, 74–5;
  journey south, 78–9; at court, 80–3; life
  in Derbyshire, 84–8, 107, 115–17,
  131–5; Catholic plot rumours, 89, 100;
  marriage proposal, 141–6; Brounker's
  visit and interrogation, 139–40, 146–8;
  Exposition (1603), 163–4, 173–4;
  attempted escape from Hardwick,179,
  180–6, 339; James's accession, 192–5;
  at Wrest Park, 201, 203; Elizabeth's
  funeral, 202; meeting with James,
  203–6; at Sheen, 206; at court, 207;
  plots involving, 211–12, 216–22; life

at court, 213–15, 223–7, 231, 234, 236;
  dedications to, 235; influence at court,
  236–7; at Hardwick again, 238;
  Gunpowder Plot, 244; Bess's death,
  251; Blackfriars house, 252, 255–6;
  journey north, 257–8; suppression of
  play, 262; first meeting with William,
  267; betrothal, 268–70, 272–3, 287;
  examination by James, 273; marriage
  plans, 274–5; in Tethys masque, 275;
  marriage, 2, 277–8; imprisonment at
  Lambeth, 279, 280–2; interrogation,
  279–80; petition, 283–5; question of
  pregnancy, 285, 290, 363; Durham
  imprisonment ordered, 290; journey
  north, 293–7; escape plans, 294, 297–8,
  299–300; flight, 1–5, 300, 306; re-cap-
  ture, 7, 306–7; in Tower, 99, 308, 309,
  318, 321, 325–6, 334; interrogation in
  Tower, 312, 314; allegations against
  Mary Talbot, 336–41; Waad's dismissal,
  341–2; death, 352–3; post mortem,
  353; funeral, 353–4; tomb, 384, 384;
FINANCES: debts, 207, 259, 262; escape
  funds, 298, 324; gifts from Bess, 132–3;
  gifts from James, 261, 274; impost,
  224; income at court, 245, 247; inheritance, 26–30, 77; James's promises,
  259, 261, 273; jewels, 30, 77, 133, 135,
  324–5, 335, 344, 348; lawsuits, 252;
  mother's dowry, 39, 133; pension, 30,
  32, 78, 133, 206–7, 225, 239, 262,
  274; petition to James, 251–2; petitions
  to Cecil, 245, 259; Tower imprisonment, 323–5;
HEALTH: explanations for her
  distraction, 166, 193–4, 340; illness in
  1595, 110; madness reports, 133, 154,
  166, 194, 340–1; measles, 238; porphyria, 166–7, 201, 206, 285, 340, 349,
  351, 375–9; self-starvation, 165–6, 352,
  353; smallpox, 256–7; in Tower, 314,
  340–1, 345, 346, 347–52;

442

Northampton, Helena, marchioness of, 206, 389
Northampton, Henry Howard, earl of, 202, 313–14, 342–3, 348–50, 356
Northumberland, Dorothy (Devereux), duchess of, 129
Northumberland, Henry Percy, eighth earl of, 43
Northumberland, Henry Percy, ninth earl of: marriage rumours, 77, 374; on Essex, 97; relationship with James, 129, 202, 244, 374; in Tower, 244, 320, 326
Nottingham, Catherine, countess of, 160, 171
Nottingham, Charles Howard, earl of (Lord Howard of Effingham), 6, 80, 216, 217, 248–9, 312
Nottingham, Margaret, countess of, 248–9

Oliver, Isaac, 256, 387
Overbury, Sir Thomas, 232, 342–3, 350–1, 353, 356
Overton, William, bishop of Coventry, 40
Owen, John, 235
Owen, Richard, 181
Oxford, Edward de Vere, seventeenth earl of, 61

Paget, Thomas Paget, third baron, 43
Palmer, Dr, 337, 338, 344
Parma, Alessandro Farnese, duke of, 68, 127
Parma, Rainutio Farnese, duke of, 68, 71, 72, 78, 83, 129
Parry, Sir Thomas, 279, 280, 282, 293, 356
Parsons, Robert, 104, 127, 194
Pembroke, Lady Mary Herbert (Talbot), 51, 53, 71, 241, 256, 357
Pembroke, William Herbert, third earl of, 51, 215, 241, 256
Percy, Thomas, 244
Pette, Phineas, 305
Philip II, king of Spain, 68, 104, 112, 118
Philip III, king of Spain, 129, 212
Pierrepont, Bessie, 260
Pierrepont, Frances (Cavendish), 144, 190, 363
Platter, Thomas, 79
Primrose, Duncan, 353–4
Proby, Peter, 100
Pusey, Timothy, 149

Ralegh, Elizabeth (Throckmorton), Lady, 83, 278, 320, 322
Ralegh, Sir Walter: dress, 60; on court life, 61; meeting with A, 66, 67; relationship with Essex, 74, 112, 212; marriage, 83, 278; religious beliefs, 92; Cadiz expedition, 112; Marlowe connection, 374;

treatment by James, 202–3; Main Plot, 211–12, 219, 222; trial, 67, 216–18; in Tower, 244, 320, 321, 326, 333, 351, 384; execution, 357–8
Ramsey (jester), 80
Reeves, Edward, 277, 283, 311, 343, 344
Rich, Lady Penelope (Devereux), 103, 125, 231, 349
Rivers, Antony, 171, 194
Rodney, Edward, 274, 277, 301–2, 303–4
Rogers, Sir Richard, 70
Rowlston (Catholic conspirator), 89
Rubens, Peter Paul, 357
Rufford Abbey, 11–13, 258, 383
Rupert of the Rhine, prince, 384
Ruthven, Patrick, 326, 343–4

St Loe, Sir William, 36–7
St Paul, Sir George, 259
Saltonstall, Sir Richard, 364
Sampson, Agnes, 81
Savill, Lady Mary, 55
Selden, John, 357
Semple, William, 89
Seton, Mary, 300
Seymour, Arbella, 271, 362, 389
Seymour, Lady Catherine (Grey), countess of Hertford: birth, 23; sister's execution, 145; marriage, 23, 24, 106, 141–2, 269, 270, 277, 286, 289, 332; in Tower, 23, 24, 309–10, 317; children, 23, 70, 309–10; relationship with Elizabeth, 72, 87; death, 142; grandson Edward's marriage, 141–2; tomb, 389
Seymour, Edward (the lord protector), earl of Hertford and duke of Somerset, 23, 141
Seymour, Edward (son of the above), earl of Hertford: betrothal, 289; marriage, 23, 106, 141–2, 269, 270, 277, 304; imprisonment, 23, 106, 141, 142, 317; children, 23, 70, 310; son's marriage, 24, 70, 278; grandson Edward's marriage, 119, 141–2; A's message to, 144, 145, 151; rumours of son's rising, 191; grandson William's escape, 304, 312, 330; grandson's allowance, 329; death, 359; tomb, 389
Seymour, Edward (son of the above), Lord Beauchamp: birth, 23, 310; legitimacy, 23, 70, 106, 269, 277; marriage, 24, 70, 278; in Tower, 106; marriage rumours, 142, 190; son Edward's marriage, 119, 141; claim to throne, 127, 141, 190–2; rumours of armed rising, 190–1; death, 192, 333, 359
Seymour, Edward (son of the above): marriage question, 119, 141–2, 145, 269, 270, 289; brother's marriage, 267, 270; death, 359